Jessie Tswarayi

Social Dominance

This volume focuses on two questions social group oppress and discrimir groups? Why is this oppressior thors approach these questio of social dominance theory. T forms of intergroup conflict, suci triarchy, all derive from the basic hu. and maintain hierarchical and group-b. ganization. In essence, social dominance ...eory presumes that, beneath major and sometimes profound differences between different human societies, there is also a grammar of social power shared by all societies. Drs. Sidanius and Pratto use social dominance theory in an attempt to identify the elements of this grammar and to understand how these elements interact and reinforce each other to produce and maintain group-based social hierarchy.

Jim Sidanius is Professor of Psychology at the University of California, Los Angeles.

Felicia Pratto is Associate Professor of Psychology at the University of Connecticut.

Social Dominance

An Intergroup Theory of Social Hierarchy and Oppression

JIM SIDANIUS

FELICIA PRATTO

CAMBRIDGE
UNIVERSITY PRESS

PUBLISHED BY THE PRESS SYNDICATE OF THE UNIVERSITY OF CAMBRIDGE
The Pitt Building, Trumpington Street, Cambridge, United Kingdom

CAMBRIDGE UNIVERSITY PRESS
The Edinburgh Building, Cambridge CB2 2RU, UK
40 West 20th Street, New York, NY 10011-4211, USA
10 Stamford Road, Oakleigh, VIC 3166, Australia
Ruiz de Alarcón 13, 28014 Madrid, Spain
Dock House, The Waterfront, Cape Town 8001, South Africa

http://www.cambridge.org

First published 1999
First paperback edition 2001

Typefaces Palatino 9.75/12.5 pt. and Optima   *System* LATEX 2$_\varepsilon$ [TB]

A catalog record for this book is available from the British Library.

Library of Congress Cataloging in Publication Data
Sidanius, Jim.
Social dominance : an intergroup theory of social hierarchy and
oppression / Jim Sidanius, Felicia Pratto.
p.   cm.
Includes bibliographical references and index.
ISBN 0-521-62290-5 (hc.)
ISBN 0-521-80540-6 (pb.)
1. Social groups.   2. Social conflict.   3. Social psychology.
4. Dominance (Psychology).   5. Oppression (Psychology).   I. Pratto,
Felicia.   II. Title
HM131.S5832   1999
305 – dc21   98-44356
                                                              CIP

ISBN 0 521 62290 5 hardback
ISBN 0 521 80540 6 paperback

Transferred to digital printing 2004

To our parents

Marlene and David Pratto, who taught me to think and to care – *Felicia Pratto*

Clarice and James Brown, for their nurturing and love – *Jim Sidanius*

Contents

Acknowledgments

The original data contained in this book have been generated over a 25-year period and with the generous support of several private and government funding agencies. In particular, we would like to thank the Swedish Council for Social Science Research, the Research Institute at the University of Texas at Austin, the University Research Institute at UCLA, the Russell Sage Foundation, and the staff at UCLA's Institute for Social Science Research.

This project also owes a great deal to the many colleagues we have interacted with over the years and who have both challenged and encouraged us to sharpen our thinking and be more precise in our formulations. This collegial interaction has been crucial to the development of our ideas (for better or worse). In particular, Professor Marilyn Brewer's wise counsel and razor-sharp mind have been very helpful to us in this regard. Special acknowledgment also goes to Professor John Petrocik. Although Petrocik and we agree very little on matters of substance, the collegial, warmhearted, and challenging nature of his disagreements with us has been very helpful in strengthening our arguments and developing the nuances of our thinking.

We are also grateful for the highly productive interactions we have had with our graduate students over the years. In particular, we would like to thank Lisa M. Stallworth, Shana Levin, Colette van Laar, Michael Mitchell, Bertram Malle, Deborah Tatar, Peter Hegarty, Jenn Orton, Progga Choudhury, Joshua Rabinowitz, John Hetts, Stacey Sinclair, Jack Glaser, Margaret Shih, Hagit Bachrach, and Sahr Conway-Lanz.

Our gratitude extends to the following research assistants on this project: Erron Al-Amin, Jill Andrassy, Nick Clements, Magda Escobar, Louis Ibarra, Amy Lee, Johanna Jensen, Jeannie Kim, Jenn Pearson, Holly Schaefer, Stacy Sinclair, Gayatri Teneja, Jack Wang, and Wes Williams. Their efforts on our behalf were crucial in getting this project completed in a timely way. Special thanks are extended to Mauricio Carvallo, whose diligence and dedication to the latter half of this project were extremely helpful and appreciated.

We are also indebted to those who read and reread drafts of this book over more than a year's time. These people include Tony Lemeiux, Christie Cathey, Jill Santopietro, Colette van Laar, and, especially, Theresa Richard.

Finally, we both extend special thanks to our respective spouses, Tom Wood and Miriam Sidanius, without whose support, understanding, and seemingly endless patience with our struggles this project could not have been completed.

FROM THERE TO HERE: THEORETICAL BACKGROUND

1 | From Viciousness to Viciousness
Theories of Intergroup Relations

I tried to defend myself but I couldn't. They took my clothes, they hit me, they were pulling my hair. A few days later six soldiers came in. All of them raped me. They cursed me, insulted me, said there were too many Muslim people and said of lot of Muslims were going to give birth to Serbian children.

18-year old Bosnian woman, 1993[1]

Despite tremendous effort and what appear to be our best efforts stretching over hundreds of years, discrimination, oppression, brutality, and tyranny remain all too common features of the human condition. Far from having escaped the grip of human ugliness in the civil rights revolutions of the 1960s, we seem only to have increased the overall level of chaos, confusion, and intergroup truculence during the post–civil rights era and the resolution of the cold war. We see signs of this brutality and oppression all around us, from the streets of Los Angeles and Brooklyn to the hills of Bosnia and the forests of Rwanda. Rather than resolving the problems of intergroup hostility, we merely appear to stumble from viciousness to viciousness. Why?

While some journalists and poets have written astute and penetrating descriptions of this nearly ubiquitous barbarism,[2] it is primarily social scientists who have tried to construct a theoretical understanding of these phenomena.[3] As a result, the social science literature on the interrelated topics of stereotyping, prejudice, intergroup relations, gender, race, and class discrimination has become enormous. Different approaches have emphasized different aspects of the problem, ranging from the functions that prejudice and discrimination serve for various psychological motivations, to limitations in human cognitive-processing abilities, to how one's social structure or social environment elicits discriminatory behavior, to how prejudice and ingroup favoritism might be evolutionarily adaptive. So many different people have written so much on these topics that one might truly wonder why anyone would bother to write further.

Part of the answer to this question lies in the fact that while a number of people have had some wise and insightful things to say about these

3

Same research as my problems, very little has been done to tie these various pieces together into a coherent whole. It is precisely because there are so many important morsels of knowledge scattered before us that we are in a position to integrate them into a larger theory.

Though both sociology and social psychology would seem equipped to explain social inequality, at present, neither discipline has what we feel is an adequate theory. Within contemporary social psychology, a researcher typically uses one main research method, usually laboratory experimentation, and examines a set of highly specific questions in great and even mind-numbing detail. Though this approach has the advantage of eliminating alternative explanations and providing a great deal of nuanced knowledge about a very specific topic, it has the disadvantage of limiting the scope of relevant theories and phenomena considered. In particular, the more research is done in these laboratory settings, rather than on real social phenomena, the less it seems to address how social processes function in the real world in which people are buffeted and pulled by enormous forces of social context, culture, and social-structural relations.

Within contemporary sociology, the heavy emphasis on social-structural relations and aggregate data analyses has meant that many sociological analyses do not address psychological phenomena in psychological terms – such as motivation and prejudice – or recognize the fact that there are still important and stable individual differences between people, even people who share the same sociological characteristics (e.g., social class, occupation, gender). The split earlier in this century between sociology and social psychology contributed to these divisions and continues to hinder a more comprehensive and rich understanding of the problems of racism, sexism, classism, and general group oppression. In addition, while a number of U.S. political scientists have also been intensely interested in the problems of prejudice and discrimination, this interest has almost exclusively and narrowly focused on the Black–White conflict. Thus, very little if any effort has been made to examine whether the lessons learned from this Black–White context might generalize to other cultural or social contexts.

While many of the theories locked within their traditional academic disciplines are able to reap the benefit of parsimony, this benefit generally comes at the cost of a good deal of cultural and theoretical parochialism. In this book we attempt to break out of this parochialism by presenting a theory of group oppression that not only relies on thinking within contemporary social psychology, political sociology, and political science, but also includes important ideas from evolutionary psychology.

Before presenting our new synthesis in Chapter 2, we shall first review the most important theories and findings relevant to group inequality. In this chapter we shall try to extract the most valuable insights and use them as components in what we hope is a more useful, comprehensive, and fruitful synthesis. For simplicity, we organize these theories into four categories: psychological models, social-psychological models, structural-sociological models, and evolutionary models.

Psychological Theories

The psychological approach to the understanding of racism, discrimination, and stereotyping focuses primarily on the internal processes taking place within the individual. These models focus on (a) personality dynamics, (b) individuals' basic values, anxieties, and beliefs, and (c) individuals' information processing.

Though these kinds of models differ in their focus, all three have been profoundly influenced by the work of Sigmund Freud and his colleagues. Although it is hard for many of us to appreciate this now, Freud introduced a revolutionary new way of understanding human behavior. Instead of regarding human choice and decision making as primarily the result of rational and logical deliberations, Freud suggested that human behavior is largely driven by subconscious and nonrational drives, and is then rationalized and justified in terms of logic and reason. Adopting this view, many scholars both inside and outside of the psychodynamic revolution, began to think of peoples' ethnic, racial, and national stereotypes as manifestations of basic features of their motivations, rather than as rationally held political philosophies.[4]

The Frustration–Aggression Hypothesis

One of the theoretically simplest versions of this new approach is the *frustration–aggression* hypothesis. In their effort to understand the outbreak of ethnic, racial, and political barbarism that had broken out in Europe in the early part of the twentieth century, an interdisciplinary group of social scientists at Yale University formulated a simple and general hypothesis of human aggression that melded drive and behaviorist theories with psychodynamic ideas.[5] They suggested that aggression, the intention to deliberately harm others, results from the individual's frustration at not achieving highly desired goals.[6] Because taking out aggression on the source of the frustration could be quite dangerous, especially when that source was a powerful person or institution (e.g., one's boss), Dollard and his colleagues suggested that people will often turn their anger against less powerful others. The Yale group applied this idea of *displaced aggression* to the analysis of political choice, intergroup prejudice, and discrimination.[7] For example, they found periodic increases in the lynching of U.S. Blacks following economic stress in the South.[8]

Despite the valuable insights that the frustration–aggression approach provided, this model still left a number of questions unanswered. First, it was not able to account for discernible levels of prejudice and discrimination by people and social institutions that have not been shown to be frustrated in any obvious fashion. Second, the frustration–aggression hypothesis appears to assume that aggression is unusual and not a normal part of social life. However, subsequent analyses of legal practices, religious practices, cultural family patterns, and other forms of institutional discrimination suggest that discrimination is extremely common, and not solely motivated by individuals' levels of frustration. To understand discrimination as more common and institutional, we will need additional theoretical machinery.

Authoritarian Personality Theory (APT)

The most ambitious application of psychoanalytic theory to the study of prejudice and discrimination was *authoritarian personality theory* (APT; see e.g., Fromm, 1941). In the first comprehensive demonstration of this theory, Adorno, Frenkel-Brunswik, Levinson, and Sanford (1950) argued that there is a personality syndrome labeled *authoritarianism*, unifying individuals' social, economic, and political convictions. As a psychodynamic theory, APT theorized that authoritarianism resulted from child-rearing practices that humiliated and deprecated the child and predicated parental affection on the child's immediate and unquestioning obedience to the parents. This kind of subjugating environment was thought to predispose children toward thinking of human relations in terms of dominance and submission and to teach a particular orientation toward hierarchy: the vilification of those thought of as weak, humane, or deviate (e.g., ethnic minorities) and the glorification of those perceived to be strong and powerful. As such, authoritarians were hypothesized to hold conservative economic and political views, and also be generally xenophobic, racist, and ethnocentric. Among the most provocative findings of this research were that (a) people who are prejudiced against one ethnic minority (e.g., Jews) also tend to be prejudiced against other minorities (e.g., Blacks, Catholics) and that (b) authoritarians – as measured by the *F-scale* – have conservative political-economic views and high levels of generalized ethnocentrism.

While authoritarian personality theory is arguably the most influential prejudice theory, it is also one of the most harshly and thoroughly criticized.[9] The original research was criticized for using attitude scales that were subject to measurement and ideological bias. The primary measurement bias in question, *agreement bias*, manifests itself when respondents agree with whatever question is being put to them, regardless of the question contents. Not only can this type of artifact result in people being falsely classified as authoritarians, but it can also produce artificially high correlations within and among attitude measures.[10] In addition, the F-scale, the measure of authoritarianism, was accused of being politically biased in measuring authoritarianism of the right, while ignoring authoritarianism of the left.

To attempt to correct this ideological bias, Rokeach (1960) constructed a *dogmatism scale*, thought to be a politically neutral measure of generalized authoritarianism. Unfortunately, repeated attempts with this alternative measure have still shown that people on the right have higher authoritarianism scores than people on the left do.[11] Not only have Robert Altemeyer's (1981, 1988) efforts to measure authoritarianism addressed problems with agreement response bias, but unlike other measures of authoritarianism, Altemeyer's (1996) measure (the Right-Wing Authoritarianism [RWA] Scale), explicitly includes the contents originally theorized to be part of authoritarianism: authoritarian submission, conventionalism, and punitiveness against deviants.[12] This new authoritarianism measure has shown itself to be highly reliable and valid and to correlate with many balanced prejudice measures, including those assessing prejudice against homosexuals, French-Canadians, immigrants, foreigners, Blacks, and Jews. Importantly, however, Altemeyer has also been unable to measure authoritarianism of the left.[13]

Despite the numerous criticisms directed against the authoritarian personality research, the use of more sophisticated and valid methodologies support several of the original claims. Three are relevant to our concerns. First, just as the authoritarianism theorists speculated, there really does appear to be a phenomenon we may call *generalized ethnocentrism*, reflecting itself in the denigration of a wide range of outgroups, including ethnic groups, political groups (e.g., communists), sexual orientation groups (e.g., gays and lesbians), and stigmatized religious groups. Second, this generalized tendency to stigmatize and denigrate the generalized "other" contains a consistent theme of dominance and submission.[14] Third, and contradicting the assertions of *principled conservatism* theorists (e.g., Sniderman & Piazza, 1993), generalized ethnocentrism is positively associated with political conservatism. This association has been found across a wide variety of cultures,[15] and has been found so consistently that some theorists have even considered ethnocentrism as a definitional component of conservatism.[16]

On the other hand, despite this broad empirical support, several other important claims either have never been put to serious empirical test or have been disproved. Among the most important claims having shortcomings is the hypothesized child-rearing origins of the authoritarianism syndrome. Aside from the highly questionable indirect support for this hypothesis that was originally offered, there has been no well-done empirical research offered to support this claim. Second, though the psychoanalytic architecture on which APT is built is rich and interesting, it may not be needed to explain the results found. Third, APT implies that the authoritarian syndrome is somehow a pathological condition that can either be treated or prevented from occurring given proper psychotherapy or child-rearing practices. Yet there is no convincing evidence that authoritarians are any more psychologically debilitated than nonauthoritarians are. Fourth, as with many other strictly psychological models of prejudice and discrimination, APT does nothing to help us understand the relation between the hypothesized psychodynamics within the individual and the dynamics of institutional behavior and ideological processes in the society.

Psychological Uncertainty and Anxiety Models

Because most evidence of authoritarianism is correlational, the robust findings that people prejudiced against one group tend to be prejudiced against other groups, and that people who are prejudiced against outgroups also tend to be politically conservative,[17] are subject to alternative interpretations. Surprisingly, such alternative theoretical explanations are few. One exception was proposed by G. D. Wilson in 1973.[18] Wilson reasoned that the fear of uncertainty is the central psychological motivation underlying conservatism. Wilson and others showed that some expressions of the fear of uncertainty, such as preference for safe and conventional vocations, fear of death, and dislike of ambiguous art, correlate with broad attitudinal measures of conservatism.[19]

Another theory that analyzes group prejudice as stemming from a kind of fear is *terror management theory* (TMT). TMT argues that because human beings can anticipate their own deaths, they are subject to the existential anxiety or terror of meaninglessness that such thoughts bring to mind. To counteract this profound anxiety, we create and work to sustain cultural worldviews that provide a meaningful way of understanding the universe and a sense that we are valuable members of this universe.[20] Self-esteem, or the sense that one is valuable within some cultural worldview, is one kind of buffer against anxiety. Solomon et al.[21] speculate that members of minority groups may experience greater challenges to the anxiety buffer because dominant cultural beliefs about those groups question their fundamental worth and value. They note that because self-esteem measures can be reactive and unstable, it is difficult to assess this hypothesis using current techniques.

Most important for intergroup relations, TMT predicts that people find those with different cultural worldviews existentially threatening and are motivated either to assimilate their views, to convert them, or to derogate or even exterminate them, all in an effort to restore the cultural anxiety buffer. The TMT team has conducted numerous experiments to test its existential threat hypothesis, which shows that being reminded of one's death leads people to denigrate culturally dissimilar others and to elevate culturally similar others. For example, after describing what would happen to them after they died and their feelings about their own death (the mortality salience condition), Christian students evaluated a Christian more positively and a Jew more negatively, a difference not found in the control group.[22]

The TMT team has also postulated and found interactions between the individual differences discussed earlier and responses to mortality salience. For example, Greenberg et al. (1990)[23] found that, following mortality salience, only participants measuring high on authoritarianism denigrated partners who expressed dissimilar attitudes, compared with a control group.

There are many praiseworthy features of TMT. It is one of very few theories to address the issue of the existential human condition, to situate self-esteem within culture rather than reducing self-esteem concerns to entirely selfish ones, and to give a predominant role to shared cultural worldviews, symbology, and ideological phenomena in understanding human existence. Its mortality salience manipulation has generated a number of provocative experimental findings that are compatible with other psychodynamic theories. However, we are not as sure that the notion of psychological threat is as novel as the theory implies. William James's (1890, p. 334) definition of *self-identity* as a "continuing sense of self-as-known" would seem to make death a threat to identity, at least in some cultures. So it may be that the mortality salience manipulation is yet another way of inducing an identity threat, of frustrating one's current goals in one's life (à la Dollard et al., 1939), or inducing fear of uncertainty.[24]

Value and Value Conflict Theories

Another psychological approach to prejudice and discrimination that focuses on people's underlying motivations concerns values theories. This approach was strongly championed by Milton Rokeach. Rokeach tried to understand people's attitudes and beliefs about politics, outgroups, and social policies relevant to outgroups by examining people's underlying values, or the priorities given to basic principles that related to attitudes and beliefs. In his critique of various approaches to liberal–conservative ideology,[25] he noted that there was little cross-cultural or cross-historical consensus on what the terms *liberal* and *conservative* mean. His proposal for saving empirical research from culturally limited and sometimes self-contradictory definitions of liberalism and conservatism was to map such attitudes and beliefs onto more enduring and general values. Rokeach hypothesized that the major twentieth-century political ideologies (i.e., communism, fascism, socialism, and capitalism) could all be classified with respect to the importance they gave to both freedom and equality values.[26] Content analyses of political writings supported this idea: Capitalism places high value on individual freedom and low value on equality. In contrast, communism places high value on equality, but low value on individual freedom. Fascism was low on both values and socialism was high on both.

However, at least in Western countries, research has shown that the importance one attaches to freedom is unrelated to one's political leanings, although equality values are quite influential. Supporters of left-wing political parties and policies place much greater emphasis on the value of equality than do supporters of right-wing political parties and social policies.[27] The value of equality has been found to be not only extremely important in determining people's political ideologies and party preferences,[28] but also quite important in determining attitudes toward specific policies (e.g., affirmative action).

Like Rokeach (1973), Katz and Hass (1988) also examined intergroup discrimination and attitudes in terms of social equality and individual freedom, but in the form of (a) humanitarianism/egalitarianism and (b) individualism, individual achievement, and the Protestant work ethic. They argued that since both values are normative, most White Americans actually hold ambivalent attitudes toward Blacks because Blacks represent good targets for humanitarianism but bad examples of individual achievement. In support of their racial ambivalence thesis, they showed that one could construct independent Pro-Black and Anti-Black attitude scales and that the Pro-Black Scale correlated positively with the Humanitarian/Egalitarian (HE) Scale but little with the Protestant ethic (PE) Scale,[29] whereas the Anti-Black Scale correlated positively with the PE Scale and negatively with the HE Scale.[30] They also showed that having White college students complete the PE Scale increased expression of anti-Black attitudes, whereas having students complete the HE Scale increased expression of pro-Black attitudes, compared with a control group.[31] Because it is assumed that most White Americans hold both sets of values and can apply both to thinking about Blacks, Katz, Wackenhut, and Hass (1986) predicted that this fundamental ambivalence would lead Whites to have exaggerated responses in dealing with Blacks. In fact, they found that Whites are sometimes being overly helpful, as the humanistic approach would prescribe, and sometimes denigrate Blacks because of Blacks' supposed rejection of the Protestant work ethic.

Besides helping us understand political choice and political ideology in a cross-situationally and cross-historically consistent fashion, the values approach has the additional advantage of relating the attitudes of individuals to the social institutions (e.g., political parties) that so powerfully determine the nature of intergroup relations.

Social-Cognitive Approach to Stereotyping

Inspired by Allport (1954), a great number of psychological studies have explored the cognitive underpinnings of prejudice and stereotyping, so many that even recent reviews are numerous and unique.[32]

Perhaps the major and overarching conclusions to be drawn from this research are that, over and above any other motives that might be at play, social stereotypes should first and foremost be seen as the result of basic and entirely normal information processing. For example, Hamilton and Gifford (1976) showed that people learn stereotypes because of a predisposition to perceive associations among events. In particular, they reasoned that people perceive relatively unusual negative traits or behaviors and relatively unusual people, such as ethnic minorities, as going together, resulting in negative group stereotypes. By presenting information about individuals in minority and majority groups having the same proportion of frequent and infrequent features, they showed that participants indeed formed an *illusory correlation* and assumed that the infrequent features were more characteristic of the minority group. Since both relatively rare and negative features[33] and social stigma increase psychological salience,[34] this would then explain why these negative features and stigmatized social groups become associated in the mind. This process would explain the association of negative characteristics not only with minority groups, but with certain stigmatized majorities as well (e.g., women, South African Blacks, Indian untouchables). Hamilton and Rose (1980) showed that holding prior stereotypes increases the likelihood of forming stereotypic illusory correlations, so the illusory correlation process seems likely to be a contributor to the existence of stereotypes, if not an ultimate origin of them. Hamilton's illusory correlation research explains how stereotypes could come about even when groups do not actually have different features.

Other research has shown that as part of normal information processing, stereotypes are often very easily activated, are used as causal explanations, are contextually sensitive, and turn out to be extremely robust and possess self-fulfilling properties. We will explore each of these factors in turn.

The Facile Activation of Social Stereotypes

There is some evidence that people learn covariations very easily, and even unconsciously.[35] For example, a child who sees that all janitors are people of color and that almost all child care givers are women is likely, then, to learn to expect such features to go together. Such associations then form the basis of a rudimentary stereotype. Similarly, a great number of experiments have shown that one feature of a person (e.g., race, mechanical ability) easily triggers expectations about features that would be unrelated if it were not for a group stereotype (e.g., education level, aggressiveness).[36]

Once learned, social stereotypes are then quite easily and facilely activated. For example, learning one feature of a person (e.g., gender) leads people to presume many other things about that person (e.g., particular hobbies and occupation).[37] The associations between such simple expectancies are so well-rehearsed that some researchers even posit that activation of a stereotype[38] and of prejudiced group attitudes[39] are completely automatic and are cued by exposure to only some stimuli.[40] Because of this facile activation, stereotypes are thought to enable people to function well enough for their own purposes, even when these stereotypes are only approximately "accurate" and even when they harm the person being stereotyped.[41]

Stereotypes as Causal Explanations

People often need to explain and understand the behavior of others who belong to a variety of social groups. Ironically, this need will often lead to the utilization of group stereotypes. For example, Levine and Campbell (1972) argued that when certain social groups disproportionately perform certain roles within the social system, people come to assume that *all* individuals within these groups have personal characteristics consistent with those roles. This suggests that when people make *internal attributions* to explain behavior, by asking themselves questions like "What kind of person would perform this role?" they are likely to come up with a stereotype they already know as an explanation.[42] Illusory correlations, real covariations, and causal attributions are processes which imply that even if people are not motivated by any particular animus against other groups, people may still form stereotypes as part of their normal cognitive functioning.

The Contextual Sensitivity of Stereotypes

We also know that there are contextual situations that will make the use of stereotypes more or less likely. For example, Erber and Fiske (1984) showed that when people's outcomes were positively linked with those of a stranger, they paid more attention to individuating features of the person and relied less on stereotypes to form an impression of that person. However, research also shows that it is more typical that members of dominant and subordinate groups are either independent or negatively interdependent (competitive) with one another.[43] Furthermore, Deprét and Fiske (1993) argue that people in positions of power, which is more typical of dominant group members, are unlikely to have to pay more attention to subordinates, and so are especially likely to stereotype. Thus, power inequalities are particularly likely to contribute to stereotyping.

The Tenacity and Self-Fulfilling Character of Social Stereotypes

Research shows that stereotypes are often quite robust, tenacious, and long-lived. For example, Devine and Elliot (1995) found that White Americans' stereotypes about African-Americans have had rather similar content over most of this century. Furthermore, and quite relevant for the possibility of social change, research has shown that rather than providing important counterexamples, the admission of *tokens* (i.e., people who are exceptional in a social context, such as a woman in a male-dominated profession), can actually lead to *more* and *not less* stereotyping and discrimination. This effect is the result of the fact that such tokens are often quite salient, and thus people are more likely to make internal rather than situational attributions for the actions of these tokens.[44]

Further, being a token can lead to more self-consciousness, resulting in underperformance. In merit judgment situations, this underperformance often confirms the stereotype and then provides additional grounds for discrimination. For example, Word, Zanna, and Cooper (1974) showed that when White interviewers had negative expectations of Black job candidates, those expectations led them to treat job candidates in interpersonally distant ways. In reaction to this cool response, job candidates appeared more flustered and unprepared and gave worse interviews than when they were treated more respectfully. Likewise, because the stereo-type about Blacks includes the notion of aggression, Bargh, Chen, and Burrows (1996) predicted that subliminal exposure to Black faces would increase the likelihood that participants would be rude to another person. This was found, and the authors argue that it might be expected that such hostility could be returned, further confirming the stereotype. Through a number of avenues, then, stereotypes act like communicable social viruses, getting the organisms they infect to replicate the virus and spread it to others.

Stereotypes not only can provoke self-confirming behavior in stereo-typed others, but also can bias memory in ways that get people to recall stereotype-confirming "evidence." For example, Snyder and Uranowitz (1978) had participants learn the life history of a woman. Those partici-pants who later learned that she was a lesbian then recalled facts about her that were consistent with their stereotype of lesbians. However, those who later learned she was straight did not recall such facts. Such recollections are only likely to provide another instance that confirms the stereotype, even though Synder and Uranowitz's experiment actually showed that it was the stereotype that confirmed the instance.

Stereotypes sometimes also filter the acquisition of information consis-tent with the stereotype, through both information-seeking strategies[45] and selective attention.[46] Though most studies exploring memory for stereotype-consistent and -inconsistent information have found greater recall of stereotype-inconsistent information than stereotype-consistent information, Hilton and von Hippel (1996) point out that this bias may lead to greater attributions for "explaining away" the incongruity, and thereby maintaining the stereotype in the face (and recollection) of in-consistent information. In other cases, incongruent information can be used to form a subtype that also functions as a stereotype.[47] Importantly, even contradictory subtypes (e.g., virgin vs. whore) seem not to discon-firm super-stereotypes.[48]

Altogether, the broad message of the stereotyping research informs us that stereotypes are a normal feature of peoples' information processing repertoire, are very easily learned and easily activated, tend to have a self-fulfilling quality, and tend to be very difficult to change.

On the other hand, the social-cognitive approach to stereotyping also has some important limitations. In analyzing individuals' cognitive pro-cesses, the research has done little to address how institutional discrimi-nation occurs. This is partly because people in institutional settings have been little studied,[49] and also because the outcomes critical to various specific theories, such as trait judgments, turn out to have little correspondence to the kinds of outcomes critical to institutional discrimination, such as hiring and firing, salary levels, and promotions.[50] Finally, in using the individual as the unit of analysis, this literature has not examined discrimination that is contingent on the cooperation of people in different roles within an organization. For example, in one Fortune 500 company we studied, White managers who were friendly with White laborers through Ku Klux Klan groups let it be known that they disapproved of the hiring of a Black manager before the Black manager even came on the job. When the White laborers filed nightly union grievances against the Black manager, they provided an apparently legitimate basis on which the Black manager could be fired. Such socially distributed responsibility has not been well analyzed by the social-cognitive approach, which would have to incorporate such elements as social role, power, and shared communications. One response to the individualistic approach to stereotyping has been to analyze social discourse around, for example, racism, to understand how the ideologies of race are spread and legitimized.[51]

Social-Psychological Theories

Whereas strictly psychological models of prejudice, racism, and discrimination concentrate on internal and psychodynamic processes within the individual, social-psychological models place greater emphasis on the individual's connection to and embeddedness in the larger social context, the individual's absorption of cultural and ideological norms, and the individual's desire to fit in and become an accepted member of the social community.

Socialization and Social Learning Theories

Perhaps the clearest example of a social-psychological model of prejudice, racism, and discrimination is the general socialization approach. This approach assumes that the primary reason that individuals exhibit hostile, racist, and discriminatory behaviors toward others is because, from early childhood on, they have been socialized and trained to feel and behave this way. Those discriminatory behaviors and hostile attitudes toward others that are deemed appropriate are rewarded and thereby reinforced, while those considered inappropriate are punished and eventually drop out of the individual's repertoire. From this perspective, one needs no complex theory of intrapsychic and psychodynamic processes, but simply must attend to what is considered appropriate and inappropriate within any given culture or context.

Modern Racism Theories

One prominent group of social learning theories of prejudice has been largely focused on Euro-American attitudes toward African-Americans. These theories have all essentially asserted that while blatant and extreme forms of racism against African-Americans are now relegated to the past, more subtle and indirect forms of racism remain. This residual racism is often conceptualized as some combination of learned emotional antipathy toward Blacks, on the one hand, and cognitively driven stereotyping mechanisms or adherence to certain U.S. values, on the other hand. These residual racism theories have gone by various names, including *aversive racism, modern racism, racial resentment*, and *symbolic racism*.[52] The most well-known and influential of these is symbolic racism theory, developed by David O. Sears and his colleagues. Like other modern racism theorists, Sears and his collaborators have argued that the U.S. civil rights movement was largely successful in eliminating classical "old-fashioned racism" from U.S. society, only to be replaced by what is called symbolic racism. Symbolic racism is defined as a combination of anti-Black affect, or emotional antipathy toward Blacks, and certain traditional U.S. values such as self-reliance, individualism, and the Protestant work ethic. Sears and his colleagues then used this "new" symbolic racism to explore White Americans' attitudes and behaviors across a series of political issues and public policy debates.

One consistent theme in this modern racism research has been the exploration of the *principle–implementation gap*,[53] or the apparent contradiction between White Americans' expressed support for the principle of racial equality and their consistent opposition to the implementation of any concrete policies that might actually promote racial equality in practice. In general, modern racism theorists have argued that this apparent contradiction can be explained by use of this new form of modern, aversive, or symbolic racism. For example, Sears, Lau, Tyler, and Allen (1980) found evidence consistent with the idea that Whites oppose ameliorative government programs not because such programs work against their own personal interest or because they believe in the racial inferiority of Blacks, but because of symbolic racism.

Despite the robust use of symbolic racism and similar measures in attitudes research, the theory has been attacked on both conceptual and methodological grounds. These criticisms concern complaints such as: symbolic racism is not really measuring anything other than political ideology, symbolic racism is simply old-fashioned racism in disguise, and there is a serious conceptual overlap between measures of symbolic racism and the various attitudes they are supposed to predict.[54] While we feel there is some merit to these criticisms, we argue that the most serious shortcoming of symbolic racism and closely related arguments is their theoretical parochialism. Although the symbolic politics approach is much broader, symbolic racism theory was specifically developed to explain the attitudes of White Americans toward Black Americans in terms of beliefs relevant to U.S. culture (e.g., individualism, the Protestant work ethic) and within the context of a particular period in U.S. history (the immediate post–civil rights era). Because of this contextual and historical specificity, these models are not easily applied to other ethnic conflicts, such as those between Hutus and Tutsis of Rwanda, the "ethnic cleansing" of Bosnia, the Holocaust of Central Europe, or even the widespread occurrence of police brutality against African-Americans in the United States.

Realistic Group Conflict Theory

Realistic group conflict theory is among the simplest of social-psychological models of intergroup relations and was developed by a number of social scientists[55] to explain intergroup phenomena such as war, domination, ethnocentrism, stereotyping, and discrimination. In contrast to symbolic racism theory, this model is quite general and simply asserts that intergroup discrimination and prejudice are the result of real groups being locked in zero-sum competition over either real material or symbolic resources. As summarized ably by Campbell (1965), the perception that one group's gain is another's loss translates into perceptions of group threat, which in turn cause prejudice against the outgroup, negative stereotyping of the outgroup, ingroup solidarity, awareness of ingroup identity, and internal cohesion, including intolerance of ingroup deviants, ethnocentrism, use of group boundary markers, and discriminatory behavior. The realistic group conflict model is supported by a large body of research, including descriptive studies of history, politics, and ethnography, as well as field experiments and survey research.[56]

Although realistic group conflict theory is powerful and parsimonious in explaining when and why prejudice and discrimination will arise, this model is still not completely satisfactory. The model is based on two primary assumptions. The first is that real groups actually exist and have a history of shared identity and shared fate. Second, it is assumed that groups believe themselves to be in zero-sum competition over valued resources. While these two conditions are certainly *sufficient* to produce discrimination and prejudice, they are by no means *necessary*.

Social Identity Theory (SIT)

The fact that neither group formation nor zero-sum structure is a necessary condition for discrimination was first discovered by Henri Tajfel and
his colleagues in the early 1970s. Tajfel tried to devise an experiment in
which the intergroup situation was quite minimal and lacked these two
primary conditions that were hypothesized by realistic group conflict theory to cause prejudice and discrimination. Tajfel and colleagues devised a
laboratory paradigm in which participants were told that they belonged to
one of two groups that they would never have heard of before. Thus, the
groups had no history of interaction, had no known stereotypic beliefs
about each other, and were not locked in a zero-sum structure. Participants were not told who was a member of which group and were asked
to allocate only "minimal" resources such as pennies or points. Since participants were given options to allocate resources to both groups, there
was no zero-sum structure to the group relationship. Furthermore, since
the participants could not allocate points to themselves, they had no direct
self-interest in how they allocated points.

The rather surprising result of this "minimal group" situation was that,
even though the groups were not formed in the traditional, socially rich
sense and were not in a zero-sum relationship, people still tended to behave in an ethnocentric and biased fashion. Though many people did try
to allocate resources as equally as the experimenters allowed,[57] they still
tended to allocate more points to the ingroup than to the outgroup. Even
more startling is that when given the choice between (a) allocating points
to both ingroup and outgroup so that both groups benefit (but where
the outgroup receives *slightly more* than the ingroup) and (b) allocating
more points to the ingroup than the outgroup (but at the cost of *absolute
loss to both groups*), people opted for strategy (b)! From a rational actor
model of human behavior, strategy (a) is quite rational, while strategy
(b) is clearly irrational. Even more depressing, discrimination outcomes
in minimal groups experiments have been found to hold over a range
of different cultures and situations.[58] However, the interpretation of this
result remains controversial.[59]

We like to think of strategy (b) as a *Vladimir's choice*, based on a well-
known Eastern European fable. Vladimir was a dreadfully impoverished
peasant. One day God came to Vladimir and said, "Vladimir, I will grant
you one wish; anything you wish shall be yours!" Naturally, Vladimir
was very pleased at hearing this news. However, God added one caveat:
"Vladimir, anything I grant you will be given to your neighbor twice
over." After hearing this, Vladimir stood in silence for a long time, and
then said, "OK, God, take out one of my eyes."

To explain the surprising findings of the minimal groups experiments, Tajfel (1978, 1981) argued that humans have a general desire for positive social identity. When it is unclear what the meaning of the minimal group membership is, they construct the meaning to be positive so that it can reflect well on themselves. They do so by presuming their group's superiority and by allocating more to ingroups than to outgroups. Tajfel discussed how this group comparison process and intergroup discrimination could be engaged for real social groups that are part of people's social identities. Consistent with the notion that prejudice and discrimination are attempts at positive self-regard, a thorough review by Brewer (1979) suggests that intergroup discrimination in the minimal groups paradigm reflects favoritism toward the ingroup rather than denigration of the outgroup.

In a further elaboration of SIT, Tajfel and Turner (1986) discussed what hierarchical social structure implies for intergroup discrimination and social identity strategies. For example, they suggested that the more stable group boundaries are perceived to be, the more members of different groups will discriminate against each other. In fact, when experimental groups differ in stable social status, members of both low- and high-status groups discriminated in favor of the high-status group.[60] Tajfel and Turner also argued that group conflict is likely to be minimized when both the superior and inferior groups accept the legitimacy of the status distinction between them. This general theory has now become the most influential theory of intergroup relations among social psychologists.[61]

Nonetheless, there are four rather serious problems with this theory. First, SIT views social identity as the primary motivator of intergroup discrimination. This implies that those who strongly identify with their ingroups should be most prone to discriminate in favor of these groups. However, as Hinkle and Brown (1990) have pointed out, the evidence in support of this expectation is rather spotty and inconsistent. Second, while SIT addresses the issue of differential social status as a determinant of intergroup relations, it does not address the issue of differential social power. Rather, SIT regards power as an instance of social status. Most other treatments define *status* as one's social-evaluative reputation, while *power* is defined as the ability to *control* another's outcomes. However, it is power rather than reputation that enables one to discriminate in the first place.[62] Moreover, experimental studies have shown that power is more important than the degree of group identification or group status in predicting intergroup discrimination.[63]

A third problem is the phenomenon of *outgroup favoritism*, especially on the part of people in low-status groups. If, as the minimal groups paradigm tradition contends, the need for positive social identity motivates discrimination, then we should expect people in low-status groups to be even more motivated to discriminate than will people in high-status groups. However, a substantial body of research shows that people in real and experimenter-created low-status groups often acknowledge the superiority of high-status groups with respect to the high-status dimension[64] and often discriminate *in favor* of high-status groups rather than in favor of their own low-status groups.[65] One of the most well-known examples of outgroup favoritism on the part of people in a low-status group is Clark and Clark's (1947) doll study in which Black children showed a distinct preference for White dolls rather than for Black dolls.

(4)   Finally, the social identity approach is limited in the scope of discriminatory behaviors it is able to explain. As mentioned earlier, Brewer (1979) found that most intergroup discrimination in the minimal groups paradigm was bias *in favor of the ingroup* rather than *denigration of the outgroup.* Unfortunately, very many of the oppressive behaviors of greatest concern to us are examples of outgroup oppression and not just simply ingroup favoritism. For example, it stretches credibility to regard slavery, torture, and mass murder, as found in the numerous instances of intergroup violence, merely as examples of ingroup favoritism. These more extreme cases of intergroup discrimination clearly denigrate and harm others. Thus, while there is good reason to accept social identity needs as *one* motive driving group discrimination, this motive cannot possibly account for the extreme levels of barbarism, brutality, and oppression often found in intergroup relations in the real world.[66]

Social-Structural and Elite Theories

While psychological and social-psychological models of prejudice, stereotyping, and discrimination focus on the motivational or cognitive processes within individuals, social-structural and elite models focus on the structural relationships among groups. In essence, elite theories argue that social systems are hierarchically and *oligarchically* organized and disproportionately controlled by a small group of people who are variously labeled as a *ruling class, a ruling elite, oligarchs,* or *dominants.*

Group Position Theory

Perhaps the simplest of all the structural, or "sociological," models of discrimination and prejudice is the *group position model.* It can be viewed as the sociological version of realistic group conflict theory. In essence, the group position model asserts that when groups are in a state of power inequality or power imbalance, the more powerful groups will endeavor to maintain their dominant position over less powerful groups. Powerful groups will do so by promoting social attitudes and policies that advantage themselves. For example, Blumer (1960) described Americans' attitudes about race as a sense of group position in which Whites will characteristically resist social policies that they perceive as redistributing power and privilege to other, rival groups (e.g., Blacks).[67]

Marxism

The most well-known and influential of all social science theories is the elite theory developed by Karl Marx in collaboration with Friedrich Engels. The core of what is now known as Marxism centers around the analysis of capitalism, including how it arose, how it works, whom it benefits, and whom it disadvantages. Marxist theory argues that capitalist societies are hierarchically organized social systems in which the economic surplus that technology and productive instruments produce is unequally distributed between the owners of this technology and those who actually produce the wealth – the workers who use the technology. Marxism argues that those with the power and control over the means of production will exploit those with little power and control. Because those who own capital have a major power advantage over those who sell labor, these owners are able to structure economic transactions in ways that almost always benefit themselves at the cost of workers. Furthermore, the owners own not only the means of economic production (e.g., manufacturing), but the means of intellectual and cultural production as well (e.g., the mass media, the universities). Because this ruling class controls the major venues of intellectual production, this gives them great power over the kinds of ideas available for public discourse and how this discourse is framed. Finally, this economic and intellectual power also translates itself into political power and control over the organs of the state. For Marxists, the ruling class's control over the state is considered so complete that the state is regarded as the "executive committee of the ruling class."

While Marxism is primarily a theory of economic, or class-based, social hierarchy and oppression, it is not completely without relevance for our understanding of race, ethnic, and gender conflict. From the Marxist perspective, racial, ethnic, and even national conflict are seen primarily as epiphenomena and derivable from the most basic and fundamental conflict in society, namely class conflict. Among other things, racism, ethnocentrism, and nationalism are seen as instruments used by the ruling class (owners of capital) to keep workers at one another's throats and thereby prevent them from correctly perceiving and understanding their real economic interests and identifying their real enemies (i.e., owners of capital).[68]

Marxism also has implications for patriarchy. Marxism argues that family structure, on the one hand, and economic and class structure, on the other hand, are inextricably linked, and that class inequality determines the nature of gender inequality. Engels (1884/1902) posited that when the family and labor market were structured to allow men greater access to capital than women had and to make people dependent on wages rather than consuming the fruits of their own labor directly, gender inequality within marriage and the exploitation of lower-class men would result. A number of studies support these conclusions across a range of societies. For example, in studying four Native American societies that had status rankings though not social classes, Jane Collier (1988) found gender inequality and the exploitation of low-ranking men by high-ranking men, even though the particular division of labor by gender differed in each society. She concluded that the way marriage was structured within each society was responsible for the exploitation of women and low-ranking men.[69]

Finally, Marx and Engels suggested that economic inequality was made possible to the degree that there was economic surplus. For societies with subsistence economies (e.g., hunter-gatherer societies), wealth, and therefore political power, will tend to be equally distributed. However, as economies become more and more efficient at producing economic surplus, this economic surplus and its attendant political power will have a tendency to become more and more unequally distributed. This assumption has also been confirmed in cross-cultural surveys. For example, in a comparison of hunter-gatherer, simple horticultural, advanced agricultural, agrarian, and industrial societies, Lenski (1984) found general support for the idea that the ability to produce economic surplus was positively associated with the general degree of social inequality.[70]

Though Marxism has been criticized from a number of perspectives, this model also contains several very insightful ideas of enduring value. Among the most important are that ideology functions to justify and support hierarchical group relations and that ruling elites largely control the contents and framing of social discourse. Because of this control of social ideology, ruling elites are able to convince not only themselves but, more importantly, their subordinates of the legitimacy of their rule. This means that the ruling class can exercise near hegemonic control over the social system without serious resistance from, and often with the cooperation of, the working class. The notion that the working class accepts the hegemonic position of the ruling class as fair and legitimate is known as *false consciousness*. While this specific label has not always been used, the basic idea of false consciousness has had a large influence on several structural models of social control. Not only has this idea had a major influence on the thinking of sociologists for some time, but it has also begun to influence the thinking of contemporary social psychologists (see, e.g., Jost & Banaji, 1994). While most social psychologists have not paid much attention to this Marxist notion of false consciousness, as we shall explore in some detail later in this book, there is reason to believe that the incorporation of this basic idea can make major contributions to psychologists' understanding of not only class conflict, but the dynamics of power differences among other kinds of groups (e.g., genders and races).

The Neoclassical Elite Approach

The early twentieth century saw other political sociologists who, like Marxists, perceived a ubiquitous conflict between ruling elites and the masses of ordinary people. However, unlike Marxists, these theorists argued that democracy and group-based social equality were inherently unachievable. The most important of these thinkers were three Italians: Gaetano Mosca, Roberto Michels, and Vilfredo Pareto. Despite important differences among these three, they shared the basic assumption that whatever the manifest content of political discourse, all social systems are *inherently undemocratic* and are ruled by a small elite who rationalize their power by use of some system of justifying ideologies.

For Mosca, the power of a ruling elite is based on its control over what he calls *social forces* (e.g., assets such as organizational skills, economic resources, and moral suasion) and, most importantly, over major social, political, and economic organizations and institutions. Given this institutional control, the ruling class is able to impose its will on the majority of the population and rationalize this rule in terms of the *political formula*, or a system of justifying and legitimizing ideologies. Instead of declaring that they rule because they simply want to rule, members of the ruling class argue that their rule is based on and justified by notions such as "divine right," assertions of their political expertise, or allusions to "the popular will." Because of its controls over both private and public organizations and institutions of the state, an organized minority will almost always triumph over a disorganized majority. Given the ruling class's organization and the ease of communication among its relatively few members, it becomes nearly impossible for the governed majority to counterorganize and resist the will of the ruling minority.[71] For Mosca, therefore, there is no essential difference between one political system and another, or between so-called democracies and traditional monarchies. Even in so-called

representative democracies, it is not the people who elect their representatives, but rather the representatives who get themselves elected by the
people.

Roberto Michels, an early activist within the radical wing of the German
Social Democratic Party (SPD) in the early part of the twentieth century,
came to very similar conclusions. Michels became frustrated with the SPD
and its constant willingness to make political compromises that violated
the party's founding principles. In his opinion, the SPD became more
anxious to preserve its bureaucratic structure, win seats in the German
Reichstag, and serve its own organizational needs than to win power for
the German working class. Based on detailed observations of the SPD and
other German parties, Michels came to the general conclusion that, out of
a desire to be effective, social organizations institute a division of labor
and select people to become specialists and experts in certain key areas of
the organization's life. Because these people soon became indispensable
to the organization, they are able to threaten the entire organization unless
"correct" decisions are made. This increasing political power of the organization's leadership then feeds the growing megalomania of the elites,
which in turn further increases their political power vis-à-vis the rank and
file of the organization. As organizations become more economically successful, they are able to appoint full-time officials and establish patronage
jobs. Because those appointed to these patronage jobs depend on these
jobs for their livelihood, this elite then becomes very conservative and
even less likely to engage in any political activity that risks the survival of
the organization. According to Michels, the accumulated effects of these
forces produces *mission drift* within organizations. This is to say, that the
longer an organization exists, the more its efforts will wander away from
its original social purpose and toward the preservation of the organization itself. This reasoning lead to Michels's assertion of the *iron law of
oligarchy*, the notion that all social organization inevitably leads to social
oligarchy, or the rule of the few.[72]

Perhaps the most important of the Italian elite theorists was Vilfredo
Pareto. Pareto also assumed that human social systems are organized and
controlled by a small group of elites ruling over a large group of disorganized masses. However, in distinction from Marx, Mosca, and Michels,
who were almost exclusively sociological in orientation in stressing elites'
control over social institutions, Pareto was slightly more psychological
and suggested that elites also rule by virtue of certain personality characteristics. Pareto distinguished between *governing elites* and *nongoverning
elites*. Nongoverning elites are those who maintain great power, influence,
prestige, and status within a social system by virtue of their superior skills,

abilities, and attributes within nonpolitical domains (e.g., great artists, scientists, inventors). Governing elites, those of primary interest to us here, are those who wield *political* power by virtue of their superior political skills, such as cunning, opportunism, or ruthlessness.

Pareto argued that the exercise of power is based on four factors: *social heterogeneity, interest, residues,* and *derivations.*[73] By *social heterogeneity,* Pareto means that all known human societies are accompanied by a separation or conflict between the mass of people who are ruled and a small and select group of individuals who are the rulers, the ruling elite. *Interests* are defined as the goals that individuals wish to attain, such as economic gain or political power. More in the spirit of Freud than most other elite theorists, Pareto asserts that human behavior is not primarily driven by either reason or logic, but rather by illogical and nonlogical drives. The part of Pareto's theory that most clearly deals with the nonlogical, psychological forces are expressed by his theory of *residues.* In essence, *residues* are defined as psychological dispositions occupying an intermediate status between human sentiments, which cannot be known directly, and observable expressions and concrete action. While Pareto distinguishes between six types of residues, only the first two of these are central for his general theory. *Class I residues* are the "instincts for combinations." These are the manifestations of sentiments of progressiveness, inventiveness, the desire for adventure, and the drawing of conclusions from abstract principle. *Class II residues* concern what Pareto calls the "preservation of aggregates." These residues express the more conservative side of human nature, including loyalty to society's norms and major institutions such as the church, the family, the military, and the nation.

It has often been pointed out that Pareto's Class I and Class II residues are really an extension of the political personalities discussed by the fifteenth-century political analyst Niccolo Machiavelli.[74] Corresponding respectively to Pareto's Class I and Class II residues, Machiavelli divided political personalities into two basic types: *Foxes* and *Lions.* Foxes are political elites who maintain their power over the masses by virtue of their cunning, manipulative abilities, opportunism, imaginative flexibility, and guile. Lions, on the other hand, are those ruling elites who maintain power by use of cohesion, threat, naked force, violence, and terror. According to Pareto, for a ruling elite to maintain itself in power, it must consist of a balance between Foxes and Lions, between guile and cunning on the one hand and ruthlessness and ferocity on the other hand.

Finally, Pareto argued that the rule of political elites demanded the presence of *derivations,* or the ostensibly logical justifications that elites employed to legitimize their essentially nonlogical, sentiment-driven reasons to rule. Although the details are slightly different, we can see that Pareto's notion of derivations is functionally equivalent to Marx's theory of *ideology* and Mosca's thesis of the *political formula*. All three concepts refer to ideational and conceptual devices by which ruling elites manage to convince subordinates and themselves that their rule is fair, right, and just. Therefore, from the Paretian point of view, democracy and "equality of opportunity for all" are merely illusions and are not possible of being realized, not even in principle.

Though Pareto, Marx, and Engels share similar views of ideology, they also have some fundamental differences. First, unlike Marxism, which tends to reduce all other elements of the social system as derivative from basic differences in economic interest, Pareto views all of the four major elements of the social system (i.e., social heterogeneity, interests, residues, and derivations) as dynamically interrelated to and mutually dependent on one another. While Pareto agrees with Marx that the class struggle is *a* fundamental fact of human history, he does not agree that it is *the* fundamental fact of human history. Second, Pareto disagrees with Marx and Engels that the modern class struggle differs in any essential degree from group struggles of the past. Pareto argues that, rather than bringing about the "victory of the Proletariat," the end of the class struggle will instead merely bring about the victory of new elites *speaking in the name of the proletariat*. In essence, the Paretian model is the ultimate statement of "Plus ça change, plus c'est la même chose."[75]

While we will take no position regarding any apparent prescriptive implications of the elite approach, given that this general approach is very consistent with the historical record, we think it would be foolish to ignore the potentially useful descriptive elements of elite theories. In fact, though elite theories have been applied primarily to analyses of European class and political systems, we suggest that some important ideas within these models may apply to systems of group domination in general, including racial, national, and gender domination.

However, there are some problems with neoclassical elite theories that are important to avoid. Chief among these is the assumption that elites rule by virtue of their meritorious personal qualities. While there are doubtless many highly gifted members of the ruling elite, it is also important to keep in mind that *meritoriousness* is not simply a matter of objective truth, but also a matter of socially constructed truth. It is often a socially constructed truth that is both defined by, and serves in the interest of, the ruling elite themselves. Dahrendorf (1959) suggests one process that might make everyone believe that elites are actually better than everyone else: He says that it is exactly those features that are more obviously exhibited by elites that will come to be defined as "meritorious."[76] Similarly, the ultimate attribution error[77] implies that people may come to believe that those with greater power or elevated social position deserve this because of some inherent, superior properties they possess. Thus, when thinking about the concept of merit, it is important that we keep in mind the socially constructed nature of this concept and the manner in which it is used to justify group domination.

Evolutionary Theory

If the elite perspectives have been largely ignored by most contemporary social scientists, recent attempts to apply evolutionary theory to human psychology and sociology have created something of a furor. In essence, the Darwinian thesis simply asserts that those organisms that possess the physiological and behavioral characteristics that allow them to produce viable offspring within certain environments will survive across time, while those organisms that are poorly suited to their environments and therefore cannot produce viable offspring will become extinct. *Evolution*, then, is the process by which organism change, largely in response to changing environmental circumstances. The construct of *evolutionary adaptation* is at once historical and dynamic and emphasizes that it is the *relationship* between organisms and their environments, not what qualities are valuable or "fit" in some absolute sense, that is what adaptation is about.

Since Darwin, there have been several major extensions of evolutionary theory, with accompanying theoretical controversies. Of relevance here is the addition of genetic theory, that selection takes place for genes rather than simply for species. Though this idea has been used to argue for genetically selfish behavior in books like *The Selfish Gene* (Dawkins, 1989), it also allowed for W. D. Hamilton's (1964) notion of *inclusive fitness*, which suggests that organisms will behave in ways that protect not only their own fitness (i.e., reproductive success), but also the fitness of organisms with whom they share a large number of genes. The greater the perceived genetic overlap between two organisms, the greater the degree of altruistic behavior among these organisms one should expect. Among other things, this implies that altruism can really be regarded as an act of genetic selfishness.

Keeping in mind that ethnic groups generally consist of genetically related individuals, the relevance that the concepts of inclusive fitness and altruism have for the study of intergroup discrimination and hostility becomes fairly clear and straightforward. The notion of inclusive fitness not only provides us with an evolutionary explanation for altruistic and self-sacrificial behavior, but also suggests that ethnic discrimination and ingroup favoritism are simply means by which genetically related organisms aid in the duplication of their common genes into successive generations. Ironically then, nepotism, ethnocentrism, and discrimination in favor of one's ingroup can be seen as manifestations of altruism, or the organism's effort to increase its inclusive fitness. The greater the degree to which organism A perceives itself to be genetically related to another organism, B, the greater the degree to which organism A will be expected to discriminate in favor of organism B. Thus, whenever people have some basis for making an ingroup–outgroup distinction, they are also likely to regard members of the ingroup to be more "related" to each other than they are to members of the outgroup, resulting in nepotism, ingroup favoritism, and outgroup discrimination.[78]

Another important Darwinian idea that has received renewed attention is the notion of *sexual selection*, or the idea that organisms may change because of features that are or are not selected by potential mates. Extended in parental investment theory (Trivers, 1972), this process implies that there will be both *intersexual* and *intrasexual* competition. In particular, as men and women bring different resources and needs to reproduction and child rearing, they will select mates who have complementary resources. This thesis implies gender differences in particular areas, such as in status-striving behavior. Moreover, the notion of sexual selection implies competition within one sex over the resources or features that the other sex values and, as we will see in Chapter 10, provides an explanation for both higher levels of violence and status ranking among males.

However, while the Darwinian theory of evolution is no longer controversial when applied to the structure and behavior of plants and animals, it is immensely controversial when applied to the behavior and psychology of human beings. Several critics have decried the misuse of evolutionary thinking and "neo-social-Darwinism" to promote the idea that certain classes, races, or genders of people are "superior" in being more "fit" than others, so that social inequalities appear justified by science and nature.[79] Examples of the misuse of such thinking can be found in the rather hair-raising history of social Darwinism during the nineteenth and early twentieth centuries (e.g., eugenics programs) and in contemporary social discourse and policy recommendations (see, e.g., Herrnstein & Murray, 1994). Thus, classical and contemporary social Darwinism present us with important lessons in how ideologies work in science as well as in political ideology. We would hope that these lessons can be taken seriously in understanding how evolutionary theory should and should not be applied.

Second, the adaptive theory of natural selection has also been widely misinterpreted by many social scientists, who have an unfortunate tendency of pitting evolutionary explanations for behavior against cultural ones. Rather than promote this either/or framing, Darwin's theory of natural selection implies that the nature versus nurture distinction is a complete illusion. Natural features (e.g., physiology, genes) and social-environmental features (e.g., culture) are both products of history and the results of one set of features acting on the other. Indeed, the adaptive process implies that behavioral predispositions may be adaptations to the environment, both its physical features (e.g., the presence of dangerous microbes) and its social and cultural features (e.g., consistent cultural norms). Similarly, certain cultural phenomena such as language and the regulation of sexual behavior are strongly influenced by evolved human predispositions. Because evolved predispositions and physical and cultural environments are constantly affecting and being affected by one another, the duality implied by the term *nature versus nurture distinction* is both misleading and nonproductive. Instead, we must regard both biological and social features as parts of the same interconnected and dynamic system.[80]

Caporael and Brewer (1991) provide an illuminating example of this perspective in the synchronicity of luteinizing hormone (LH) cycles in certain mammals, including rodents, primates, ungulates, and humans. When the females of such species live in close proximity to one another over an extended period of time, they tend to exhibit synchronized LH cycles, increasing the chance they will conceive and give birth at or near the same time. One benefit of this outcome is that it allows for cooperative rearing of the young and increases the probability that each youngster will survive to maturity. This synchronicity can be seen as the effect of a "social" arrangement (i.e., group living) on the physiological and social outcomes of the mothers and children. At the same time, LH synchronization can be seen as a "physiological" influence that helps maintain the utility of group living. Clearly, then, the context within which evolution takes place consists of not only the physical environment but also the social environment.

Summary and Conclusions

In this chapter we have reviewed a very rich array of theories concerning the complex and related issues of prejudice, stereotyping, discrimination, and oppression. We grouped the theories into four categories: psychological models, social-psychological models, structural-sociological models, and evolutionary models. Most psychological and social-psychological work has attempted to explain these phenomena in terms of personality variables, cognitive processing, or the exigencies of specific social situations, whereas the social-structural models have attempted to understand these phenomena from the perspective of conflicts between real groups for material and symbolic resources. Evolutionary theory suggests that certain behaviors such as intergroup competition, ingroup cooperation, and coordination may be adaptive. This general approach promises to offer a fresh and potentially useful way of understanding essentially ubiquitous human phenomena such as ethnocentrism, patriarchy, and class inequality. In broad terms, this perspective regards these phenomena as stemming from human predispositions that evolved to increase inclusive fitness or reproductive success.

While each of the approaches we have reviewed has its shortcomings, they also offer a number of important insights. First, reliance on social stereotypes is common because of the constraints placed on human information processing. Second, despite the normalcy of stereotyping, there are important individual differences between people in their propensity to hold negative stereotypes and related group attitudes and to discriminate against or oppress other people. Third, socialization and other cultural transmission processes are important to understanding how both individuals and societies teach and spread social ideologies and social practices. Fourth, the actions of social and political institutions, and not just the actions of individuals, must be included to explain stable oppression. Fifth, social ideologies and stereotypes are consensual and shared by members of dominant and subordinate groups alike. These shared ideologies are central to the perpetuation of oppressive intergroup relations by legitimizing these relations in the past and re-creating them in the future. Sixth, we must open ourselves to the possibility that phenomena such as patriarchy, ethnocentrism, and group discrimination are due to evolved behavioral predispositions. At the same time, however, we must not allow this thinking to degenerate into simple-minded geneticism or function as one more apology for oppression. With all of these points in mind, we shall now present our attempt to synthesize these ideas into the new model called *social dominance theory.*

2 | Social Dominance Theory

A New Synthesis

As we saw in the preceding chapter, a number of classical and contemporary theories of social attitudes and intergroup relations have given us some important insights into the nature and dynamics of intergroup conflict, stereotyping, and group oppression. However, there has yet to be a serious effort to integrate these insights into one coherent and comprehensive theoretical model. In an effort to accomplish this and gain a firmer purchase on the almost boringly repetitive nature of human oppression, we have developed social dominance theory (SDT). While this approach is new in many ways, its primary virtue is that it ties together the most critical and useful components and models reviewed in Chapter 1. The most important sources for our new synthesis can be found in the ideas of (a) authoritarian personality theory,[1] (b) Rokeach's two-value theory of political behavior,[2] (c) Blumer's group positions theory,[3] (d) Marxism and neoclassical elite theories,[4] (e) results from political attitude and public opinion research, (f) social identity theory (SIT),[5] and (g) modern thinking within evolutionary psychology.[6] While SDT has been influenced by models within personality psychology, social psychology, and political sociology, it is neither strictly a psychological nor a sociological theory, but rather an attempt to connect the worlds of individual personality and attitudes with the domains of institutional behavior and social structure. Thus, SDT is an attempt to integrate several levels of analysis into one coherent theoretical framework.

Some Basic Observations

SDT begins with the basic observation that all human societies tend to be structured as systems of *group-based social hierarchies*. At the very minimum, this hierarchical social structure consists of one or a small number of dominant and hegemonic groups at the top and one or a number of subordinate groups at the bottom. Among other things, the dominant group is characterized by its possession of a disproportionately large share of *positive social value*, or all those material and symbolic things for which people strive. Examples of positive social value are such things as political authority and power, good and plentiful food, splendid homes, the best available health care, wealth, and high social status. While dominant groups possess a disproportionately large share of positive social value, subordinate groups possess a disproportionately large share of *negative social value*, including such things as low power and social status, high-risk and low-status occupations, relatively poor health care, poor food, modest or miserable homes, and severe negative sanctions (e.g., prison and death sentences).

After making the observation that human social systems are structured as group-based social hierarchies, SDT then attempts to identify the various mechanisms that produce and maintain this group-based social hierarchy and how these mechanisms interact.

Group-Based Versus Individual-Based Social Hierarchies

By the term *group-based social hierarchy* we mean something quite distinct from an individual-based social hierarchy. In an individual-based social hierarchy, individuals might enjoy great power, prestige, or wealth by virtue of their own highly-valued *individual* characteristics, such as great athletic or leadership ability, high intelligence, or artistic, political, or scientific talent or achievement. Group-based social hierarchy, on the other hand, refers to that social power, prestige, and privilege that an individual possesses by virtue of his or her ascribed membership in a particular socially constructed group such as a race, religion, clan, tribe, lineage, linguistic/ethnic group, or social class. This is not to imply that the power, prestige, and privilege of individuals in group-based social hierarchies are completely independent of the individuals' personal characteristics and qualities. We only wish to imply that such achievements and status of individuals are not completely independent of the status and power of the groups to which they belong. With ascribed, or group-based, hierarchies, on the other hand, one's social status, influence, and power are also a function of one's group membership and not simply of one's individual abilities or characteristics. Of course, in complex human social systems, individual- and group-based social hierarchies will not be completely independent. Access to the means of individual achievement (e.g., education, specialized skills) is differentially available to ascribed social groups. For example, two children may both have the same level of native talent, individual drive, and personal ambition. However, if one child is of the upper class, has ambitious and well-connected parents, and attends the "right" schools, the chances are that this child will do quite well in life. On the other hand, for the other child growing up in an impoverished, dangerous, and sociogenic neighborhood and afflicted with inferior schools, chances are that that child will not do quite as well in life. This, of course, is simply to state the obvious. Even in modern, democratic, and multigroup societies, the achieved component of social status is, to a very significant degree, dependent on the social status and power of one's ascribed group membership.

The Trimorphic Structure of Group-Based Social Hierarchy

Pierre van den Berghe[7] was among the first to observe that human group-based social hierarchies consist of distinctly different stratification systems. While he distinguished among four stratification systems,[8] for our purposes these can be collapsed into three: (a) an *age system*, in which adults and middle-age people have disproportionate social power over children and younger adults,[9] (b) a *gender system* in which males have disproportionate social and political power compared with females (*patriarchy*), and (c) what we shall label an *arbitrary-set* system. The arbitrary-set system is filled with socially constructed and highly salient groups based on characteristics such as clan, ethnicity, estate, nation, race, caste, social class, religious sect, regional grouping, or any other socially relevant group distinction that the human imagination is capable of constructing.

In such systems, one group is materially and/or politically dominant over the other. As we shall see later, while there are a number of similarities in the structural and functional characteristics of these three stratification systems, each of them is unique and plays a different role in the overall construction and maintenance of group-based social hierarchies. For example, if a person lives long enough, he or she can occupy every level of the age system, from the role of low-status, small child to the role of high-status elder. This continually changing social role is quite distinct from one's position in either the arbitrary-set or, especially, the gender systems, in which one's position in the social hierarchy tends to be relatively fixed throughout life. This *fixedness* of status position is particularly dramatic with respect to the gender system.

While the age and gender systems certainly have at least some degree of malleability in terms of who is defined as young or old, male or female, the arbitrary-set system is characterized by an unusually high degree of arbitrariness, plasticity, flexibility, and situational and contextual sensitivity in determining which group distinctions are socially salient and the manner in which ingroups and outgroups are defined. For example, the salient arbitrary-set ingroup–outgroup boundaries may be defined in terms of membership in street gangs (e.g., Bloods vs. Crips), nationality (e.g., American vs. Iraqi), race (White vs. Black), or social class (e.g., working class vs. upper class). Furthermore, even using a particular arbitrary-set dimension (e.g., race), the criteria for membership in one category or another is highly dependent on the cultural and situational context. For example, a given person would be classified as Black in early-nineteenth-century America (i.e., having at least $\frac{1}{8}$ African heritage), classified as mulatto during the same period in the Caribbean or in South Africa, and White in late-twentieth-century Sweden.

The arbitrary-set system is also, by far, associated with the greatest degree of violence, brutality, and oppression. While the age and gender systems are certainly no strangers to very brutal forms of social control, the brutality associated with arbitrary-set systems very often far exceeds that of the other two systems in terms of intensity and scope. For example, besides the infamous Holocaust, the twentieth century alone has witnessed at least seven major episodes of genocidal, arbitrary-set violence, including (a) the episodic massacres of the Kurds by Turkey in 1924, Iran in 1979, and Iraq in 1988, (b) Stalin's wholesale slaughter of the Kulaks in 1929, (c) the widespread massacre of the inhabitants of East Timor in the late 1990s, (d) the Khmer Rouge terror in the late 1970s, (e) ethnic cleansing of Muslims in Bosnia and other regions of the former Yugoslavia in the late 1990s, (f) the widespread killing of Kasaians in Zaire,[10] and (g) the most recent massacres of Tutsis and Hutus in Rwanda and Burundi in the late 1990s. Furthermore, Gurr and Harff cataloged some 63 ethnic and armed conflicts around the world in 1993 alone.[11] These conflicts were not restricted to any particular part of the world, being found in Europe, the Middle East, North and Sub-Saharan Africa, Central, South, and East Asia, the Pacific Islands, and the Americas. This level of barbarism and blood lust is rarely, if ever, observed within the age and gender systems of social stratification.

Another difference between the arbitrary-set system and the age and gender stratification systems is that with the exceptions of the social roles of headman and shaman, arbitrary-set stratification systems are generally not found among small hunter-gatherer societies.[12] It is widely assumed that one major reason for the lack of arbitrary-set, group-based social hierarchy among hunter-gatherer societies is because such societies lack sufficient economic surplus. The technologies of food production and storage within hunter-gatherer societies do not permit long-term storage of food.[13] Similarly, because hunter-gatherer societies tend to be nomadic, people within such societies are not able to accumulate large amounts of other, nonedible forms of economic surplus such as animal skins, weapons, and armaments. This lack of economic surplus does not allow for the development of highly specialized social roles, such as professional armies, police, and other bureaucracies facilitating the formation of expropriative political authority. Because of the absence of military and "coercive specialists," all adult males within hunter-gatherer societies are essentially the military equals of all other adult males. Therefore, the extent to which political authority among adult males exists, this authority tends to be based on mutual agreement, persuasion, and consultation rather than coercion. Although hunter-gatherer societies are generally not *completely* egalitarian, when social and political hierarchy does exist among adult males, it tends to be based on the general skills and leadership capacities of particular *individuals*. As a result, this hierarchy tends not to be transgenerational or hereditary in nature.

In contrast, societies producing substantial and stable economic surplus (i.e., horticultural, agrarian, industrial and postindustrial societies) are also those that have arbitrary-set systems of social hierarchy.[14] Because of economic surplus, not all adults need to devote most of their time to food procurement and survival. Certain males are then freed to specialize in the arts of coercion (e.g., warlordism, policing) or spiritual and intellectual sophistry. These specialists are used by political elites to establish and enforce expropriative economic and social relationships with other members of the society. Once these role specializations and expropriative relationships are in place, arbitrary-set, group-based hierarchies then emerge. Examples of societies containing systems of stable, arbitrary-set, group-based hierarchies abound and can be found in both the ancient and modern worlds and on every continent. A partial list would include nations and societies such as Mexico, Japan, Sumeria, Nigeria, Germany, Israel, France, Canada, the United States, Taiwan, Zaire, Korea, Israel, the Zulu empire, the former USSR, South Africa, ancient Rome, ancient and modern Egypt, Greece, China, Scandinavia, Benin, Persia, and the pre-Colombian societies of the Inca, Aztec, and Maya. For example, as late as the Edo period (1603–1867) essentially five hierarchically arranged social classes were formed in Japan. In order of social status and power, these groups were the Shi (samurai), Nou (farmers), Kou (industrial professionals, craftsmen), Shou (merchants, retailers), and the Burakumin (or nonhumans; i.e., Eta and Hinin).[15] Even if attention is restricted to nonsubsistence societies, one is truly hard pressed to find a society anywhere in the world that does *not* have an arbitrary-set stratification system.

Furthermore, every attempt to abolish arbitrary-set, group-based hierarchy within societies of economic surplus have, without exception, failed. These failures have ranged from attempts at massive, revolutionary change (e.g., in France, Russia, Mexico, China, and the U.S. civil rights movement) to transformatory experiments within small and iso-lated utopian communities (e.g., New Harmony, Indiana; New Lanark, Scotland; the Oneida Community, New York). This apparently perfect correlation between the production of sustainable economic surplus and the emergence of arbitrary-set social hierarchy appears to imply that sys-tems of arbitrary-set hierarchy will emerge *whenever the proper economic conditions allow.*

While arbitrary-set hierarchy tends to be restricted to those societies producing economic surplus, age and gender systems of social stratifica-tion appear to be completely universal. Adults generally have more power and privilege than children and younger people.

In both hunter-gatherer and early agricultural societies, while women contributed substantially to the subsistence of the group by frequently collecting and controlling the essentials for survival, there is no known society in which women, as a group, have had control over the political life of the community, the community's interaction with outgroups, or the technology and practice of warfare, which is arguably the ultimate arbiter of political power. While some scholars have argued that matriarchy is the foundation of human society (see, e.g., Bachofen, Gimbutas),[16] most anthropologists and social historians dispute this claim. Although there are several known examples of matrilineal societies (i.e., where descent is traced through the family of the mother), matrilocal or uxorilocal soci-eties (i.e., where newly married couples reside with the wife's kin), and societies in which women have near economic parity with men,[17] there are no known examples of matriarchal societies (i.e., where women, as a group, control the political and military authority within the society).[18]

We have evidence of women being excluded from significant politi-cal and military power as far back as 5,000 years. For example, by 3000 B.C., women in Sumer were excluded from almost all important political and military decisions. Similarly, approximately 3,700 years ago, the legal code of ancient Babylon (i.e., the Code of Hammurabi) built on the patri-archal tendencies of Sumer and prescribed rather draconian punishments for women who challenged male dominance.[19] Even though some soci-eties were occasionally ruled by very powerful individual queens, in the aggregate the ultimate military power has always been in the hands of men. Furthermore, patriarchy in the ancient world was not restricted to Islamic societies or areas in and adjacent to the Near East, but has also been documented among the ancient and traditional cultures in Middle and South America, Africa, the ancient Germanic tribes, and the ancient cul-tures in India, China, and Japan.[20] In his discussion of the role of women in hunter-gatherer societies, Gerherd Lenski (1984) remarks:

Women invariably occupy a position inferior to men, though in some societies, the differential is not great. Women are almost always excluded from the role of headman and usually are ineligible to become shamans or participate in council meetings. (p. 111)

While not as stable as age and gender hierarchies, the evidence suggests that arbitrary-set stratification systems also display a remarkable degree of stability. One example of this stability is the Indian caste system, which has remained relatively intact for at least 3,000 years. While caste is no longer part of the legal order of Indian society and "untouchability" was outlawed after Indian independence in 1947, caste remains an extremely important aspect of Indian social and political life. For example, most marriages are still made within castes, politicians rely on the "caste vote," castes continue to act as economic and political pressure groups, castes are still ranked in terms of purity and pollution, and intercaste violence continues to the present day.

While the United States is a more socially dynamic nation than India and is, of course, not nearly as old, the U.S. version of the caste system shows every sign of being highly stable as well. Despite intense efforts to eliminate racism from U.S. life, the relative dominance of Euro-Americans over African-Americans has remained unchanged since the European occupation of the New World more than 400 years ago. Although not nearly as impressive as the Indian example, some empirical evidence of the stability of the U.S. ethnic hierarchy can be found in recent public opinion polling assembled by Tom Smith (1991). Using national probability samples, Smith tabulated the perceived social standing of a long array of U.S. ethnic groups, once in 1964 and again a quarter of a century later in 1989. What makes this particular period of U.S. history so interesting is that it embraces the era when the modern civil rights movement was at its height and the United States had embarked on its most intense and ambitious efforts to eliminate racism and actualize the promise of U.S. democracy. Close inspection of these data discloses a very high degree of hierarchical stability. While the social status ranking of a number of ethnic groups increased during this period (e.g., Negroes: 2.75 in 1964 to 4.17 in 1989), the *relative* ethnic group rankings and, thereby, the hierarchical structure within this arbitrary-set system remained essentially unchanged.

Basic Assumptions of Social Dominance Theory

After observing the ubiquitousness and stability of group-based social hierarchy and having identified the trimorphic nature of this social hierarchy, we can now introduce the three primary assumptions on which social dominance theory (SDT) is based:

(1) *While age- and gender-based hierarchies will tend to exist within all social systems, arbitrary-set systems of social hierarchy will invariably emerge within social systems producing sustainable economic surplus.*

This first assumption follows from our review of the anthropological literature on human social structure.

(2) *Most forms of group conflict and oppression (e.g., racism, ethnocentrism, sexism, nationalism, classism, regionalism) can be regarded as different manifestations of the same basic human predisposition to form group-based social hierarchies.*

The second assumption touches on a subtle yet extremely important distinction between SDT and one of its intellectual parents, namely, SIT. While SIT clearly recognizes and, in part, accommodates itself to the reality of social hierarchy and power differences between social groups, SDT is centrally focused on and built around the notion of group-based social hierarchy. In contrast to SIT, originally developed to explain ingroup favoritism within the context of essentially equal and arbitrarily defined social groups, SDT was originally conceived as a model of social hierarchy. Because of this, SDT focuses on the way that both social discourse (e.g., ideology, attitudes, and stereotypes) and individual and institutional behavior contribute to and are affected by the nature and severity of group-based social hierarchy.

In situations in which hierarchical group relations cannot be identified, SDT would, in principle, have little to explain, and one might be content to understand the nature of prejudice and discrimination in terms of some combination of earlier models, such as authoritarian personality theory, realistic group conflict theory, and SIT. The social dominance synthesis states not only that group-based social hierarchy will tend to be ubiquitous, especially within social systems producing economic surplus, but more importantly, that most if not all forms of group prejudices, stereotypes, ideologies of group superiority and inferiority, and forms of individual and institutional discrimination both help produce and are reflections of this group-based social hierarchy. In other words, phenomena such as prejudice, racism, stereotypes, and discrimination simply cannot be understood outside the conceptual framework of group-based social hierarchy, especially within social systems of economic surplus.

(3) *Human social systems are subject to the counterbalancing influences of hierarchy-enhancing (HE) forces, producing and maintaining ever higher levels of group-based social inequality, and hierarchy-attenuating (HA) forces, producing greater levels of group-based social equality.*

A perusal of recorded history across all known non-hunter-gatherer societies testifies to clear and sometimes extreme levels of group-based social inequality. The relatively recent system of chattel slavery in the United States is perhaps one of the most brutal examples in human history. Group-based social inequality is often directly produced by the unequal distribution of social value (both positive and negative) to various groups within the social system. This unequal distribution of social value is, in turn, justified and defended by use of various social ideologies, beliefs, myths, and religious doctrines. At the same time, a fair reading of the historical record also reveals consistent attempts to create more egalitarian and inclusive social systems. Evidence of these HA forces can be seen in everything from early Christian discourse,[21] to the widespread sociopolitical discourse emanating from social democratic, socialist, and Marxist movements of the nineteenth century, to the civil and human rights activists of the middle and late twentieth century. However, for the most part, these counterdominance, or HA, tendencies within non-hunter-gatherer societies appear to function to moderate the degree of *inequality*.

Schematic Overview of Social Dominance Theory

Given our three basic assumptions of SDT, the body of SDT concerns identifying and understanding the specific intrapersonal, interpersonal, intergroup, and institutional mechanisms that produce and maintain group-based social hierarchy and how, in turn, this hierarchy affects these contributing mechanisms. In very broad terms, SDT argues that the general processes producing and maintaining group-based social hierarchy are those sketched out in Figure 2.1.

As shown in the extreme right-hand side of Figure 2.1, SDT argues that group-based social hierarchy is driven by three proximal processes: *aggregated individual discrimination, aggregated institutional discrimination, and behavioral asymmetry*. These proximal processes are regulated, in part, by legitimizing myths. The extent to which an individual endorses legitimizing myths depends on whether he or she generally endorses, desires, and supports a system of group-based social hierarchy or not. We call the generalized orientation toward group-based social hierarchy *social dominance orientation* (SDO).

Aggregated Individual Discrimination

By the term *aggregated individual discrimination*, we are referring to the simple, daily, and sometimes quite inconspicuous individual acts of

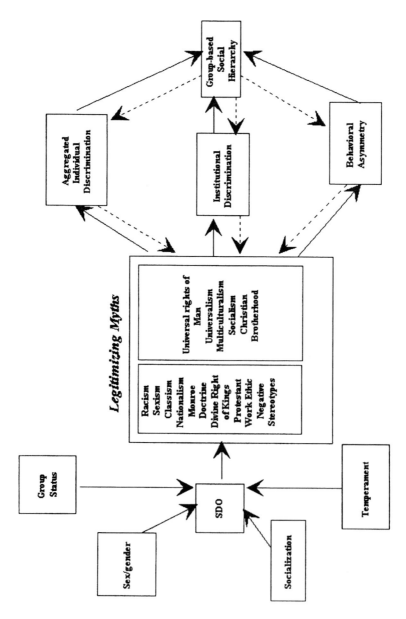

Figure 2.1. Schematic overview of social dominance theory.

Legitimizing Myths

Racism
Sexism
Classism
Nationalism
Monroe
Doctrine
Divine Right
of Kings
Protestant
Work Ethic
Negative
Stereotypes

Universal rights of
Man
Universalism
Multiculturalism
Socialism
Christian
Brotherhood

Group-based
Social
Hierarchy

Aggregated
Individual
Discrimination

Institutional
Discrimination

Behavioral
Asymmetry

Group
Status

Sex/gender

SDO

Socialization

Temperament

discrimination by one individual against another. Examples of such discrimination can be found in the decision of an employer not to hire or promote a person from a given minority group or the decision of a voter not to vote for a given candidate because of race, ethnicity, or gender. When thousands of such individual acts of discrimination are aggregated over days, weeks, years, decades, and centuries, they contribute to the clear and salient differences in the power between social groups.

Aggregated Institutional Discrimination

Group-based social hierarchy is produced not only by individual and private acts of discrimination, but also by the rules, procedures, and actions of social institutions. These institutions may be public or private, including courts, lending institutions, hospitals, retail outlets, and schools. Sometimes this institutional discrimination is conscious, deliberate, and overt, and sometimes it is unconscious, unintended, and covert. Whatever form it takes, it can be identified by whether institutional decisions result in the disproportionate allocation of positive and negative social value across the social status hierarchy, all other factors being equal.[22]

Systematic Terror

Besides the unequal distribution of social value, institutions also help maintain the integrity of the social hierarchy by the use of *systematic terror*. By systematic terror we refer to the use of violence or threats of violence disproportionately directed against subordinates. Systematic terror functions to maintain expropriative relationships between dominants (i.e., members of dominant groups) and subordinates (i.e., members of subordinate groups) and enforce the continued deference of subordinates toward dominants. As we shall discuss in more detail in Chapter 8, systematic terror is likely to be most ferocious when subordinates directly challenge and confront the hegemonic control of dominants. There are three basic forms of systematic terror: *official terror, semiofficial terror*, and *unofficial terror*.

Official terror is the public and legally sanctioned violence and threat of violence perpetrated by organs of the state and disproportionately directed toward members of subordinate groups. The most contemporary examples of official terror are the disproportionate use of the death penalty against subordinates in nations such as apartheid South Africa and the United States, and the acts of collective punishment used against the Palestinians of Gaza and the West Bank by Israel. Rather than being a relatively uncommon occurrence in the modern world, the evidence suggests that official terror is quite widespread. For example, in a 1997 study of 151 countries, Amnesty International reported general, comprehensive, and widespread state violence against ethnic and racial minorities in the form of mass arrests, trials without due process of law, extended detention without trial, beatings, the torture of children in front of their parents, and the like.

Semiofficial terror is the violence or intimidation directed against subordinates, carried out by officials of the state (e.g., internal security forces, police, secret police, paramilitary organizations) but not publicly, overtly, officially, or legally sanctioned by the state. Examples of semiofficial terror can be seen in the death squad activities that have played such a prominent role in the politics of Asia, Central and South America, and Africa. Some of the most recent evidence of semiofficial terror can be found in the systematic and routine beatings, bombings, rapes, and murders perpetrated against opponents of the Apartheid regime by members of the Vlakplass, or South African secret service.[23]

Unofficial terror is that violence or threat of violence perpetrated by *private individuals* from dominant groups against members of subordinate groups. While this terror does not enjoy the active approval or sanction of official government agencies, it usually does enjoy the tacit approval if not active participation of members of the security forces (e.g., lynchings by the Ku Klux Klan). This type of terror can be quite widespread in scope and comprehensive in its effects. For example, unofficial terror resulted in the deaths of at least 3,400 African-Americans in the United States between 1882 and 1927.[24]

One finding from the study of institutional discrimination and associated forms of terror is that the legal and criminal justice systems are among the major instruments used in establishing and maintaining the hierarchical structure of intergroup relations. Admittedly, the internal security and criminal justice systems are designed to maintain "law and order." However, from a social dominance perspective, in the aggregate, *law* is often written and enforced so as to favor the interests of dominants, and *order* is often defined as those social conditions that disproportionately protect and maintain the interests of dominants. Therefore, contrary to the commonly held assumption that discrimination against subordinates within the criminal justice system is relatively rare, nonsystematic, and completely overshadowed by the everyday realities of basic fairness and equity, SDT suggests that discrimination within the criminal justice system is quite systematic and comprehensive in its effects.

SDT expects that discrimination against subordinates is to be found in all societies with economic surplus, including societies with democratic and egalitarian pretensions. However, in general, the level of brutality and discrimination against subordinates within so-called democratic societies will tend to be somewhat constrained, indirect, and covert due to the cultural ideals espousing equality before the law. As a consequence, although the criminal justice system will still behave in a discriminatory manner, the elites within these systems will be under some pains to justify the presence and extent of this discrimination. In other words, it is crucial that such democratic social systems maintain *plausible deniability*, or the ability to practice discrimination, while at the same time denying that any discrimination is actually taking place.

Behavioral Asymmetry

Group-based social hierarchy is also produced and maintained by a mechanism known as *behavioral asymmetry*. On average, there will be differences in the behavioral repertoires of individuals belonging to groups at different levels of the social power continuum. More importantly, however, these behavioral differences will both contribute to and be reinforced by the group-based hierarchical relationships within the social system. This behavioral asymmetry will also be affected by socialization patterns, stereotypes, legitimizing ideologies, psychological biases, and the operation of systematic terror.

The construct of behavioral asymmetry highlights one of the major ways in which SDT differs from other closely related structural models of group oppression, such as classical Marxism, neoclassical elitism theory, or group position theory. These latter models emphasize the manner in which people within elite, dominant, and ruling classes actively oppress, manipulate, and control people within subordinate groups. While SDT does not dispute, and indeed incorporates many of these ideas, it places greater emphasis on the manner in which subordinates *actively* participate in and contribute to their own subordination. Within SDT, we do not regard subordinates merely as *objects* of oppression, but also as people who usually retain some *agency* and actively participate in the oppressive exercise. In other words, within SDT, group oppression is very much a co-operative game.

On the other hand, we do not mean to imply that subordinates do not resist their own oppression, for they most certainly do. At times, this resistance can be quite intense, leading to active rebellion and even social revolution. Nonetheless, successful social revolution is a rare event indeed, and most group-based systems of social hierarchy remain relatively stable over long swaths of time. Therefore, while we recognize that there will always be some element of resistance and resentment within subordinate groups,[25] contrary to the arguments of more traditional elitism theorists, we suggest that within relatively stable group-based hierarchies, most of the activities of subordinates can be characterized as cooperative of, rather than subversive to, the system of group-based domination. Furthermore, we suggest that it is subordinates' high level of both passive and active cooperation with their own oppression that provides systems of group-based social hierarchy with their remarkable degrees of resiliency, robustness, and stability. Therefore, seen from this perspective, social hierarchy is not maintained primarily by the oppressive behavior of dominants, but by the deferential and obsequious behavior of subordinates.[26]

Thus far, we have been able to identify at least four varieties of behavioral asymmetry: (a) *asymmetrical ingroup bias*, (b) *outgroup favoritism*, or *deference*, (c) *self-debilitation*, and (d) *ideological asymmetry*.

With regard to *asymmetrical ingroup bias*: As Sumner (1906) remarked generations ago, and as has been found to hold across most cultures, people generally tend to be *ethnocentric* and to favor their own ingroups over outgroups.[27] However, within a given social system, not all groups will show ingroup bias to the same degree. Dominant groups will tend to display higher levels of ingroup favoritism or bias than subordinate groups will.

Deference, or *out-group favoritism*, can be regarded as a special case of asymmetrical ingroup bias and be said to occur when the degree of asymmetrical ingroup favoritism is so strong that subordinates actually favor dominants over their own ingroups. A well-known example of such outgroup favoritism can be found in the Uncle Tom-ing behavior of certain African-Americans toward Euro-Americans.[28]

Self-debilitation occurs when subordinates show higher levels of self-destructive behaviors than dominants do. These self-debilitating and self-destructive behaviors are often consistent with, but not exclusive to, the negative stereotypes associated with subordinate groups. As we shall discuss in much more detail in Chapters 4 and 9, these lower expectations and stereotypes are consensually shared across the social status hierarchy and exist within the minds of both dominants and subordinates alike. From a social dominance perspective, the negative stereotypes of subordinates are important, not only because of the discriminatory behavior they induce among dominants, but also and perhaps even more importantly, because they serve as behavioral scripts or schemas for subordinates. This is to say that the negative stereotypes that subordinates have about themselves induce them to behave in ways that reinforce these stereotypes. Stereotypes thus become *self-fulfilling prophecies*.[29]

Not only should we expect to find asymmetry in the type and degree of ingroup bias across the social status hierarchy, but the social dominance model also posits the existence of a much more subtle form of asymmetry, labeled *ideological asymmetry*. As we see in Figure 2.1, our theory assumes that a host of HE legitimizing ideologies, such as racism, sexism, classism, and meritocracy, are driven by one's acceptance of and desire for group-based social hierarchy (i.e., SDO). Not only is one's desire for group-based social dominance related to one's social ideologies, but both of these factors help drive group-relevant social policies. Those holding HE social ideologies are also those who are most likely to support social policies perceived to increase the degree of group-based social inequality (e.g., punitive social welfare legislation). In addition, these are also the same individuals who are most likely to oppose those social policies perceived to decrease the degree of group-based social inequality (e.g., affirmative action, protective discrimination).[30] However, the ideological asymmetry hypothesis suggests that the degree to which HE and HA social ideologies and social policies are related to and driven by group dominance values will systematically vary as a function of one's position within the group-based, hierarchical social structure. Everything else being equal, the social attitudes and policy preferences of dominants are more strongly driven by social dominance values than is the case among subordinates.

Altogether, within SDT these various forms of behavioral asymmetry are thought to be important because they illustrate the *cooperative* nature of intergroup oppression and group-based social hierarchies. Systems of group-based social hierarchy are not maintained simply by the oppressive activities of dominants or the *passive* compliance of subordinates, but rather by the coordinated and collaborative activities of both dominants and subordinates.

Legitimizing Myths

Group-based social hierarchy is also affected by what we term *legitimizing myths*. Legitimizing myths (LMs) consist of attitudes, values, beliefs, stereotypes, and ideologies that provide moral and intellectual justification for the social practices that distribute social value within the social system. As we shall see in more detail in Chapter 4, our theory of LMs owes much to Marxist notions of "ideology," Mosca's concept of the "political formula," Pareto's notion of "derivations," Gramsci's idea of "ideological hegemony," Moscovici's notion of "social representations," and Durkheim's notion of "collective representations."[31] Within SDT, LMs can be distinguished by two independent characteristics: *functional type* and *potency*.

Functional type refers to whether a particular LM justifies either group-based social *inequality* or its exact opposite, social *equality*. LMs that justify and support group-based social inequality are referred to as hierarchy-enhancing LMs, while LMs that support and justify greater levels of group-based social equality are referred to as hierarchy-attenuating LMs.

There are many different examples of HE-LMs, including sexism and classical racism, the notions of the "white man's burden," fate, and the doctrine of meritorious karma, Confucianism, negative stereotypes of subordinate groups, traditional forms of classism, the thesis of papal infallibility, nationalism, the Monroe Doctrine and the notion of manifest destiny, the thesis of the divine rights of kings, and speciesism (the idea that humans have the right to rule the planet and all living creatures on it).

While these are all fairly obvious examples of HE-LMs, there are also more subtle, yet no less powerful examples of HE-LMs. In contemporary U.S. and Western cultures, among the most important of HE-LMs are the notions of individual responsibility, the Protestant work ethic, internal attributions of the misfortunes of the poor, and the set of ideas and assumptions collectively referred to as "political conservatism." What all these ideas and doctrines have in common is the notion that each individual occupies that position along the social status continuum that he or she has earned and therefore deserves. From these perspectives then, particular configurations of the hierarchical social system are fair, legitimate, natural, and perhaps even inevitable.

While HE-LMs are often associated with what is regarded as conservative political beliefs, this need not always be the case. For example, there are also left-wing versions of HE-LMs. One such ideology is Lenin's theory of the leading and central role of the Communist Party. This theory asserted that since members of the Communist Party were the only individuals who truly understood the "real interests" of the working class, it was only right and just that they also exercise near complete monopolistic control of the state. This was the theoretical justification for the existence of the nomenklatura.

The set of beliefs, values, ideologies, and attitudes known as HA-LMs have social functions directly contradicting HE-LMs. While HE-LMs serve to exacerbate and maintain group-based social inequality, HA-LMs serve to promote greater levels of group-based social egalitarianism. Examples of HA-LMs are as readily available as HE-LMs. They include political doctrines such as socialism, communism, feminism, and the universal rights of man, as well as major themes in the U.S. Declaration of Independence, and even portions of the New Testament.[32]

The potency of an LM refers to the degree to which it will help promote, maintain, or overthrow a given group-based hierarchy. The degree to which an LM is potent is a function of at least four factors: *consensuality, embeddedness, certainty,* and what we shall call *mediational strength.*

Similar to arguments proposed by Gramsci, Durkheim, and Moscovici, by the term *consensuality* we are referring to the degree to which social representations and social ideologies are broadly shared within the social system. However, as we shall see in Chapter 4, within SDT, the notion of *consensuality* is given a much more precise and focused definition than has been generally provided in the past. Among other things, we argue that the notion of consensuality is particularly directed at the degree to which HE- and HA-LMs are shared across the continuum of social power and within both dominant and subordinate groups alike. For example, for most of U.S. history, classical racism, or the belief that Blacks were inherently inferior to Whites, was not simply a belief held by most Whites, but arguably a belief shared by a substantial number of Blacks as well. Among other things, this implies that Blacks have endorsed anti-Black racism almost as intensively and thoroughly as Whites have. As we shall argue in more detail later in this book, this suggests that from the point of view of system stability, the largest and most important component of anti-Black racism is not simply the beliefs held by Whites, but rather the anti-Black racism shared by Blacks.

Everything else being equal, we postulate that the greater the degree to which dominants can induce subordinates to endorse self-demeaning ideologies such as anti-Black racism, the less physical force or threat of force (i.e., terror) will be necessary in order to keep the hierarchical group relationships in place. Similarly, within the contemporary United States and Western Europe, one of the reasons that the Protestant work ethic is such a potent HE-LM is because it is widely embraced across broad swaths of the social power continuum, by rich and poor, Black and White, men and women.[33]

By *embeddedness* we mean that the LM is strongly associated with and well anchored to other parts of the ideological, religious, or aesthetic components of a culture. For example, classical racism against Blacks can be seen as rather well embedded within Western and U.S. culture. While the color black is most often associated with implications of evil, filth, depravity, and fear, the color white is most often associated with notions of purity, truth, innocence, goodness, and righteousness. These two contrasting color symbols permeate a great deal of Western culture and can be discerned in everything from classical fairy tales to popular film and literature.

By *certainty*, we are referring to whether a given LM appears to have a very high degree of moral, religious, or scientific certainty, or truth. For example, belief in inherent white superiority was a very robust LM in nineteenth-century Western Europe in general, and the antebellum South in particular. One of the reasons this classical racism appeared to be so "obviously true" is that it was consistent with the emerging "scientific" literature of the time, including the new evolutionary thinking and its social Darwinist offshoots (see, e.g., Gobineau).[34] Furthermore, rather than having died out, this type of social Darwinist and "scientific racism" continues to be produced by U.S. and Western European intellectuals such as Shockley, Rushton, Gottfredson, Murray and Herrnstein, and Rasmussen.[35] Collectively, these intellectuals continue to exert significant influence on the direction and tenor of social discourse in the United States and Western Europe.

Finally, by *mediational strength* we refer to the degree to which a given LM serves as a link between the desire to establish and maintain group-based social hierarchy on the one hand and endorsement of HE or HA social policies on the other hand. For example, as we shall discuss in more detail in Chapter 4, those who strongly support the Protestant work ethic are also those most opposed to help for the poor and the less fortunate. According to SDT, part of the reason that people endorse the Protestant work ethic is because it is an accessible and socially acceptable means of justifying group-based social inequality. The stronger an LM mediates the relationship between the desire for group-based hierarchy and a given social policy, the more potent the LM is said to be.

While the ideas of Marx, Gramsci, Pareto, Mosca, and Moscovici all suggest that ideology justifies group dominance, these ideas provide us with no empirical standard for testing whether any given ideology actually does so in any given situation. In contrast, as we shall see in more detail in Chapter 4, the notion of mediation provides us with a relatively crisp empirical standard by which to judge whether a given ideology or belief is functioning as an LM. Namely, a given belief, attitude, opinion, or attribution can be classified as an LM if and only if it is found to have a mediational relationship between the desire for group-based social dominance on the one hand and support for HE or HA social policy on the other hand.

The Nature of Social Dominance Orientation

Perhaps the most psychological component of SDT concerns the construct of social dominance orientation (SDO). SDO is defined as the degree to which individuals desire and support group-based hierarchy and the domination of "inferior" groups by "superior" groups. As a general orientation, SDO pertains to whatever group distinctions are salient within a given social context. These group distinctions may involve sexes, genders, races, social classes, nationalities, regions, religions, estates, linguistic groups, sports teams, or any of an essentially infinite number of potential distinctions between groups of human beings.

SDO is thought to have a widespread influence over the nature and intensity of group-based social hierarchy, not only because it influences a wide range of social ideologies and LMs, but also and perhaps most importantly, because it influences the output of HE and HA public policies. The empirical and conceptual scope of SDO is expected to be extremely broad because it is related to attitudes toward *any* social ideology, attitude, belief, career path, or social policy with strong implications for the distribution of social value between social groups. This social value comes in a variety of forms, including wealth, power, status, jobs, health, and prestige.

SDO is significantly affected by at least four factors. First, SDO will be driven by one's membership in and identification with arbitrary, highly salient, and hierarchically organized arbitrary-set groups. In general and everything else being equal, one should expect that dominants and/or those who identify with dominants will have higher levels of SDO than subordinates and/or those who identify with subordinates have. Second, one's level of SDO is also affected by a series of background and socialization factors, such as one's level of education, religious faith, and a whole set of other socialization experiences (e.g., war, depression, natural disasters). Third, there is reason to believe that people are born with different "temperamental predispositions" and personalities.[36] One such predisposition is empathy. As we shall see in Chapter 3, there is reason to believe that the greater one's empathy, the lower one's level of SDO.

Fourth, one's level of SDO depends on one's gender. Everything else being equal, males will have significantly higher average levels of SDO than females will. This thesis is known as the *invariance hypothesis*. As we shall discuss in much more detail in Chapter 10, this greater level of SDO among males is not due simply to the fact that they occupy dominant social roles, but also to factors that are largely independent of these social roles. For this and other reasons to be discussed in more detail later in this chapter and in Chapter 10, the gender system of social hierarchy is related to, yet quite distinct from, the arbitrary-set system.

The Intersecting Psychologies of Gender and Arbitrary-Set Conflict

Since there is overwhelming evidence that intergroup aggression is primarily a male enterprise (see Chapter 10), there is also reason to expect that arbitrary-set aggression is primarily directed at outgroup males rather than outgroup females. If we regard normal forms of intergroup discrimination as mild forms of intergroup aggression, then there is also reason

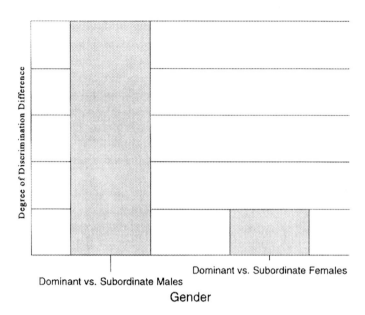

Figure 2.2. Difference in level of discrimination between dominant and subordinate males versus dominant and subordinate females.

to suspect that it will be primarily males rather than females who are the targets of this arbitrary-set discrimination. We label this thesis as the *subordinate-male target hypothesis* (SMTH).

Note, the SMTH does *not* imply the absence of discrimination against women, for such discrimination clearly occurs and is part of the gender system of group-based social hierarchy (i.e., patriarchy). Rather, what we are suggesting is that, everything else being equal, subordinate males rather than subordinate females are the primary objects of arbitrary-set discrimination. In Figure 2.2, we ignore the absolute level of discrimination directed at any group and show the expected *difference* in discrimination directed against members of dominant and subordinate groups within each gender. Thus, for example, Figure 2.2 shows more discrimination directed against dominant and subordinate women. However, the SMTH expects the difference in discrimination experienced by subordinate males as opposed to dominant males to be much greater. The SMTH is both counterintuitive and stands in direct contradiction to the generally accepted double-jeopardy hypothesis. This hypothesis suggests that since both subordinate ethnic groups and women are discriminated against, women from subordinate ethnic groups are then at a double disadvantage.[37]

The SMTH highlights another major difference between previous theories of intergroup relations and SDT. Namely, SDT incorporates the political psychology of gender into the larger story of arbitrary-set conflict. Rather than regarding the psychology of intergroup conflict and the psychology of gender as being independent domains, we regard the psychology of the one as an important and fundamental component of the psychology of the other. Seen from the perspective of SDT, the psychology of intergroup conflict is intimately connected to and bound up with the male predisposition for group boundary maintenance, territorial defense/acquisition, and the exercise of dominion. This implies that an understanding of the psychology of gender is incomplete without an incorporation of the dynamics of intergroup relations, and an understanding of intergroup relations is incomplete without incorporating important lessons of the psychology of male–female differences. We shall be discussing this issue in greater detail in Part III and Chapter 10.

Hierarchical Equilibrium and Hierarchy Constraints

Given the historical record of both human and hominoid social structure, it seems most reasonable to assume that hominoid social systems are predisposed to organize themselves within some range of group-based inequality. Furthermore, the historical record also seems to suggest that under normal circumstances and everything else being equal, the degree of this group-based social hierarchy will tend to stabilize around a given level that we can refer to as the *point of hierarchical equilibrium*. In broad terms, we suggest that this point is established at the fulcrum between HE forces and HA forces.

Besides the HE-LMs already mentioned, HE forces also consist of important social institutions and roles such as the internal security forces (e.g., local and secret police), major elements of the legal and criminal justice system (e.g., prosecutors), and major elements within the business community (e.g., banks, insurance companies). Besides the HA-LMs already mentioned, other examples of HA forces would be social institutions and roles such as civil rights and social welfare organizations, charities, the public defender's office, and religious denominations such as the Society of Friends.

In sum, the counterbalancing and mutually constraining effects of HE and HA forces are thought to be among the factors helping to maintain hierarchical equilibrium in any society over time. Furthermore, we posit that within relatively stable social systems, hierarchical equilibrium is found at the point at which the social system is organized in a hierarchical and trimorphic fashion, where the degree of group-based social

hierarchy has yet to become either morally offensive or structurally destabilizing.

Other Structural Implications of Social Dominance Theory

The mechanisms already described not only tend to make group-based
social hierarchies ubiquitous and stable, but also provide these social hierarchies with a number of other common characteristics. Among the
most important of these are features such as *increasing disproportionality,
hierarchical consensuality,* and *resiliency.*

Increasing Disproportionality

One defining feature of group-based social hierarchies is what Robert
Putnam (1976) has labeled the *law of increasing disproportion.* This law
suggests that the more political authority exercised by a given political
position, the greater the probability that this position will be occupied by
a member of the dominant group.[38] In addition, the law of increasing
disproportion operates within all three forms of group-based stratification (i.e., age system, gender system, and arbitrary-set system).

For example, Putnam shows that the higher the post held by any given
individual in the British government (e.g., prime minister vs. member of
Parliament), the greater the likelihood that this individual attended one of
the two elite British universities (Oxford or Cambridge). Putnam presents
evidence showing that this increasing disproportionality is not restricted
to particular nations or cultures, but is found cross-culturally, including
in countries such as the United States, the former Soviet Union, Israel,
Italy, and Tunisia.[39]

Hierarchical Consensuality

Group-based social hierarchies are also characterized by a high degree of
hierarchical consensuality, by which we mean that there is a high degree of
consensus within the social system as to which groups are dominant and
which subordinate. This consensuality characterizes not only the beliefs
of dominants, but, more importantly, those of subordinates. This high
degree of cross-group consensuality is critical for the orderly and relatively peaceful coordination of dominant and submissive behaviors and
the maintenance of an ongoing system of group-based social inequality.

One example of this high degree of hierarchical consensuality can be
found in our analysis of a sample of 723 UCLA undergraduates in 1989.[40]
We asked these students to rate the social status of five ethnic groups on
a scale from "1 = *very low status*" to "7 = *very high status.*" Results showed

that the ethnic groups were perceived to have highly significant differences in social status.[41] The average social status ratings were ordered: (a) Whites ($M = 6.42$), (b) Asians ($M = 4.80$), (c) Arabs ($M = 3.59$), (d) Blacks ($M = 3.31$), and (e) Latinos ($M = 3.00$). Use of an agreement coefficient known as the *intraclass correlation coefficient*[42] showed a very high level of consensus in the ethnic status ratings of these five groups across all respondents (intraclass $r = .999$). In addition, the degree of consensus among raters within each of the four ethnic groups was high (Euro-Americans: intraclass $r = .998$; Asian-Americans: intraclass $r = .997$; Latino-Americans: intraclass $r = .995$; African-Americans intraclass $r = .988$).[43] Most importantly, however, the consensuality in perceived social status of U.S. ethnic groups was largely impervious of the ethnic group to which one belongs. Inspection of the mean status ratings of each of these five ethnic groups within each of four ethnic groups in Figure 2.3 shows a very high degree of cross-ethnic consistency in how U.S. ethnic groups are perceived.[44] The same basic results were found using a second sample of UCLA students and four ethnic groups four years later.[45]

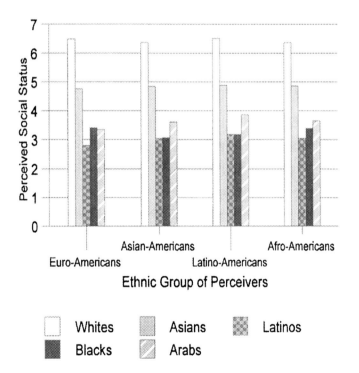

Figure 2.3. Perceived social status of U.S. ethnic groups as a function of ethnic group membership (UCLA Sample 31).

Resiliency

While group-based social hierarchies tend to be highly stable over time, this cross-temporal stability is not absolute. Not only does the *degree* of social hierarchy within any given social system vary across time, but at least within the arbitrary-set system, there are also rare yet dramatic occasions when a given group-based social hierarchy will be completely overthrown. While these "regime smashing" social revolutions are exceedingly rare, there have been at least seven such events within the last 300 years, including (a) the French revolution of 1789, (b) the Mexican revolution of 1910, (c) the Russian revolution of 1917, (d) the Chinese revolution of 1949, (e) the Vietnamese revolution (1954–1975), (f) the Cuban revolution of 1959, and (g) the Sandinista revolution of 1979. However, despite all these attempts at egalitarian social transformation, one is struck by the fact that there is not a single case in which an egalitarian transformation has actually succeeded. Even in the few cases in which the ancien régime was overthrown (e.g., in the French, Russian, Mexican, and Chinese revolutions), like the myth of the phoenix, some new arbitrary-set order soon rose up to take its place. In other words, even though a given arbitrary-set stratification system might collapse or be overthrown, the phenomenon of arbitrary-set stratification itself appears to be extremely resilient.

Consistencies in Social Organization Across Primate Species

The evolutionary perspective suggests not only that humans will tend to live in group-based and hierarchically organized social systems, but also that this form of social organization should tend to be found among other species closely related to humans. Studies of other primate species tend to support this expectation.[46] Not only do all primates within the hominoid clade (i.e., chimpanzees, bonobos, gorillas, and baboons) have systems of social dominance, but there is a group-based nature to these systems. Several group-based primate systems outside of the hominoid clade also have a trimorphic structure not unlike that found among humans, indicating that social status is a function of age (older animals dominating younger animals),[47] sex (males dominating females,[48] though there is one major exception),[49] and position in kinship and friendship groups, which might be considered rudimentary arbitrary-set systems.[50]

Among most primates, these kinship groups are most closely associated with mother–offspring lineage bonds. Besides age, sex, size, and intelligence, in certain primate species such as yellow baboons (*Papio cynocephalus*) the social rank of the offspring is influenced by the social rank of the mother.[51] Studies among olive baboons (*Papio anubis*) have shown that the death or loss of social status of the mother affects the social status of her offspring.[52] Similarly, research has shown that when the social rank of rhesus monkey mothers was experimentally manipulated by the introduction or removal of higher-ranking animals, the offspring showed changes in their level of aggressive behavior congruent with their changed social rank.[53] Another manifestation of the arbitrary-set system can be seen in the formation of political coalitions and alliances among high-status primate males. It is not uncommon for certain *alpha males* (i.e., dominant males) to achieve their dominant positions by forming and maintaining "ruling coalitions" with other high-status males.[54]

Considering only closely related primates in the hominoid clade, there are a number of other common and relevant features of social organization, including (a) the existence of closed social networks, or what might be called *ingroups*, (b) communal territoriality, (c) male domination of intergroup relations, (d) male domination of hostile and agonistic relations between groups, and (e) male domination of stalking, attacking, and killing of outgroup males.[55] This list suggests that the hominoid clade appears to be predisposed toward an *ingroup-centric*, or *ethnocentric*, orientation in which the boundary maintenance toward outgroups is enforced largely by males. We shall explore the further implications of this fact in some detail in Chapter 10.

Now that the broad outlines of SDT have been explored, the remainder of this book will examine the specific mechanisms thought to produce and maintain group-based social hierarchy and how these mechanisms affect and are affected by each other.

Summary

SDT begins with the observation that surplus-producing human social systems are structured as trimorphic, group-based social hierarchies. The three forms of group-based system are an age system, a gender system (i.e., patriarchy), and an arbitrary-set system. The arbitrary-set system consists of socially constructed group distinctions that happen to be relevant within specific situational and historical contexts. Not only does this trimorphic structure appear to characterize human social systems that produce economic surplus, but there are also rudimentary signs of this trimorphic structure within other groups of primates as well.

After noting the ubiquitousness of group-based social hierarchy, SDT goes on to make three primary assumptions: (a) While age- and gender-based hierarchies tend to exist within all social systems, arbitrary-set systems of social hierarchy invariably emerge within social systems producing sustainable economic surplus; (b) most forms of group conflict and oppression (e.g., racism, ethnocentrism, sexism, nationalism, classism, regionalism) are different manifestations of the same basic human predisposition toward group-based social hierarchy; (c) human social systems are subject to the influences of HE forces, which promote group-based social inequality and are partially counterbalanced by opposing HA forces, which promote group-based social equality.

Based on these assumptions, SDT then goes on to explore the manner in which psychological, intergroup, and institutional processes interact with one another in the production and maintenance of group-based, hierarchical social structures.

Unlike most previous models of intergroup discrimination and prejudice, SDT operates at several levels of analysis. While being influenced by many of the perspectives within evolutionary psychology and sociobiology, it does not make the assumption that the dynamics of intergroup conflict and oppression can be reduced to individual strategies of reproductive success or inclusive fitness maximization. Unlike classical psychological and individual differences theories such as authoritarian personality theory, SDT does not restrict its explanation of discrimination and prejudice to the intrapsychic conflicts and mechanics of individual actors, but rather examines how psychological orientation and individuals act and are acted on by a group-based hierarchy. Unlike situational and cognitively oriented theories in social psychology, SDT does not restrict itself to the nature and dynamics of the individual's self and social categorizations, but situates these processes in the context of motivational differences between individuals and the broader social context within which individuals find themselves. Finally, unlike classical sociological theories, SDT utilizes but does not restrict itself to the structural relations between groups or the operations of social institutions.

Therefore, as a general and synthetic perspective, SDT attempts to take elements from the individual, group, institutional, and structural levels of analysis and integrate them into a new, more comprehensive, and more powerful theoretical framework. From evolutionary psychology come the notions that the ubiquitousness of social hierarchy and ethnocentrism are most parsimoniously understood in terms of survival strategies adopted by hominoids, including *Homo sapiens*. From authoritarian personality theory and Rokeach's two-value theory of political ideology comes the notion that the importance that people place on the values of equality, dominance, and submission are of fundamental importance to our understanding of a whole range of sociopolitical beliefs and behaviors. From realistic group conflict and group position theories comes the notion that the political choices and attitudes of individuals must often be seen within the context of group conflict over both real and symbolic resource allocation. From SIT come the important notions that conflict between groups is not necessarily or even primarily designed to maximize the absolute material return to the ingroup, but rather to maximize the *relative* return to the ingroup, sometimes even at the cost of substantial material loss to both the self and the ingroup. Finally, from classical and neoclassical elitism theories comes the notion of the functional value of ideology in the dynamics of hierarchical social control.

To these basic ideas, we have added some new theoretical elements: (a) the notion of SDO as a ubiquitous motive driving most group-relevant social attitudes and allocative decisions, (b) the notion of behavioral asymmetry, or the different yet coordinated behavioral repertoires of dominants and subordinates that help maintain the stability of group-based hierarchy, (c) the notion that the dynamics of the political psychology of gender is an essential and universal element in the dynamics of hierarchical relationships among social groups in general, and (d) the notion that hierarchical stability is affected by the equilibrium-producing functions of HE and HA social forces. Among other things, we argue that this theoretical catholicism will allow us to get a firmer grip on the general dynamics of intergroup relations and to more clearly appreciate the underlying similarities in a wide array of social phenomena within one comprehensive theoretical framework. The phenomena of concern can range from simple acts of mobbing in the playground, to mild forms of prejudice and street gang violence, to instances of genocide.

OPPRESSION AND ITS PSYCHO-IDEOLOGICAL ELEMENTS

3 | The Psychology of Group Dominance

Social Dominance Orientation

Systems of group-based social hierarchy and oppression do not just fall from the sky, nor do they merely result from the accidents and vicissitudes of human history. Rather, while the proximal forces constructing and maintaining oppressive systems are complex and multifaceted, they are also the expressions of human will, agency, and mind. However, perhaps psychology's greatest insight is that the human mind both forms and is formed by human society. Therefore, understanding the nature and dynamics of group-based social inequality requires that we understand the psychology of group dominance. In this chapter we will argue that one of the ways in which this psychology of group dominance expresses itself is in a form we call social dominance orientation (SDO).

SDO is defined as a very general individual differences orientation expressing the value that people place on nonegalitarian and hierarchically structured relationships among social groups. It expresses general support for the domination of certain socially constructed groups over other socially constructed groups, regardless of the manner in which these groups are defined. These groups may be defined on the basis of race, sex, nationality, ethnicity, religion, social class, region, skin color, clan, caste, lineage, tribe, minimal groups, or any other group distinction that the human mind is capable of constructing. Individuals differ in the degree to which they desire group-based inequality and dominance for any number of reasons. However and whatever the reason, understanding the intensity and distribution of SDO within any given society is important to understanding the internal dynamics and overall hierarchical structure of societies in general.

The groups most likely to be the targets of social dominance drives will be those groups that are the most salient and that define the sharpest power differential within any given society at any given time. Social class defined the primary continuum for social stratification for much of modern European history, and therefore has been the group distinction most likely to engage social dominance drives, while for most of U.S. history, race rather than social class has been and remains the primary basis of social stratification, and therefore is most likely to engage SDO.

Overview

In the first part of the chapter, we explain our conception of SDO and its relation to group status. We show that SDO can be reliably measured, that these measures are valid, and that understanding SDO adds to our knowledge over and above other constructs. In the second part of the chapter, we show how SDO relates to political attitudes, values, beliefs, social hierarchy roles, and prejudice toward groups and then show how SDO influences discrimination against groups.

Descriptions of Samples and Scale Forms

To measure individuals' levels of SDO, we have developed value scales across 45 samples and 18,741 respondents from 11 nations, including the United States, Australia, Canada, Israel, "Palestine" (i.e., West Bank and the Gaza Strip), the Peoples' Republic of China, Mexico, New Zealand, Sweden, Taiwan, and the former USSR. While some of these samples are probability samples, most are convenience samples. However, since our aim has not been to describe populations but to relate SDO to other measures within samples, use of convenience samples is an acceptable strategy for us. Most of our respondents were either secondary school students or college students, while some 4,562 were randomly sampled adults. The population base, year collected, location, number of participants, and SDO measure for each sample are shown in Table 3.1. The sample numbers provided in Table 3.1 are used throughout the book.

Anti-Egalitarianism and SDO Scales

We refined our measures of SDO as we refined our understanding of it. Our earliest studies used measures close to Rokeach's[1] concept and measures of a general value for (or against) equality. Since these earliest anti-egalitarianism scales, our measures have more pointedly assessed one's values toward *group-based* dominance. The items and item formats for the AE[2] and SDO scales can be found in the appendix to this chapter. Much of our discussion involves the most recent SDO_5 and SDO_6 scales, shown in Table 3.2.

The SDO_5 Scale was developed by extensive item selection and criterion testing (see Pratto, Sidanius, Stallworth, & Malle, 1994, for details). The SDO_6 Scale is quite similar to the SDO_5 Scale but emphasizes orientations toward *intergroup relations*, rather than unspecified or interpersonal relations, and also particularly assesses orientations toward *group domination* rather than just toward equality. Both scales are balanced so that

Table 3.1. Data Sources and Brief Descriptions of Samples

Sample Number	Brief Sample Description	Nation	Year of Survey	Sample Size	Scale Version	Response Scale
1	Cluster sample of gymnasia students from Stockholm County	Sweden	1979	783	Anti-egalitarianism (AE-1)	7-point
2	Students: University of Wisconsin, Madison	United States	1982	267	AE-1	7-point
3	Convenience sample of high school students from Melbourne	Australia	1985	274	AE-1	7-point
4	Students: University of Texas at Austin	United States	1986	5,655	AE-2	5-point
5	Students: University of California at Los Angeles (UCLA)	United States	1989	723	Social dominance orientation (SDO$_1$)	7-point
6	Students: Stanford University	United States	1990	81	SDO$_5$	7-point
7	Students: Stanford University	United States	1990	57	SDO$_5$	7-point
8	Students: University of California at Berkeley	United States	1990	98	SDO$_5$	7-point
9	Students: Stanford University	United States	1990–1991	46	SDO$_5$	7-point
10	Students: San Jose State University	United States	1990–1991	463	SDO$_5$	7-point
11	Students: Stanford University	United States	1991	100	SDO$_5$	7-point
12	Students: Stanford University	United States	1991	190	SDO$_5$	7-point

(Continued)

Table 3.1. (*cont.*)

Sample Number	Brief Sample Description	Nation	Year of Survey	Sample Size	Scale Version	Response Scale
13	Convenience sample of Los Angeles adults	United States	1991	154	SDO_{2a}	7-point
14	Convenience sample of adults from Leningrad	USSR	1991	171	SDO_1	7-point
15	Students: Stanford University	United States	1991	224	SDO_5	7-point
16	Students: Stanford University	United States	1991	49	SDO_5	7-point
17	Students: San Jose State University	United States	1991	144	SDO_5	7-point
18	Students: Stanford University	United States	1992	115	SDO_5	7-point
19	Convenience sample of Los Angeles public defenders	United States	1992	56	SDO_3	7-point
20	Convenience sample of police from the Los Angeles Police Department	United States	1992	59	SDO_3	7-point
21	Adults called to jury duty in Los Angeles County	United States	1992	116	SDO_3	7-point
22	Students: UCLA	United States	1992	382	SDO_3	7-point
23	Students: San Jose State University	United States	1992	97	SDO_5	7-point
24	Students: Stanford University	United States	1992	139	SDO_5	7-point
25	Students: Stanford University	United States	1992	231	SDO_5	7-point

	Sample	Country	Year	N	SDO	Scale
26	Stratified random sample of Los Angeles County adults (computer assisted telephone interview – CATI survey)	United States	1992	1,897	SDO_4	4-point
27	Stratified random sample of Los Angeles County adults (CATI survey)	United States	1993	983	SDO_{5b}	4-point
28	Convenience sample of Vancouver adults	Canada	1992	67	SDO_5	7-point
29	Convenience sample of adults from Taipei and surrounding countryside	Taiwan	1992	46	SDO_5	7-point
30	Students: University of Guadalajara	Mexico	1992	49	SDO_5	7-point
31	Students: UCLA	United States	1993	823	SDO_6	7-point
32	Students: Hebrew University, Bar-Ilan University, and Haifa University (Israeli Jews)	Israel	1994	705	SDO_6	7-point
33	Students: Hebrew University and Haifa University (Israeli Arabs)	Israel	1994	181	SDO_6	7-point
34	Students: Bethlehem University, Nablus, Hebron Gaza, and Palestinians from the West Bank and the Gaza Strip	Palestine	1994	159	SDO_6	7-point

(Continued)

Table 3.1. (cont.)

Sample Number	Brief Sample Description	Nation	Year of Survey	Sample Size	Scale Version	Response Scale
35	Students: University of Shanghai	People's Republic of China	1994	300	SDO_6	7-point
36	Students: Stanford University	United States	1994	235	SDO_6	7-point
37	Students: Stanford University	United States	1994	103	SDO_6	7-point
38	Students: Victoria University of Wellington	New Zealand	1995	209	SDO_6	7-point
39	Stratified random sample of Los Angeles County adults (CATI survey)	United States	1996	706	SDO_6	4-point
40	Students: University of British Columbia	Canada	1994	93	SDO_6	7-point
41	Students: UCLA undergraduates	United States	1993	45	SDO_6	7-point
42	Students: Stanford University undergraduates	United States	1995	207	SDO_6	7-point
43	Students: UCLA undergraduates	United States	1991	198	SDO_{2b}	7-point
44	Students: Stanford University graduate students	United States	1995	583	SDO_6	7-point
45	Bay Area voters	United States	1992	478	SDO_6	7-point
Total				18,741		

Table 3.2. Items on The SDO$_5$ and SDO$_6$ Scales

Social Dominance Orientation Scale (SDO$_5$)

1. Some groups of people are simply not the equals of others.
2. Some people are just more worthy than others.
3. This country would be better off if we cared less about how equal all people were.
4. Some people are just more deserving than others.
5. It is not a problem if some people have more of a chance in life than others.
6. Some people are just inferior to others.
7. To get ahead in life, it is sometimes necessary to step on others.
8. Increased economic equality.[a]
9. Increased social equality.
10. Equality.
11. If people were treated more equally we would have fewer problems in this country.
12. In an ideal world, all nations would be equal.
13. We should try to treat one another as equals as much as possible. (All humans should be treated equally.)
14. It is important that we treat other countries as equals.

Social Dominance Orientation Scale (SDO$_6$)

1. Some groups of people are simply inferior to other groups.
2. In getting what you want, it is sometimes necessary to use force against other groups.
3. It's OK if some groups have more of a chance in life than others.
4. To get ahead in life, it is sometimes necessary to step on other groups.
5. If certain groups stayed in their place, we would have fewer problems.
6. It's probably a good thing that certain groups are at the top and other groups are at the bottom.
7. Inferior groups should stay in their place.
8. Sometimes other groups must be kept in their place.
9. It would be good if groups could be equal.[b]
10. Group equality should be our ideal.
11. All groups should be given an equal chance in life.
12. We should do what we can to equalize conditions for different groups.
13. Increased social equality.
14. We would have fewer problems if we treated people more equally.
15. We should strive to make incomes as equal as possible.
16. No one group should dominate in society.

---

[a] Items 8–14 should be reverse coded. The response scale was 1 = *very negative* to 7 = *very positive*.

[b] Items 9–16 should be reverse coded. The response scale was 1 = *very negative* to 7 = *very positive*.

responses to half the items index approval of inequality and dominance and half of the responses index approval of equality and dominance.[3] We have intermixed the order of the items in various ways in different samples, and we have never noticed that the order of items influenced the results.

Reliability of Anti-Egalitarianism and SDO Scales

One of the ways that we establish the existence of general orientations toward social dominance is by showing that they can be measured reliably. Most social scientists accept two kinds of reliability measures: one showing that separate measures of the same construct converge (usually measured by Cronbach's coefficient α-coefficient), and the other showing that measures are stable over time. Table 3.3 shows the α-reliability of the anti-egalitarianism and SDO scales in all 45 samples.[4] The median reliability of the anti-egalitarianism scales and early SDO scales was .78, while the median reliability was .79 for the SDO_5 Scale and .89 for the SDO_6 Scale. Such reliabilities are considered acceptable to excellent.

The SDO_5 and SDO_6 scales are also highly stable over time. The SDO_5 scores of 25 university students (subsample of Sample 6) show a substantial correlation over a three-month interval ($r = .81$, $p < .01$) and did not change reliably from Time 1 to Time 2; the average change was 0.09 on a seven-point scale.[5] Quite similarly, in Sample 9, the correlation between participants' SDO_5 scores over a several month interval was .84 ($p < 001$), with no reliable change. Over a month, SDO_6 scores also correlated highly ($r = .86$, $p < .001$) in Sample 41. Similar convergent validity shows that the two versions of the SDO scale (SDO_5 and SDO_6) measure the same construct. Sample 36 was given the SDO_5 Scale and then given the SDO_6 Scale four weeks later.[6] The correlation between these two scales was .75, which is only slightly lower than test–retest reliabilities of either scale.

Dimensionality of the SDO Scales

In showing how SDO influences intergroup relations, we will show that it relates to a number of other constructs. It is therefore important to show that SDO is not simply an amalgam of all powerful political attitudes, ideologies, or values, but is a unitary construct, distinct from others. Two kinds of analyses of the SDO_5 Scale showed it to be unitary. First, analyses within all samples using the scale showed that a single dimension captured the bulk of the variance.[7] Second, we subjected our largest sample using the SDO_5 Scale (Sample 10) to a confirmatory factor analysis, to test the fit of a unidimensional model.[8] The results showed that all 14 items loaded reliably (all values of $p < .0001$) on a single dimension and an

Table 3.3. Alpha Reliability Coefficients, Means, and Standard Deviations of Anti-Egalitarianism and Social Dominance Scales over Independent Samples

Scale version

	AE-1			AE-2	SDO$_1$		SDO$_{2a}$	SDO$_{2b}$	SDO$_3$	
Sample	1	2	3	4	5	14	13	43	19	20
α	.76	.63	.74	.80	.79	.77	.83	.84	.79	.80
M	2.93	2.20	2.47	1.72	2.47	3.73	2.86	2.87	1.59	3.83
SD	1.24	1.14	1.31	0.71	0.97	0.73	1.12	0.73	0.75	1.89

	SDO$_3$		SDO$_4$	SDO$_5$						
Sample	21	22	26	6	7	8	10	11	12	15
α	.70	.83	.65	.84	.85	.85	.83	.81	.84	.89
M	2.76	1.93	2.59	2.55	2.31	2.44	2.74	2.91	2.59	2.59
SD	1.09	0.86	0.87	0.42	0.41	0.37	0.47	0.51	0.46	0.48

	SDO$_5$									SDO$_{5b}$
Sample	16	17	18	23	24	25	28	29	30	27
α	.84	.81	.82	.80	.83	.83	.85	.76	.70	.64
M	2.50	2.97	3.02	3.12	2.60	3.13	2.71	2.67	2.62	1.97
SD	0.49	0.63	0.42	0.60	0.48	0.81	0.19	0.80	0.91	0.58

(*Continued*)

Table 3.3. (*cont.*)

| | | | | | Scale version | | | | | |
| | | | | | SDO$_6$ | | | | | |
Sample	31	32	33	34	35	36	37	38	39	40
α	.89	.83	.84	.66	.66	.91	.89	.88	.82	.90
M	2.04	2.71	2.27	1.98	3.27	2.35	2.49	2.25	1.51	2.71
SD	0.87	1.09	0.75	0.78	0.71	0.82	0.88	0.90	0.41	1.09

| | | SDO$_6$ | | |
Sample	41	42	44	45
α	.92	.90	.80	.72
M	2.15	2.39	2.32	1.85
SD	0.89	0.85	0.95	0.64

acceptable fit of the model to the data. Additional analyses of all samples using the SDO$_6$ Scale also showed that the first dimension accounted for the bulk of the variance, and confirmatory factor analysis of large samples (i.e., Samples 31, 32, 39) showed that all items loaded reliably on one dimension.

Finding a single dimension for a scale that is balanced is not easy because the two semantic dimensions (here, equality vs. dominance) may appear as separate factors, even if the factors are highly correlated. In some of our largest samples (31 and 32), we have found the SDO$_6$ Scale to consist of two subdimensions: (a) group-based egalitarianism (items 9–16) and (b) group-based dominance (items 1–8). A confirmatory factor analysis of Sample 31 revealed that this two-factor solution provided an acceptable fit to the data, but that the two factors were highly correlated ($r = .60$, $p < .001$). In Sample 32, the fit of the two-factor model was poorer but still acceptable, and again the two factors were highly correlated ($r = .74$, $p < .001$). Though this issue may bear further exploration, at present we have no research evidence that it would be useful to consider the two subdimensions of SDO as independent.

Distinctions Between SDO and Related Concepts

To convince the reader of the usefulness of SDO, we must show that it is not redundant with familiar personality or political variables.

Rokeach's Two-Value Model

Rokeach's two-value model of sociopolitical attitudes[9] assumes that almost all political attitudes and behaviors are heavily influenced by two fundamental human values: the importance people give to *social equality* and to *individual freedom*. SDT gives no major importance to the value of individual freedom, which as we saw in Chapter 1 has not proved empirically robust as a predictor of social and political attitudes. We have followed Rokeach's emphasis on equality values,[10] but have particularly focused on *group* dominance, rather than on abstract, or *individual*, equality. Most importantly, our theory is more comprehensive than others because we incorporate not just individual values, but how such psychological orientations and social ideologies interact with social institutions in producing and maintaining group-based hierarchies.

Using values scales improved on by Braithwaite and Law (1985) and the SDO$_6$ Scale in Sample 42, we tested whether our measures of SDO were empirically distinguishable from the political values that Rokeach identified. The values scale conceptually closest to the SDO$_6$ Scale is the

Table 3.4. Correlations Among SDO$_6$ and Braithwaite and Law's Value Scales

Scale	SDO$_6$	IHES	IHES$_2$	NSOS	PGIHS	SSS
IHES	−.40**					
IHES$_2$	−.36**	.98**				
NSOS	.14*	.35**	.37**			
PGIHS	−.14*	.45**	.46**	.21**		
SSS	.17*	.20**	.20**	.65**	.27**	
IRS	−.03	.49**	.47**	.38**	.48**	.41**

* $p < .05$, ** $p < .01$.

International Harmony and Equality Scale (IHES), which measures the desire to achieve a more cooperative, equitable, and humanistic social order. In addition, we used the National Strength and Order Scale (NSOS; emphasizing the attainment of economic and political might and internal order),[11] the Personal Growth and Inner Harmony Scale (PGIHS; the pursuit of self-knowledge and wisdom),[12] the Social Standing Scale (SSS; measuring one's economic well-being and status in the community),[13] and the Individual Rights Scale (IRS; concerning the individual's rights of autonomy and private enjoyment), all of which used rating rather than Rokeach's ranking formats. We also removed two items with very similar content from the SDO scales to compute the IHES$_2$.[14]

Not unexpectedly, Table 3.4 shows that there was a reliable negative correlation between the SDO$_6$ Scale and the IHES. However, the size of the correlation is too small to consider SDO redundant with IHES. Further, SDO was independent of values for individual rights and was largely independent of the national strength, personal growth, and social standing values, despite the fact that these values correlated rather substantially with IHES.

Political Conservatism

The constellation of beliefs and attitudes associated with SDO may sound like intuitive definitions of political conservatism. To presume that SDO is simply conservatism, however, would be wrong. SDO has a specific definition as a person's general value for group dominance and group inequality. Conservatism, in contrast, has numerous definitions, including (a) resistance to change,[15] (b) a political philosophy or attitude emphasizing respect for traditional institutions, (c) distrust of *any* government activism,

(d) resistance to *centralized* government bureaucracy and the promotion of localized social control, (e) the principles and policies of the Conservative Party in the United Kingdom or of the Progressive Conservative Party in Canada,[16] (f) cautiousness and the avoidance of risk taking,[17] (g) the internalization of parental prohibitions and conformity to socially acceptable beliefs and behaviors,[18] (h) pessimism about the chances of improving people's behavior through social change, (i) opposition to universal suffrage, social and political equality, and popular democracy, (j) opposition to the "excesses" of personal freedom and emphasis on personal responsibility, (k) resistance to planned economies, the promotion of free-market, laissez-faire capitalism, and the sacrosanct status of private property rights, (l) support for lower taxes, and (m) the support of "true" religious belief. None of these definitions overlap with SDO except for the idea of opposition to sociopolitical equality or democracy. Many of these conservative principles were articulated by Edmund Burke in his book *Reflections of the Revolution in France* (1790), where he argued against radical egalitarianism and social leveling.[19] It may be some testament to the general liberal nature of Western societies that most contemporary conservatives will not support Burke's argument against social equality of results, but instead argue for equality of opportunity.[20]

SDO and political conservatism are not only conceptually distinct, but also empirically distinct. This can be seen in two ways. First, the average correlations between SDO and political conservatism are much too small for us to consider these two constructs synonymous (i.e., SDO_5: median $r = .26$; SDO_6: median $r = .30$; see Table 3.10).

Second, partial correlation analysis[21] allows us to conclude whether SDO has marginal utility above the effects of political conservatism when trying to predict other variables such as respondents' social policy attitudes. The results of these analyses are found in Tables 3.12 and 3.13. Whereas the correlations between SDO and the social and political policy attitudes were naturally somewhat attenuated after we controlled for the effects of political conservatism, for the most part these correlations remained reliable even after controlling for conservatism. For example, in Table 3.12, the median correlation between SDO_5 and the desire to provide more support to the military dropped from .33 (no controls for conservatism) to .31 (with controls for conservatism). In total, Table 3.10 shows that of the 57 reliable correlations between SDO and the various social and political policy attitudes, 47 of them (i.e., 82%) remained reliable after controlling for political conservatism. The same pattern was found in the relationship between SDO and the social policy attitudes among Israelis regarding the Israeli–Arab conflict (see Table 3.12). While

all the partial correlations between SDO and policy attitudes were somewhat attenuated, all remained reliable when controlling for the effects of
religiosity and political conservatism. Such results show that the association of these variables with conservatism is not sufficient to explain their
association with SDO.

Authoritarianism

Authoritarianism and SDO are similar in that authoritarians and those
scoring high on SDO are both expected to be relatively racist, sexist, homo-
phobic, ethnocentric, and politically conservative, and to show little empathy for lower-status others. But as Pratto et al. (1994) showed, SDO and authoritarianism are still theoretically and conceptually distinct. The authors
of authoritarian personality theory viewed authoritarianism as an aberrant and pathological condition resulting from harsh child-rearing practices and as an ego defense against feelings of inadequacy and vulnerability.[22] SDT lacks as detailed an explanation for the development of SDO,
but we suspect that nearly all observed levels of SDO reflect normal human variation, in combination with normal socialization experiences, and
partly resulting from inherited personality predispositions. Conceptually,
authoritarianism concerns submission to the authority of the ingroup,[23]
whereas SDO concerns attitudes toward hierarchical relationships *between*
groups.

Empirical research has confirmed these conceptual distinctions. As
Pratto et al. (1994) reported using Sample 23, SDO correlated only
.14 (n.s.) with Altemeyer's 30-item Right-Wing Authoritarianism (RWA)
Scale and .18 ($p < .10$) with Goertzel's personality measure of authoritarianism.[24] Similarly, in two southern samples, McFarland and Adelson[25]
found that SDO_5 and authoritarianism (RWA) correlated only .21 ($p < .01$)
in their adult sample and not at all in the student sample ($r = .07$, n.s.).
Independently, Altemeyer has also confirmed that RWA and our SDO
scales assess separate constructs. Using 1,556 Canadian university students and adults in five independent samples, Altemeyer found that the
correlations between the SDO and RWA scales varied between .08 and .28
(median = .17).[26]

As with political conservatism, partial correlations of Sample 23 showed
that SDO correlated reliably with social policy attitudes even after controlling for RWA, conservatism, and Goertzel's authoritarianism measure.[27]
Because authoritarian personality theory was developed to explain general ethnocentrism, phenomena that SDT also tries to explain, it is especially important that we demonstrate the marginal utility of SDO over authoritarianism within this domain. Using Sample 9 we examined whether
the relationships between SDO, on the one hand, and measures of racism,

Table 3.5. Stepwise Regression of Latent Prejudice on Four Predictors Across Two Independent Samples

Predictor in Order of Selection	Simple Correlation r	Final β	Multiple Correlation R
Adult sample (N = 283)			
SDO$_5$	.53	.29	.53
Authoritarianism	.47	.44	.64
Universalism	−.4	−.19	.71
Gender	−.24	−.17	.73
Student sample (N = 438)			
SDO$_5$	.48	.29	.48
Authoritarianism	.47	.42	.64
Gender	−.31	−.21	.69
Universalism	−.3	−.1	.74

Source: McFarland and Adelson (1996).

nationalism, and conservatism, on the other hand, would remain reliable after we controlled for the RWA and Goertzel measures. Consistent with expectations, all of the significant zero-order correlations between SDO and the ideological measures remained significant after controlling for the effects of both authoritarianism measures.

In an even broader study of the predictors of general group prejudice, McFarland and Adelson (1996) used 20 psychological predictors of a latent prejudice dimension, defined as a composite of pseudopatriotism and prejudice against gays, Blacks, and women. The predictor variables included measures of (a) authoritarianism (i.e., Altemeyer's RWA Scale), (b) attributional complexity, (c) need for structure, (d) self-esteem, (e) collective self-esteem, (f) neuroticism, (g) psychoticism, (h) just-world beliefs, (i) impression management, (j) self-deception, (k) hostile aggressiveness, (l) life satisfaction, (m) self-direction, (n) universalism, (o) traditionalism, (p) conformity, (q) security, and (r) SDO (SDO$_5$ Scale) and several demographic variables.

Their results showed that SDO had the strongest zero-order correlations with the latent prejudice measure in both samples (adults: $r = .53$; students: $r = .48$). In addition, stepwise multiple regression analysis showed that, even after controlling for the effects of all other predictor variables, only four predictors made statistically significant and unique contributions to latent prejudice in *both* samples, namely authoritarianism, SDO, gender, and universalism (see Table 3.5). The fact that

Table 3.6. Correlations of SDO$_5$ Scale with Assorted Personality Measures Across Samples

Personality Traits	Median *r*	Significance Ratio
CPI dominance	.05	1:4
JPRF dominance	−.03	0:5
Empathy	−.31	5:6
Concern	−.46	6:6
Distress	.14	2:6
Perspective taking	−.18	3:6
Fantasy	−.22	4:6
Altruism	−.24	2:3
PAQ communality	−.33	2:2

Note: CPI = California Psychological Inventory; JPRF = Jackson Personality Form; PAQ = Personal Attributes Questionnaire.

authoritarianism and SDO were both strong predictors of latent prejudice indicates that the constructs are not redundant. Altemeyer (1998) found similar results in several Canadian samples using SDO and RWA to predict prejudice against Blacks, women, and homosexuals.

Standard Personality Variables

SDO is also conceptually and empirically distinct from standard personality variables. Because SDO concerns one's attitude toward relations between groups, we expected it to be distinct from concern for one's personal standing. In fact, Pratto et al. (1994) found SDO to be independent of two standard measures of interpersonal dominance and of the standard Rosenberg self-esteem scale (see Table 3.6 for a summary). Thus, whether one thinks well of oneself, or is efficacious, confident, assertive, task-oriented, or influential, which are associated with interpersonal dominance,[28] is unrelated to whether one likes or dislikes group dominance. Altemeyer (1998), however, has found SDO to relate to a darker form of interpersonal dominance: the propensity for cruelty. Not surprisingly, Pratto et al. (1994) found that SDO was negatively related to empathy, communality, and tolerance: Those scoring high versus low on SDO were less concerned with the well-being of others or their community (see Table 3.6).

In order to summarize the results across many samples, we show the median correlation between support for each ideology and SDO, and we also indicate the proportion of samples in which the correlation was found to be significantly different than zero, which is called the significance ratio. Pratto et al. (1994) also confirmed that SDO was distinct from self-monitoring, self-consciousness, and the Big Five personality dimensions (extroversion, openness to experience, neuroticism, conscientiousness, and agreeableness).

The Roots of SDO

Though we have not thoroughly researched the question of how people acquire different levels of SDO, we suspect that there are at least three major influences: socialization experiences, situational contingencies, and temperament. While we do not have data concerning the possible temperamental influences on SDO, we do have evidence concerning possible socialization and situational, or context, effects. For example, as one possible socialization source, we expect that people from dominant groups (i.e., dominants) will adopt higher levels of SDO than people from subordinate groups (i.e., subordinates) will. One reason is that people's general desire for positive self-esteem is compatible with hierarchy-legitimizing myths for people in high-status and dominant groups, making group superiority seem appropriate to them. Because dominants are generally treated better than subordinates, dominants should then feel more comfortable with group inequality. In addition, because societies define social standards in ways that benefit people in dominant groups, such groups do indeed seem better to many people, affirming the "rightness" of inequality in dominants' minds.

Though we have not explored the processes involved, we do have substantial evidence that group status is related to SDO. In student Samples 5, 8, 10, 31, 42, and 44, Pratto and Choudhury[29] found that those in higher-status groups had reliably higher levels of SDO than those in lower-status groups, whether group status was operationalized as gender, ethnicity, or sexual orientation (see means in Table 3.7; see Chapter 10 for gender differences). That is, men, Whites, and heterosexuals had higher SDO levels than women, Blacks, Hispanics, gays, lesbians, and bisexuals. We found similar group-status differences on SDO comparing native-born Euro- and African-Americans in a random sample of Los Angeles County residents (Sample 39).[30] Such differences have also been found between New Zealand police officers of differing ethnic status: 62 White police officers (M = 2.87) scored reliably higher on the SDO_6 Scale than 19 minority police officers (i.e., Maori, Samoan, or "other"; M = 2.11). Similarly, White Los Angeles police officers scored reliably higher on the SDO_3 Scale (M = 4.41) than did Black and Hispanic officers (M = 3.13).[31]

Table 3.7. Mean SDO Scores by Group Status

Sample	Group Comparison	Low-Status Group	High-Status Group
5	Race	2.4	2.6
10	Race	2.4	2.6
8	Race	2.0	2.9
31	Race	1.7	2.3
44	Sexual orientation	1.9	2.3
5	Gender	2.4	2.8
10	Gender	2.5	3.0
8	Gender	2.2	2.7
31	Gender	1.9	2.3
42	Gender	2.1	2.6
44	Gender	1.9	2.3

Note: All groups were different at $p < .05$.

Where there are several stratified groups, SDO remains linked to the relative status of each group. As we showed in Chapter 2, the status of U.S. racial groups ascends in the order Latino-Americans, African-Americans, Asian-Americans, and Euro-Americans. Shadowing this pattern, in Sample 31 we found that each racial group's mean SDO level increased with group status (see Figure 3.1). Trend analysis showed this relationship to be purely and reliably linear ($r = .32$).[32]

Israel also has several stratified racial/ethnic groups.[33] Combining the data from Samples 32–34, we tested whether SDO_6 differences among the groups followed their social status, which in descending order is (a) Ashkenazic Jews ($n = 414$), (b) Sephardic Jews ($n = 182$), (c) mixed Jews ($n = 89$), (d) Israeli Arabs (Arabs with Israeli citizenship, $n = 169$), and (e) Palestinian Arabs (Palestinians living in the occupied West Bank or the Gaza Strip, $n = 156$). Generally following our expectations, the high-status Ashkenazim showed the highest levels of SDO, and the low-status Palestinian Arabs showed the lowest levels of SDO, with the intermediate-status groups falling in between.[34] In particular, pairwise comparisons showed that Palestinian Arabs had reliably lower SDO scores than both Ashkenazic Jews and Israeli Arabs and Sephardic Jews had reliably lower SDO scores than Ashkenazic Jews.[35]

In sum, previous studies show that increasing group status is linked to increasing SDO, robustly across samples, population, culture, and group status designation. However, because the data are naturally occurring,

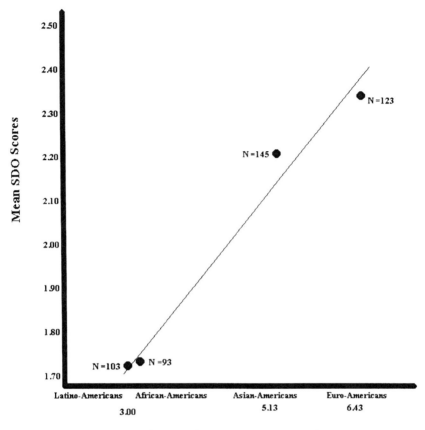

Figure 3.1. SDO as function of perceived ethnic status (UCLA Sample 31).

they do not demonstrate that holding higher group status *causes* SDO to increase. To test whether one's relative group status actually increases SDO levels, we conducted an experiment in which we manipulated the salience of the relative status of the real status group to which participants belonged. This technique is preferable to manipulating the relative status of artificial groups because it is unclear whether such manipulations reflect the psychology of real group status. In Jewish Israeli Sample 32, our colleague Shana Levin primed participants for two real, group status situations: the ethnic division between Ashkenazic and Sephardic Jews, and the nationality division between Israelis and Palestinians.[36] In the ethnic priming condition, respondents answered a series of questions about relations among the Ashkenazim and Sephardim in Israel, and then completed a random half of the 16-item SDO_6 Scale. In the nationality priming condition, the same respondents answered a series of questions about Palestinian–Jewish relations, followed by a second set of 8 SDO_6 items.[37] The order of the half-SDO scales was counterbalanced.

She examined the SDO scores for Ashkenazi Jews, mixed Jews, and Sephardic Jews. She reasoned that following the ethnic prime, the SDO scores of each group should reflect the ethnic group's social status and differ. Following the nationality prime, however, when Jews were primed to think about an outgroup substantially lower in status than all three Jewish groups, the SDO differences among these three groups should disappear, and all three groups would have higher SDO scores.

Figure 3.2 shows that all three hypothesis were confirmed. Following the ethnic prime, high-status Ashkenazic Jews had the highest SDO scores (M = 2.36), low-status Sephardic Jews had the lowest SDO scores (M = 2.05), and the intermediate-status, mixed Jews were found in between (M = 2.28).[38] Following the nationality prime, the SDO differences among the three groups were no longer statistically significant.[39] In addition, there was a marked increase in the level of SDO of all groups.[40] This experiment suggests that considering the real, group status differences

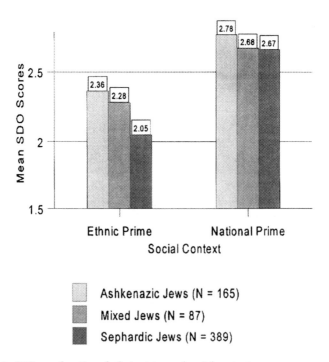

Figure 3.2. SDO as a function of ethnic status and social context.

that one confronts in everyday life from the vantage of the high-status group helps to create higher levels of SDO. Nonetheless, individual levels of SDO are still robust; the two SDO subscales correlated $r = .56$.

SDO and Other Demographic Indicators

We also explored the connection between SDO and gender, education, socioeconomic status, ethnicity, religiosity, and employment status in four of our largest and most diverse samples (Samples: 1, 31, combined Samples 32 and 34, and 39) using multiple regression analysis. While only the UCLA, Los Angeles, and Israeli samples employ modern SDO scales, the Swedish sample (Sample 1) is useful because it was random and had several demographic indicators.

The results, shown in Table 3.8, show that demographic variables accounted for a nontrivial portion of SDO's variance (varying between 6 and 21%). However, across samples and nations, only gender and group status were reliably related to anti-egalitarianism or SDO scales. Men and boys were consistently higher on SDO or anti-egalitarianism than women and girls (see Chapter 10). Noting that group status is defined in different ways in different societies (e.g., as social class in Sweden, the Black–White distinction in the United States, and the Jewish–Arab distinction in Israel), the results were always the same. The salient dominant group was found to have higher average SDO than the salient subordinate group. Coupled with the results of the context experiment, these results imply that the experience of having higher group status leads people to be more favorably oriented toward group dominance compared with having low group status.

Filling Out the Psychology of Group Dominance

The preceding results have shown that people have consistent orientations toward group dominance, and that SDO levels are reliably related to one's own group status. But the important consequences of this orientation are shown in people's beliefs about particular intergroup relations, their support or opposition to social practices that influence intergroup relations, what kinds of attitudes they have toward social groups, and whether they embrace or discriminate against outgroups.

Because SDO represents support for group domination, people scoring high on SDO should most prefer high-status groups and least prefer low-status groups. We tested the prediction that SDO would be positively correlated with positive feelings toward high-status groups and negatively correlated with positive feelings toward low-status groups in two

Table 3.8. Forward Regression Analyses of SDO as a Function of Demographic Factors in Four Independent Samples (entries are standardized regression coefficients)

Variables	Sample			
	Swedish Sample 1 (AE-1 Scale)	UCLA Sample 31 (SDO$_6$ Scale)	Israeli Samples 32–34 (SDO$_6$ Scale)	Los Angeles Adult Sample 39 (SDO$_6$ Scale)
Gender	0.28**	0.17**	0.22**	0.13**
Age	−0.02	−0.06	0.07	0.05
Education	0.02	−0.08	−0.03	−0.16**
Social class	0.27**	0.03	−0.05	−0.07*
Native born	n.a.	n.a.	n.a.	−0.27**
Language of interview	n.a.	n.a.	.01	.00
Ethnic status	0.01	0.32**	0.13**	0.09*
Religiosity	−0.06	n.a.	0.11**	0.03
Employment status	n.a.	n.a.	n.a.	0.00
Conservative parental ideology	0.17**	n.a.	n.a.	n.a.
Percentage of total variance accounted for (R^2)	21	13	6	15

Note: Entries are standardized regression coefficients.
$^+p < .10$, $^*p < .05$, $^{**}p < .01$, n.a. = not available.

large random samples of Los Angeles residents (Samples 26, 39) and in a large UCLA sample (Sample 31), which used either the SDO$_4$ or SDO$_6$ scales. Using standard public opinion techniques, respondents indicated how warmly they felt toward various groups, usually on a cold–warm temperature scale (i.e., "0 degrees" = *Very cold* to "100 degrees" = *Very warm*).

Table 3.9 shows that the SDO measures were reliably negatively correlated with 12 of the 13 measures of affect toward low-status groups. Conversely, the higher that people scored on SDO, the more they liked high-status groups: 8 out of 11 correlations between SDO and affect toward high-status groups were reliably positive. This result indicates that

Table 3.9. Correlations Between Measure of Affect Toward Low- and High-Status Groups and SDO$_4$ and SDO$_6$ Scales

Group Affect and Group Identification	SDO$_4$		SDO$_6$	
	Median Correlation	Significance Ratio	Median Correlation	Significance Ratio
Affect toward low-status groups and their supporters				
Women	—	—	−.37	1:1
Poor people	—	—	−.39	1:1
Democrats	—	—	−.3	1:1
Blacks	−.13	1:1	−.41	2:2
Hispanics	−.16	1:1	−.38	2:2
Asians	−.1	1:1	−.38	—
Hispanic civil rights groups	−.2	1:1	—	—
Black civil rights groups	−.24	1:1	—	—
Affect toward high-status groups and their supporters				
Republicans	—	—	.24	1:1
Whites	.1	1:1	.09	—
Business executives	.16	1:1	—	—
Politicians	.15	1:1	—	—
Identification				
Ingroup identification	—	—	.18	2:2
Differential affect (Whites–Blacks)	.25	1:1	.39	1:1

Note: "—" means that data were unavailable.

SDO is not a measure of general misanthropy because it distinguishes between people based on their group status.

SDO and Legitimizing Myths

One of the most important habits associated with SDO is people's use of social ideologies. People can use ideologies to guide their own actions, justify their own behavior, and decide what behavior in others they feel is justified and ultimately approvable. Ideologies may be especially important when people are confronted with the possibility of social change, either welcoming it or opposing it. In the next section, we review how SDO

relates to ideological habits to either approve or disapprove of existing ideologies and to support or oppose various kinds of social change.
Regardless of whether a social practice is traditional or new, we expect
people who score high on SDO to use and prefer social ideologies that
enhance group inequality, and we expect people who score low on SDO
to use and prefer ideologies that would attenuate group inequality. That
is, *it is the social implications for intergroup relations that ideologies have, rather
than their specific contents, that we believe orient people toward those ideologies
in ways compatible with their SDO levels.* As such, both within and between
cultures we predict that support for a variety of group-relevant ideologies
will correlate with SDO.

We first examine correlations between the SDO_5 and SDO_6 scores and
an array of legitimizing ideologies in the U.S. samples (see Table 3.10).
As Table 3.10 shows, those scoring higher on SDO were the strongest
endorsers of racism, sexism, nationalism, cultural elitism, and patriotism.
These robust findings indicate one of the ways that SDO is a general orientation: it orients people to many kinds of intergroup relations that they
confront. SDO was also reliably related to several other ways of thinking
about specific intergroup relations. We discuss each in turn.

Ethnic prejudice

Because different races or ethnic groups often serve as the basis of
arbitrary-set group dominance, we expect SDO to correlate highly with
beliefs that demean subordinate ethnic groups. In Sample 12 we found
that anti-Arab racism, assessed while the United States was going to war
against an Arab country,[41] correlated .22 ($p < .05$) with the SDO_5 Scale.
Within every U.S. sample, SDO scales correlated highly and reliably with
various measures of anti-Black attitudes and opinions. In Sample 23 the
SDO_5 Scale correlated .53 ($p < .01$) with McConahay's seven-item Modern
Racism Scale,[42] $-.38$ ($p < .01$) with Katz and Hass's Pro-Black Scale, and
.30 ($p < .01$) with their Anti-Black Scale.[43] Though Katz and Hass showed
these two scales to be independent, the generality of SDO is shown in that
SDO correlated in the expected directions with each. In Sample 39, we
found SDO_6 to be correlated .32 ($p < .01$) with four items from Sears's
Symbolic Racism Scale.[44] Thus, the association between SDO and anti-
Black racism in the United States is robust across different kinds of racism
measures.

SDO also correlated with the forms of ethnic prejudice most relevant
in other cultural contexts. For Canadians, SDO correlated strongly with
prejudice against Asian immigrants and native Canadians ($r = .67$ and
.56, respectively). For Taiwanese, SDO correlated with prejudice against

Table 3.10. Relationships Between SDO$_5$ and SDO$_6$ Scales and Support for Legitimizing Ideologies Across U.S. Samples

Legitimizing Ideologies	SDO$_5$		SDO$_6$	
	Median Correlation	Significance Ratio	Median Correlation	Significance Ratio
General ideologies in the United States				
Racism/ethnic prejudice	.56	7:7	.55	6:6
Noblesse oblige	−.54	10:10	—	—
Sexism	.47	12:12	—	—
Nationalism	.52	8:8	.42	1:1
Cultural elitism	.44	2:3	—	—
Patriotism	.43	3:3	.11	1:1
Rape myths	.43	2:2	—	—
Denial of racial discrimination	—	—	0.18	4:4
Blacks get fair trials	.33	1:1	—	—
Perceived zero-sum competition	.31	3:3	.40	2:2
Just world beliefs	.26	—	—	—
Political conservatism	.26	8:9	.30	5:6
Protestant work ethic	.08	2:4	.23	3:3
Social legitimacy	—	—	.35	2:2
Social attributions				
External attributions for poverty	−.22	1:1	−.29	2:2
Internal attributions for poverty	.34	1:1	.49	2:2
Protest riot attributions	—	—	−.19	1:1
Criminal riot attributions	.19	1:1	.26	1:1

Aborigines ($r = .57$), and for Israelis, SDO correlated with prejudice against Palestinians ($r = .36$, see Table 3.11). Clearly, then, SDO is not a construct based only in U.S. racism, but appears to be a psychological response to intergroup dominance in whatever form it takes. The only sample in which ethnic prejudice was not related to SDO was in the

Table 3.11. Correlations Between SDO and Support for Legitimizing Ideologies in Non-U.S. Samples

Legitimizing Ideologies	Nation/Race (Sample Number)								
	Canada (28)[a]	Canada (40)[b]	Taiwan (29)[a]	Mexico (30)[a]	China (35)[b]	New Zealand (38)[b]	Israeli Jews (32)[b]	Israeli Arabs (33)[b]
Political conservation	0.29	0.22	0.04 n.s.	—	—	0.19	0.29	—
Sexism	0.58	0.69	0.40	0.52	0.35	0.59	—	—
Racism/ethnic prejudice	0.56	0.67	0.57	0.27	−0.03 n.s.	—	0.36	—
Denial of racial discrimination	—	—	—	—	—	—	0.11	0.19
Nationalism	—	—	—	—	—	—	0.13	0.12
Patriotism	—	—	—	—	—	—	−0.05 n.s.	0.20
Protestant work ethic	—	—	—	—	—	—	—	0.23
Social legitimacy	—	—	—	—	—	—	0.43	0.22
Internal attributions of ethnic inequality	—	—	—	—	—	—	0.41	—
External attributions for ethnic ineqality	—	—	—	—	—	—	−0.11	—

Note: [a] = SDO_5 Scale, [b] = SDO_6 Scale; – indicates that attitude measure was not available in sample.

People's Republic of China ($r = -.03$), where assessing social and political attitudes is highly problematic because of the repressive political climate.[45]

Sexism

Arbitrary-set group oppression occurs differentially from society to society, yet we have seen that belief in myths that legitimize a variety of group dominance relations correlate with SDO. Similarly, sexism is legitimized differentially across cultural contexts, but support for such sexist ideologies are expected to correlate with SDO. In the United States, we used three standard sexism measures that test beliefs about different abilities, occupational roles, or temperaments between men and women; these sexism measures were reliably related to SDO in all 12 samples, with a median correlation of .47. In two samples we also found SDO to be related to the belief that women are to blame for being raped and sexually assaulted.[46] Sexism measures with quite different contents, but which were also culturally appropriate, correlated with SDO in other nations as well (median $r = .55$). For example, belief in Confucian conceptions of gender roles correlated with SDO in Taiwan and China. These correlations were found to be strong and reliable even after we controlled for the effects of gender.

Political Conservatism

Another robust relationship was that between SDO and political conservatism, measured in standard ways, using some combination of respondents' political party preferences and their self-classifications along a liberal–conservative continuum on several issue domains, such as foreign policy, economic policy, and social policy. This relationship was robust within the United States, Canada, New Zealand, and Israel. Though conservatism was not correlated with SDO in Taiwan ($r = .04$), support for the existing ethnic/political hegemony was correlated with SDO. Thus, SDO is related to political affiliations that favor hegemony. Nonetheless, the sizes of the correlations between SDO and conservatism were too small to regard these two constructs as equivalent or redundant with one another.

Causal Attributions

In U.S. political culture, people's attributions for social inequality are important because they legitimize either remedial action or inaction. External attributions place the blame for misfortune on factors beyond the individual's or group's control, such as impoverished background, brutal

childhood experiences, or lack of job opportunities, and help to justify remedial prescriptions.[47] Internal attributions, such as laziness or inability,
locate the blame on the individual or group and, in the political sphere,
are used to argue against remediation. Given how internal and external attributions are used to argue for or against programs that might
reduce inequality, we expect SDO to be positively correlated with the
tendency to make internal attributions for the misfortunes of low-status
others and negatively correlated with the tendency to make external attributions for the same. In one survey, we asked respondents to indicate
which of several factors were responsible for Blacks and Hispanics having lower incomes than Whites.[48] We presented the respondents with a
set of eight attributions: four *internal attributions* (e.g., laziness, less intellectual ability) and four *external attributions* (e.g., poor schools, effects
of past discrimination).[49] As expected, SDO was positively associated
with endorsement of internal attributions (SDO$_5$: median $r = .34$; SDO$_6$:
median $r = .49$) and negatively associated with endorsement of external attributions (SDO$_5$: median $r = -.22$; SDO$_6$: median $r = -.29$; see
Table 3.10). We found similar results when asking about the causes of the
civil disturbances in Los Angeles in 1992. There was a negative correlation
between SDO and the belief that the disturbances were a protest against
injustice (SDO$_6$: $r = -.19$) and positive correlations between SDO and the
belief that the disturbances were due to criminal elements (SDO$_5$: $r = .19$;
SDO$_6$: $r = .26$).

In Israel, respondents were asked for explanations for the differential
status of high-status and low-status groups of Jews – the Ashkenazim and
Sephardim. SDO was positively, strongly, and significantly correlated with
internal attributions ($r = .41$), but the expected negative correlation with
external attributions was not quite reliable ($r = -.11$). Taiwan provides an
important complementary case. There, traditional religious beliefs suggest
that the gods and fate determine one's poverty or wealth, and in our
Taiwanese sample, support for this external attribution correlated strongly
and positively with SDO ($r = .62$, $p < .01$).[50] Across the cultures studied,
then, it is clear that SDO is not a particular habit of making internal or
external attributions. Rather, SDO orients people to find the most socially
acceptable way of rationalizing inequality.

Legitimizing Rationales for Social Policies

The kinds of beliefs we have discussed are important because they
influence whether people accept or reject social policies that influence intergroup relations. This analysis has led us to two general predictions.
First, those scoring highest on SDO should most oppose social policies

understood to favor low-status groups (hierarchy-attenuating [HA] policies) and to most support social policies that favor high-status groups (hierarchy-enhancing [HE] social policies). We have found such correlations between SDO and a variety of attitudes toward HE or HA social policies. For example, Table 3.12 summarizes the correlations between the SDO_5 and SDO_6 scales and attitudes toward 20 group-relevant social policies in the United States. As expected, attitudes toward policies detrimental to low-status groups, such as tougher law and order policies, were positively correlated with SDO, whereas attitudes toward policies that would aid low-status groups, such as gay and lesbian rights, were negatively correlated with SDO.

Similarly, in Israel we expected SDO to correlate with negative attitudes toward Palestinians and social policies justifying Jewish hegemony over former Arab lands and Arab peoples. Table 3.13 shows the expected correlations between SDO and policy attitudes among Israeli Jews (Sample 32).

Our second general expectation is that rationales for policies that are hierarchy-enhancing should appeal most to those scoring high on SDO, whereas rationales for policies that are hierarchy-attenuating should most appeal to those low on SDO. This implies an even more specific relationship between SDO and policy attitudes: Feelings about HE rationales will correlate positively with SDO, and feelings about HA rationales will correlate negatively with SDO – even for different rationales about the same policy.

In one test of this hypothesis, we asked a random sample of Los Angeles respondents (Sample 39) how much their views on affirmative action were driven by six rationales commonly used in U.S. discourse.[51] Two of these rationales could be classified as HA beliefs and four could be classified as HE beliefs. As expected, the SDO_6 Scale was negatively correlated with agreement with the HA beliefs and positively correlated with agreement to the HE beliefs. The two HA beliefs and their correlations with SDO were "Affirmative action will provide equal opportunity for all groups" ($r = -.11$, all $ps < .01$) and "Affirmative action allows us to increase diversity" ($r = -.21$). The four HE beliefs were "Affirmative action is reverse discrimination" ($r = .30$), "Affirmative action is basically unfair" ($r = .30$), "Affirmative action will increase racial conflict" ($r = .30$), and "Affirmative action just increases the idea that certain groups are not as good as others" ($r = .30$). Note that despite the fact that the content of these latter two reasons appears oppositional to SDO, because they were reasons to legitimize what is seen as an HA policy, these reasons correlated positively with SDO.

Table 3.12. Simple and Partial Correlations Between Social Policy Attitudes and SDO

Group-Relevant Social Policy Attitudes	SDO$_5$ Scale				SDO$_6$ Scale			
	Product Moment r		Partial Correlation		Product Moment r		Partial Correlation	
	Median r	Significance ratio	Median r	Significance ratio	Median r	Significance ratio	Median r	Significance ratio
Tougher law and order measures	.24	5:6	.20	3:6	.28	2:2	—	—
More money for the military	.33	4:5	.31	4:5	.31	1:1	—	—
Opposition to gay and lesbian rights	.41	6:6	.37	4:6	.22	1:1	.10	0:1
Opposition to women's rights	.39	6:6	.34	6:6	—	—	—	—
Opposition to universal health care	.08	1:1	.01	0:1	.42	1:1	.22	1:1
Opposition to social welfare programs	.50	6:6	.34	6:6	.49	1:1	.33	1:1
Opposition to miscegenation	.28	5:6	.21	4:6	.29	2:2	.27	1:1
Opposition to civil rights policies (e.g., integration, public accommodations)	.44	6:6	.32	6:6	.33	1:1	.22	1:1
Opposition to affirmative action	.18	1:1	.10	0:1	.36	2:2	.19	2:2

Opposition to immigration	.30	1:1	.26	1:1	—	—	—	—
More money to prisons vs. schools	—	—	—	—	.23	1:1	.21	1:1
Chauvinism	.37	2:3	.16	1:3	—	—	—	—
Favor U.S. military action against Iraq	.48	1:1	—	—	—	—	—	—
Willingness to make sacrifices for the sake of war with Iraq	.45	1:1	—	—	—	—	—	—
Favor suspension of civil liberties for the sake of war against Iraq	.45	1:1	—	—	—	—	—	—

Types of Affirmative Action One Would Oppose

Quotas	—	—	—	—	.25	1:1	.15	1:1
Group membership as one of several factors to consider	—	—	—	—	.22	1:1	.13	1:1
As a tie-breaker	—	—	—	—	.23	1:1	.14	1:1
Train so that groups can compete	—	—	—	—	.29	1:1	.23	1:1
Outreach	—	—	—	—	.31	1:1	.26	1:1
Giving preference to less qualified people	—	—	—	—	.16	0:1	.11	0:1

Table 3.13. Simple and Partial Correlation Between SDO_6 Scale and Social Policies in Israel

Social Policies	Correlation with SDO_6	Partial Correlation
Jewish right to all land of Israel	.26**	.15*
Preserve Israel as a Jewish state	.15*	.13*
Equal rights for Arab citizens	−.41**	−.34**
Compromise with the Palestinians	−.35**	−.27**
Strong-arm policy toward Arabs	.46**	.34**

Note: Partial correlations controlled for the effects of political conservatism and religiosity.
* $p < .05$, ** $p < .01$.

Our strongest evidence that it is the perceived HA or HE effects of social policies that differentially appeal to those scoring high and low on SDO comes from persuasion experiments. In these, we asked college students selected for having a very high or very low SDO to consider a new social policy designed to address some of the problems of immigration.[52] The policy was to put new immigrants into a housing facility for a short time after arriving in the United States so that they could be screened and educated. There was no initial relation between attitudes toward this new, ambiguous policy and SDO level. After participants had read a persuasive essay either for or against the policy (or, in some experiments, both), they indicated their attitude toward the policy again. If participants had read an essay citing HE reasons for the policy, those with a high SDO were persuaded to support it more than those with a low SDO. If participants had read an essay citing HE reasons against the policy, those with a high SDO were persuaded to oppose the policy more than those with a low SDO. That is, it was the HE contents of the persuasive arguments that appealed to high-SDO people, not the policy itself. The converse effects were found for essays that used HA reasons, whether the essays were for or against the policy.[53] Similar results were found in an experiment using voters as participants, suggesting that when political discourse relies on HE or HA legitimizations, it can differentially persuade those with a high or low SDO that social policies are right.

We conducted three field surveys as political events unfolded to test this idea. Following Iraq's invasion of Kuwait in 1991, we surveyed college students about their support for the impending war that the United States and its allies would wage against Iraq. Both immediately after the invasion and just prior to and during the war, those with the highest SDO favored warring with Iraq, particularly to regain U.S. dominance in the Middle East.[54]

In spring 1991, President George Bush nominated Clarence Thomas, a Black conservative and opponent of affirmative action, to serve on the Supreme Court. As the Senate Judiciary Committee was about to complete its hearings concerning Thomas's nomination, a news story broke that Thomas had sexually harassed two former subordinates. As a result, the Senate Judiciary Committee held additional hearings scheduled over an entire weekend, including subpoenaed testimony from Professor Anita Hill.

On the day of Thomas's confirmation and for two days following, we recontacted 149 of the respondents in Sample 15 (Stanford students), who had filled out the SDO_5 Scale a month earlier, and asked them four additional questions. We asked how much they favored Bush's nomination of a Black to the Supreme Court, which we expected to correlate negatively with SDO, and how much they favored Bush nominating a conservative to the Supreme Court, which we expected to correlate positively with SDO. Because Senator Arlen Specter and other Judiciary Committee members accused Anita Hill of lying, we also asked respondents how much they believed Anita Hill's testimony. We expected belief in Hill's testimony to correlate negatively with SDO because it provided a rationale against Thomas's confirmation.[55] As expected, those with a higher versus lower SDO were less supportive of a Black nominee ($r = -.20$, $p < .05$), more supportive of a conservative nominee ($r = .32$, $p < .001$), more disbelieving of Anita Hill's testimony ($r = -.26$, $p < .001$), and more supportive of the confirmation of Clarence Thomas ($r = .22$, $p < .01$).

As we will argue in Chapter 8, the death penalty is generally used in a HE manner, so we measured attitudes toward it in March 1992 as California was preparing to reinstitute use of the death penalty after a hiatus of 16 years. In Sample 25, we used the SDO_5 Scale. Two weeks later and a day after the execution of Robert Alton Harris,[56] we assessed the students' attitudes toward the death penalty. As expected, the students' SDO scores predicted their support for the execution of Harris ($r = .36$, $p < .01$), their belief in the deterrent value of capital punishment ($r = .35$, $p < .01$), their belief in execution as retribution ($r = .51$, $p < .01$), and their belief that executions should be as painful as possible ($r = .42$, $p < .01$).

SDO and Hierarchy-Enhancing and Hierarchy-Attenuating Social Roles

Like social practices, social roles can be classified as hierarchy-enchancing or hierarchy-attenuating, depending on what bias they have toward high- or low-status groups. HE roles maintain and enhance group status and power distinctions – for example, by channeling positive resources up in the social hierarchy, by channeling negative resources down in the social hierarchy, by accentuating group boundaries, and by generally supporting the relative advantages for dominant groups. HA roles discriminate in the opposite direction by differentially favoring subordinate groups and by reducing group inequality through reduction in status and power differentials between dominant and subordinate groups.

Examples of HE roles include prison guard, police officer, internal security officer (e.g., FBI, KGB, Shinbet), prosecutor, and corporate lawyer, while examples of HA social roles generally include civil rights and human rights advocates, charity workers, public interest and labor lawyers, social workers, labor organizers, and public defenders.[57]

We expect people in HE roles to have higher SDO levels and people in HA roles to have lower SDO levels. Using an earlier version of the SDO scale (SDO$_3$ Scale), we found that Los Angeles police officers (HE occupation) had significantly higher SDO scores than a random sample of adults picked for jury duty in Los Angeles County. In addition, a sample of public defenders from the Los Angeles County Public Defender's Office (HA occupation) had not only significantly lower SDO scores than the police officers did, but significantly lower SDO scores than the jurors as well. These differences held even after controlling for such demographic differences among groups as age, education, income, ethnicity, and gender.[58] Likewise, when we classified voters' occupations, we found that their SDO levels reflected their holding of HE, middling, or HA occupations.

There are a number of processes that we expect to lead to such a confluence between hierarchy role and SDO level. First, we suspect that when people can pick their careers, they will choose them in part to reflect their SDO values. For example, using the SDO$_5$ Scale, Pratto, Stallworth, Sidanius, and Siers (1997) tested the idea that people will be differentially attracted to HE and HA roles.[59] In these tests, we asked the students which sectors of the society they intended to work in after graduation. We provided respondents with a list of 20 careers, which we sorted into three different categories: (1) HE careers (e.g., prosecutors, police officers, business executives), (2) HA careers (e.g., social workers, public defenders), and (3) "middlers," or those whose career aspirations could not be classified as either HE or HA (e.g., scientists, sales managers). Because women tend to be more attracted to HA careers than men, we controlled for the possible effects of gender.[60] The results were as expected; those intending to work in HA roles had lower SDO scores than middlers, whose scores were below those intending to work in HE roles.[61]

We replicated these findings using the SDO_6 Scale and a slightly different method. In Sample 31, we examined the correlation between SDO and the perceived attractiveness of four HE careers (i.e., criminal prosecutor, police officer, FBI agent, and business executive) and four HA careers (i.e., public defender, civil rights lawyer, social worker, and human rights advocate).[62] SDO was positively correlated with perceived attractiveness of HE roles and negatively correlated with perceived attractiveness of HA roles. SDO maintained its significant relationship with career attractiveness, even when socioeconomic status and political conservatism were also considered.[63]

More direct tests of whether SDO leads people to select HE or HA occupations were conducted by Pratto et al. (1997). They created an HA and an HE job description with the same occupation, matching the salary level, prestige, and pay of the jobs, and also basic duties. They compared how many HE versus HA jobs across several occupations each respondent chose and found that number to correlate .58 with respondents' SDO scores taken previously. In complementary experiments, respondents pretended to hire recent college graduates into such positions. Both business people and college students had strong biases to hire job applicants who appeared to be low on SDO into HA jobs and applicants who appeared to be high on SDO into HE jobs – at a ratio of about 2 to 1. Both self-selection and hiring procedures may ensure that high-SDO people obtain HE jobs and low-SDO people obtain HA jobs.

SDO, Group Discrimination, and Intergroup Context

The main reason that we consider SDO the key to understanding individuals' influence on social hierarchy is that, coupled with the ideological habits and social roles that go with it, it explains who discriminates against which social groups. People with a high SDO readily apply ideologies that tell them to discriminate in favor of group inequality and find themselves in social roles in which they are expected to do so. People with a low SDO readily apply ideologies that tell them to discriminate to reduce group inequality and find themselves in social roles that suggest they do so. This orientation has even been observed in fairly ambiguous intergroup situations. In a laboratory experiment in which people were arbitrarily assigned to one of two groups, but not told the meaning of these groups, SDO (Scale 2a) predicted who was most biased in favor of their own group.

People with a high SDO were more likely to want the group distinction to be used for social segregation, including in job applications and choosing dates and friends, and preferred competing rather than cooperating with people in the minimal outgroup.[64]

In another pair of minimal group discrimination experiments,[65] we selected people with a high or low SDO to participate, and then assigned them to a minimal group. Participants were measured for how they would allocate resources between the two groups, using four alternative allocation strategies: giving the most points to both groups, giving an equal number of points to each group, giving one's own group the maximum number of points, or making sure that their group had as many *more* points relative to the other group as they possibly could. Because this last strategy maximizes group differences, we expected it to differentiate between people with a low versus a high SDO. Moreover, we expected this to occur most when aspects of the experimental situation made the intergroup context most salient because it would "activate" SDO.

In the first experiment, the experimenter brought little attention to the minimal group distinction and included a low group-salience condition and a group-salience condition in which participants read an essay threatening the status of a real group to which they belonged. In this experiment, about two-thirds of both low- and high-SDO people then discriminated against the minimal outgroup in the standard condition using the relative group-gain strategy. But in the group-salience condition, 72% of high-SDO participants discriminated, but only 38% of low-SDO participants discriminated. In another experiment, the experimenter heightened the participants' focus on the minimal group in the high-salience condition, and in the low-salience condition, reduced the salience of this group distinction with an essay about real groups. In that experiment, as in the preceding one, when the intergroup situation was most salient, there was a marked difference in who discriminated against the outgroup. The overwhelming majority (90%) of high-SDO participants used the relative group-gain strategy, whereas only 28% of low-SDO participants did. When the intergroup situation was less salient, however, both groups discriminated at the same rate (37%). These experiments show that when social situations emphasize the intergroup situation, people's SDO levels are more likely to influence whether they discriminate against outgroups.

SDO as a Unifying Construct

Although we have shown that SDO is not just another measure of authoritarianism, interpersonal dominance, or political conservatism, we suggest that their mutual commonality with SDO can largely explain the persistent correlations among such variables. For example, despite the claims of "principled conservatism theorists,"[66] political conservatism has consistently been found to be related to racism, ethnocentrism, and generalized xenophobia. This pattern is so robust that it has been found even among the intellectually sophisticated,[67] in numerous countries not sharing America's particular history of racism (such as Holland, New Zealand, Australia, Great Britain, France, Germany, Sweden, Japan, and Korea),[68] and most profoundly in Sweden, an ethnically homogeneous country that has little experience with more than one race.[69]

We argue that the robust empirical relationship between conservatism and ethnic prejudice is due to the common psychological motive that both ideologies share, namely the desire for the dominance of one group over another. If this reasoning is correct, then when one controls for SDO, the correlation remaining between political conservatism and racism should largely disappear. We tested this hypothesis using the SDO or anti-egalitarianism scales in our five largest samples (Sample 1 ($N = 783$), Sample 26 ($N = 1,897$), Sample 31 ($N = 823$), Sample 32 ($N = 705$), and Sample 39 ($N = 706$)). Consistent with substantial research, we found significant and positive correlations between racism and political conservatism in each sample (Sample 1: $r = .28$;[70] Sample 26: $r = .29$;[71] Sample 31: $r = .23$;[72] Sample 32: $r = .15$;[73] Sample 39: $r = .47$[74]).[75] But as Model 1 in Figure 3.3 shows for Sample 39, when racism and political conservatism were modeled as dependent on SDO, the residual correlation was no longer reliable ($r = .19$, n.s.).[76] In other words, the correlation between political conservatism and racism is largely attributable to their joint association with SDO. In Model 2, we see that the correlation between racism and SDO cannot be attributed to joint association with political conservatism ($r = .27$, $p < .05$). Similarly, Model 3 indicates that racism is also unable to account for the correlation between SDO and political conservatism ($r = .30$, $p < .05$). The same findings held in Samples 31 and 26 from the United States and, using anti-egalitarian items, in Swedish Sample 1.[77]

We replicated this pattern of relationships among SDO, political conservatism, and anti-miscegenation attitudes in Israel (Sample 32). In Model 1 of Figure 3.4, we found SDO to completely account for the correlation between political conservatism and anti-miscegenation attitudes ($r = .03$, n.s.). In the depicted alternatives, (Models 2 and 3), the residual correlations were reliably greater than zero ($r = .29$, $p < .05$, and $r = .32$, $p < .05$, respectively). Thus, we have consistent evidence that the robust association between ethnic prejudice and political conservatism is due to their mutual association with SDO.

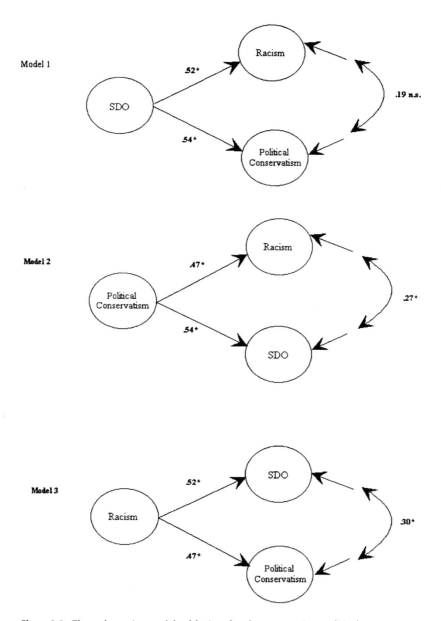

Figure 3.3. Three alternative models of the interface between racism, political conservatism, and SDO (Los Angeles Sample 39; * p < .05).

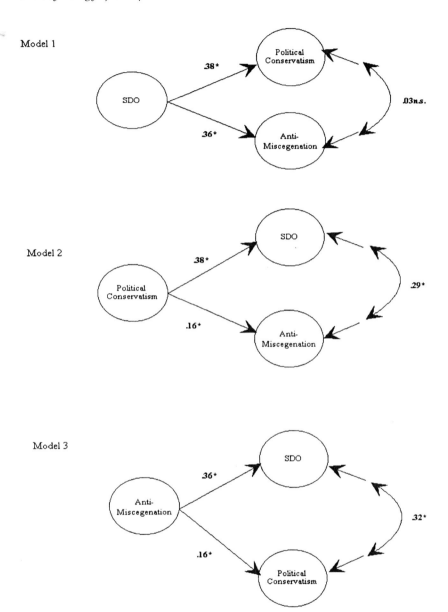

Figure 3.4. Three alternative models of the interface between anti-miscegenation attitudes, political conservatism, and SDO (Israeli Sample 32; * p < .05).

Summary and Conclusions

In this chapter we illustrated the way that societies help to replicate social dominance through the psychological orientation toward group dominance called SDO. We showed that people having low group status or power were more likely to acquire low levels of SDO, including opposition to group-based inequality, whereas those having high group status or power were more likely to favor the domination of "inferior groups" by "superior groups." After reviewing evidence for measurement validity, we showed that SDO predicts who within a society will use ideologies to enhance versus attenuate hierarchy, who will acquire social roles that do the same, and who will discriminate against groups in social segregation or resource allocation. The psychology of group dominance turns out to be a useful lens through which to examine the social processes that reify group inequality.

Appendix. Anti-Egalitarianism and Early Social Dominance Orientation Scales

The general instructions to all scales read: "Below are a series of statements with which you may either agree or disagree. For each statement, please indicate the degree of your agreement/disagreement by *circling* the appropriate number from 1 to 7. Once again, remember that your first responses are usually the most accurate."

Anti-Egalitarianism Scale (AE-1)

1. Increased social equality.*
2. White superiority.
3. Social equality.*
4. Racial equality.*

Anti-Egalitarianism Scale (AE-2)

1. Increased equality.*
2. Each ethnic group should stay in its own place.
3. Racial equality.*
4. White superiority.

(Continued)

Appendix. *(cont.)*

Social Dominance Orientation Scale (SDO$_1$)

1. Equality.*
2. This country would be better off if we cared less about how equal all people were.
3. If people were treated more equally we would have fewer problems in the country.*
4. Increased social equality.*
5. Increased economic equality.*

Social Dominance Orientation Scale (SDO$_{2a}$)

1. Some groups of people are just more worthy.
2. Winning is more important than how the game is played.
3. If people were treated more equally we would have fewer problems in the country.*
4. It is really not a big problem if some people have more of a chance in life than others.
5. To get ahead in life, it is sometimes necessary to step on others.
6. This country would be better off if inferior groups stayed in their place.
7. All people should be given an equal chance in life.*
8. I feel much better after defeating someone in competition.
9. Being at the top is the only place to be.
10. Increased social equality.*

Social Dominance Orientation Scale (SDO$_{2b}$)

1. Some groups of people are just more worthy than others.
2. Winning is more important than how the game is played.
3. Getting ahead in life by almost any means necessary.
4. This country would be better off if we cared less about how equal all people are.
5. If people were treated more equally we would have fewer problems in this country.*
6. It is really not a big problem if some people have more of a chance in life than others.
7. To get ahead in life, it is sometimes necessary to step on others.
8. This country would be better off if inferior groups stayed in their place.
9. Being on top is the *only* place to be.
10. It is important that our country continue to be the best in the world.
11. Sometimes war is necessary to put other countries in their place.
12. In an ideal world, all nations would be equal.*
13. This country must continue to lead the free world.

(Continued)

Appendix. (*cont.*)

Social Dominance Orientation Scale (SDO_{2b})

14. It's about time that we put Japan in its place.
15. We should do anything necessary to increase the power of our country, even if it means war with smaller countries.
16. The United States should proceed with disarmament regardless of what the Soviet Union does.*
17. Increased social equality.*
18. Equality.*
19. Competition.
20. Nice guys finish last.

Social Dominance Orientation Scale (SDO₃)

1. We have gone too far in pushing equal rights in this country.
2. This country would be better off if we worried less about how equal people are.
3. It is really not a big problem if some people have more of a chance in life than others.
4. Increased social equality.*
5. Social equality.*

Social Dominance Orientation Scale (SDO₄)

1. Winning is more important than how the game is played.
2. Getting ahead by any means necessary.
3. Sometimes war is necessary to put other countries in their place.
4. Inferior groups should stay in their place.

Social Dominance Orientation Scale (SDO₅ₛ)

1. Winning is more important than how the game is played.
2. Getting ahead in life by almost any means necessary.
3. Sometimes violence is necessary to put other groups of people in their place.
4. This country would be better off if inferior groups stayed in their place.
5. Social equality between groups.*
6. If we treated people more equally we would have fewer problems in this country.*
7. To get ahead in life, it is sometimes necessary to step on other groups of people.
8. We should strive for increased social equality between groups.*

Note: The early anti-egalitarianism and SDO scales are sometimes referred to as *group dominance orientation* scales. All items marked with * should be reverse-coded.

4 | "Let's Both Agree That You're Really Stupid"

The Power of Consensual Ideology

There are two primary means by which dominant groups maintain their hegemonic position over subordinate groups: the threat or actual exercise of naked force, and control over ideology and the contents of "legitimate" social discourse.[1] Of these two mechanisms, control over discourse and ideology are much to be preferred. Maintaining hegemonic control by the use of violence alone carries at least two critical dangers.

First, use of naked force can further stiffen resistance and resentment within subordinate groups. If deemed "excessive," the use of force will only delegitimize the dominant group's right to rule in the eyes of subordinates and dominants alike. The more illegitimate the dominants' power is seen to be, the more violence dominants will be required to use, leading to even greater delegitimation and thus into an ever spiraling downward cycle. For example, France's loss of Algeria in 1962 was not actually the result of military defeat, but rather the result of the inability of certain critical segments of the French elite to morally justify further slaughter in the service of continued French hegemony.[2] Second, if the level of violence inflicted on subordinates is too severe, their psychological and economic usefulness to dominants can be severely impaired.

Rather than resort to naked force, group-based social hegemony is more efficiently and safely maintained by the exercise of power over ideology and discourse. The exercise of power over discourse has gone by different labels by different scholars. Some have referred to it as the production of "ideology" or "false consciousness" (e.g., Marx & Engels, 1846/1970), or "the political formula" (e.g., Mosca, 1896), or "ideological hegemony" (e.g., Gramsci, 1971). Although there are differences in how these various scholars have defined these terms, they all share the common notion that ideologies and social attitudes are often used to convince both dominants and subordinates alike of the purported righteousness, justice, and fairness of hierarchically organized social relations.

However, our notion of justifying ideologies is somewhat broader than these traditional conceptualizations. Marxist scholars define *false consciousness* as "the holding of false or inaccurate beliefs that are contrary to one's own social interest and which thereby contribute to the maintenance of the disadvantaged position of the self or the group."[3] We would modify both parts of this definition. First, we suggest that the so-called truth or falsity of legitimizing beliefs may be difficult to ascertain and have nothing to do with their power to legitimize inequality. Ideologies can serve as justifying instruments whether or not they are epistemologically true (e.g., "There has never been a woman president of the United States") or unverifiable (e.g., "Jews are in alliance with the Devil"). What, in part, gives justifying beliefs their power is not their truth value per se, but rather the degree to which people accept these beliefs as true, right, and just. The more firmly myths are tied to the basic values and points of view of their culture, the more difficult they will be to change.

Second, the focus on beliefs that work against the disadvantaged omits another important class of legitimizing beliefs: those that delegitimize inequality and legitimize equality. Examples of such myths are "All men are born with certain unalienable rights" and the doctrine of the universal rights of man. Such beliefs also have power to influence social practices and are communicated and shared within communities.

The Construct of Legitimizing Myths

Our theory of social ideology therefore has expanded from traditional notions of false consciousness. We define legitimizing myths (LMs) as values, attitudes, beliefs, causal attributions, and ideologies that provide moral and intellectual justification for social practices that either increase, maintain, or decrease levels of social inequality among social groups. Our use of the term *myth* is not meant to imply that these beliefs are epistemologically true or false, but rather that they appear true because enough people in the society behave as if they are true. Thus, our notion of ideologies resembles Sanday's[4] description of gender stereotypes as cultural scripts, Merton's[5] idea of the self-fulfilling prophecy, and other analyses that link social practice to social beliefs.

Second, recognizing that ideologies can push societies to be more or less hierarchical, we also distinguish between two classes of LMs. Hierarchy-enhancing (HE) LMs are those that enhance social hierarchy by justifying it or the practices that sustain it. On the other hand, hierarchy-attenuating (HA) LMs are those that reduce social hierarchy by delegitimizing inequality or the practices that sustain it, or by suggesting values that contradict hierarchy (e.g., inclusiveness).

Third, within social dominance theory (STD), in order for a belief or ideology to be considered an LM at all, it must be shown to serve a mediating role between the desire to establish group-based social hierarchy

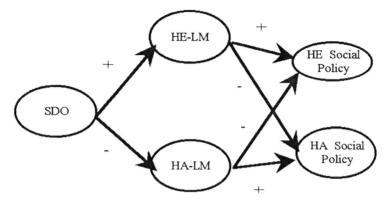

Figure 4.1. The effects of SDO on HE and HA social policies as mediated by HE- and HA-LMs.

(e.g., SDO), on the one hand, and either the support of or opposition to some HE or HA social policy, on the other hand (see Figure 4.1). If a belief cannot be shown to serve such a mediating role, then it does not qualify as an LM. For example, the abolition of affirmative action can be considered an HE social policy because it can be demonstrated that it will generally be perceived as impeding the upward social mobility of subordinate groups (e.g., Blacks and women). One of the arguments often used against affirmative action is that it violates the norms of equity and individual achievement. However, while the Protestant work ethic might indeed function as a genuinely principled basis for opposition to affirmative action, we would argue that this ideology is also serving as an HE-LM as well. To support this statement, three conditions must be found to hold: (a) The Protestant work ethic must be positively correlated with the desire for group inequality and dominance (e.g., SDO); (b) the Protestant work ethic must be positively correlated with opposition to affirmative action; and (c) there must be a significant *indirect* or *mediated* effect of the desire for dominance on opposition to affirmative action via the Protestant work ethic. In other words, we must be able to demonstrate that the effect of the dominance motive works through its relationship to the Protestant work ethic.

Fourth, as mentioned in Chapter 2, LMs will be potent to the extent that they are *central* and consistent with other critically important and basic religious, political, economic, and social beliefs and ideologies within the social system. The more firmly tied they are to the basic values of the society, the more difficult these LMS will be to change and the more powerfully they will drive social policy.

Finally, to the extent that people in societies believe in and act in accordance with LMs, their societies will be organized in kind. *Consensuality* on such ideas within a society helps to coordinate behaviors, makes social practices meaningful, gives people psychological security, and provides standards for judging people's behavior or potential changes within the society. Consensual ideologies are therefore the thread that weaves the fabric of social relations together.

Dissensual and Consensual Ideologies

The effectiveness of consensual ideologies was brought home to us when, on June 10, 1997, the Gallup organization held a press conference and released the first results of a major study of U.S. public opinion on race relations in the United States. The Gallup organization asked a large number of Whites and Blacks to indicate the degree to which they believed that "Blacks in your community have as good a chance as Whites" to get (a) "any kind of job," (b) "education," and (c) "housing." As can be seen in Figure 4.2, the results of this survey showed that an overwhelming percentage of Whites felt that Blacks had the same opportunities as Whites had in all three areas (jobs: 79%, education: 79%, and housing: 86%). However, the Gallup organization seemed most impressed by the *differences* in the opinions of Blacks and Whites. In its press release, the Gallup organization highlighted the fact that Black–White opinion gaps in the three domains were 33, 16, and 28 percentage points, respectively.

From our perspective, these numbers really are impressive indeed, but for three entirely different reasons. First, as we shall demonstrate in detail in Part III of this book, given the objective reality that Blacks *really do not*, in fact, have equality of opportunity in any major sector of U.S. life, one cannot but be impressed by the overwhelming percentage of Whites who insist otherwise.

Second, given this discriminatory reality, we are also impressed by the fact that a majority of Blacks also believe that U.S. society offers equality of opportunity in these three domains (56% on average). Because, as we shall demonstrate later in this book, the belief in the existence of equal opportunity in U.S. life is clearly inconsistent with reality, these Gallup results among Blacks represent one of the clearest examples of false consciousness likely to be found.

Third, and what shall be at the heart of our discussion in this chapter, rather than being impressed by the *gap* between Black and White opinions concerning discrimination in U.S. life, we shall argue that the most important story in these data concerns the degree to which Whites and

Blacks actually agree. Without exception and across all three domains (i.e., jobs, education, and housing), there is a higher degree of *agreement*, or consensus, than *disagreement*, or dissension, between Whites and Blacks concerning the equality of opportunity in U.S. life. Our theoretical analysis suggests that this is not coincidental, but is a self-perpetuating feature of the continued hierarchical relationship between Blacks and Whites in U.S. society.

The Notion of Consensual and Dissensual Beliefs

Within a given society, one can analyze variability in support of LMs as indicating the potential for cultural change, ideological schism, or cultural stability. Marxists and other structural theorists have often emphasized the group differences in attitudes toward LMs, just as the Gallup organization did in its press conference. Considering all the variation of opinion within a society, this component of the variation can be called *dissensual*. That is, dissensual variance is the portion of total variation in attitudes that is due to the fact that people belong to different groups.

That variation in social attitudes that is not attributable to differences in group membership, or the variance that remains, save random error, is therefore the *consensual* component of opinion. For example, suppose four people (two women and two men) were discussing the stereotypic belief that women are emotional. All four may vary in their opinions. To the extent that men and women, as groups, have different opinions, there is dissensual variance. Even allowing for that, the two women may disagree with each other about this idea, and once the dissensual variance is considered the remaining variance that exists, save measurement error, is considered consensual with respect to the distinction between men and women as distinct groups. This consensual variance is important because when people disagree about an idea, but still think about it in the same terms, they can be said to share the same ideological framework and are thus able to communicate with each other. Sharing the framework in which the question of whether women are emotional is seen as legitimate and important means that social discourse takes place within certain terms, and not within others. This shared conceptual framework not only aids in intergroup communication, but also helps promote the stability of the social system.

As a matter of fact, we argue that when the hierarchical social structure is relatively stable, the consensual variance of an LM should be considerably larger than its dissensual variance. This implies that the amount of variance in LMs that dominant and subordinate groups share in common will be considerably larger than the amount of variance that divides them.

As a result, the greater the size of the consensual variance relative to the dissensual variance, the smaller the degree of ideological and political conflict we should find between groups.

Combining our analysis of consensual and dissensual myths with classical measurement theory,[6] we can separate the total variance of opinion on any LM (e.g., racism, sexism) into two components: a *dissensual* component, or that portion of the LMs that distinguishes among social groups (e.g., races, classes, or genders), and a residual portion that does not separate groups from one another. Furthermore, the residual LM scores can be broken down into two additional components: a part that is simply due to random error, and a part that is true, consensual, and shared in common across all pertinent social groups.

Within measurement theory, the reliability (r_{tt}) of any variable is defined as the proportion of that variable's variance that is considered *true variance* (i.e., not stochastic, random error). This implies that what we are calling consensual variance is merely the reliable portion of the residual variance of the LM. This is to say:

$$r_{tt\,\text{Residual (LM)}} = \frac{\sigma^2_{\text{Consensual (LM)}}}{\sigma^2_{\text{Residual (LM)}}} \tag{1}$$

Therefore, once we have found the variance and reliability of a residual LM, the variance of the consensual LM score can be simply defined as:

$$\sigma^2_{\text{Consensual (LM)}} = r_{tt\,\text{Residual (LM)}}\,\sigma^2_{\text{Residual (LM)}} \tag{2}$$

To summarize, the total variance of any LM can then be divided into the following three components:

$$\sigma^2_{\text{Total (LM)}} = \sigma^2_{\text{Dissensual (LM)}} + \sigma^2_{\text{Consensual (LM)}} + \sigma^2_{\text{Random error (LM)}} \tag{3}$$

The components in Equation 3 can also be used to define another potentially useful construct (see Equation 4), which we call the *ideological conflict coefficient (ICC)*. If there is complete consensus between all relevant social groups with respect to any ideology, the degree of dissension will be zero, and thus the ideological tension or conflict between these social groups will be essentially nonexistent. If, on the other hand, there is absolutely no consensus, or ideological overlap, between social groups, the consensual variance will tend to approach zero, and ideological conflict between the relevant social groups will be extreme. Given our thesis that ideological consensus coordinates group discrimination and the integrity of the social hierarchy, we predict that societies in which the ICC index is relatively high should also experience relatively high levels of group conflict, and societies in which this ICC index is relatively low should experience little group conflict and intergroup violence. Because testing this hypothesis would necessitate sampling relevant myths from representative samples within a variety of societies and comparing them to a measure of intergroup conflict (e.g., the number of terrorist acts or political prisoners), we have yet to test this idea empirically.

$$ICC = 1 - \frac{\sigma^2_{Consensual\,(LM)}}{\sigma^2_{Dissensual\,(LM)} + \sigma^2_{Consensual\,(LM)}} \tag{4}$$

Finally, applying the logic of classical measurement theory and expressing scores in standard form,[7] the estimated consensual LM score for any individual can be found as:

$$z_{Consensual\,(LM)} = r_{tt_{Residual\,(LM)}} z_{Residual\,(LM)} \tag{5}$$

Some Empirical Demonstrations

We shall apply these ideas to some empirical evidence to make three major points. First, we will show that the true variances of legitimizing ideologies are far from completely explained by the differences between highly relevant and socially constructed groups, such as gender, social class, and race. We will show that within relatively stable societies such as the United States and the former USSR, the variances of consensual legitimizing beliefs are considerably larger than the variances of the dissensual legitimizing beliefs, such that:

$$\sigma^2_{Consensual\,(LM)} > \sigma^2_{Dissensual\,(LM)} \tag{6}$$

Second, rather than merely being inert and benign, we will show that consensual LMs are related to attitudes toward a series of HE and HA social policies. Third, and consistent with Figure 4.2, we will show that these consensual LMs actually work to mediate the relationship between SDO, on the one hand, and support for and opposition to HE and HA social policies, on the other hand.

To demonstrate these effects, we will use data from four data sets: (a) the large University of Texas data set (Sample 4), (b) the 1993 UCLA data set (Sample 31), (c) the 1991 Soviet data set (Sample 14), and (d) a random sample of white adults from Los Angeles County (Sample 39).

Issue 1: The Relative Sizes of Consensual and Dissensual Legitimizing Myths

Our first question concerns the issue of whether or not people from different status groups agree more than they disagree with each other with respect to controversial issues generally thought to separate them.

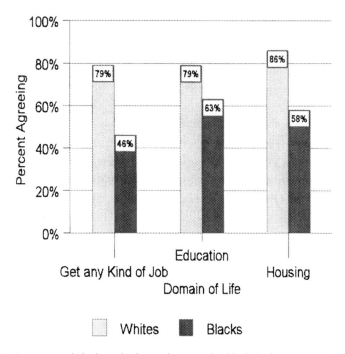

Figure 4.2. Percentage of Blacks and Whites who agree that blacks in their community have the same chance as Whites (Source: Gallup, 1997).

Examples of such controversial social issues would be ideologies such as racism, thought to separate Whites from Blacks, and sexism, thought to separate men from women. We will attack this first question using two comprehensive measures of the legitimizing ideologies (classical racism and sexism) and the large Texas data set (Sample 4; see Table 4.1). The question asked was "Which of the following objects, statements, or events do you have a positive or a negative feeling toward?"

As with the Gallup Poll findings reviewed earlier, these Texas data show that Blacks and Whites display highly significant differences in how they feel about classical racism.[8] Restricting ourselves to the four largest ethnic groups in the United States, the data in Figure 4.3 show the degree to which different ethnic groups had above average (anything above zero) or below average (anything below zero) racism levels. Not surprisingly, the results showed Euro-Americans to have above average and the highest levels of racism, while African-Americans had below average and the lowest levels of racism. However, as we shall shortly demonstrate, the racial attitude differences between these ethnic groups still pale in comparison to the degree to which all ethnic groups actually agree with one another on this dimension.

Table 4.1. Racism and Sexism Scales in Sample 4

Racism

Racial equality.
A Black president of the USA.
Black neighbors in your neighborhood.
Foreigners.
Interracial dating should be avoided.
Each ethnic group should stay in its own place.
There are too many Black students at the university.
White superiority.
A Black supervisor.
Mexican immigrants.
Interracial marriage.

Sexism

A real man should avoid showing weakness.
Most feminists are a little too aggressive.
Traditional sex roles.
Women are probably not as good in engineering as men.
Female auto mechanics.
Only men should be allowed to play professional football.
Male nurses.
Homosexuality.
Men who cry in public (weep, etc.).
Female fighter pilots.
Women supervisors.
Male secretaries (e.g., typists, receptionists).
A man who stays at home to take care of the house while
    his wife earns the money.

Similarly, men were found to be significantly more sexist than women.[9]
Once again, however, we will show that the degree to which men and
women disagree on sexism is quite small in comparison to the degree to
which both genders actually agree.

The degree to which racial and gender groups actually agree with each
other can be calculated by use of consensual racism and sexism scores. To
compute these scores, we determined the degree to which each item of the
racism and sexism scales could be determined by one's membership in
racial and gender groups. Use of regression analyses showed that a substantial portion of the LMs (i.e., racism and sexism) could be explained
in terms of the students' racial and gender group memberships.[10] For

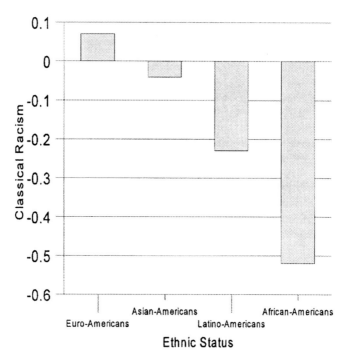

Figure 4.3. Classical racism scores (expressed as deviations from the grand mean) as a function of ethnic status (University of Texas Sample 4).

example, approximately 13% of the variance in the racism scores could be accounted for by these racial group distinctions, while fully 22% of the variance in sexism scores could be accounted for by gender group distinctions. That portion of these LMs that could not be accounted for constituted the residual LM scores. To estimate the portion of these residual scores that consisted of a relatively uniform and unidimensional construct, we computed the reliability of these residual scores (by use of Cronbach's α-coefficient). This α-coefficient essentially measures the degree to which these residual racism and sexism scores were homogeneous and reliable.

The results of these analyses showed that these residual racism and sexism ideologies were not merely random noise, but were quite reliable and homogeneous. For example, the reliability of the residual racism scores was .88, while that of the sexism scores was .83. These reliabilities compare quite favorably with the reliabilities of the original and total racism and sexism scores of .89 and .86, respectively. In other words, even after one removes the effects of group distinctions such as race and gender, the residual and remaining scores are still highly reliable. This is to say that

Table 4.2. Components of the LMs of Racism and
Sexism (Sample 4)

Components	LMs	
	Racism	Sexism
Total variance	56.63	72.21
Dissensual variance	7.36	16.07
Consensual variance	43.54	46.59
Error variance	5.73	9.55
Reliability of total scores	.89	.86
Reliability of residual scores	.88	.83

there are coherent and highly reliable dimensions of racism and sexism
that are completely independent of distinctions between group factors
such as race and gender.

We estimated the variance of the consensual LMs and then compared
these with the variances of the dissensual LMs. The major results from
these analyses are found in Table 4.2.[11]

To briefly remind ourselves of what some of these variance components
mean, recall that the dissensual scores are those LM indices with respect
to which different genders and ethnicities differ from one another. The
consensual LMs, on the other hand, are those racism and sexism scores
with respect to which different groups do not differ, but rather share in
common.

Therefore, in response to our first inquiry and consistent with what we
would expect within stable societies, the data in Table 4.2 clearly indicate
that *the variances of the consensual LMs are substantially larger than the variances of the dissensual LMs.* For example, the variance of consensual racism
was found to be almost 6 times that of dissensual racism, while the variance of consensual sexism was almost 3 times that of dissensual sexism.
In other words, with respect to both racism and sexism, the different races
and genders all agree much more than they disagree.

To assure ourselves that the effects of consensual ideology were functionally similar across very different sociopolitical systems, we repeated
these consensual analyses using a Soviet sample (Sample 14). Here we had
access to the SDO_1 Scale and measures of racism, political conservatism,
and support for government policy to aid ethnic and national minorities.[12]
We repeated the same type of analyses used with the U.S. Sample 4, this
time computing consensual scores for SDO and the two legitimizing beliefs of racism and political conservatism. In computing these consensual

Table 4.3. Variances and Reliabilities of Various Components of
SDO and LMs. (Soviet Sample 14)

| | Ideologies | | |
| | | Political | |
Components	SDO	Conservatism	Racism
Total variance	91.45	13.41	29.16
Dissensual variance	25.51	4.22	6.92
Consensual variance	52.70	7.34	17.87
Error variance	13.24	1.85	4.37
Reliability of total scores	.766	.742	.769
Reliability of residual scores	.734	.710	.751

scores, we had access to a much wider array of background and demographic variables to control for. There were 13 such variables altogether,
including: age, gender, length of military service, ethnicity (i.e., 21 different ethnic categories), religious affiliation, membership in organized
religion (i.e., yes vs. no), marital status, area of academic specialization
(if university student), social class (i.e., middle class vs. working class),
number of social science courses taken, membership in Communist Party,
highest level of education achieved, and number of children. SDO, racism,
and political conservatism measures were each regressed on these 13 demographic and background variables and residual and consensual scores
calculated. The results of these analyses are found in Table 4.3.

These results show that even when parsing out the effects of a very
wide array of demographic and background variables, the consensual
variance of the ideologies (SDO, racism, and political conservatism) was
still substantially larger than the dissensual variance. Second, these residual scores are not just random noise, but largely represent true variance.[13]
Most importantly, however, Table 4.3 once again shows that the variance
of the consensual legitimizing ideologies was considerably larger than the
variance in the dissensual legitimizing ideologies.

In other words, people from different Soviet ethnicities, genders, social
classes, political groupings, and so forth are in substantially more agreement than disagreement about sociopolitical ideologies.

Issue 2: Legitimizing Ideologies and Support for Public Policy

Second, we claim that consensual ideology is neither socially nor politically inert. Rather, consensual ideology is quite active in helping to

Table 4.4. Correlations Between Consensual Ideologies, Political Conservatism, and Opposition to Affirmative Action and School Busing (Sample 4)

Social Attitude	Consensual Racism	Consensual Sexism
Political conservatism	.34***	.38***
Opposition to affirmative action	.18***	.16***
Opposition to school busing	.24***	.24***
Consensual sexism	.59***	—

***$p < .001$.

determine the types of social policies a society is likely to implement. To demonstrate this, we need merely to examine the correlations between dimensions of consensual ideology and support for various redistributive public policies.

We start this inspection with data from the Texas sample. In these analyses, we examine the relationships between consensual racism and sexism, on the one hand, and political conservatism, opposition to affirmative action, and school busing to achieve racial integration, on the other hand (see Table 4.4)

Table 4.4 confirms our expectations and shows that even after controlling for group differences, consensual racism and sexism are still very active ideologies and are substantially related to other HE social attitudes such as political conservatism ($r = .34$ and $r = .38$, respectively), opposition to affirmative action ($r = .18$ and $r = .16$, respectively), and opposition to school busing ($r = .24$ in both cases).[14] In addition, the data also showed that consensual racism and sexism were strongly related to one another ($r = .59$).

We replicated these correlation analyses with the UCLA sample and examined the correlations among the consensual ideologies and consensual SDO. The correlations in Table 4.5 are consistent with the Texas findings and confirm expectations. We found that the consensual LMs were strongly related to the entire vector of HE and HA social policy attitudes such as: (a) aid to the helpless (i.e., the poor, the unemployed, the sick and the homeless),[15] (b) increased taxation of the rich, (c) support of government aid to minorities,[16] (d) support of government measures for equal access to public accommodations,[17] (e) support of severe prison sentences for the police officers involved in the Rodney King beating (i.e., officers

Table 4.5. Correlations Between Redistributive Social Policy Attitudes and Consensual LMs

Redistributive Social Policies			Consensual SDO and LMs			
	SDO	Racism	Protestant Work Ethic	Political Conservatism	Justice Doctrine	Discrimination Denial
Opposition to increased taxes on the rich	.23***	.18***	.24***	.32***	.28***	.26***
Opposition to government policies to aid minorities	.38***	.25***	.33***	.31***	.41***	.39***
Opposition to aid to the helpless	.42***	.32***	.34***	.37***	.38***	.34***
Opposition to government antidiscrimination efforts	.34***	.25***	.22***	.18***	.27***	.17***
Support for officers Powell and Koon	.32***	.26***	.27***	.24***	.35***	.29***
Support for prisons vs. schools	.22***	.27***	.27***	.07 n.s.	.30***	.24***
Support for Whites vs. minority student groups	.13**	.15**	.12**	.12**	.18***	.15***

** $p < .05$, *** $p < .001$.

Table 4.6. Correlations Between Opposition to Affirmative Action and Consensual Attitudes (Los Angeles County Sample 39)

Variable	Variable 1	2	3	4	5	6	7
1. Affirmative action opposition	1	.22	.12	.10	.23	.22	.23
2. Consensual SDO		1	.13	.44	.08	.25	.21
3. Consensual Protestant work ethic			1	.16	.25	.18	.42
4. Consensual internal attributions for Black poverty				1	n.s.	.17	.30
5. Consensual external attributions for Black poverty					1	.15	.36
6. Consensual political conservatism						1	.26
7. Consensual symbolic racism							1

Note: Unless indicated, all correlations were significant at the .05 level or beyond.

Lawrence Powell and Stacy Koon),[18] (f) public spending on prisons versus education,[19] and (g) support for White versus minority student organizations.[20] Table 4.5 shows that, with only 1 exception, all 42 of these correlations between the LMs (plus consensual SDO) and the social policy attitudes were statistically significant and in the expected direction. For example, the data showed that consensual denial of the existence of discrimination in U.S. society is positively associated with opposition to government aid to minorities ($r = .39$) and the helpless ($r = .34$) and support for police officers Koon and Powell[21] ($r = .29$). Similarly, the greater one's consensual belief in the justice doctrine, the more opposed one was to higher taxes on the rich ($r = .28$).

We found similar results using the random sample of adults from Los Angeles County (see Table 4.6). Despite the fact that a significant portion of SDO and the five group-relevant social ideologies could be accounted for by the social status and demographic differences among the groups (i.e., race, gender, income level, educational level), the consensual scores were still related to one's attitude toward affirmative action and to each other in ways we expected. The greater one's opposition to affirmative action, the more one (a) rejected external attributions for Black poverty ($r = .23$), (b) had relatively high levels of symbolic racism ($r = .23$), (c) was politically conservative ($r = .22$), (d) endorsed the Protestant work ethic ($r = .12$), and (e) endorsed internal attributions for Black poverty ($r = .10$).

Issue 3: The Mediating Role of Legitimizing Ideology

Finally, our theory of ideology assumes that even consensual LMs serve as conduits, or mediators, between the desire to assert and maintain group-based social hierarchy and opposition to redistributive social policies. If this thesis is true, then not only should consensual SDO and the consensual LMs be related to the entire set of redistributive social policies, but most importantly, we should also find evidence of a mediated relationship between consensual SDO and redistributive social policies across a wide number of social policies. In other words, besides possible direct influences (as depicted in Figure 4.1), the desire for group dominance (e.g., SDO) should also have an *indirect* or *mediated* effect on the social policies via one of a number of consensual LMs.

To test this idea, we conducted several analyses of the type depicted in Figure 4.1, one for each redistributive social policy attitude with the UCLA sample. For each analysis, a specific social policy attitude was modeled as a function of the direct effects of the LMs, plus the direct and indirect effects of SDO (via the LMs). While we have no strong expectations as to whether there should be significant and *direct* effects of consensual SDO on any given social policy attitude, we do expect that the *indirect* effects of consensual SDO should be statistically significant in each and every case.[22] In other words, consensual and legitimizing ideologies serve as the means by which social dominance motives help to drive social policy. Table 4.7 contains the results from these analyses.

To get a better idea of exactly what the results in Table 4.7 are telling us, we have drawn a model in which "opposition to aid for ethnic minorities" is considered a function of the five consensual LMs, plus consensual SDO (see Figure 4.4). As we can see in Figure 4.4, four of the five consensual LMs made independent contributions to peoples' opposition to government aid to minorities. Thus, the more that people (a) believed that society was just and fair, (b) believed that there is no discrimination, (c) were politically conservative, and (d) believed in the Protestant work ethic, the more those people opposed government aid to minorities (i.e., $\beta = .19; \beta = .18; \beta = .12$, and $\beta = .10$, respectively).

However, the real point of the analyses in Table 4.7 is to discover if consensual SDO has *indirect*, or *mediated*, effects on the policy attitudes, via the consensual LMs. The results were quite consistent with this expectation. As can be seen in Table 4.7, consensual SDO had its most powerful mediated effect on attitudes toward aid to the helpless (i.e., .22) and its weakest mediated effect on attitudes toward support for White versus minority student groups and opposition to government antidiscrimination

Table 4.7. Direct and Indirect Effects of Consensual SDO and Consensual LMs on Redistributive Social Policy Attitudes

Social Policy Attitudes	Effects of Consensual SDO		Direct Effects of Consensual LMs				
	Direct Effects	Mediated Effects (Indirect Effects)	Racism	Protestant Work Ethic	Political Conservatism	Justice Doctrine	Discrimination Denial
Opposition to increased taxation on rich	.04	.19***	.03	.08	.22***	.11*	.10
Opposition to government aid to minorities	.18***	.20***	−.02	.10*	.12**	.19***	.18***
Opposition to aid to the helpless	.20***	.22***	.07	.14**	.19***	.11**	.10**
Opposition to antidiscrimination efforts	.22**	.12***	.06	.10*	.05	.10*	−.01
Support for Powell and Koon	.14**	.18***	.05	.10*	.09*	.15**	.10**
Support for prison vs. schools	.04	.19***	.15**	.16***	−.07	.15**	.07
Support for White vs. minority student groups	.01	.12***	.07	.03	.05	.09	.06

$p < .05$, ** $p < .01$, *** $p < .001$.

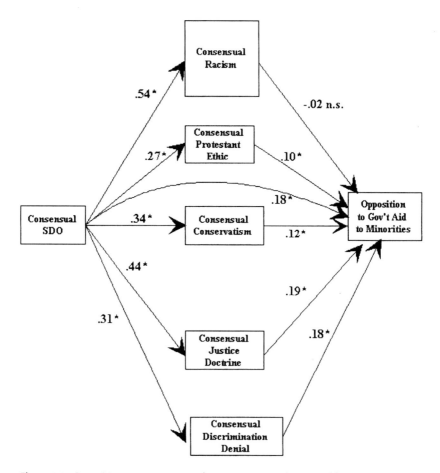

Figure 4.4. Opposition to government aid to minorities as a function of five consensual LMs and consensual SDO (UCLA Sample 31).

efforts (.12 in both cases). In other words, there is evidence consistent with the idea that one of the major ways in which the desire for group dominance influences people's HE public policy attitudes is indirect and via a long array of different socially acceptable and seemingly reasonable legitimizing beliefs.

A second finding of note is that, even after considering the simultaneous effects of all five consensual LMs, consensual SDO still had reliable direct effects on four of the seven social policy attitudes. In order of magnitude, these direct effects involved (a) opposition to government antidiscrimination efforts (.22), (b) opposition to aid to the helpless (.20),

(c) support for police officers Stacey Koon and Lawrence Powell (.19), and (d) opposition to government aid to minorities (.18).

Finally, while consensual racism was not found to make independent contributions to redistributive policy attitudes, the consensual Protestant work ethic, the consensual justice doctrine, and consensual political conservatism were found to make reasonably consistent and independent contributions to the redistributive social policy attitudes. For example, one's attitude toward aiding the helpless was found to have multiple and independent sources. Opposition to such aid was strongly related not only to one's degree of SDO (both directly and indirectly), but also to one's level of (a) political conservatism (.19), (b) belief in the Protestant work ethic (.14), (c) endorsement of the justice doctrine (.11), and (d) denial of racial discrimination in the United States (.10).

We replicated these basic findings using the random adult sample from Los Angeles County. A path analysis was computed between consensual SDO, the set of consensual LMs, and respondents' opposition toward affirmative action. Once again, these consensual attitudes were found to be far from inert. Without exception, the analysis disclosed that consensual SDO was significantly related to all of the consensual legitimizing ideologies in the manner expected. This is to say that the greater the respondents' consensual SDO scores, the more they: (a) endorsed the Protestant work ethic, (b) endorsed internal attributions for Black poverty, (c) rejected external attributions for Black poverty, (d) were politically conservative, and (e) had relatively high levels of symbolic racism ($\beta = .20$; see Figure 4.5). However, it is also interesting to note that, even though all five LMs were significantly related to opposition to affirmative action, when the direct effects of consensual SDO and the five consensual ideologies were considered simultaneously, only three of the five LMs were found to have independent and statistically significant effects on opposition to affirmative action: (a) rejection of external attributions for poverty ($\beta = .16$), (b) political conservatism ($\beta = .13$), and (c) symbolic racism ($\beta = .11$). Furthermore, even when considered individually, the consensual Protestant work ethic and consensual internal attributions were still not found to have statistically significant mediating roles between consensual SDO and affirmative action opposition. Thus, these results imply that, within this population, consensual Protestant work ethic and internal poverty attributions cannot be said to qualify as true LMs.

In addition, while there was evidence for the indirect effects of consensual SDO on affirmative action opposition (primarily thru the mediating roles of three of the five LMs; indirect effect $= .06$, $p < .01$), most of

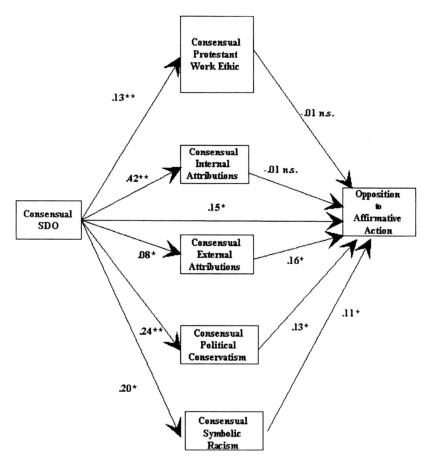

Figure 4.5. Opposition to affirmative action as a function of concensual ideology and consensual attitudes (Los Angeles County Sample 39; * p < .05, ** p < .01).

consensual SDO's effect on affirmative action attitudes appeared to be direct rather than mediated (direct effect = .15, $p \leq .01$).

Finally, we also replicated these mediational analyses using the Soviet sample. We estimated a model in which government support for minorities was pictured as a function of consensual SDO, consensual conservatism, and consensual racism, and where consensual racism and consensual conservatism were both driven by consensual SDO (see Figure 4.6). Figure 4.6 shows that consensual SDO was found to be reliably and positively related to both consensual LMs (consensual conservatism: $\gamma = .18$, and consensual racism: $\gamma = .48$) and to have a direct relationship to opposition to goverment aid to minorities ($\gamma = .25$). Not surprisingly, the

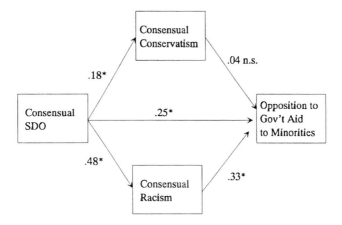

Figure 4.6. Opposition to government aid to minorities as a function of consensual conservatism, consensual racism, and consensual SDO (Soviet Sample 14).

greater the level of consensual racism, the greater the Soviets' opposition to government-sponsored aid to ethnic and national minorities ($\beta = .33$). Most importantly, however, while consensual racism's mediational role was slight, it was still found to be statistically significant (i.e., indirect effect $= .16$, $p < .05$).

In sum, across different types of populations and in both the United States and the former Soviet Union, these analyses offer consistent support for the basic idea that social ideologies identified as LMs function, in part, as mediators between the desire to maintain group-based social hierarchy in society (i.e., SDO) and opposition to redistributive social policies. While these data clearly do not support the idea that group-relevant social ideologies are completely and solely determined by the desire to establish group-based social hierarchy and relations of dominance and submission among social groups, the data are consistent with the idea that these dominance motives are *partly* implicated in many of these social ideologies.

Summary and Conclusions

While socially constructed groups (ethnic groups, races, genders, social classes, etc.) at different points along the social power continuum are naturally expected to differentially endorse legitimizing ideologies in relatively predictable ways, there will remain a substantial portion of these legitimizing ideologies that these socially constructed groups qua groups will still share in common. We have referred to these as consensual LMs.

Given this, we then emphasized three points. First, in situations in which there is relative peace between socially constructed groups, the importance of these consensual LMs will be substantially larger than the importance of the dissensual LMs, or that portion of the ideological space that different socially constructed groups do not share in common. Second, rather than being inert, these consensual ideologies are still important in helping to drive a long array of HE and HA social ideologies. Third, these consensual LMs not only will be related to a whole series of group-relevant public policy positions, but also will serve as mediational links between the desire to establish group-based social hierarchy among relevant groups and the social policies that will achieve these hierarchical relationships.

Finally, and perhaps even more importantly, our residualizing approach to the measurement of false consciousness, consensual ideology, and the political formula may offer us a relatively simple and flexible empirical purchase on a general construct that has been of central concern within many paradigms of political sociology and political theory for a very long time. The importance of having a straightforward and simple means of operationalizing an abstract concept such as false consciousness or consensual ideology goes far beyond any implications for SDT. Not only is this residualizing approach relatively simple and well grounded in measurement theory, but it is extremely flexible as well. It allows one to easily parse out the effects of any number of socially constructed group distinctions (ethnicity, gender, social class, national origin, religious faith, sexual preference, etc.), regardless of the precise mathematical forms these relationships may take.[23]

Another advantage of the residualizing approach to consensual ideology is that it allows for a precise definition of ideological tension or conflict between groups. In principle, for any given set of group distinctions, when the proposed ideological conflict coefficient is close to zero, the degree of potential violence and conflict between these groups should be at a minimum. Likewise, the greater the degree of social tension between groups, the greater the relative size of dissensual LMs to consensual LMs. This monotonic relationship between social conflict and the ratio of dissensual/consensual variance should occur both within given societies, vis-à-vis specific group comparisons (e.g., Whites vs. Blacks), and with respect to socially constructed groups across societies (e.g., ethnic distinctions in the United States vs. ethnic distinctions in Sweden). However, whether or not the degree of intergroup conflict actually bears such a monotonic relationship to the relative sizes of dissensual/consensual ideologies has yet to be determined and appears to be a good target for future research.

On the other hand, this residualizing approach to the construct of consensual ideology is not without its limitations. Most importantly, while this approach does allow one to define a consensual ideological space with respect to any number of possible group distinctions, it does not allow one to meaningfully define a consensual ideological space with respect to all *individuals* within a given social system. For those interested in attitudes shared by all individuals, this is perhaps the most pertinent space of all. With our approach, however, we are limited to defining consensual beliefs with respect to groups qua groups and not with respect to individuals within groups. However, for the purposes of understanding *intergroup* conflict, this limitation is not critical because most forms of socially destabilizing conflict are expressions of *group* rather than *individual* identities.

THE CIRCLE OF OPPRESSION: THE MYRIAD EXPRESSIONS OF INSTITUTIONAL DISCRIMINATION

One of the primary means by which societies produce and maintain group-based social hierarchy is through the use of institutional discrimination. By *institutional discrimination* we are talking about the way that social institutions such as schools, businesses, and government bureaucracies disproportionately allocate positive social value (e.g., high social status, good health care, good housing) to dominants and disproportionately allocate negative social value (low social status, poor housing, long prison sentences, torture, and executions) to subordinates.

There are at least two major distinctions one may make concerning institutional discrimination: *individual-mediated* and *standard-of-practice-mediated*[1] *institutional discrimination*. In addition, one may distinguish between *overt* and *covert institutional discrimination*.[2]

Individual-mediated institutional discrimination may be said to occur when individuals with biased, or dominance-oriented, attitudes and beliefs allow these to influence the decisions they make and the actions they take as agents of public or private institutions. For example, a highly prejudiced loan officer might decide not to grant a home mortgage loan to an Asian-American family for no other reason than the fact that he or she dislikes Asians. Standard-of-practice institutional discrimination occurs when an institution's rules and procedures have discriminatory effect, even if it is claimed that there is no discriminatory intent. For example, a fire department might have regulations stipulating that no one may be hired who is not able to carry a sixty-five-pound hose up a two-story ladder within 20 seconds. Because men have more upper-body strength than women, everything else being equal and in the long run this rule will result in substantially more men than women being hired by this fire department. While the distinction between individual-mediated and standard-of-practice discrimination is a useful one in many circumstances, in this discussion we shall primarily concern ourselves with the concrete outcomes of institutional decisions rather than with the precise sources of these decisions.

Overt discrimination consists of institutional rules and procedures that *explicitly* and *openly* target dominants and subordinates for differential treatment. Examples include restrictive housing covenants (e.g., prohibiting the sale of property to Blacks and Jews in the United States during the Jim Crow period) and the pass laws found in apartheid South Africa. In covert institutional discrimination, there are no explicit and open policies allocating different treatments for dominants and subordinates. Rather, institutional rules and procedures are structured in such a way that institutions end up allocating a disproportionate amount of positive value to dominants and a disproportionate amount of negative value to subordinates.

Overt institutional discrimation was very common within horticultural, agrarian, and even early industrial societies. This discrimination was generally justified in terms of the assumed moral, spiritual, or intellectual superiority of dominants, as exemplified by principles such as the notion of karma and the doctrine of the divine right of kings, or by theories of male and racial superiority. However, since the seeming triumph of democratic principles (e.g., liberté, égalité, fraternité) and the extension of citizenship rights to previously excluded groups that took place in many parts of the world between the latter half of the eighteenth century and the first half of the twentieth century, overt institutional discrimination has tended to disappear. However, we will argue that rather than putting an end to institutional discrimination, the emergence of the modern era has simply meant that overt institutional discrimination has been replaced by its covert shadow. Despite the fact that almost all so-called democratic states now have more or less comprehensive legislation prohibiting institutional discrimination, in the chapters to follow we will show that covert discrimination is a very powerful and comprehensive force helping to maintain the structural integrity of group-based hierarchies.

Covert institutional discrimination is the discriminatory method of choice within societies with democratic and egalitarian pretensions for at least two reasons. First, this technique generates differential allocations to dominants and subordinates while still maintaining the fiction of even-handedness and fairness. Second, because the discriminatory nature of these covert processes is often very subtle and difficult to prove, both dominants and subordinates are often not even aware that discrimination has actually taken place. As a result, it is difficult for subordinates to employ collective action to bring this discrimination to an end.

The effectiveness of covert discrimination in shielding dominants from the reality of institutional discrimination was seen in the 1997 Gallup poll of 1,680 randomly selected Euro-Americans already mentioned in Chapter 4. As we recall, an overwhelming majority of the Whites claimed that Blacks had the same opportunities as Whites within U.S. society.

Jennifer Hochschild's[3] analysis of Euro-American public opinion between 1986 and 1991 shows much the same thing. The belief that modern "democratic" societies are largely, if not completely, free from racial, ethnic, and gender discrimination is not only very widespread among the lay public, but is also held by a number of scholars, public intellectuals, and political commentators.[4]

Despite the widespread belief in the equality of opportunity for all citizens, in the chapters to follow, we present powerful evidence proving that this belief is, in fact, false. We will show that the widespread assumption of equality of treatment fails to be consistent with the best empirical evidence available not only in the United States, but in every other so-called democratic nation in which serious research on these questions can be found. Furthermore, this largely covert institutional discrimination is not limited to a few areas of an individual's life, but is comprehensive and all-encompassing. In fact, covert institutional discrimination can be found to affect all of the major areas of an individual's life, including employment, financial opportunities, the housing and retail markets, education, health care, and the criminal justice system. In others words, covert institutional discrimination against subordinates constitutes a total environment, or what might be described as the *circle of oppression*.

5 | "You Stay in Your Part of Town, and I'll Stay in Mine"

Discrimination in the Housing and Retail Markets

If subordinate groups are to be kept in "their place," it is then crucial that they also be restricted in the places they are allowed to live and in the quality of the goods and services they have access to. This implies that, among the many other ways in which subordinates will be discriminated against, discrimination in both the housing and retail markets will form important and essential arcs in the circle of oppression.

Discrimination in the Housing Market

Housing discrimination literally gets people where they live. Despite wide-scale attempts by most modern states to eliminate the more blatant and overt forms of housing discrimination, covert housing discrimination remains an extremely powerful force in helping to isolate subordinates into residential areas that are impoverished, underserviced, and dangerous. As we discuss in more detail ahead, isolation within these areas further erodes the ability of subordinates to exploit their full potential and to become equal members of civil society.

Perceived Housing Discrimination

The first evidence we consider are people's reports of housing discrimination taken from recent studies conducted in Sweden, the United States, and the United Kingdom. In 1996, a large sample of foreign immigrants to Sweden were asked about their perceptions of discrimination within Swedish society, including the housing market (i.e., being denied home ownership, home financing, or apartment rental).[1] As Figure 5.1 shows, certain immigrant groups perceived more housing discrimination than others.[2] Substantially more Africans and Arabs perceived discrimination than Asian and, especially, European immigrants (i.e., Yugoslavs).

There is reason to believe that the fact that Africans and Arabs report the most discrimination probably reflects the relative social status of these groups in other parts of Europe.[3] What makes the high level of perceived discrimination against Arab and African immigrants to Sweden particularly interesting is that they are the best educated of all major

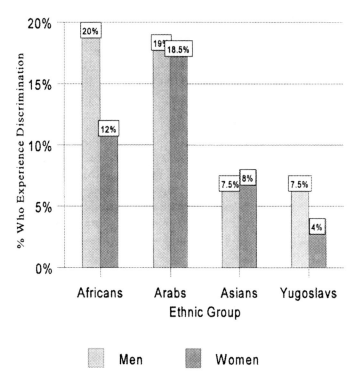

Figure 5.1. Percentage of immigrants to Sweden who experienced housing discrimination (Source: Lange, 1996).

minority groups. For example, while only some 15% of Yugoslavs and 23% of Asians were university educated, 28% of Arabs and approximately 30% of Africans were university educated. While 6.9% of Arabs, 2.8% of Yugoslavs, and 2.6% of Asian immigrants lacked primary school education, only 1.4% of the African immigrants lacked such basic education. Furthermore, the occupational prestige of the African and Arab immigrants was correspondingly higher than that of Asian and Yugoslav immigrants. Therefore, whatever is driving the relatively high degree of perceived discrimination against the African and Arab immigrants clearly has nothing to do with the low educational or occupational achievement of these groups.

Also, consistent with the subordinate-male-target hypothesis, with the exception of Asians, women immigrants tended to perceive *less* discrimination than their male counterparts. This gender difference was particularly marked among African immigrants.

Consistent with our assumption concerning the general nature of outgroup discrimination, similar results have been found in a series of major

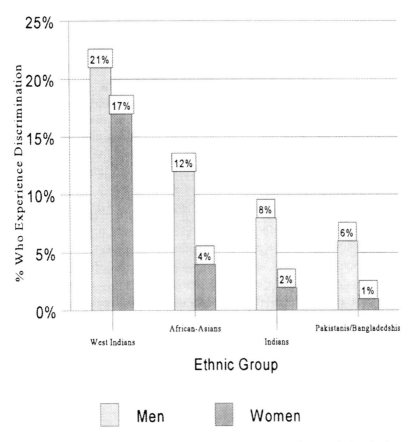

Figure 5.2. Percentage of immigrants who experienced discrimination at the hands of private landlords as a function of ethnicity and gender in Great Britain (Source: D. J. Smith, 1976).

British and U.S. studies. For example, in 1974, the British Social and Community Planning Research Organization and Political and Economic Planning (PEP) conducted a national survey among 3,292 West Indian and Asian immigrants (i.e., East Indians and Pakistanis) to England. Among other things, this survey assessed experiences of discrimination in the private housing market. As shown in Figure 5.2, the rate of perceived discrimination against people of African descent or those with any strong African connection (i.e., African-Asians) was substantially greater than that experienced by other immigrant groups. A series of studies conducted in the United States by Farley and his colleagues found similar results. For example, in a 1990 national survey, 48% of African-Americans believed that there was a lot of housing discrimination against Blacks, while an additional 38% believed that Blacks encountered some housing discrimination.[4] However, the British findings, like the Swedish results, show a clear tendency for subordinate males to experience substantially higher levels of housing discrimination than subordinate females.

Such perception data probably *underestimate* rather than *overestimate* the actual rate of housing discrimination for at least two reasons. First, as Smith and his colleagues (1976) note, whenever possible most subordinates will try to seek housing from people within their own ethnic communities, rather than venture beyond these communities and risk experiencing discrimination at the hands of others. In fact, the English PEP study showed that the rate of housing discrimination experienced by immigrants who sought housing from White landlords was especially high. Smith reported that approximately two-thirds of West Indians, Pakistanis, and African-Asian men and about half of Indian men seeking housing from White landlords experienced housing discrimination. The idea that the more that subordinates interact with dominants, the more discrimination they will experience, is also supported by data from the United States. For example, using a random sample of Blacks from Los Angeles in 1992 (Sample 21), we found that the more educated and wealthier Blacks were, the more strongly they felt that they were subject to racial discrimination by Whites (see also Hochschild, 1995).[5]

A second reason why the perceived level of housing discrimination probably underestimates rather than overestimates the actual level of housing discrimination is that most landlords are not likely to tell subordinates that they are refusing to rent or sell to them because of their racial, ethnic, or religious background. Rather, they are more likely to say that the housing unit is no longer available or simply not show the subordinates all of the housing available. Therefore, without other information, the subordinates will have no way of knowing that they have been actually discriminated against.

Of course, the fact that subordinates often perceive themselves to be discriminated against in the housing market is far from *proof* that they really are discriminated against. To prove the existence of housing discrimination, we will need to consider much harder evidence than that provided by these subjective reports.

Harder Evidence of Housing Discrimination: Mortgage Lending Data

There has been evidence for some time that one of the means by which home ownership has been restricted for subordinates is through difficulty in obtaining home financing from banks and mortgage companies (see, e.g., Feagin & Feagin, 1978). For most potential home buyers, the ability to obtain a home mortgage is crucial because very few families have the ability to purchase homes outright. Scholars and specialists in the field have been aware of the relative difficulty for ethnic minorities and women to obtain mortgage loans for a generation. For example, a 1974 survey of over 100,000 loan applications found that African-Americans were more than twice as likely to face rejection of their home mortgage applications than were Euro-Americans.[6] However, this survey lacked the necessary information to know whether these differences were due to racial discrimination rather than a myriad of other economic or situational factors.

More recent U.S. data suggest that subordinates face discrimination not only in obtaining loans for home mortgages, but also in getting loans to run the family farm. Furthermore, the nature of these data make it more difficult to explain this differential rate of success in obtaining farm loans in other than racial terms. Specifically, despite the fact that the U.S. Department of Agriculture (USDA) prohibits racial and ethnic discrimination, according to a 1997 report by the Civil Rights Action Team (CRAT) of the USDA, on average, it took Black farmers in several U.S. states three times as long even to have their loan applications processed as it took White farmers. Similar disparities were found in the loan-processing times for Native American farmers as opposed to White farmers. The same report also found a pattern in which USDA officials told Black farmers that they could not even apply for loans that were routinely issued to White farmers. For example, it was often found that Farm Service Agency officials might claim to have no applications on hand when Black farmers inquired, and ask the Black farmers to return later. Upon returning, the Black farmers would receive no assistance in filling out these loan applications, and then would be asked repeatedly to correct mistakes or oversights in the application. This process would often be stretched into months, and by the time the loan application process was completed, and even if the loan was approved, planting season would have already passed. Because the Black farmers had not been able to plant at all, or had obtained only limited credit to buy fertilizer and other necessary supplies, their yields and profits were subsequently reduced.[7]

Intense interest in the issue of home mortgage lending and race in the United States was spurred by a four-article series by Bill Dedman in the *Atlanta Journal and Constitution* entitled "The Color of Money." Despite the passage of the Fair Housing Act of 1968 (amended in 1974) and the Equal Credit Opportunity Act of 1974 (amended in 1976), this series documented that, on average, mortgage loan applications from African-Americans were rejected by savings and loan associations at twice the rate as those from Euro-Americans. Furthermore, using six years of Home

Mortgage Disclosure Act (HMDA) data for Atlanta lenders, supplemented with information on loan applications, analyses showed that loans were made to predominantly White middle-class census tracts at approximately five times the rate they were made to predominantly Black middle-class census tracts – a clear example of redlining.

Interest in this issue was further stimulated in 1991 by the release of data required by the Home Mortgage Disclosure Act of 1975. The original 1975 HMDA required mortgage lenders to provide detailed information concerning all loan applications, including the degree to which lenders practiced redlining – refusing to make mortgage loans to certain neighborhoods regardless of the creditworthiness of the applicants or the quality of the properties. In 1989, Representative Joseph Kennedy instigated an amendment to the HMDA that required that loan data be provided not only by depository institutions and their subsidiaries, but also by the larger mortgage companies. Most importantly, however, the 1989 amendment also required lending institutions to provide outcomes of loan applications for all home purchases, home improvements, and refinancing, as well as the race, ethnicity, and income level of each loan applicant, the name of the lender, and the census tract within which the home was located.

When these new data were inspected for the first time in 1990, they showed dramatic differences in mortgage loan refusal rates as a function of race. Specifically, the evidence showed that while only 14.4% of mortgage applications from Whites for conventional loans were refused, the refusal rate was 22.4% for Latinos and 33.9% for Blacks. Blacks were refused at more than twice the rate as Whites. The refusal rates for government-insured mortgage loans were 12.1% for Whites, 18.4% for Latinos, and 26.3% for Blacks. As Figure 5.3 shows, these dramatic differences in conventional loan denials were also found in subsequent years. It should also not be missed that the mortgage loan approval rate for each ethnic group shows a very strong correspondence to each ethnic group's overall social status in U.S. society (see Chapter 2).

Although these differences are not prima facie proof of discrimination, they did stimulate further research into whether or not discrimination was actually occurring. Both the banking industry and banking regulators have argued that these differences do not represent racial discrimination, but rather result from differences in income, wealth, credit history, and overall creditworthiness of the applicants. To address such alternative interpretations, the Boston Federal Reserve Board research team (led by Alicia Munnell) conducted an unprecedented study of over 3,000 loan applications made in the Boston area during 1990. In addition to using

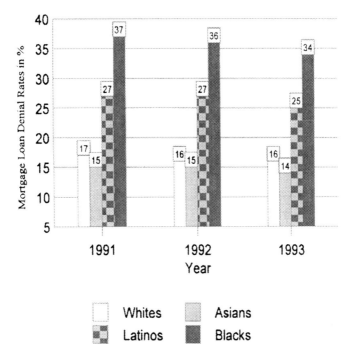

Figure 5.3. Mortgage denial rates as a function of ethnicity and year (Source: Duncan & Wachter, 1995).

all of the information in the new HMDA data set, the Boston Fed also engaged in extensive discussion with lenders and other experts to identify all other relevant variables hypothesized to affect loan decisions. Munnell et al. compiled a list of 38 variables to consider, including characteristics of the applicant (e.g., age, employment history, credit history), factors associated with the risk of default (e.g., net wealth, liquid assets, poor credit history), factors associated with the cost of default (e.g., rent/value in tract, loan/appraisal value), and characteristics of the loan itself (e.g., length, fixed interest rate). Altogether, this research was the most comprehensive and thorough study of mortgage lending ever done.[8]

Even using all of these relevant variables and testing several loan decision models, Munnell et al.'s analyses showed that the applicant's race still made a substantial difference in the probability of gaining loan approval. For example, using their preferred model specification, Munnell et al. found that, after controlling for the entire set of variables, the probability of loan denial was still 8.2 percentage points higher for Blacks and Latinos than for Whites. However, considering the fact that the refusal rate for Whites was only 10%, this means that, everything else being equal, the rejection rate for the two subordinate groups (Blacks and Latinos) is 82% higher than for dominants (i.e., Whites).

The publication of these results stimulated intense debate within banking, lending, and civil rights circles in the United States. Despite the power, sophistication, and thoroughness of the Munnell et al. (1992) Boston Fed study, the conclusions of this work did not go unchallenged. Critics of the work, predominantly associated with the banking and lending industries, have attacked this work on four grounds.[9]

The first objection can be labeled the *omitted variable bias*. This argument basically suggests that some other "economically rational" variable (i.e., a variable related to loan performance) must have been omitted from the Boston Fed's equations. Critics argued that if this omitted variable had been included in the equations, the effect of race would have disappeared. Furthermore, if lenders are aware of the correlation between race and this so-called omitted variable, then race could be reasonably used as its proxy. This latter phenomenon is called *statistical discrimination*. While statistical discrimination is illegal in the United States, it could still be considered "economically rational" behavior. However, it should be recalled that the Boston Fed research team took extreme pains to identify all possible variables that lenders consider in making lending decisions. Besides the factor of race itself, no such omitted variable has yet been named or identified.

Second, some critics argued that the equations used to control for all other variables other than race were "misspecified." *Misspecification* is a statistical concept that basically means that the form of the relationship between some dependent variable of interest (e.g., loan approval) and a set of determining factors (e.g., personal characteristics) has not been correctly identified.[10] However, as has already been mentioned, the Munnell team examined a large number of alternative specifications and each time still found that race made a substantial and independent difference in the probability of loan approval.[11]

The third major criticism concerns the integrity of the data. Some critics asserted that the Boston Fed study contained erroneous data points, was miscoded, contained erroneous information about some variables (e.g., wealth), contained outliers (i.e., extreme data points), and was otherwise contaminated in important ways.[12] Nonetheless, follow-up analyses have revealed that removal of all such offending data points resulted in only marginal changes, leaving the basic conclusion of racial discrimination intact.[13]

Finally, some objected to the Boston Fed study on what could be considered theoretical or even theological grounds. Those with a "homo-economicus" view of human nature insist that the only color that economic actors are truly interested in is not the color of peoples' skin, but rather the color of their money. From this perspective, racial discrimination in the mortgage lending market is economically "irrational" because it would lead the economic agent to forgo potentially profitable transactions. Presuming that people are economically rational, one must conclude that since racial discrimination is economically irrational, it could not possibly be a stable outcome. However, as we saw in minimal groups experiments reviewed in Chapter 1[14] (e.g., Vladimir's choice) and as Gupta (1990) has shown with respect to political violence, people are often quite willing to give up economic profit for the privilege of discriminating against others. Thus, using all of the standard and highly stringent scientific criteria available for social survey research, the Boston Fed study[15] and its basic conclusions stand.[16] Subordinate ethnic groups experience substantially poorer outcomes in mortgage lending than dominants do.

Nonetheless, despite the scientific rigor of the Boston Fed study, survey methods, by their very nature, are still limited. No matter how many mis-specifications one tries to control for, one can never be *completely* sure that one's dependent variable is actually caused by a given set of independent variables, rather than by other factors that one either has not thought of or is unable to control for. To build a completely convincing demonstration of discrimination, one must use controlled field audits or field experimentation instead. While researchers specializing in mortgage lending have yet to employ audit methods in any substantial way, researchers within the subfield of housing rental and sales have been employing these experimental methods for some time.

Very Hard Evidence of Housing Discrimination: Audit Studies

In housing audit studies, one tries to isolate the effect of an applicant's subordinate status by pairing the subordinate with an otherwise equivalent member of a dominant group. Special effort is made to see that the members of each audit pair are equivalent with respect to all *relevant* criteria such as income, creditworthiness, appearance, education, family configuration, job history, and applicant behavior. The only *systematic* difference between the auditors within any pair is that one is a dominant and the other is a subordinate. Over a large number of trials, one then sends these paired auditors to apply for housing to the same housing agent. If there are any systematic differences in the manner in which one member of the pair is treated, these differences cannot be attributed to anything other than discrimination. As is now customary with audit studies in general, the primary measure of discrimination is defined as the *net* degree of unfavorable treatment of subordinates compared with dominants.

It is possible to observe discrimination at three major stages in a housing search. The first is the *information stage*. This is the point where a housing agent may simply lie to a subordinate auditor and state that there is no housing available, when there is, in fact, housing available. Similarly, a housing agent may also show the subordinate auditor fewer housing units than are actually available. Second, at *the transaction stage*, a housing agent and a customer have already decided to pursue a housing purchase or rental. Discrimination at this stage may be observed in the degree of enthusiasm and earnestness with which the housing agent tries to complete the transaction. For example, the housing agent may offer significantly less favorable terms to subordinate auditors, demand application fees, request income and employment histories, not return phone calls from customers quickly or at all, and make more negative comments about the housing units. In the final stage, known as *the location stage*, subordinate auditors may be steered to less desirable locations than they originally requested.

Among the very few housing audits outside the United States are two relatively small British studies, one conducted in 1967, before passage of the British 1968 Race Relations Act, and one conducted in 1973. Both studies examined both the rental and housing sales markets. The 1967 study examined possible housing discrimination against only West Indians, while the 1973 study explored reactions to West Indians, Asians (i.e., Indians, Pakistanis), and Greeks.[17] The results of both studies showed clear evidence of net housing discrimination against the subordinates. The 1973 data revealed that housing discrimination was most extreme against darker-skinned foreigners. The net level of discrimination against the dark-skinned subordinates (i.e., West Indians, Indians, and Pakistanis) was 17% for home purchases and 27% for rentals, whereas the net level of housing discrimination against the Greeks was 12% for purchases and 11% for rentals.[18]

Though audit studies of housing discrimination are rare elsewhere, there have been at least 74 such audits conducted within and across several regions of the United States. The U.S. studies are also generally of substantially higher scientific quality, especially those we review below. The U.S. studies have almost exclusively examined housing discrimination against African- and Latino-Americans.[19] While such audits have been conducted since the mid-1950s,[20] the first major one was conducted by the U.S. Department of Housing and Urban Development (HUD) in 1977. This study, known as the Housing Markets Practices Survey (HMPS), was a national survey of housing discrimination against African-Americans and selected 40 nationally representative metropolitan areas using 3,264 separate audits.[21] Pairs of identical auditors, one Black and one White, responded separately to randomly selected newspaper advertisements from major metropolitan newspapers.[22] After each application, the manner in which each auditor was treated by the housing agent was recorded. The second major U.S. housing audit, the Housing Discrimination Study (HDS), was also a national survey conducted by HUD of 3,800 audits during the spring and summer of 1989.[23] Among other things, the purpose of this second audit study was to (a) see if the results of the earlier study could be replicated, (b) see if there was a pattern of national discrimination against Latinos as well as Blacks, and (c) measure the degree of "ethnic steering," or the process by which Blacks and Latinos are guided away from predominantly White neighborhoods. The results from these two audits were quite consistent with the broad findings of the two earlier British studies already reviewed briefly. To illustrate these patterns, we use John Yinger's analysis of the HDS study to substantiate discrimination in the three major stages of the housing search process.

Stage 1: Housing Availability

After contacting a housing agent, the prospective customer then largely depends on the housing agent to provide accurate information about such things as the availability, cost, conditions, and location of housing. At this first, or information, stage of the housing search, the data from the 1989 HDS study revealed results that were quite consistent with the 1977 HMPS study. Namely, when trying to get information about available housing, subordinate auditors were systematically discriminated against by being given substantially less information than dominant auditors.

Like the HMPS research, the 1989 HDS study found substantial discrimination against African- and Latino-Americans in both the sales and rental markets. The major results from the HDS study (see Table 5.1) show the net rate of discrimination against the subordinates. Here, the *net rate of discrimination* is defined as the proportion of audits in which the dominant is treated more favorably minus the proportion of audits in which the subordinate is treated more favorably.

Table 5.1. Net Rate of Housing Discrimination Against African- and Latino-Americans at the Information Stage (HDS, 1989 Study)

Specific Audit Measure	White/Black Audits: Percent Difference	White/Latino Audits: Percent Difference
Sales audits		
Advertised unit available	5.45*	4.51*
Advertised unit inspected	5.63*	4.20*
Similar units inspected	9.04*	6.26*
Excluded	6.34*	4.51*
Number of units recommended	11.09*	13.12*
Number of units shown	14.00*	9.68*
Number of units available	19.44*	16.50*
Rental audits		
Advertised unit available	5.48	8.37
Advertised unit inspected	12.50*	5.09
Similar units inspected	2.47*	1.61
Excluded	10.66*	6.52*
Number of units recommended	11.09*	5.36
Number of units shown	17.16*	7.94
Number of units available	23.25*	9.76

Source: Reproduced by permission from Yinger, 1995.
* $p < .05$ for two-tailed test.

For example, Table 5.1 shows that the net discrimination against African-Americans in the number of housing units available (i.e., the sum of the units recommended and actually shown) was 23.3% with respect to rental audits. What this means is that, in more than one in five times, White customers had more housing made available to them than to comparable Black customers. The corresponding level of discrimination in number of housing units available with respect to sales audits was 19.4%. While the net discrimination rates were less severe for Latinos, the same general pattern appeared for them as well. Furthermore, the data in Table 5.1 are clear testimony to the fact that subordinates were always at a disadvantage compared with dominants when looking for housing, regardless of whether they were interested in buying or renting. All 14 of the comparisons were statistically significant for the sales audits, while half of the comparisons were statistically significant for the rental audits. In total, the net rate of discrimination against African-Americans was approximately 5.5% in both the sales and rental markets. Furthermore, exclusion from the market – being lied to by the housing agent and told that there was no housing available when there was in fact housing available – was also substantial. The highest rate of exclusion was found for Blacks within the rental market (i.e., 10.7%).

While the rates of discrimination in the sales and rental markets were similar, the rate of discrimination against Blacks was higher than that against Latinos. What was not expected was that the rate of discrimination against Latinos did not vary as a function of their skin color or degree of Spanish accent. However, Latino housing agents, but not White housing agents, tended to discriminate more against dark-skinned Latino auditors and less against Latino auditors with heavy Spanish accents.[24]

In addition to the net rate of discrimination, Yinger (1995) also examined the *severity* of housing discrimination. Yinger computed a *discrimination severity index* defined as the average number of units shown to White auditors minus the average number of units shown to Black auditors. He then went on to explore whether or not discrimination severity depended on the housing agent's opportunity to discriminate. For example, if an agent has no housing units to show in the first place, he or she then has no opportunity to discriminate against the subordinate auditor. Similarly, if a housing agent has only one unit to show, then the severity of discrimination cannot be greater than one unit. Yinger thus defined the *opportunity to discriminate* as the total number of housing units available to be inspected.[25] Using these two indices, he found that discrimination severity did indeed increase as a function of the opportunity to discriminate. The more opportunity there was to discriminate, the more discrimination was found for both the White/Black audits and the White/Latino audits, and within both sales and rental markets.

This opportunity to discriminate phenomenon is not only interesting in its own right, but theoretically important because it is consistent with one of the assumptions of social dominance theory (SDT). As we recall from Chapter 2, group-based hierarchy is most common under conditions of economic surplus; *the more positive social value available, the more this positive social value will be unequally distributed.*

Stage 2: The Transaction Stage

Once a customer has made a decision to pursue a transaction, self-interest suggests that the housing agent should close the deal and earn his or her commission as efficiently as possible. But in contradiction to these homo-economicus presumptions, the data showed that the transaction phase was also associated with clear evidence of substantial housing discrimination.

For example, housing agents were more likely to make positive comments on prospective homes to dominant than to subordinate auditors, less likely to give subordinates special incentives to take a rented apartment, and more likely to ask the subordinates to call back later, rather than pursue the transaction immediately. In general, housing agents pursued the completion of transactions with much less enthusiasm for their subordinate clients than for their dominant clients. This also implies that in order to complete transactions, subordinates also needed to expend considerably more time and energy than dominants.

Stage 3: Steering

Finally, even when housing agents decided to complete a transaction with subordinate home seekers, these agents were much more likely to direct, or steer, the customer to an area other than the one the customer originally requested. The results from the HDS indicated that housing agents tended to direct subordinates to housing tracts with greater minority populations, lower incomes, lower housing values, and generally less desirable neighborhoods. Blacks were much more likely to be steered to Black neighborhoods, while Latinos were much more likely to be steered to neighborhoods with low per capita incomes, *despite* the fact that the Black and Latino auditors had the same level of income and wealth as the White auditors.

In comparing the HDS audits in 1989 with the HMPS audits conducted in 1977, we see very little improvement in the overall level of housing discrimination in the United States. While some individual measures showed less discrimination in 1989 – due in part to certain methodological differences between the studies – other specific indicators of housing discrimination were just as high or even higher in 1989 than in 1977. On balance, therefore, there is no evidence of any improvement in the level of housing discrimination over this 12-year period.[26]

The Subordinate Male Target Hypothesis

The results of the national 1989 and 1977 housing audits and a smaller 1981 sales and rental audit in selected Boston neighborhoods all disclosed gender effects that were quite consistent with the findings from Sweden and Great Britain and the subordinate male target hypothesis (SMTH;

see Chapter 2). Namely, in general, housing discrimination was found to be significantly higher against subordinate men than against subordinate women.[27]

The Costs of Discrimination

The fact that subordinates face substantial barriers in the housing market is not simply embarrassing and frustrating for them. It also imposes substantial additional direct and indirect costs on them. Among the most significant direct costs of housing discrimination are an array of extra *opportunity and transaction costs.*[28] In a housing search infected with discrimination, these extra costs include less than optimal economic transactions being concluded and extra time and effort to close a deal. In his analysis of the costs of discrimination, Yinger has estimated that Black and Latino households pay a "discrimination tax" of approximately $3,000 every time they search for a home to buy.[29]

Coupled with these direct economic costs, one must also consider a series of quite serious indirect costs. Because housing discrimination tends to reinforce preexisting housing segregation and to locate even economically strong subordinates into neighborhoods with relatively high levels of social and economic dislocation, such subordinates then pay the additional economic, social, and psychological costs of being exposed to the sociogenic and destructive problems associated with these neighborhoods. Among these extra costs are the problems brought about by being exposed to neighborhoods offering fewer employment opportunities and social services and having one's children locked in inferior schools. The fact that these areas suffer from poor schools harms the ability of children to excel academically and thereby achieve social mobility for themselves as the next generation. The fact that these highly segregated areas are often cut off from employment opportunities hurts the ability of teenagers from these areas to contribute to the families' economic well-being, gain work experience, and eventually escape from these hypersegregated conditions. The fact that members of subordinate families are then more likely to suffer from poor academic performance and higher rates of poverty only reinforces the strength and potency of the hierarchy-enhancing legitimizing myths (HE-LMs) and stereotypes about them, leading to further housing discrimination and segregation. In other words, housing discrimination, poor public schools, poor access to the labor market, and HE-LMs all feed and grow on one another. The net result of these mutually reinforcing mechanisms is the continuation of group-based hierarchy stretching from one generation to the next into the indefinite future.[30]

Discrimination in the Retail Market

A substantial amount of anecdotal and journalist evidence suggests that retail outlets serving the poor and ethnic minorities often charge higher prices for the same products than retail outlets serving dominants and members of the middle class. Systematic research into this issue began in the early 1960s with the publication of David Caplovitz's book *The Poor Pay More*. In this work, Caplovitz studied 464 families in three New York settlement houses and found that they paid higher prices for most of the things they bought, paid higher interest rates, and were given poorer quality goods. Similar conclusions were reached by the Governor's Commission on the Los Angeles Riots of 1965 and studies of retail discrimination in Los Angeles and Portland, Oregon.[31] Since this time, however, there have been surprisingly few systematic studies of discrimination in the retail market.

Ian Ayres and his colleagues have provided two noteworthy exceptions. In the first of these studies, a small team of White and Black male and female auditors were sent into the same 90 Chicago car dealerships to negotiate the best deals they could for new cars. Because audit methodology was used, the auditors were completely equivalent in all respects except for the characteristics of race and sex. The results showed that car dealerships offered substantially lower prices to White male auditors than to equivalent Black male auditors or to women of either race.[32] However, even though this original study was based on 165 car negotiations, this study was still somewhat flawed because there was a very small number of auditors per auditor type. That is, there were only six auditors altogether (one White female, one Black female, one Black male, and three White males), so the results showing discrimination against Black males were based on reactions to a single Black male. To correct this methodological flaw, Ayres repeated the study, using 38 auditors (including five Black males, seven Black females, and eight White females) and negotiations for over 400 automobiles.[33]

The results of this larger study mirrored the results of the first. Controlling for all other differences between the auditors, including bargaining strategy, the results showed that car dealers made significantly higher initial and final offers to all subordinates (i.e., women and Blacks) than to dominants (i.e., White males). The data in Figure 5.4 show how much more money subordinates had to pay on average for a new car in comparison with White males, after controlling for all other factors.[34] For example, everything else being equal, initial offers made to White women were $209.6 higher than the those made to White men, while final offers (after negotiation) made to White women were $215.7 higher than those made

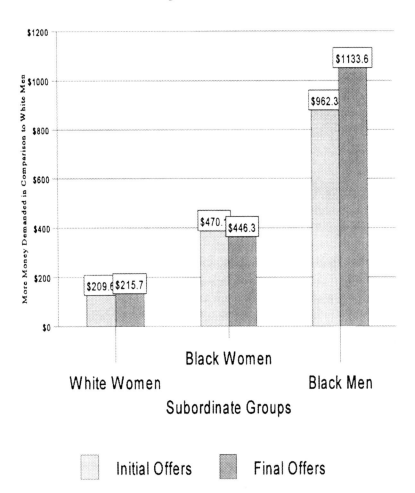

Figure 5.4. Net amount of additional money in car sales demanded of subordinates in comparison with dominant males (Source: Ayres, 1995).

to White men. Though these differences are not statistically significant,[35] the differences between the offers to White men and Blacks were. As can be seen in Figure 5.4, Black women had to pay $470 more than White men on initial offers and $446.3 more than White men on final offers (about 4% more in both cases). The data also strikingly showed that the most impressive differences were found between offers to White and Black men. Compared with White men, Black men were required to pay $962 more on initial offers and $1,133.6 more on final offers. Altogether, these results are quite consistent with the SMTH and quite contrary to the double-jeopardy hypothesis.

Ayres speculated that these discrimination effects might be driven by four primary motives: (a) Sellers may have higher costs for negotiating with certain buyer types ("associational animus"), (b) sellers may desire to directly harm or disadvantage certain buyer types (while Ayres labels this motive "consequential animus," it is akin to "group dominance drive"), (c) certain buyer types may have higher per-period negotiating costs ("cost-based statistical discrimination"), and (d) certain buyer types may have higher reservation prices,[36] in other words, are least willing to walk away from an expensive deal (i.e., revenue-based "statistical discrimination"). Using game-theoretic strategies and carefully analyzing the sellers' behavior, Ayres attempted to uncover which of these motives was most responsible for these discriminatory results.

Ayres' additional analyses lead to three primary conclusions. First, it appears that sellers discriminate against different buyer types for different reasons. While cost-based inferences appear to explain part of sellers' discrimination against Black females, consequential animus, or what we would label *group dominance orientation*, appears to explain sellers' discrimination against Black males. Second, analysis of the sellers' bargaining behavior did not support an associational animus interpretation. Third, the sellers' bargaining behavior was consistent with revenue-based statistical inferences as a partial cause of the sellers' discrimination. In other words, sellers also discriminated against the subordinates for reasons of pure profit maximization[37] – because they guessed that Whites were not willing to pay higher prices.

Summary and Conclusions

Despite the predominant belief that subordinates are treated equally in the housing market, a consistent body of suggestive and direct evidence shows that this is not even close to being true. Even though housing discrimination has been illegal in almost all nations with democratic pretensions for over a generation, the evidence suggests that there is widespread and systematic covert discrimination in the housing and retail markets across a number of modern states, including the United States, Great Britain, and Sweden. Housing discrimination is found at each stage of the housing search, from initial information concerning housing availability, to efforts made to conclude transactions, to the availability of financing, and to the final location of housing.

Besides being limited in their choices of a place to live, subordinates pay rather large direct and indirect costs for this discrimination. As well as paying substantial direct costs in terms of added time, expense, and lost economic opportunity, they also experience nontrivial indirect costs in the form of living in neighborhoods with higher crime and unemployment rates and having substandard education for their children.

Hand in glove with discrimination in the housing market is discrimination within the retail market. Retail outlets located in subordinate group areas charge higher prices for the same goods as retail outlets located in largely dominant group areas. Furthermore, subordinates are forced to pay more than dominants for purchases that appear to involve any amount of negotiation, even when one controls for the location of retail outlets.

As will be seen in the subsequent chapters on institutional discrimination, our review of discrimination in the housing and retail markets revealed the presence of an interaction between gender and subordinate arbitrary-set status. Compared with males from the dominant arbitrary-set groups (e.g., White males), all women were at a disadvantage, and subordinate males were at a *particular* disadvantage. This finding is clearly inconsistent with the double-jeopardy hypothesis. But as we will see in greater detail in the chapters that follow (see Chapter 10 in particular), this finding is consistent with the SDT thesis of the gendered nature of intergroup conflict and oppression (i.e., SMTH).

Finally, the fact that our review of housing and retail discrimination was limited to the United States, Great Britain, and Sweden is due to the fact that no comparable studies have been published in other nations. We would be surprised if such discrimination were not common in other societies as well. However, this expectation awaits further empirical substantiation and would appear to be a good target of future empirical research.

6 | "They're Just Too Lazy to Work"

Discrimination in the Labor Market

Because the nature of one's work is strongly tied to one's general perceived worth in society, work will also be an important determinant of one's general well-being and social status. By institutionalizing the differential allocation of various kinds of jobs to different social groups, societies create and maintain group-based social dominance.

In this chapter we examine evidence concerning the second arc in the circle of oppression, employment discrimination. In addition to arguing that disparate outcomes in employment are a major cause of group dominance, this review will enable us to test certain key theoretical hypotheses. First, we will test social dominance theory's (SDT's) prediction that institutional discrimination is systematically directed against women. Second, we will test SDT's prediction that discrimination against subordinate men is greater than that against subordinate women, the subordinate male target hypothesis (SMTH). Third, by surveying studies conducted across as many societies as have been systematically studied, we can then explore the robustness of gender discrimination, arbitrary-set discrimination, and the SMTH across different nations and particular dominance–subordinate relations.

A secondary goal of this review is to examine possible factors that will either mitigate or exacerbate employment discrimination. In addition, this review will allow us to assess other theoretical explanations for employment discrimination, as well as to reveal where further research on employment discrimination is needed. As in the preceding chapter, we will begin this exploration with soft evidence and then progress to increasingly harder evidence of employment discrimination against members of subordinate groups.

Self-Reports of Employment Discrimination

Once again, the best source of soft evidence for employment discrimination is the reports of subordinates themselves. Lange's (1996) study (see also Chapter 5) also examined Swedish immigrants' perceptions of employment discrimination as a function of national origin and gender (see

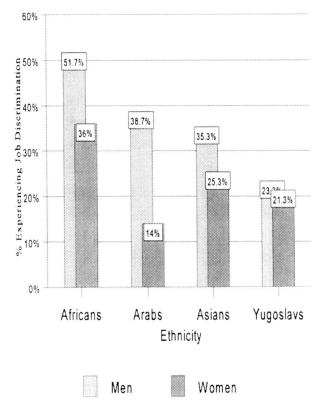

Figure 6.1. Mean percentage of immigrants experiencing discrimination in Sweden within the past two or three years as a function of ethnic group and gender (Source: Lange, 1996).

Figure 6.1). The researchers asked immigrants to recall whether they had been personally discriminated against in hiring, promotion, dismissal, or racial harassment on the job.[1]

There are at least three issues of note in these results. First, even in Sweden, a nation with, arguably, the finest human rights and civil rights records in modern times, the level of experienced employment discrimination must be regarded as quite high by any standard. This is especially true for African immigrants, and African men in particular. Slightly more than half (52%) of African men reported experiencing some form of discrimination in the labor market within the past five years. Second, consistent with what we have already seen with housing data (see Chapter 5), there seems to be a clear rank order in the level of perceived discrimination. European immigrants experienced the least amount of labor market

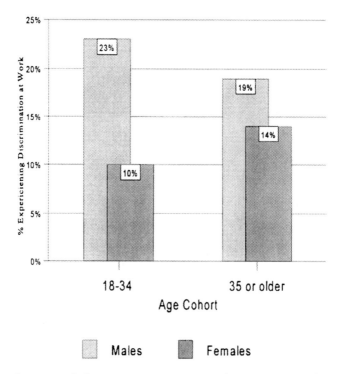

Figure 6.2. Percentage of African-Americans experiencing discrimination at work within the past 30 days as a function of age and gender (Source: Gallup, 1997).

discrimination, while African immigrants experienced the greatest. These results are especially noteworthy because, as already mentioned in the preceding chapter, the African immigrants to Sweden are also the most highly educated of all major immigrant groups. Third, consistent with the SMTH, there was a general tendency for subordinate males to experience greater labor market discrimination than subordinate females.

The gender differences in the perception of labor market discrimination among subordinates in Sweden are also replicated in the major 1997 Gallup poll of race relations in the United States. When asked if they had been personally discriminated against at work within the last 30 days, Black men, especially young Black men, reported higher rates of discrimination than Black women (see Figure 6.2).

Evidence of employment discrimination against subordinates is also found in many other countries of Western Europe and the Third World. For example, in the major English study of discrimination described in Chapter 5 (the 1976 PEP study), a substantially higher proportion of

West-Indian and Asian immigrants than native White workers rated their chances of job promotion as being poor.[2] Similarly, in a study of 81 Black workers in São Paulo, Brazil, Sandoval[3] found unambiguous and widespread evidence of discrimination against Black workers. Black office workers were disproportionately placed out of sight from White clients. White women were preferred to Black women for domestic service. Black clerks were sent to retail departments in which they would serve customers with lower incomes, and Blacks were the first to be fired. The level of discrimination appeared to be little better in the professional and academic sectors, where Blacks often worked in positions for which they were overqualified.

As Table 6.1 shows, even in nations possessing comprehensive antidiscrimination laws, (e.g., Sweden, Canada, the Netherlands, the United Kingdom, and the United States), the unemployment rate among subordinates is consistently higher than that among dominants or the population as a whole. On the whole, the unemployment rate among subordinates is approximately twice as high as that among the rest of their societies.

There are also subgroups within certain nations for which the unemployment rate is extreme. For example, in Australia the unemployment rate among young (20–24 years) Aborigines and Torres Strait Islanders is as high as 46%.[4] In 1988, the unemployment rate for subordinate workers in Belgium[5] was more than 40% higher than that for workers as a whole. The ratio of African- to Euro-Americans unemployed has remained approximately 2 to 1 over the past 25 years (see Turner, Fix, & Struyk, 1991). In Sweden, the unemployment rate of immigrants is 63% higher than that of native Swedes.

Even the passage of the 1976 British antidiscrimination law (i.e., Race Relations Act) has not produced progressive improvement of the unemployment ratio between Whites and subordinate ethnic groups (i.e., largely West Indians, Pakistanis, and Indians).

Consistent with what some people have argued, it is quite possible that these employment differences between dominants and subordinates might be due solely to human capital differences between the groups.[6] These human capital factors include things such as familiarity with the language and customs of the host country, education level, and job skills. If a deficit of human capital factors were the sole cause of higher unemployment rates among subordinates, then among immigrants one should observe lower rates of unemployment among the second generation, who generally possess higher levels of human capital than their parents. However, the data show that the unemployment rate for second-generation immigrants is as high or even higher than that among first-generation

Table 6.1. Relative Unemployment Rates of Subordinates (Migrants and Ethnic Minorities) Across Eight Modern Industrial States

| Nation | Subordinate Groups | Unemployment Rate (percentage) | | | |
		Total Population	Dominant Group	Subordinate Group	Year
Australia	Aborigines and Torres Strait Islanders	8.4[a]	—	38.0[b]	1994
Belgium[c]	Italians, Moroccans, Italians, Turks	10.9	—	15.3	1998
Canada[d]	West Indians, Chinese, Indians, Pakistanis	10.3	—	12.4[e]	1986
France[c]	Algerians, Portuguese, Moroccans, Italians	—	8.4	14.0	1982
Germany[c]	Turks, Yugoslavs, Italians	9.4	—	14.7	1989
The Netherlands[c]	Surinamese, Turks, Moroccans	13.0	—	45.0	1989
Switzerland[c]	Italians, Yugoslavs, Spaniards	0.7	—	1.4	1987
United Kingdom[f]	West Indians, Indians, Pakistanis, Africans	—	8.0	19.0	1996
United States[g]	African-Americans	5.4	4.7	10.5	1996
Sweden[h]	Finns, Turks, Yugoslavs	—	16.0	26.0	1995
New Zealand[i]	Maori	—	8.1	25.8	1992

[a] Bodman (1995).
[b] ATSIC (1994).
[c] Data on unemployment in Belgium, France, Germany, the Netherlands, and Switzerland, are from Zegers de Beijl (1990).
[d] 1986 Canadian census (Raskin, 1993).
[e] Subordinate group defined as Blacks.
[f] Commission for Racial Equality (1996).
[g] U.S. Bureau of Labor Statistics (1994).
[h] SCB Statiska Centralbyrån (1998).
[i] Kelsey (1995).

immigrants. For example, while the unemployment rate in the late 1980s among Belgian youth as a whole was approximately 23%, the corresponding rates were 40% for second-generation Italians and 50% for second-generation Turks and Moroccans. The only group of second-generation immigrants in Belgium who had an unemployment rate similar to that of the national average were Spaniards.[7] In 1982, while the unemployment rate among people under 25 years of age in France was 20%, the corresponding rate among young immigrants was 33%. Furthermore, the relatively high degree of unemployment among young immigrants in France persists, even after controlling for job qualifications.[8] Similarly, in 1996, the unemployment rate among young Whites in Great Britain (16–24 years) was 18%, while the rate among corresponding ethnic minorities was 51%.[9] The same general trends are found in the Netherlands.[10]

Familiarity with language and culture are even less plausible explanations for unemployment differences between young Euro- and African-Americans. Nevertheless, the unemployment disparities between dominant and subordinate U.S. youth look much the same as those between dominants and subordinates in Western Europe.

Despite the presence of antidiscrimination laws in most Western nations, employment discrimination not only is common, but often remains overt. Several surveys among Dutch employers have shown that a substantial number of these employers indicated that they would refuse to hire immigrant workers. For example, using a representative sample of some 300 employers, Lagendijk (1986) found that when given a choice between a Dutch job applicant and an equally qualified minority applicant, the majority of employers (53%) voiced preference for the Dutch applicant.[11] Not surprisingly, Holland is not the only country in which such a result has been found. A 1985 study of 2,000 vacancies advertised on the British Labor Exchange found that 7% contained explicitly discriminatory language and specifications.[12] In a recent U.S. survey, Wilson and his colleagues interviewed 179 employers from Chicago and surrounding Cook County, Illinois. Of those willing to voice a direct opinion, 74% voiced negative attitudes about hiring inner-city Blacks, especially Black men. Employers felt that a home address indicating that an applicant lived in a Black neighborhood was sufficient reason not to consider an applicant for employment (for similar findings, see Kirschenman & Neckerman, 1991).[13]

Once employed, subordinates are overrepresented in jobs having poor working conditions such as shift work, long hours, repetitive tasks, physical dangers, and high accident rates.[14] Subordinates also show a disproportionately low mobility out of lower-end jobs. One factor keeping subordinate workers in low-end jobs is restricted access to on-the-job training.

For example, in a 1982 French study, Thomas found that less than 1% of immigrant workers employed by firms with 10 or more employees was engaged in on-the-job training. This compares with a more than 10% on-the-job training rate found among native French workers.[15] Being locked into the lower end of the job market also makes subordinates more vulnerable to the vicissitudes of the business cycle. For example, during the economic downturn in Germany during the 1970s, while immigrant workers represented only some 10% of the labor force, they accounted for nearly 50% of those who lost their jobs.[16]

Not only are subordinates less likely to hold desirable jobs, but they are virtually excluded from jobs with power. When subordinate workers are promoted, they are usually only promoted to positions of authority over other subordinate group members and very rarely to positions of authority over dominants.[17] For example, recent U.S. data show that not only are Black men less likely to occupy positions of authority compared with White men, but when Black men do achieve authority positions, they tend to have a smaller "span of control" (i.e., number of subordinate workers) and a smaller "span of responsibility" (e.g., power over promotions and salary) than comparable White men.[18] Despite the increase in the number of African-American managers in recent years, the data show a consistent trend for these managers to be restricted to highly racialized domains in which their authority tends to be restricted to "minority issues" as opposed to mainstream tracks within the firm.[19] Furthermore and consistent with the SMTH, in a major study of U.S. firms between 1972 and 1994, Smith[20] found that the authority gap is greater between White and Black men than between White and Black women, and while the net authority gap between White and Black women has tended to attenuate over time, the net authority gap between White and Black men *has not* tended to shrink over time.

The conclusion that arbitrary-set subordinates are disproportionately found in the low-skill sector of the labor market strongly contributes to their lower average salaries. For example, in 1978 the average salary of migrant male workers in France was 25% lower than that of their French counterparts.[21] However, the relatively low salaries of subordinates are not simply due to their being disproportionately represented at the low end of the labor market and having lower levels of education. Subordinates receive lower salaries than dominants even after one controls for employee assets (e.g., education, skill level) and job type. For example, a 1982 study of French construction workers found that the average hourly wage for skilled migrant workers was 7.5% lower than that for skilled workers as a whole.[22] Male immigrants to Canada suffered incomes 9.5 to

22% below that of native-born Canadians, even after controlling for age and education differences.[23] Similarly, the hourly wages of migrant workers in Germany was 10% lower than that of their German counterparts performing the same kinds of jobs.[24]

The fact that relative employment positions of dominant and subordinate workers is not simply due to human capital factors is also found once one establishes very strong statistical controls for these factors. Thus, for example, after imposing statistical controls for human capital and structural differences between groups, DeFreitas (1985) concluded that discrimination could account for approximately one-third of the higher unemployment rate among Latino-American men.

Not only is there now widespread evidence that subordinates are discriminated against in terms of being the last hired, being the first fired, not being hired at all, getting lower salaries for the same work, getting less on-the-job training, and getting lower rates of promotion, but the work environment is also far less welcoming. Subordinates experience greater social isolation at work, greater supervisory control of their work, disproportionate criticism from fellow workers and supervisors, assignment to the dirtiest and most dangerous work details, being made to work with the oldest machinery and materials, having their mistakes reported immediately to management, being exposed to humiliating and threatening comments (e.g., "Niggers go home!!" and "Ausländer raus!!"),[25] and generally being treated as inferior by both supervisors and fellow workers. As Zegers de Beijl (1990) suggests in his review of this literature and consistent with the general thrust of SDT, this generally hostile and deprecating work environment often takes its toll on the state of mind of those subjected to it.[26] One possible consequence of such treatment may be that subordinates become discouraged and drop out of the labor force completely. Even when employed, subordinate workers are more likely than dominant workers to fall behind in their work schedules, be involved in industrial accidents, take sick leave, and be absent from work.

The Subordinate Male Target Hypothesis in Employment Discrimination

As we recall, the SMTH suggests that while both dominant and subordinate females will be equally subject to gender discrimination, arbitrary-set discrimination will be particularly severe against subordinate males rather than subordinate females. There is a good deal of data in the employment discrimination literature that is consistent with the SMTH. For example, in the 1974 English PEP study, it was found that although dominant women (i.e., British-born Whites) earned a weekly wage about

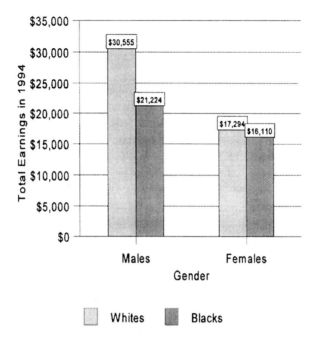

Figure 6.3. Total earnings in 1994 in the United States as a function of gender and ethnic status (Source: U.S. Bureau of the census, 1998a).

3% higher than subordinate women for full-time employment, dominant men earned a weekly wage 10% higher than subordinate men.[27] Similarly, the 1994 U.S. census shows that although White women showed an average total yearly earnings about 7% higher than that of Black women, the average total earnings of White men was almost 44% higher than those of Black men (Figure 6.3).

Similar patterns can be found even when one controls for educational achievement. For example, in Figure 6.4 we have plotted yearly income as a function of ethnicity (Whites, Latinos, and Blacks), gender, and educational achievement using data from the 1994 U.S. Census. There are at least three issues of note in these data: (a) As one would expect, at each educational level, men earned substantially more than women, (b) at each level of educational achievement, African- and Latino-American men earned less than Euro-American men, and (c) most consistent with the SMTH, while there are great disparities in income at each level of education between dominant (i.e., White) and subordinate (i.e., Black and Latino) males, these ethnic disparities are not nearly as pronounced among females. Quite the contrary, among those with advanced degrees,

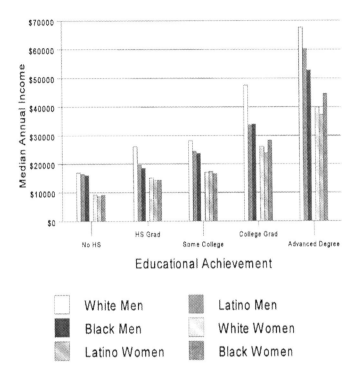

Figure 6.4. Mean earnings in 1994 for Americans 18 years and older as a function of educational achievement and race (Source: U.S. Bureau of the Census, 1998b).

African-American women earn *even more money* on average than Euro-American women (i.e., $44,618 vs. $39,816 per year, respectively).

Further support for the SMTH can be found in more detailed analyses of the relation between additional education and salary conducted by Farley and Allen (1987) using U.S. census data from 1960 and 1980. The data in Figures 6.5 and 6.6 show the average increase in one's hourly wage for every additional year of education. In broad terms, these data confirm what we all know, namely that investment in education increases one's earning potential. However, not only do the data show that return on investment is greater for dominants than for subordinates, but more interestingly, the specific combination of gender *and* ethnicity is quite important. For example, Figure 6.5 shows that the average White male in 1980 could expect to earn an additional $0.63 per hour for every additional year he stayed in school, while the average Black male could only expect to earn an additional $0.36 for each additional year. Among women, there was a smaller disparity between Whites ($0.27) and Blacks ($0.16) in 1960,

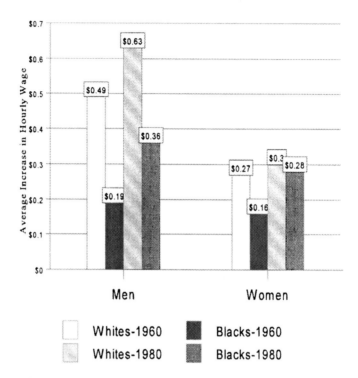

Figure 6.5. Value of one additional year of elementary or secondary education for Whites and Blacks (Source: Farley & Allen, 1987).

becoming marginal by 1980. This differential gender effect is even more pronounced among those with a college education (see Figure 6.6). While White men continue to receive greater economic benefit from advanced education than Black men ($0.96 vs. $0.69 per hour for each additional year of education), the *exact opposite* tends to be true among women, especially by 1980. At that point, White women received an additional $0.64 per hour for every additional year of college education, while Black women received an additional $0.79 per hour for every additional year of college education!

In fact, evidence consistent with the SMTH can be found in census data stretching back to 1949. In Figure 6.7 and using U.S. census data, we plot the Black/White earnings ratio for people with different levels of education and different genders between the years 1949 and 1984. Thus, for example, if highly educated Black men earned the same amount of money as highly educated White men, the earnings ratio would be 1.00. Controlling for educational attainment, we see that there has been a general

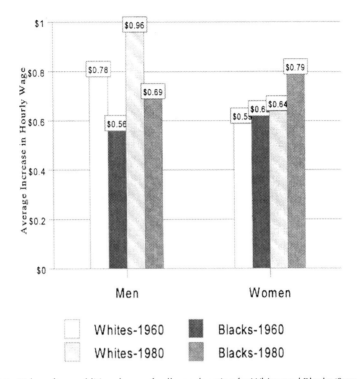

Figure 6.6. Value of one additional year of college education for Whites and Blacks (Source: Farley & Allen, 1987).

improvement in the relative Black/White income ratio since the 1940s. However, evidence in support of the SMTH is found in the fact that, ever since 1949, the income disparity between well-educated White and Black women has been consistently smaller than that between well-educated White and Black men.

Even within a given profession, evidence reflecting the SMTH has been reported. Using the 1985 American Chemical Society membership data, Koelewijn-Strattner analyzed differences in income and authority levels for Black and White men and women, while controlling for differences in factors such as education, professional experience, marital status, and occupational role. The results showed that while professional advancement as a chemist was strongly affected by being female, there was no evidence of a double-jeopardy effect of being Black *and* female.[28]

There is also some evidence that the "extra" discrimination against subordinate men is further exaggerated by the business cycle. Two U.S. studies of the Black/White income ratio found that while the relative salaries

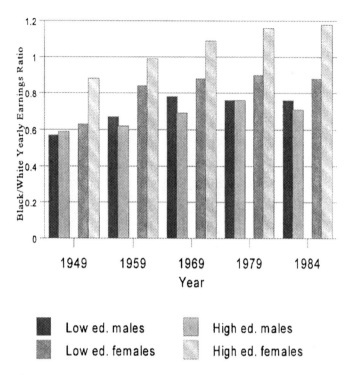

Figure 6.7. Black/White earnings ratio for low education (i.e., less than 8 years) versus high education (i.e., college graduates) for U.S. males and females (Source: Farley & Allen, 1987).

of Black men compared with White men decreased when the economy worsened, there was no corresponding decrease for Black women in comparison with White women.[29]

Definitive Evidence for Job Discrimination

While the data reviewed thus far very strongly suggest employment discrimination, especially against subordinate males, they do not provide *definitive proof* of employment discrimination. As such, some people continue to argue that the differential outcomes in employment, promotion rates, and salaries between dominants and subordinates are the result of behavioral deficiencies on the part of the subordinates themselves, rather than the result of institutional discrimination (e.g., D'Souza, 1995; Thernstrom & Thernstrom, 1997).

Fortunately, the scientific use of *employment audits* allows one to establish the reality of employment discrimination beyond any reasonable doubt. As with housing audits, the *job audit*, or *employment audit* (also known as a *situation test*), essentially consists of simultaneously sending out equally qualified and matched job applicants for the same job vacancy. The matched pair of job applicants are made to be equivalent in all essential ways including education, age, job experience, letters of recommendation, skill level, and behavioral demeanor. The only systematic difference between the applicants within each pair is that one auditor is a dominant while the other is a subordinate.

There are three basic types of job audits: *correspondence audits*, in which auditors apply for the same job by mail; *telephone audits*, in which the auditors apply for the job over the telephone, but usually do not appear for an in-person interview; and *in-person audits*, in which auditors apply in person for the job vacancy and go through the entire job application process, including presenting themselves for interviews. In each case, if the matched pair of job auditors receive different treatment by employers, this difference can be directly attributed to discrimination. Of the three types of job audits, the correspondence audit probably offers the greatest amount of experimental control over extraneous factors because any differences in the demeanor, appearance, and interpersonal style of the applicants cannot affect the outcome. In correspondence audits, the only information the prospective employer has to react to is the applicant's job résumé. However, correspondence audits also run the risk of being less sensitive because the auditors' differing social statuses are less likely to be noticed by the prospective employer compared with telephone and, especially, in-person audits.

In job audits, discrimination is defined by the difference between the dominant and subordinate auditors' success in job seeking, as defined by who proceeds farthest in the job application process, who is given the friendliest and most encouraging treatment, who receives a job offer, and who is offered the higher starting salary.

Because all of the job-relevant characteristics of the auditors are equal, absence of employment discrimination would be found when the success rates of the auditors within a pair are equal. The *net* rate of job discrimination is defined as the difference between the proportion of job applications in which the dominant and subordinate auditors are successful across all job applications.

Since the 1970s, a number of employment audits have been conducted by the International Labor Office (ILO). The ILO research format assesses discrimination at three distinct stages of the job-seeking process: the application stage (having one's application accepted), the interview stage (being invited for an interview), and the job offer stage (being offered a job). The ILO format also assesses *cumulative net discrimination*, assessed over the three job application stages.[30]

Research conducted in other countries has used research designs close enough to the ILO research design format[31] to permit us to summarize all the results together. The major English study of employment discrimination, known as the PEP study, was carried out in a series of employment audits during the mid-1970s.[32] The PEP study covered almost 300 plants and examined the job success of native Whites and immigrants from the West Indies, East Asia (i.e., Indians and Pakistanis), Greece, and Italy. Henry and Ginzberg (1985) conducted an employment audit in Toronto using in-person audits on a total of 201 jobs and White and Black auditors. In the United States, two studies were conducted by the Urban Institute – one with White–Hispanic pairs and one with White–Black pairs. And two were conducted by the Fair Employment Council (FEC) of Greater Washington – again one with White–Hispanic pairs and one with White–Black pairs.[33] Besides these, we will compare the results of a series of ILO employment audits from Germany and the Netherlands. Altogether, we have been able to examine the results of 19 employment audits across five nations (Canada, Britain, Germany, Holland, and the United States), using three testing techniques (correspondence, telephone, and in-person audits) and over 2,600 paired testers.

Despite the wide differences in some of the circumstances under which these audits were conducted, the overall results are remarkably consistent. Namely, controlling for all job-relevant factors and across all 19 studies, there was clear evidence of job discrimination favoring dominants.[34] The cumulative discrimination rate varied from 8.9% in Canada to as high as 46% in Great Britain (Table 6.2). With only a very few exceptions, each case of employment discrimination against subordinates was statistically greater than zero. Another way of understanding the cumulative implications of these results is to realize that the probability of all 19 studies showing evidence of discrimination against subordinates being due to chance alone is essentially zero (i.e., on the order of 0.0001). Therefore, we can be sure beyond a reasonable doubt that employment discrimination against subordinates is a very real phenomenon.

The weighted average degree of net discrimination across all studies and nations was a rather substantial 23.7%. What this number means in plain English is that, in any given job search, a subordinate has an almost 1 in 4 chance of being discriminated against. In addition, since most people apply for more than one job in any given job search, the probability of being discriminated against in at least one of these job applications is extremely high. As can be seen in Figure 6.8, if a subordinate applies for 5 jobs, the probability of being discriminated against at least once is as high as 75%; if a subordinate applies for 12 jobs, the probability approaches

Table 6.2. Overview of Employment Audit Results from Canada, Germany, Great Britain, the Netherlands, and the United States

Research Team	Country	Group Contrasts	Cumulative Net Discrimination (percentage)
Correspondence audits			
R. A. Smith, 1977	Britain	Native Whites vs. West Indians and East Asians	30.0
R. A. Smith, 1977	Britain	Native Whites vs. Italians	10.0
Bovenkerk, Gras, and Ramsoedh, 1994	Netherlands	Dutch vs. Surinamese men	19.2
Bovenkerk et al., 1994	Netherlands	Dutch vs. Surinamese women	12.8
Goldberg, Mourinho, and Kulke, 1996	Germany	Germans vs. Turks	9.7
Telephone audits			
Bendick, Jackson, Reinoso, and Hodges, 1991	United States	White vs. Latino men and women	25.1
R. A. Smith, 1977	Britain	Native Whites vs. West Indians and Asians	20.0
R. A. Smith, 1977	Britain	Native Whites vs. West Indians and Asians	46.0
R. A. Smith, 1977	Britain	Native Whites vs. Greeks	9.0
R. A. Smith, 1977	Britain	Native Whites vs. Greeks	10.0
In-person audits			
Bendick, Jackson, and Reinoso, 1994	United States	White vs. Black men and women	14.1
Cross et al., 1990	United States	White vs. Latino men	39.8
Turner, Fix, and Struyk, 1991	United States	White vs. Black men	22.3
Henry and Ginzberg, 1985	Canada	Whites vs. Blacks	8.9
Bovenkerk et al., 1994	Netherlands	Dutch vs. Moroccan men	36.6

(Continued)

Table 6.2. (*cont.*)

Research Team	Country	Group Contrasts	Cumulative Net Discrimination (percentage)
Bovenkerk et al., 1994	Netherlands	Dutch vs. Moroccan women	34.8
Bovenkerk et al., 1994	Netherlands	Dutch vs. Surinamese men	40.0
Bovenkerk et al., 1994	Netherlands	Dutch vs. Surinamese women	36.0
Goldberg et al., 1996	Germany	Germans vs. Turks	19.0

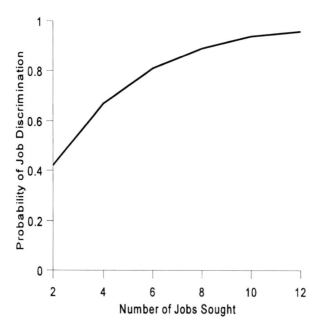

Figure 6.8. Probability of being discriminated against as a subordinate job applicant as a function of job applications, increase.

100% (specifically 96.1%).[35] Given these odds, it is surprising that even more subordinates do not report experiences of personal discrimination in the labor market.

It also important to note that despite the claims of "reverse discrimination" heard in both Europe and the United States, there was not a single study in which evidence for net reverse discrimination could be found. Net discrimination was *always in favor of dominants.*

A more detailed examination of the employment audit literature reveals evidence of discrimination at each step of the job application process. For example, in studying native Dutch and Moroccan job applicants, Bovenkerk et al. (1994) found that the net discrimination against Moroccans was 23.4% at the job application stage, 8.6% at the interview stage, and 4.6% at the job offer stage. This resulted in a cumulative net discrimination rate of 36.6%. In summarizing the cumulative discrimination against Hispanics and Blacks in employment audits in the United States, Bendick (1996) found that: (a) Whites obtain interviews at a 22% higher rate than Blacks, (b) Whites receive job offers at the interview stage at a 415% higher rate than Blacks, (c) once made a job offer, there is a 17% chance that Whites will be offered a higher salary than will Blacks for the same position, (d) once an employer expresses interest in a job candidate, the likelihood that a White applicant will be steered to a less qualified job is 37% lower than that of a Black applicant, and (e) access to additional job vacancies is 48% greater for White than for Black job applicants.[36] Similar results were obtained in four other U.S. employment audits that used much smaller samples or different methods.[37]

Factors Moderating the Degree of Employment Discrimination

To examine what factors are associated with lower or higher levels of discrimination, we performed a small *meta-analysis* of the data. Meta-analysis involves treating each study as a unit of analysis and examining a dependent variable, usually some type of "effect size," as a function of the various characteristics of the studies. In this case, the effect size is the degree of net discrimination found in each study.

For all 19 employment audits, we had information concerning (a) the research technique involved (i.e., correspondence, telephone, or in-person audit), (b) the applicants' gender, (c) the skill level of the job in question, and (d) the nation in which the test was conducted. We used these variables to predict the discrimination effect size in a multiple regression equation,[38] and the results revealed the following:

Research Method. The lowest levels of employment discrimination were found in correspondence audits ($mean_W = 17.1\%$),[39] with no substantial difference between telephone audits and in-person audits ($mean_W = 27.5\%$ vs. 26.6%). But even the level of discrimination in correspondence audits (17%) was not trivial. As described earlier, job applicants' group status may be less apparent and less salient in correspondence audits, leading to lower rates of discrimination.

Skill Level.   There was a substantially higher level of job discrimination for unskilled jobs than for skilled jobs (mean$_W$ = 26.8% vs. 13.3%). This difference held even after controlling for research method and gender of the job applicants (mean$_W$ = 27.1% vs. 12.4%). It is possible that discrimination against subordinates in the more restricted skilled labor pool may be more costly to employers.

Consistent with this "opportunity cost" interpretation of discrimination, in a study comparing unemployment in the Netherlands, Veenman (1990) found that the gap in unemployment between Moluccans and native Dutch was almost nonexistent at the peak of the Dutch business cycle, while it was quite severe during periods of recession. Similarly, a number of studies from the United States, Canada, and Australia have found that the relative earnings of subordinates tend to increase when the economy is good and labor is tight, and to decrease when the economy is sluggish and labor is plentiful.[40]

Gender.   Consistent with our SMTH, the data also showed that subordinate men were discriminated against at slightly higher rates than subordinate women (mean$_W$ = 28.6% vs. 27.4%), and controlling for experimental method and skill level only exacerbated this difference (mean$_W$ = 29.5% vs. 22.5%).[41]

National Differences.   To compare the degree of job discrimination across nations, we used only those countries in which two or more independent employment audits had been conducted, which included Great Britain, the Netherlands, Germany, and the United States, but not Canada. The data showed a substantial level of job discrimination against subordinates in all four nations: 29.9% in Holland, 26.8% in Great Britain, 26.36% in the United States, and only 13.1% in Germany. This national pattern remained essentially unchanged after controlling for research method, skill level, and gender of applicant. It is interesting that the only country that has no special legislation protecting ethnic minorities or immigrants from job discrimination also had the lowest level of discrimination (i.e., Germany). One of the primary reasons for the lack of antidiscrimination laws in Germany is that, despite its large number of foreign workers, Germany does not consider itself to be an "immigration nation" (Goldberg et al., 1996). Rather, Germany has considered its foreign labor as temporary *Gastarbeiter* (guest workers).

Other Moderating Variables

While all 19 studies reviewed provided information regarding gender of applicant, skill level of job, research method used, ethnicity of applicant, and nation, only some of the studies also contained information regarding the specific occupation sought, firm size, job advertising, use of employment agencies, whether the job was in the public or private sector, and the presence of affirmative action programs. Therefore, while we cannot perform a formal meta-analysis considering these additional factors, we had enough information concerning these additional variables to come to some tentative conclusions regarding their relevance for employment discrimination.

Occupation. In general, and over and above the effects of skill level, job discrimination appears more severe in jobs involving contact with the public. For example, in a correspondence audit using native Dutch and Surinamese applicants for highly skilled jobs, Bovenkerk et al. (1994) found a higher level of job discrimination for the occupations of financial manager (22.6%), teacher (17.3%), and personnel manager (30.5%) than for laboratory assistant (−6%).

Firm Size. One might expect larger firms with professional human resource departments to discriminate less than smaller firms. However, the U.S. FEC study involving Blacks and Whites showed only a marginally lower discrimination rate in large firms compared with small firms (21.9% vs. 25.5%), and studies in Germany[42] and Holland[43] showed a slightly larger, though nonsignificant, rate of discrimination in larger than smaller firms.

Job Advertising. Results from the U.S. audits show that discrimination is lower when jobs are widely advertised. For example, the rate of discrimination experienced by applicants for jobs advertised in major newspapers (i.e., 14.7% for Blacks, 19.7% for Latinos) was lower than that experienced when jobs were listed in locally distributed suburban newspapers (i.e., 22.3% for Latinos), or during "walk-in" applications, where there had been no newspaper advertising (i.e., 34.3% for Blacks).[44]

Private Versus Public Firms. In the first major economic theory applied to employment discrimination, Gary Becker (1957) argued that employers will incur economic costs by not hiring equally productive members of subordinate groups at lower salaries than they would have to pay members of dominant groups, or from not hiring more qualified subordinates at the same cost they would have to pay less qualified dominants.[45] As forcefully argued by Sowell (1981) and other neoconservatives, one of the implications of Becker's analysis is that a good antidote to employment discrimination would be more open and competitive markets, rather than antidiscrimination laws.[46] In markets free of discrimination laws, it is argued, discrimination would be too costly and would therefore decline. However, the fact that there has not been an increase in U.S. discrimination after the antidiscrimination laws of the 1960s were enacted appears to contradict this reasoning.

A better test of the neoconservative argument would be to compare public and private firms. According to the neoconservative position, because private firms are more subject to free market forces than are public firms and government agencies, one should expect *less* employment discrimination within the private sector than within the public sector. However, the empirical evidence offers no support whatsoever for this reasoning. As a matter of fact, whenever employment audits have been used to compare the discriminatory behavior of private versus public firms, private firms have been consistently found to display substantially higher rates of employment discrimination than public firms. The best tests of this have used correspondence audits in Holland and Germany. For example, Bovenkerk et al. (1994) compared the discrimination rates for private and semipublic firms with respect to the treatment of native Dutch and Surinamese job applicants. In this analysis, firms comprising the semipublic sector consisted of all companies and organizations predominantly funded *but not run by* the government, such as denominational primary schools. Government funding supposedly frees such firms from market pressure, but they have the same level of legal accountability as other private firms. Contrary to Sowell's argument, discrimination within the private sector (31.0%) was greater than that within the semipublic sector (13.7%). Similar results have been found in Germany, where the rate of job discrimination in private firms was more than $6\frac{1}{2}$ times the rate of employment discrimination within public firms (25.0% vs. 3.7%).[47]

Consistent with data and arguments presented in Chapter 3,[48] we believe that a major reason for the substantially higher levels of discrimination found within these private versus semipublic firms is that the goals of the institutions and the people in them probably differ dramatically between the two types of firms. Our data showed that those attracted to careers within the commercial and business sectors, often HE jobs, have substantially higher levels of SDO than those attracted to careers oriented toward helping the less fortunate (HA jobs). These latter jobs are substantially, though not exclusively, within the public sector.

City Versus Suburbs.   In the United States one might expect that (predominantly White) suburban areas would be less welcoming of minority job applicants than central cities. However, the empirical support for this thesis is mixed and inconclusive.

Employment Agencies. The U.S. FEC studies also found that the use of employment agencies had a substantial effect on the level of job discrimination.[49] U.S. employment agencies are for-profit businesses that place workers with other firms. The FEC studies found that when they tried to place workers through private employment agencies, the subordinate auditors experienced substantially higher rates of job discrimination than dominant auditors; the discrimination rate was 33.7% for Latinos and 66.7% for Blacks. As Bendick (1996) points out, these data imply that private employment agencies perceive part of their function as screening out "less desirable" (e.g., subordinate) workers for their client firms. However, it is still not clear whether this very high rate of discrimination by employment agencies is a function of their character as private firms or their perceptions of the desires of their private client firms.

Finally, employment audits in the United States have found that firms announcing themselves to be "equal opportunity employers" were just as likely to discriminate against subordinates as firms not making such public announcements (23.0% vs. 22.0% using Latino auditors).[50]

Affirmative Action Programs. Perhaps the most fascinating and provocative results concern affirmative action programs (sometimes called "positive action" programs). Such programs are designed to take affirmative steps to increase underrepresented groups in the workforce. Such programs have been accused by politicians and some litigants (e.g., Bakke in *Bakke v. University of California*, 1978) of producing reverse discrimination (i.e., discrimination against dominants). Despite the great controversy these policies have generated, it is remarkable how little research has been done to test whether reverse discrimination actually occurs. The only audit study we know of to explore this question was conducted in Holland by Bovenkerk et al. (1994). This Dutch team used correspondence audits for jobs requiring a college education (e.g., teachers, laboratory assistants, administrators) using native Dutch and Surinamese testers. The researchers examined 17 usable cases in which firms had affirmative action programs and 165 usable cases in which firms did not have affirmative action programs. What makes this Dutch case particularly interesting is the nature of the affirmative action decision rule used in Holland: "When two job candidates are equally qualified, always hire the minority candidate." Given this decision rule in the context of controlled audit studies (i.e., using equally qualified candidates), one would expect to find reverse discrimination.

The results showed that in firms using this affirmative action decision rule, the Surinamese applicant was favored over the Dutch applicant in 17.6% of the cases, and the Dutch applicant was favored over the

Surinamese applicant in 17.6% of the cases. In other words, for firms practicing *preferential* affirmative action (i.e., preference for the equally qualified minority candidate), the net rate of job discrimination was zero. However, in firms that did not practice affirmative action, the Surinamese applicant was preferred over the Dutch applicant in 14.5% of the cases, while the Dutch applicant was preferred over the Surinamese applicant in 35.8% of the cases (a net discrimination rate in favor of dominants of 21.3%). The difference in the discrimination rate between these two types of firms was statistically significant.[51]

There are at least three major points of interest in these results. First, contrary to popular opinion, even using a rather severe affirmative action decision rule (i.e., always prefer the equally qualified minority candidate), there was still no empirical evidence of reverse discrimination. On the contrary, these programs appear to generate the results that critics of affirmative action claim to want, namely, complete equity and fairness: a situation in which two equally qualified candidates have an equal chance of being hired. Second, while there is no evidence that antidiscrimination legislation actually eliminates employment bias, there is now some evidence that affirmative action programs *can* eliminate such bias. Because discrimination against the "subordinate other" is the default rule, or general background condition, it takes an active and counterdiscriminatory decision rule in order to neutralize this default rule. Despite this fact, such programs are still highly unpopular among dominants and consequently, we suspect, politically unsustainable over the long run. For example, in a 1997 Gallup poll of Americans, a plurality of Whites wanted affirmative action programs reduced. Further, in November 1996, California voters, including 60% of the Euro-American voters, passed a referendum, upheld by the U.S. Supreme Court, making affirmative action by the state illegal (Proposition 209).

Furthermore, experimental research shows that opposition to affirmative action is even more likely when the intended recipients of this policy are members of subordinate, arbitrary-set groups. Surveying a random sample of White, Black, and Latino respondents from Los Angeles County in the spring of 1996, we assessed support for affirmative action in job hiring when respondents were told, randomly, that the recipients of affirmative action were either women, poor people, or Blacks. The results showed that respondents' attitudes toward affirmative action depended on which group the policy benefited. All three ethnic groups (Whites, Blacks, and Latinos) supported affirmative action most when the recipients were women. The only marked opposition to affirmative action among Whites was when the recipients were Blacks (Figure 6.9).[52]

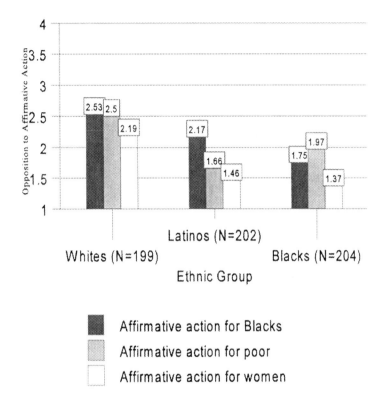

Figure 6.9. Opposition to affirmative action in hiring and promotion as a function of target and ethnicity of respondent among random sample of Los Angeles County residents (1 = *strongly support*; 4 = *strongly oppose*; Sample 39).

It appears that dominants in particular are most opposed to policies that eliminate discrimination against low-status, arbitrary-set subordinates in particular.[53] As already suggested in Chapter 4, opposition to effective antidiscrimination policies (e.g., affirmative action) among dominants is not driven simply by perceptions of unfairness, but also by the desire to maintain the hegemonic position of one's group within the social structure.

To explore this hypothesis we examined the factors associated with affirmative action opposition for each of the affirmative action beneficiaries. We expected SDO to be particularly associated with opposition to affirmative action when the target of affirmative action was Blacks. To test this idea, we performed three multiple regression analyses,[54] once with respect to each recipient group. The independent variables used were (a) gender (male = 1, female = 2), (b) income, (c) education level, (d) anti-Black affect (i.e., more positive feelings toward one's own ethnic group than toward

Table 6.3. Degree of Opposition to Affirmative Action as a Function of Affirmative Action Target and Seven Predictor Variables (Sample 39)

Variables	Target		
	Women	Blacks	Poor People
Gender	.04	.00	−.01
Education	.22**	.12*	.12*
Income	.03	.05	.03
Anti-Black affect	.00	.00	−.01
Protestant work ethic	.21*	.03	−.02
Political conservatism	.04	.23**	.06
SDO	.17	.63**	.11
N	128	133	147
Adjusted R^2	.13**	.20*	.04*

Note: Blacks were excluded from analyses; entries are unstandardized regression coefficients.
* $p < 0.05$; ** $p < .01$.

Blacks),[55] (e) political conservatism, (f) support for the Protestant work ethic (i.e., the notion that people will succeed by their own efforts), and (g) SDO (see Table 6.3).

The results showed that some of the factors associated with affirmative action opposition were dependent on who the beneficiary of affirmative action was. For example, net of the other factors, the people most opposed to affirmative action for women were better educated ($b = .22$) and held to the Protestant work ethic ($b = .21$). However, few participant variables were related to opposition to affirmative action for poor people, besides the slight effect of education level ($b = .12$). However, when the target of affirmative action was America's classic subordinate group (Blacks), not only are education and political conservatism significantly associated with opposition to this social policy ($b = .12$, and .23, respectively), but SDO was strongly associated with this opposition as well ($b = .63$). In other words, not only are people more opposed to affirmative action when the beneficiaries of this policy are the major subordinate group (i.e., Blacks), but this opposition is also significantly and strongly associated with the public's level of SDO.

Taken as a whole, we fear that all of these findings imply that it is exactly those social policies that are most effective in eliminating discrimination that will be most politically unsustainable. Though political discourse has made affirmative action appear to violate principles of equity and individualism, these are not the only motives involved. Rather, as we saw in Chapter 4, the more that members of dominant groups are interested in maintaining their group's relative position in the social hierarchy, the more they perceive antidiscrimination policies as unfair.

Psychological and Economic Consequences of Employment Discrimination

Despite protestations to the contrary, there is widespread and convincing evidence that subordinates face a rather daunting situation in the labor market. The level of stress this situation is likely to produce may even interfere with the way in which they perform their jobs and result in things like higher levels of job alienation and less commitment to their employers. These forms of behavioral asymmetry are all perfectly understandable given the manner in which subordinates are treated within the labor market. The problem is that such asymmetry, whether actual or imagined, will become a self-fulfilling prophecy by serving to reinforce the prejudices of dominants against subordinate workers and thereby feed another cycle in the production and maintenance of the hierarchical relationships between dominant and subordinate groups.

Finally, one of the most important long-term consequences of systematic labor discrimination against subordinates is its contribution to the enormous differences in net wealth between dominants and subordinates (see, e.g., Oliver & Shapiro, 1995). For example, according to the U.S. Bureau of the Census, the median net wealth of Euro-American households in 1993 was $45,740, while that of African- and Latino-Americans households was $4,418 and $4,656, respectively, a ratio of essentially 10 to 1. What is so important about these differences is that the privileges that wealth produces tend to be passed on from one generation to next, a process that contributes to the stability of the group-based nature of social hierarchy.

Summary

In this chapter we examined evidence of the means by which employment discrimination produces and maintains group-based social hierarchy. Consistent with the major assumptions of SDT, the evidence shows widespread discrimination against both women and members of arbitrary-set groups. Furthermore, the discrimination against arbitrary-set groups is quite general across different arbitrary-set distinctions (e.g., race, ethnicity, religion, nationality) and across different social and political systems. Employment discrimination has been found in all countries in which the issue has been seriously investigated: in developed as well as third world nations and in nations with strong as well as weak antidiscrimination legislation. While we have not been able to examine every society in the world, there is *not one* society where the issue has been seriously studied in which employment discrimination has failed to appear.

Furthermore, evidence supporting employment discrimination against subordinates can be found at every level of scientific certainty: from the relatively soft evidence based on subordinates' perceptions of discrimination, to fairly hard survey evidence using various statistical controls, to the very hard evidence based on well-controlled field experiments (e.g., correspondence audits). All three research methods yielded consistent evidence of discrimination at nontrivial and sometimes substantial levels. In addition, group-based discrimination occurs systematically through every phase of employment. Subordinates have substantially less chance of being hired. Once hired, they are likely to get less pay for the same work, less chance for on-the-job training, and less chance for promotion to positions of responsibility, and they are at greater risk for dismissal during periods of economic recession than dominants. Most labor market discrimination is covert. However, there is still a substantial proportion of firms in which job discrimination is quite overt, even when such discrimination is patently illegal.

There are a number of factors that appear to moderate the degree of discrimination. In general, the level of employment discrimination is greater (a) for jobs requiring less rather than more qualifications, (b) in private versus public firms, (c) in jobs requiring more rather than less contact with the public, (d) in jobs narrowly versus broadly advertised, (e) when employment agencies versus other firms are used, and (f) during periods of economic recession rather than expansion.

This last condition concerning economic expansion appears to contradict our earlier remarks that discrimination is most likely under conditions of surplus rather than scarcity. However, this contradiction is actually more apparent than real. In periods of great economic expansion and growth, there are more jobs than job applicants. This creates a situation of surplus for applicants and one of scarcity for employers. On the other hand, in periods of economic contraction, there are often more job applicants than jobs. This creates a situation of scarcity for applicants and one of surplus for employers. Since the employer has considerably more power in any one-on-one job negotiation than the individual job applicant, in understanding the dynamics of employment discrimination we must primarily attend to the constraints imposed on the employer rather than those imposed on the job applicant. Because economic growth places the employer in a situation of employee scarcity, the employer does not generally have the option of discriminating without suffering great economic costs. But during periods of economic contraction, employers are often faced with employee surplus. However, under these surplus conditions, employers are then free to follow their personal preferences and discriminate against certain categories of job applicants without having to suffer adverse economic consequences.

In addition, examination of the employment discrimination data also shows rather consistent support for the SMTH. While there is strong evidence of gender discrimination against women from both dominant and subordinate arbitrary-set groups, arbitrary-set discrimination appears to be primarily directed against arbitrary-set men rather than arbitrary-set women.

Finally, we have shown that while there are social policies (e.g., affirmative action) that show promise of being able to completely eliminate or seriously attenuate labor market discrimination, these are the very policies that happen to be politically unpopular among dominants and, therefore, politically unsustainable in the long run.

7 | "They're Just Mentally and Physically Unfit"

Discrimination in Education and Health Care

Despite the fact that a very large proportion of both dominants and subordinates are convinced that both groups are treated equally within the domains of education and health care, the evidence we review next shows these beliefs to be significantly out of touch with reality.

Discrimination in Education

Confucius (551–479 B.C.), a sage and high-level bureaucrat, was one of the earliest documented examples of a poor person rising to fame and prominence by virtue of fortuitous access to higher education. In many hierarchical societies, education has been a key element in social mobility. Because of their power and value as scarce resources, education and literacy have tended to be reserved exclusively for ruling elites and their agents for most of human history. For example, many slave states in the United States made it illegal to teach slaves to read.[1]

Mass literacy did not begin to emerge until around A.D. 1000 in Europe, and even then was largely restricted to the ruling elites out of a fear of what impact it might have on the general social order. To the extent that subordinates were given literacy instruction at all, this instruction stressed rote memorization, rather than the ability to process information critically. It was not until the Industrial Revolution of the nineteenth century that basic literacy was extended to broad sections of the population. Though the twentieth century has seen an even further extension of literacy, this training still tends to be rather rudimentary and to stress rote learning rather than critical reasoning abilities.[2]

While the precise mechanisms by which relatively inferior education is delivered to subordinates vary across different social systems, regardless of social system the outcomes are all essentially the same. Subordinates are given relatively poor literacy training, and subsequently have relatively poor reading and math skills, low intelligence test scores, and relatively high rates of academic failure. For example, in their recent book *Inequality by Design*, Fischer and his colleagues (1996) show the association between group status and academic performance across several societies.

Supplementing their data with some additional findings, we found that in 21 comparisons between dominant and subordinate groups across 14 nations, members of dominant groups had higher levels of academic and intellectual achievement than members of subordinate groups (see Table 7.1). While the sizes of these differences vary somewhat from nation to nation, the basic pattern is quite unambiguous and cross-culturally consistent.[3]

For example, in Japan, Koreans have been a subordinated group for several generations, and their academic performance is clearly inferior to that of Japanese. Lee reports that in 1976, Korean students attended university at less than half the rate of the Japanese population as a whole (i.e., 12.7% vs. 29.4%). However, in the United States, where Koreans are not a subordinate group relative to the Japanese, the academic performance of Koreans and Japanese are essentially equivalent.[4] The Burakumin (or Eta-Hinin people) is an "indigenous" Japanese group that has held subordinate status in Japan since the Tokugawa Period (1603–1868). Like other subordinate students around the world, Burakumin children have lower academic achievement than non-Burakumin children. For example, in data from Shiga Prefecture in 1978, while 30% of non-Burakumin children earned high grades in ninth-grade math classes, only 10% of the Burakumin children earned such grades. Similarly, while 23% of non-Burakumin children earned poor grades, as many as 60% of the Burakumin children did so.[5] However, in the United States, where Burakumin background carries no social stigma, the academic performance of Burakumin children does not differ from that of other Japanese-Americans.[6]

Mechanisms Producing Poor Academic Achievement

As John Ogbu[7] has noted, the inferior performance of subordinates is commonly attributed to internal and inadequate characteristics of the subordinates themselves. However, the fact that the Burakumin can change their academic performance so dramatically when not placed in a subordinated role belies such inherency explanations. Instead, we suggest that there are three other major processes by which subordinate social status becomes transformed into relatively poor academic performance (see Figure 7.1).

First and most obviously, poor academic performance among subordinates is the result of the meager economic and social assets available to children from subordinate families. For example, the parents of subordinate children are less able to provide their children with intellectually stimulating environments, private schools, private tutors, computers, and extra help at home.

Table 7.1. Association Between Arbitrary-Set Group Status and Academic Success Across Countries

	Group Status/Academic Success	
Country	High/High	Low/Low
Australia	Whites	Aborigines
Belgium	French	Flemish
Canada	Whites	Native Americans
Czechoslovakia	Slovaks	Gypsies
France	Native French	Portuguese immigrants
Great Britain	English	Irish, Scots
India	Nontribals	Tribal people
	Brahmins	Harijans
	High caste	Low caste
Israel	Jews	Arabs
	Ashkenazis	Mizrachis
Japan	Non-Burakumins	Burakumins
	Japanese	Koreans
New Zealand	Whites	Maoris
Northern Ireland	Protestants	Catholics
South Africa	English	Afrikaners
Switzerland	Native Swiss	Immigrants
United States	Whites	Blacks
	Whites	Latinos
	Whites	Native Americans
	Northern European immigrants	Southern European immigrants

Sources: Modified and adapted from Fischer et al., (1996). Specific sources for each country are Australia (Klich, 1988; Stoneman, 1929), Belgium (Raven, 1989), Canada (Gotowiec & Beiser, 1993; Wilson, 1991), Czechoslovakia (Adamovic, 1979), France (Neto & Mullet, 1982), Great Britain (Benson, 1995), India (Das, 1994; Das & Khurana, 1988; Das & Padhee, 1993; Gupta & Jahan, 1989; Shyam, 1986), Israel (Dar & Resh, 1991; Gross, 1978; Kugelman, Lieblich, & Bossik, 1974), Japan (DeVos & Wetherall, 1983; Shimahara, 1991), New Zealand (Beck & St. George, 1983; Ogbu, 1978), Northern Ireland (Lynn, Hampton, & Magee, 1984), South Africa (Verster & Prinsloo, 1988), Switzerland (Lanfranchi, 1993), and the United States (Kolb, 1932; U.S. Department of Education/NCES, 1988).

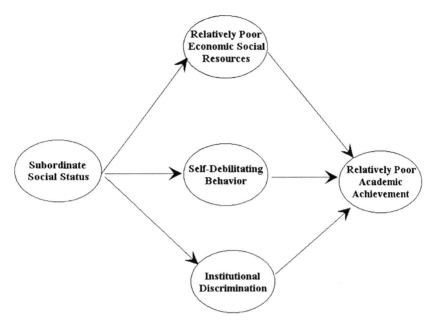

Figure 7.1. Mechanisms mediating the relationship between subordinate social status and relatively poor academic performance.

Second, as we discuss in more detail in Chapter 9, the academic outcomes of subordinates also result from *self-debilitating behaviors* such as school truancy, not doing homework assignments, not doing extra reading at home, and generally not taking school and academic work very seriously. John Ogbu's analysis of African-American inner-city youth suggests that such behaviors are not due to inherent intellectual inadequacy, but rather are a response to their subordinated status as expressed by the development of *oppositional identity*.[8] Oppositional identity leads subordinate children to regard the school and its teachers as representatives of an "oppressive enemy" and, therefore, as forces to be resisted and rejected. Among other ways, this oppositional identity is expressed as ingroup loyalty and a refusal to cooperate with school authorities or the dominant group's definition of academic success and achievement. Therefore, striving for academic excellence is regarded as "putting on airs" and "acting White." In other words, academic success becomes tantamount to an act of treason to one's group.

The third means by which subordinate social status is transformed into substandard academic achievement is through direct and indirect forms of institutional discrimination. This institutional discrimination takes several forms: *differential funding, differential referral, differential track-ing,* and *differential teacher expectations.*

Mechanisms of Institutional Discrimination in Schools

Differential Funding. Because of the greater political power that dominants exert over institutions that allocate social resources (e.g., legis-latures, courts, and government bureaucracies), the children of dominants receive a larger proportion of public assets for their education than do the children of subordinates. For example, under the apartheid regime in South Africa, the White/Black per pupil funding ratio exceeded 15 to 1. Differential academic outcomes in South Africa were also aided by wide disparities in average class size within Black and White schools. It was not uncommon for Black schools to have average class sizes of 80 students or more, whereas the average class size in White South African schools was 20 students.[9] Similarly, it was not until 1883 that U.S. court required equal distribution of school funds on a per capita basis to Black and White children. However, as we shall see later, despite the fact that the doctr-ine of "separate but equal" (*Plessy v. Ferguson,* 1896) was overturned in the famous *Brown v. Board of Education* decision of 1954, the phrase *separate and unequal* still describes the state of U.S. education to this day.

The United States continues to institutionalize very wide disparities in the funding of public schools primarily serving dominant and sub-ordinate children. The primary mechanism by which this is done is by basing school funding on local property taxes. Because property values are much higher in wealthier areas than in poorer areas, even though peo-ple in poorer areas often tax themselves at substantially higher rates than people in wealthier areas, the amount of money raised for school funding tends to be substantially higher in wealthier districts. The net result is that the per pupil expenditure provided to dominants' children is often more than twice as much as that provided to subordinates' children (see Figure 7.2 for a New York City area example). In addition, because the property taxes can be counted as a tax deduction, the federal government in essence subsidizes this unequal allocation of resources to dominant and subordinate children.

Consequently, the schools attended by the children of dominants are generally much better equipped, are in better physical condition, are staffed by more experienced, more competent, and better-paid teachers, have smaller class sizes, contain a larger number of up-to-date computers, have larger libraries, and have better and more up-to-date textbooks.[10] Schools serving subordinate children often do not even have enough

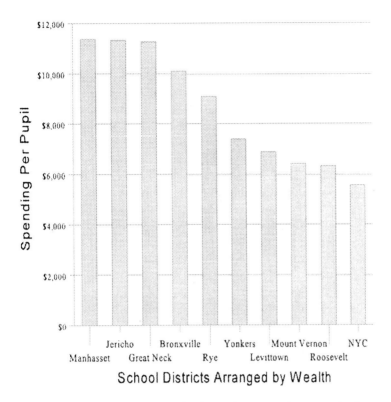

Figure 7.2. Per pupil public school funding in the New York City area for the years 1986–1987 (Source: Kozol, 1991, Table III, p. 237).

textbooks for each student. For example, a recent U.S. survey by the Association of American Publishers and the National Education Association found that 39% of teachers nationwide and as many as 54% of teachers in California did not have enough textbooks for all of the students in their classes.[11] This study also showed that while the state of California spends an annual average of $33 per student for textbooks, the Los Angeles Unified School District, largely serving poor and minority students, spends only $23 per student on textbooks annually. The fact that subordinate students do not have access to an adequate number of textbooks limits the amount of homework teachers can assign, the amount of substantive reading that students can do, and, consequently, the amount of learning that can take place. Finally, the fact that wealthier school districts spend more money per pupil than poor school districts also helps to produce a self-reinforcing feedback loop. The school quality of wealthier areas makes such areas more attractive, further driving up home prices and leading, in turn, to even greater disparities in the educational opportunities available to dominant versus subordinate children.[12]

Most states in the United States have taken steps that, at first blush, appear aimed at attenuating these funding discrepancies by providing extra funds to poorer districts in order to raise them to a "foundational" level. However, as Jonathan Kozol points out, rather than defining a "foundation" as the funding level found in the richest districts, state legislatures often define a foundation as "a level of subsistence that will raise a district to a point at which its schools are able to provide a 'minimum' or 'basic' education."[13] As a result, these state remedies rarely, if ever, actually eradicate the funding discrepancies between richer and poorer districts. To make matters worse, to get even these very mild tax redistributions passed by state legislatures, legislators often feel compelled to provide state aid to *all* school districts rather than just the poor districts. Such state allocations usually perpetuate rather than alleviate the disproportionate school funding between rich and poor.[14]

Though many government and private commissions studying this funding issue appear to value the notion of *equity* across the social status continuum, Kozol notes that when the concrete recommendations of such commissions are carefully examined,

we realize that they do not quite mean "equity" and that they seldom ask for "equity." What they mean, what they prescribe, is *something that resembles equity but never reaches it*; something close enough to equity to silence criticism by approximating justice, but far enough from equity to guarantee the benefits enjoyed by privilege. The differences are justified by telling us that equity must always be "approximate" and cannot possibly be perfect. But the imperfection falls in almost every case to the advantage for the privileged.[15]

Perhaps even more importantly, two U.S. Supreme Court decisions have eviscerated almost all legal remedies for differential funding between rich and poor school districts. On March 21, 1973, the Court made what is generally considered the most important decision concerning schools and civil rights since *Brown v. Board of Education* in 1954. This decision, *San Antonio Independent School District v. Rodriguez*, dealt with a class action suit filed by Demetrio Rodriguez and other parents of children enrolled in a very poor school district in San Antonio, Texas. Although the residents of this poor district paid one of the highest tax rates in the state, this tax rate could raise only $37 annually per pupil. Even after including the state's reallocation subsidy, the allocation still only came up to $231 per pupil. On the other hand, even at a lower tax rate, Alamo Heights, one of the wealthier districts in San Antonio, was able to raise $412 per pupil. After the state legislature's "equalizing reallocation" of tax funds, the allocation for children in the wealthier Alamo Heights rose to $512 per pupil. While the federal district court ruled in 1971 that this disparate funding scheme was a violation of the equal protection clause of the U.S. Constitution, this decision was later overruled by the U.S. Supreme Court. Among other things, the Court argued that "the equal Protection Clause does not require absolute equality" and it is not the states' duty to provide such equality.

School integration is another method of distributing educational resources more equally. In an effort to achieve racial integration, a federal district court ruled that because the schools in metropolitan Detroit were both separate and unequal, it would approve a plan to integrate the schools across school district lines and mix the children in the predominantly White suburban schools with the children in the predominantly Black Detroit urban schools. However, on appeal in 1974, the U.S. Supreme Court struck down that order in *Milliken v. Bradley*, holding that suburban districts could not be ordered to help desegregate a city's schools unless those suburbs had been involved in illegally segregating them in the first place, a case that could not be established.

Altogether then, not only is it now legal in the United States to have racially separate schools (*Milliken v. Bradley*), but it is also legal for these schools to provide unequal educations (*San Antonio v. Rodriguez*).

In addition to receiving substantially less educational funding than dominant students, subordinates also receive less attention from school administrators. For example, studies show that supervisors, who provide curricular aid to teachers, spend substantially more time aiding schools with mainly dominant student populations than schools with mainly subordinate student populations.[16] In one extreme case, Sedlacek and Brooks (1976) found that supervisors spent at least twice as much time at White schools than at Black schools.

Differential Referral. In both the United States and Scandinavia, teachers and school administrators are more likely to regard subordinate children as having behavioral problems or as being intellectually "retarded" or emotionally disturbed. As a result, school authorities often refer these subordinates to some form of "special education" or "remediation."[17] For example, in the United States, while Black children are three times as likely as White children to be placed in classes for the mentally retarded, they are only half as likely to be placed in classes for the intellectually gifted.[18] In addition, the degree to which African-American students are placed in programs for the "emotionally handicapped" depends on the proportion of White to Black teachers in the schools; the greater the proportion of White teachers, the more likely Blacks students are classified as emotionally handicapped.[19]

These conclusions are supported not only by a great deal of statistically controlled survey evidence, but also by experimental evidence. For example, Lanier and Wittmer used 359 elementary school teachers to determine whether or not race was associated with students' classification as "educable mentally retarded (EMR)." Each teacher was assigned to review identical student profiles, except for the race and gender of the student. The results revealed that Black students were referred to EMR classes significantly more often than White students. Furthermore, this bias was *consensual* across both Black and White teachers. The data also showed that teachers were more likely to request conferences with White than with Black parents.[20]

Differential Tracking.   Students from subordinate groups are disproportionately "tracked" into less academically enriching classes, while students from dominant groups are disproportionately tracked into more academically enriching classes, regardless of the students' actual intellectual abilities.[21] This differential tracking effect has also been found in other multiethnic nations such as Israel and Brazil. For example, in a Brazilian study, White teachers were found to direct Black students toward manual or service occupations, while directing White students toward higher-status occupations.[22] Similarly, in Israel, students of Ashkenazic origin (i.e., dominants) tend to be tracked into academic study, while students of Sephardic origin (i.e., subordinates) tend to be tracked into vocational study.[23]

Tracking can have profound consequences for a child's future intellectual development. For example, Gamoran examined data from a 1982 survey of U.S. public high school sophomores and seniors. Controlling for other factors, the data showed that tracking had significant and substantial effects on student achievement, exceeding even the difference in achievement between students remaining in school and school dropouts. Remarkably, these data suggested that academic development was affected more by which school students attended than by whether or not they attended school at all.[24] Similar results have been shown for tracking in Israel. Eligibility for higher education was enhanced among students placed in the academic track (predominantly Ashkenazic students), while vocational track placement of the subordinate students (predominantly

Sephardic students) further reduced their already low likelihood of receiving higher education.[25]

Finally, there are data which suggest that whether or not teachers decide to use tracking depends, in part, on their attitudes about racial and ethnic integration. For example, a study of 5,284 fifth-grade U.S. students and 886 teachers in 94 elementary schools showed that teachers with negative attitudes toward racial integration tended to promote the use of resegregative practices, such as tracking and within-class grouping. However, teachers with positive attitudes toward racial integration tended to deemphasize tracking and instead promoted equal-status programs and cooperative learning environments. Most importantly, the data also showed that there was higher Black achievement in classrooms using equal-status programs, cooperative activities, or more flexible tracking.[26]

Differential Teacher Expectations. Discrimination against subordinate school children also expresses itself through teachers' lower academic expectations of students. Now-classic research by Rosenthal and Jacobson showed that, even when students begin with the same academic talents, students whom teachers regard as bright become more academically successful than those students whom teachers regard as dull.[27] This "self-fulfilling prophecy effect" has been replicated in a great deal of research.[28] Follow-up research has shown that there are at least three avenues by which teachers' negative expectations are communicated to so-called dull students: teachers give them less time to answer questions, give them more criticism for failure and less praise for success, and establish less eye contact with them.[29] Once these students understand that less is expected of them, they live down to these diminished expectations.

Reinforcing the teacher–student feedback loop, there is evidence that teachers reward students who fulfill their expectations and punish students who violate these expectations, *regardless of whether these expectations are positive or negative*. For example, Rosenthal and Jacobson found that when those students labeled "dull" showed substantial academic improvement, they were considered to be more maladjusted, less appealing, and less curious and were evaluated more negatively. This suggests that even when subordinates attempt to transcend the negative expectancies others hold of them, they will still be strongly sanctioned. Subsequent research has shown that these effects manifest themselves with respect to race as well. For example, some experimental research shows that teachers give preferential treatment to "gifted" students, but only if the students are White. In contrast, non-gifted Black students are treated more positively than are gifted Black students, who are generally treated negatively.[30]

Some Qualifying Conditions

Voluntary Versus Involuntary Subordinates

While subordinates generally have worse academic performance than dominants, there are two major qualifications that must be mentioned. First, as John Ogbu has convincingly argued, the degree to which subordinates display lower levels of academic performance depends on whether their social position is voluntary or involuntary.[31] *Voluntary* subordination is usually the result of immigration from one society to another, often undertaken to improve one's economic and/or social circumstances. Examples of voluntary subordinates include Sikh immigrants to Great Britain; Asian immigrants to the United States; and African, Arab, Asian, and Yugoslav immigrants to Sweden. These voluntary subordinates usually have the advantage of being able to move into the host country with their feelings of self-worth and cultures intact (e.g., languages, social relations, religions). Most importantly, these voluntary immigrants also move into the new country with substantial levels of human capital (e.g., education, specialized skills, mutually supportive social networks). While one can argue that few people will voluntarily chose to put themselves in a subordinate position, the very act of immigration from one society to another almost invariably entails some initial degree of subordination vis-à-vis the native and dominant population. These immigrants are usually at a disadvantage in terms of command of the language and customs of the host society and are almost always discriminated against by the host population. However, despite these handicaps, because these subordinates are able to transfer much of their economic and human capital into their new societies and have a rather optimistic conception of the future and their capacities to succeed in this future, they often emphasize education for their children and expect their children to perform in school. Rather than adopting an oppositional identity, these children are encouraged to submit to and obey school and sociopolitical authorities within the host country.[32]

Involuntary subordinates, on the other hand, have usually acquired their subordinate status as a result of military conquest, colonization, enslavement, or some other form of externally enforced subjugation. Examples of involuntary subordinates are African-Americans and Native Americans, the Maori of New Zealand, Palestinian Arabs of Israel, and Australian Aborigines. Unlike the situation of voluntary subordinates, for many of the reasons already explained (e.g., oppositional identity), the relatively low levels of academic performance among involuntary subordinates is often quite severe and of long standing.

Studies of acculturation illustrate how the transformation to subordinate status influences educational outcomes. Though voluntary immigrants usually display higher levels of academic achievement than native-born subordinates, recent data from the United States show that the more acculturated immigrants become to U.S. society, the worse their school performance becomes. For example, in a 10-year study of more than 20,000 U.S. high school students from nine high schools, Laurence Steinberg discovered that the longer Asian and Latino immigrant families had been in the United States, the less their children were committed to school work, the less time they spent on homework, the less attentive they were in class, and the less likely they were to have friends who thought that academic achievement was important.[33] As we will discuss in more detail in Chapter 9, these data further support the idea that the relatively poor school performance of subordinates is not due to cultural or biological deficiencies, but is better seen as a response to their group's relative status position within the social structure of the host nation.

Subordinate Male Target Hypothesis and Educational Achievement

The second major qualification to the general principle of low academic performance for subordinates concerns gender. While subordinates generally display less academic success than dominants, once again and consistent with the subordinate male target (SMTH), it is generally *not* the case that subordinate females are at greater risk for academic failure than subordinate males.

For example, Figure 7.3 shows the high school completion rates and college enrollment rates for U.S. dominants (i.e., Whites) and two groups of U.S. subordinates (i.e., Blacks and Latinos). The data show that dominants have higher high school completion and college enrollment rates than both groups of subordinates. However, these data also show that while these rates for male and female dominants are essentially the same, there is a slight tendency for female subordinates to display higher rates of success than the male subordinates. Rather than subordinate females experiencing a double handicap based on arbitrary-set status and gender, it is rather the males of arbitrary-set subordinate groups who are at the greatest risk. A study of African- and Euro-American junior high school students found similar results.[34] Even after controlling for social class and age, there were relatively few academic differences between Black and White students. Where there were significant differences between

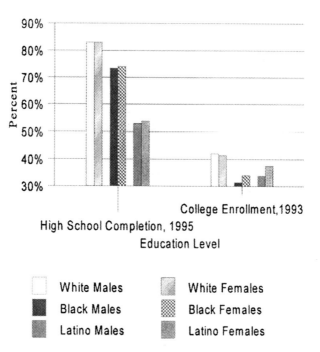

Figure 7.3. High school completion rates and college enrollment rates as a function of ethnic status and gender (Source: Carter & Wilson, 1994).

the races, however, it was the African-American boys who seemed to be experiencing problems. These boys showed signs of oppositional identity and greater conflict with school authorities. Similar results have been found outside of the continental United States, such as on the tiny island of St. Croix.[35]

An even clearer example of the SMTH pattern can be seen at the very highest levels of educational achievement. For example, Figure 7.4 shows that, in 1979, of all the Euro-Americans who received doctorates, only 30% were women (and by implication 70% were men). This is in sharp contrast to the situation among African-Americans. In the same year, almost half (i.e., 48%) of the doctorates awarded to African-Americans went to women. Since 1979 and without exception, more than half of all doctorates going to African-Americans have been awarded to women. This trend has increased over time. Thus, by 1989, 61% of all African-Americans receiving doctorates were female and only 39% were male. While the proportion of women receiving doctorates among Euro-Americans has also shown a tendency to increase since 1979, unlike the data for African-Americans, at no point did the proportion of Euro-American females

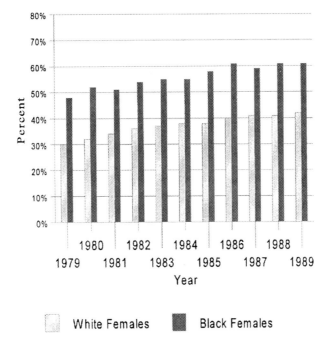

Figure 7.4. Percentage of doctoral degrees awarded to African-American and Euro-American White females within each ethnic group between 1979 and 1989 (Source: National Research Council, Doctorate Records File, 1995).

receiving Ph.D.s exceed the proportion of Euro-American males receiving these degrees.

In conclusion, across many different social systems, the evidence shows a very clear positive association between one's social status and one's academic achievement. While discrimination is clearly not the only reason for the association between social rank and academic success (see Chapter 9 for a fuller discussion), the evidence clearly suggests that institutional discrimination is substantially involved in this discrepancy. This discrimination primarily expresses itself in substantially greater resources (e.g., money, time, encouragement) being allocated for the education of dominants than of subordinates.

Social Status and Health

Dominants are privileged not only with relatively high academic success, but also with relatively better health. There is a consistent and impressive amount of data across both human societies and different primate species showing that those at the top of the social hierarchy are generally in better psychological and physical health than those at the bottom. This is particularly true of highly stratified societies (see Wilkinson, 1996). Similar to the processes shown in Figure 7.1, we have strong reason to believe that subordinate social status becomes transformed into poor health outcomes via at least three broad paths. First, because of their relatively limited economic and political power, subordinates are less likely to have access to the economic and social resources that promote good physical health and psychological well-being. Such resources include plentiful and high-quality food, the ability to avoid dangerous and stressful living and work environments, and greater access to immediate and high-quality medical care.

Second, as we shall detail in Chapter 9, the poor health outcomes of subordinates also result from self-debilitating behaviors such as various forms of drug abuse, cigarette smoking, consumption of harmful foods, and lack of adequate physical exercise (see also Chapter 9). Third, institutional discrimination, within the society in general and within the health care system in particular, also contributes to the relatively poor physical and psychological health of subordinates.

The Social Status–Health Gradient

To get a rough idea of the power of the relationship between social status and physical and psychological health, one need only consider the following. The average life expectancy of Australian Aborigines is 17 years less than that of non-Aboriginal Australians. The infant mortality rate for Aborigines is 3 times that of other Australian children, and the maternal mortality rate of Aborigines is 5 times that of non-Aboriginal women. The rate of illness from diseases such as leprosy, tuberculosis, and hepatitis, as well as sexually transmitted diseases, is 10 times that found among non-Aboriginal people in Australia.[36]

Similar, if less dramatic, health disparities exist in the United States. In 1991 Euro-Americans had a seven-year-longer life expectancy than African-Americans and suffered significantly lower death rates from heart disease, breast cancer, and prostate cancer. In addition, Euro-Americans have also been found to have lower rates of hypertension, diabetes, other forms of cancer, low-weight births, and nervous and mental disorders than African-Americans.[37]

A substantial portion of the differential health outcomes between Euro- and African-Americans is attributable to differences in social and economic resources. However, class differences alone cannot account for all of this variance. For example, though the differences in health outcomes between Whites and Blacks are especially acute at low levels of socio-economic status, work by Pappas et al. (1993) shows that Blacks have significantly higher mortality rates than Whites *throughout the entire social status continuum.* In other words, even well-off Blacks have less positive health outcomes than equally well-off Whites.

If we regard social status as a general, hypothetical construct with several related, yet slightly independent manifestations (e.g., race, income, education, occupation), then it becomes clear that these White–Black differences in health outcomes are simply a special case of a much broader and more general phenomenon. This more general phenomenon is the essentially ubiquitous and completely linear association between social status and health outcomes. For example, it is not the case that only the very poor have worse health than the wealthy, after which the health differences disappear. Rather, the association between social status and health status is essentially linear and constant throughout the social status continuum. This association is known as the *socioeconomic status–health gradient.*[38] However, because we argue that social status is not simply a function of standard economic, educational, and occupational factors, but also includes the independent effects of socially constructed group distinctions in rank as well (e.g., race and ethnicity), we shall refer to this as the *dominant/subordinate–health gradient.*

The relationship between general health and social status – over and above access to health-related resources – has been found in several studies using different indicators of social status. For example, the famous Whitehall Study examined 17,350 British civil servants over a period of 10 years. The British Civil Service ranked grades of employment, the lowest consisting of unskilled workers (e.g., messengers) and the highest consisting of top administrators. Despite the fact that this sample was relatively homogeneous and *all* employees had access to the National Health Service, high-ranking civil servants had a substantially lower mortality rate than low-ranking civil servants.[39] Similar relationships have been found in other nations.[40] For example, using a large sample of White men and women 25 to 64 years old, Kitagawa and Hauser (1973) examined the relationship between mortality[41] and years of education. Their data also showed a clear and monotonic dominant/subordinate–health gradient (Figure 7.5). However, Wilkinson[42] found that though health and mortality are strongly associated with relative income differences *within* various countries, health and mortality are only weakly associated with average income differences *between* various countries. This implies that one's *relative* position within the social status hierarchy is more important to one's health than one's absolute level of access to material resources. In fact,

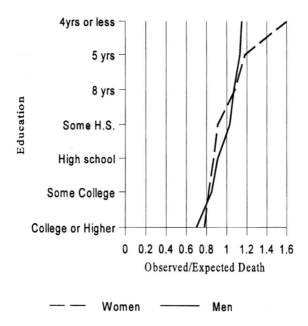

Figure 7.5. Ratio of observed to expected deaths as a function of educational status and gender (Source: Kitagawa & Hauser, 1973).

because health outcomes are strongly linked within a society, reducing inequality within a society can improve the health not only of subordinates, but of dominants as well (Wilkinson, 1996).

Although the relationship between social status and psychological health is much less consistent, in at least two areas the data are similar to what is generally found with physical health. For example, in a national epidemiological study of Americans published in 1991, Robins and Regier found that though somatization disorder is found almost exclusively in women, Black women suffer particularly high levels of this disorder.[43] In the same database, Blazer and colleagues found that African-Americans also suffered significantly higher rates of generalized anxiety disorder (excluding panic and depression disorders) than either Whites or Latinos.[44]

The Dominant/Subordinate Health Gradient in Other Primates

The relationship between social status and general health is also found among other primate species. For example, in a series of studies of wild baboons, Sapolsky and his colleagues[45] found that within stable social hierarchies, low-status animals have substantially and chronically higher concentrations of glucocorticoids (i.e., hormones resulting from stress) than high-status animals. The same relationship between social status and basal glucocorticoid levels is found among a variety of other species. Chronically high levels of these stress hormones are associated with a wide range of deleterious health outcomes[46] such as attenuated immune function (as indexed by circulating lymphocytes), a low ratio of high-density/low-density lipoprotein cholesterol,[47] and significant damage to the hippocampus.

Similar relationships between social status and health outcomes have been found among cynomolgus monkeys (macaques, *Macaca fascicularis*).[48] What makes cynomolgus monkeys a relevant animal model here is that they develop a form of atherosclerosis very similar to that in humans and also experience myocardial infarction (heart attacks) at rates similar to those of humans.[49] Furthermore, macaques also serve as an interesting psychosocial model because their behavioral repertoires are also highly complex and, as in humans, are defined by patterns of agonistic and affiliative behaviors. The social organization of macaques is also hierarchically structured.[50] Work by Manuck and his colleagues has shown that within stable social hierarchies, subordinate male macaques show significantly higher levels of coronary artery atherosclerosis than dominant male macaques. However, the reverse trend is found within unstable social hierarchies. While female macaques suffer less extensive coronary artery atherosclerosis than males, just as in humans, lower-status female macaques also suffer significantly higher levels of atherosclerosis than higher-status females.[51]

Discrimination in the Health Care System

Overt Institutional Discrimination

Part of the differential health outcomes between dominant and subordinate human groups is due to institutional discrimination within the health care system. Perhaps the clearest examples of overt discrimination within this system is found in the eugenics policies that began around the turn of the century and continue to this day in some nations. The forced sterilization program of undesirables and "defectives" in Nazi Germany is well known and needs no further comment here. However, less well known were the similar programs in several so-called democracies of the Western world. For example, the first recorded eugenics sterilization in the United States was performed on a man at Jeffersonville State Prison, Indiana, in 1899.[52] Forced sterilization laws were first enacted in Indiana in 1907, and by 1931 such laws were in place in 30 states of the United States. Between 1919 and 1943, some 4,310 people were forcibly sterilized in California's

Sonoma State Home. Not surprisingly, in the United States, these forced sterilization laws were primarily used against the poor, Blacks, and other ethnic minorities.[53] At around the same time, very similar laws were also passed in Austria, Belgium, Czechoslovakia, Denmark, Finland, Norway, Sweden, and Switzerland. Just as in the United States and Nazi Germany, forced sterilization policies in Scandinavia were primarily directed against the poor, "social deviates," and ethnic minorities such as the Tattare and Gypsies. The intellectual justification for such racist eugenics programs was further developed by the world's first academic department devoted to the preservation of racial purity: Statens Institut för Rasbiologi (State Institute for Racial Biology), established in Sweden's Uppsala University in 1921.[54] This academy was the forerunner of the German equivalent established in Berlin under the Nazi regime (i.e., Kaiser Wilhelm Institut für Rassenhygiene).

These racist eugenics programs were promulgated not only by the political right, but by the political left and center as well. For example, the very active, forced sterilization programs of Scandinavia were largely the result of policies promoted by leading figures within the region's social democratic parties. These prominent figures included such notables as Tage Erlander, Sweden's prime minister between 1946 and 1969, Gunnar and Alva Myrdal, the well-known and highly respected Swedish intellectuals of the left,[55] K. K. Steincke, a leading figure within the Danish Social Democratic Party in the 1920s, and Johan Scharffenberg, a leading figure in the Norwegian resistance movement against the Nazi occupation. Racist eugenics programs were also supported by leading socialist intellectuals from Great Britain, including George Bernard Shaw and Bertrand Russell.[56]

These forced sterilization policies were far from modest in scope. Between 1934 and 1976, 6,000 Danes, 40,000 Norwegians, and 60,000 Swedes were forcibly sterilized.[57] These programs did not completely die out in the mid-1970s, but are still used in New Zealand[58] and Austria.[59] Since forced sterilization programs began in Austria during the 1930s, it is estimated that between 20,000 and 30,000 Austrians have been forcibly sterilized.

Finally, it is instructive to point out that the "scientific" arguments supporting these eugenics programs of the early part of the century have not disappeared, but have been reaffirmed in recent scholarship. For example, within the two years of its publication in 1994, *The Bell Curve*,[60] a treatise on the inherent intellectual inadequacies of the poor and Blacks, is reported to have sold some 500,000 copies and has been widely quoted and debated in the popular press.[61]

However, perhaps the most notorious example of institutional discrimination by the health care system is the Tuskegee syphilis study. Starting in 1932 and under the auspices of the U.S. Public Health Service, 400 Black men from rural Alabama were diagnosed as having syphilis. To study the long-term effects of untreated syphilis on the human body and mind, the researchers deliberately decided not to inform the men of their condition, or that they could infect their wives and children. Furthermore, although penicillin had become widely available for the treatment of syphilis in the 1940s and was the standard treatment by 1951, the government doctors still withheld all treatment from these men. The experiment was finally halted in 1972, and only after a federal health worker made the experiment public.[62]

Covert Institutional Discrimination

While such blatant and overt forms of institutional discrimination are now less common, as we shall see later, there is reason to believe that covert discrimination is quite prevalent. Because the interface between social status and health outcomes is one of the least thoroughly researched areas of discrimination and field experiments have not yet been conducted, all of the evidence suggesting such discrimination is necessarily indirect. Nonetheless, when the available evidence is aggregated, there is little reasonable doubt of either the existence or power of covert institutional discrimination on health outcomes.

The epidemiological evidence collected over the past 10 years seems to suggest that, aside from the effects of access to money or medical insurance, subordinates are simply not given the same level of medical care and attention afforded to dominants. For example, Peterson and his colleagues[63] found that Blacks undergo fewer coronary revascularization procedures than Whites. To determine if these differences were due to the clinical differences between the two patient groups, Peterson et al. examined a sample of 12,402 patients with coronary heart disease, 10.3% of whom were Black. The research team calculated the rates of angioplasty and bypass surgery in Blacks and Whites after cardiac catheterization. The team examined patterns of treatment after stratifying the patients according to the severity of disease, anginal status, and estimated survival benefits due to revascularization. Finally, they compared five-year survival rates in Blacks and Whites. Even after adjusting for the severity of disease and other clinical characteristics, Blacks were still 13% less likely than Whites to undergo angioplasty and 32% less likely to undergo bypass surgery. There was also a statistically significant race difference in rates of bypass surgery even among patients with very severe anginal symptoms (i.e., 31% of Blacks vs. 45% of Whites).[64] Finally, the data showed that both unadjusted and adjusted five-year survival rates were significantly lower among Blacks than among Whites. While not directly concluding that these treatment differences were due to racial discrimination, the research team *could not come up with any other plausible alternative explanation.*

Similar differences in the access that Blacks and Whites have to treatment have been found with extreme kidney failure[65] and cancer.[66] In some of the most comprehensive research conducted in this area, McBean and Gornick (1994) found that Blacks were significantly less likely than Whites to have received therapeutic medical procedures for several severe illnesses. The largest differences were found for what were termed "referral-sensitive surgeries" such as percutaneous transluminal coronary angioplasty, coronary artery bypass graft surgery, total knee replacement, and total hip replacement. On the other hand, Black patients were significantly *more* likely to receive "mutilative," deforming, and disfiguring treatments such as amputation of the lower limb, surgical debridement (removing of tissue), and bilateral orchiectomy (i.e., total castration).

Similarly, Gornick et al. (1996) have found wide disparities between Blacks and Whites in the use of many Medicare services. Examining census and Medicare administrative data for 26.3 million beneficiaries 65 years of age or older (24.2 million Whites and 2.1 million Blacks), they found that the mortality rate of Black men was 19% higher than that for White men. The mortality rate for Black women was 16% higher than that for White women.[67] Blacks were also discharged from hospitals at a rate 14% higher than that of Whites,[68] but Blacks visited physicians for ambulatory care 9% less than Whites.[69] Adjusting the mortality and utilization rates for differences in income reduced the racial differences only slightly.

The data also showed that there were 26.0 mammograms for every 100 women among Whites and only 17.1 mammograms for every 100 women among Blacks. Similar differential rates of mammography between upper- and lower-income groups were found within each race. Among Whites, mammography rates were 33% lower for the least affluent as compared with the most affluent, and among Blacks the corresponding mammography rates were 22% lower. For every 1,000 Medicare beneficiaries, there were 515 influenza immunizations among Whites and only 313 among Blacks. Once again, the data also showed income differences independent of racial differences. Specifically, the immunization rate was 26% lower among the least affluent Whites as compared with the most affluent Whites, while the immunization rate was 39% lower among the least affluent Blacks as compared with the most affluent Blacks. Finally, as in the McBean and Gornick study, Gornick et al. found that disfiguring medical procedures were more likely to be performed on Blacks than on Whites. For example the Black:White ratio for bilateral orchiectomy (i.e., castration) was 2.45:1, while the Black:White ratio for amputations of all or part of the lower limb was 3.64:1.[70]

In other words, even though the Medicare health insurance program was not obviously or ostensibly designed to deliver different levels of care to dominants and subordinates – defined in either racial or class terms – the fact is that the delivery of care is significantly related to these social status differences. Although this issue has not been widely explored in other nations, a study in Australia also found similar differential medical treatment data for dominants (i.e., Whites) and subordinates (Aborigines).[71]

Thus far we have discussed medical care administered by health care providers. But medical professionals also provide information and advice about self-care that can influence health. For example, data have long showed that subordinates have higher levels of infant mortality and prematurity than dominants. One way to combat these relatively poor birth outcomes is for health professionals to provide comprehensive and timely prenatal advice in areas such as tobacco use, alcohol consumption, drug use, and breast-feeding. However, in a study of 8,310 White and Black women, Kogan and colleagues found that even when exposed to prenatal health professionals and even after controlling for sociodemographic, utilization, and medical factors, Black women still received significantly less advice than White women about smoking cessation and alcohol use.[72]

Does Racism Make You Sick?

Finally, studies suggest that the differential health outcomes for dominants and subordinates result not only from discrimination by health care institutes, but also from physiological responses to discrimination. For example, Krieger and Sidney (1996) examined the association between blood pressure and self-reported experiences of racial discrimination. Blacks were found to have higher systolic blood pressure than Whites, but this difference in blood pressure was substantially reduced after considering the reported experiences of racial discrimination. In other words, there is at least some indication that the psychological experience of racial discrimination actually helps to produce the negative health consequences so widely observed within subordinate groups (see also Chapter 9 for a further discussion of this point). Further, Krieger and Sidney (1996) found that systolic blood pressure was lower among Blacks who reported challenging racial discrimination than among Blacks who reported accepting what they regarded as unfair racial discrimination.[73] These latter findings present some of the first evidence supporting Franz Fanon's (1963) thesis that resistance to oppression has positive physical and psychological consequences for the oppressed.

There is also relatively consistent evidence from Australia, Canada, Ghana, Jamaica, the United States, and Western Europe that those with darker skin complexions are evaluated as being less valuable, experience higher levels of discrimination, and have lower socioeconomic status than those with lighter skin complexions.[74] Following up on these findings in a large sample of African-Americans, Gleiberman and colleagues found that people with darker skin had significantly higher levels of diastolic blood pressure than did people with lighter skin. Together, these findings suggest that discrimination based on skin tone influences blood pressure.[75]

Health data also show a familiar pattern concerning gender and arbitrary-set group status. For example, Hahn et al. examined the effects of poverty on mortality among Blacks and Whites between 25 and 74 years of age between 1971 and 1984 and in 1991.[76] They found that approximately 6% of U.S. mortality was attributable to poverty in 1973 and 5.9% in 1991. More to the point, however, mortality attributable to poverty was lowest among White women, 2.2 times higher among White men, 3.6 times higher among Black women, and as much as 8.6 times higher among Black men. Once again, the group most disadvantaged appear to be subordinate men.

Summary

In this chapter we have explored two additional arcs in the circle of oppression, namely discrimination in the domains of education and health care. Not only has the historical evidence shown that both the quantity and quality of education provided to subordinates was substantially lower than that provided to dominants, but this unequal distribution of educational resources persists, even within so-called democratic states and public institutions. We identified four major mechanisms helping to produce these differential outcomes: differential funding, differential referral, differential tracking, and differential teacher expectations.

The data also show that relatively poor academic outcomes for subordinates are moderated by two major factors: whether the subordinates are voluntary or involuntary, and whether the subordinates are male or female. A consistent body of evidence shows that academic outcomes are generally better for voluntary rather than involuntary subordinates. Furthermore, and consistent with the SMTH, academic performance is generally better for subordinate females than for subordinate males.

Finally, this chapter discussed the ubiquitous fact that arbitrary-set subordinates have higher morbidity and mortality rates than arbitrary-set dominants. While this dominant/subordinate–health gradient has yet to be fully understood, we argue that part of the explanation is due to differential access to medical care, differential treatment by health care professionals, differential dissemination of health care information, and the physiological effects of discrimination.

8 | "The More of 'Them' in Prison, the Better"

*Institutional Terror, Social Control, and
the Dynamics of the Criminal Justice System*

If, on their first visit to Earth, extraterrestrial beings wanted some quick and easy way to determine which human social groups were dominant and subordinate, they would merely need to determine which groups were over- and underrepresented in societies' jails, prison cells, dungeons, and chambers of execution. As we look around the world and across human history, we consistently see that subordinates are prosecuted and imprisoned at substantially higher rates than dominants. The disproportionate imprisonment of subordinates can be seen across a wide variety of cultures and nations, including the Maori of New Zealand,[1] the Aborigines of Australia,[2] Native Americans in the United States[3] and Canada,[4] native Algerians under the French occupation,[5] Caribbean immigrants in England,[6] foreign immigrants in the Netherlands[7] and Sweden,[8] the Lapps of Finland,[9] the Burakumin and Koreans of Japan,[10] the Tutsi of Rwanda and Zaire,[11] and the Arabs of Israel,[12] just to name a few.

Recent data from Australia and the United States show what can only be regarded as an *extreme* overrepresentation of subordinates as targets of the criminal justice system. For example, the indigenous people of Australia are imprisoned at a rate more than 15 times that of nonindigenous people. According to a recent U.S. State Department human rights report, more than 45% of the Aboriginal men between the ages of 20 and 30 have been arrested at some time in their lives. Furthermore, the incarceration rate for Aboriginal young people is 21 times greater than that for non-Aboriginal young people.

Data from the United States are almost equally grim. In California there are more than five times as many young African-American males under the control of the criminal justice system as African-Americans of *all ages* enrolled in four-year college programs.[13] Almost 40% of California's young African-American males are either in prison, on parole, on probation, or wanted by the police. For Latinos, the comparable figure is 11%, while for White males the criminalization rate is only 5%. Whereas African-Americans make up only 7% of California's population, they make up 18% of those arrested and 32% of the prison population.[14]

Two-thirds of the men of color in California were arrested at least once between the ages of 18 and 30.[15] The rate of imprisonment of African-Americans under California's "three-strikes" law[16] was 17 times the rate for Euro-Americans in Los Angeles County.[17] The data are even worse for the District of Columbia, where it is estimated that as many as 50% of young Black men (18–35 years) were targets of the criminal justice system in some form.[18] Data collected in 1997 indicate that 12 states in the United States imprisoned African-Americans at more than 10 times the rate for Euro-Americans.[19] Even more impressive is Espy and Smykla's compilation of all documented executions carried out in the United States between 1608 and 1991.[20] Despite the fact that African-Americans have never constituted a majority of the U.S. population and today represent only some 12% of the population, they still make up more than 51% of the 14,634 people executed throughout U.S. history. Furthermore, the differential rates of imprisonment in the United States shows signs of high consistency across time. The data in Figure 8.1 show incarceration rates

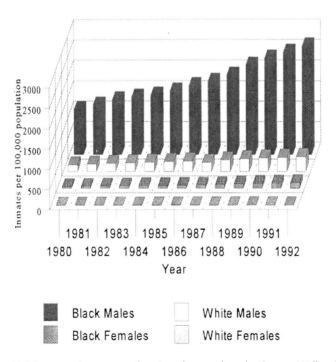

Figure 8.1. U.S. incarceration rates as a function of race and gender (Source: Walker, Spohn, & Delone, 1996, Table 8.3, p. 210).

in the United States between 1980 and 1992. Consistent with the findings from all other countries, males have very much higher incarceration rates than females. In these U.S. data, on average males are incarcerated at more than 21 times the rate of females. During this 13-year period, however, the average incarceration rate for Blacks was more than 6.8 times that for Whites, with Black males being especially likely to be imprisoned.[21]

Given such data, the question that immediately pops to mind is why? What are the forces responsible for producing this vast disproportion in imprisonment across the social status continuum? The manner in which one answers this question largely depends on which of three broad models of the law one chooses to use: the *value consensus model*, the *pluralistic model*, or the *class conflict model*.[22]

The value consensus model views the law as the impartial expression of the common will directed toward the common good. Here, the law in general and the criminal justice system in particular serve to maintain good order, mediate between competing groups in an impartial fashion, and protect the lives and property of all citizens in a value-neutral and equitable fashion, all without regard to one's social station.[23] This model of the law is thought to be particularly applicable to modern, democratic societies. For example, a 1997 Gallup poll showed that a plurality of Euro-Americans were convinced that Blacks and Whites were given equal treatment by the U.S. criminal justice system.[24]

While not completely denying the importance of the general will in the production and enforcement of law, the pluralist model emphasizes that the production and enforcement of law is a compromise between the competing economic, social, and symbolic interests of rival elites, rather than being primarily directed toward promotion of the common good.[25] Thorsten Sellin (1938) was among the earliest members of the pluralist school and succinctly expressed the flavor of this position when he wrote:

The character of [the criminal laws], the kind or type of conduct they prohibit, the nature of the sanctions attached to their violations, etc. depend upon the character and interests of those groups in the population which influence legislation. ... The social values which receive the protection of the criminal law are ultimately those which are treasured by dominant interest groups. ... The criminal norms ... change as the values of the dominant groups are modified or as the [forces of social change] cause a reconstitution of these groups themselves and shifts in their focus of power. (pp. 21–22)

The class conflict model, primarily derived from the Marxist perspective, argues that the law is primarily controlled by owners of capital and wealth and is designed to protect and expand these economic interests.[26]

In many ways, the class conflict model of law and society can be seen as a special case of the pluralist model. In particular, both models share the view of law as an instrument designed to protect and expand the power and privileges of powerful groups and to restrict and control the activities of subordinate and powerless groups. Because of this essential communality, both the pluralist and class conflict models can be regarded as members of a general dominance approach to law.

If one uses a value consensus approach to law, the overrepresentation of subordinates in society's prisons is simply due to the higher rate of criminality among subordinates. On the other hand, if one uses a general dominance approach, this overrepresentation is to be substantially explained in terms of dominants' desire to protect and maintain their positions of power and privilege. However, rather than make a mutually exclusive choice between these competing perspectives, we suggest that there is substantial truth to both of these general views. In part, the law does function in the interests of the common good, *and* the law also functions to protect and maintain the status, privileges, and power of dominants. More importantly, we shall argue that the fact that subordinates may indeed commit a disproportionate number of crimes is not independent of the dynamics of hierarchical group control and the legal protection of privilege. Rather, we regard both of these processes as dynamically interconnected. However, in this chapter we shall primarily concentrate on the law as a protector of privilege, and in the following chapter we shall concentrate on the disproportionate criminality of subordinates and how it is related to and dependent on the dynamics of hierarchical group organization.

Law and the Exercise of Terror

While it is perfectly obvious that criminal justice systems, just like all other human systems, cannot be perfectly fair or impervious to error, unlike proponents of the value consensus model[27] we argue that the errors that the criminal justice system commits are not purely random, or unsystematic. Rather, the criminal justice system's differential treatment of dominants and subordinates is clearly *systematic* and essentially inseparable from the expression of group-based power. Not only does the law function to maintain the group-based social order, but it also helps to reproduce this group-based social order.[28]

One of the primary means by which the social hierarchy is maintained is through *terror*. One standard dictionary defines terrorism as the "practice of using violent or intimidating methods, esp. to achieve political ends."[29] While most people usually think of terrorism in connection with small bands of political ruffians, the standard definition of terror applies equally well to the behavior of states and governments. In the hands of the state, terror is usually directed toward the suppression of any organized and symbolic activities of subordinates perceived as posing concrete or symbolic threats to the continued power of dominants. Because states are disproportionately controlled by dominants, it is natural to expect that state terror will be directed disproportionately against subordinates rather than dominants. Viewed in this way, state terror can be seen as a special case of intergroup conflict.[30]

There are three major forms that this intergroup terror can take: *official terror, semiofficial terror,* and *unofficial terror.* Official terror is the legally sanctioned and publicly displayed violence and the threat of violence perpetrated by the state's security forces and the justice system. Examples of official terror abound: the repression of the Shiite minority by the Iraqi government in the 1990s,[31] the massacre of thousands of Armenians by the Turkish government during the early part of the twentieth century, the massacre of the Cheyenne at Sand Creek by the Colorado militia in 1864,[32] and the public executions of opponents of the apartheid regime of South Africa. Besides these extreme forms of violence against subordinates, official terror also manifests itself in more subtle ways, such as disproportionate punishment severity directed against members of subordinate ethnic, economic, racial, and religious minorities.

Semiofficial terror is disproportionately directed against subordinates by members of internal security forces (e.g., police, secret police) and is usually performed under color of law. However, unlike official terror, semiofficial terror lacks official, public, and legal sanction by the state. Examples of semiofficial terror can be found in the death squad activities that have played such a prominent role in Central and South American and South African politics during the 1970s and 1980s.[33] A slightly milder form of semiofficial terror can be found in the U.S. program of the late 1960s called COINTELPRO. According to an FBI memorandum, this counter-intelligence program was designed "to expose, disrupt, misdirect, discredit, *or otherwise neutralize* the activities of Black nationalist, hate-type organizations and groupings, their leadership, spokesmen, membership, and supporters" (emphasis added). Included in the FBI's definition of "hate-type organizations" were groups such as Martin Luther King's Southern Christian Leadership Conference and the Congress of Racial Equality.[34]

Finally, unofficial terror is violence or threat of violence that is perpetrated by private individuals from dominant groups and directed against members of subordinate groups, and that lacks either explicit or implicit support by the state. Examples of unofficial terrorism can be found in the activities of ethnic militias in Bosnia of the mid-1990s and groups like the White Citizens' Council and Klu Klux Klan across the U.S. South and Midwest in the latter half of the nineteenth century and the beginning of the twentieth century. The most recent and well-known U.S. case of unofficial terror was the brutal 1998 lynching of James Byrd Jr. in Jasper, Texas. Even though unofficial terror is not openly sanctioned or organized by the state, it can still be quite widespread and comprehensive in its effects. For example, between 1882 and 1927, at least 3,400 African-Americans were lynched.[35]

Official Terror and the Criminal Justice System

While semiofficial and unofficial terror are relatively rare within states with democratic pretensions, official terror is both more common and often quite subtle. The primary means by which official terror is exercised is through discrimination within the criminal justice system.

How would one go about demonstrating this discrimination? For both ethical and legal reasons, the use of definitive and well-controlled field audits to study discrimination within the criminal justice system is clearly not feasible. Therefore, we are necessarily restricted to somewhat less definitive methodologies such as the use of case records, archival data, mock trial experiments, and survey data employing statistical controls. Even though no given piece of such evidence should be considered definitive in and of itself, when the evidence is accumulated across different techniques, different social systems, and different researchers, the case for the existence of systematic and institutionalized discrimination against subordinates is both powerful and compelling.

The Laws of Law

The manner and conditions in which the criminal justice system discriminates against subordinates follows five basic principles. These principles are so applicable across different social systems that we refer to them as the *laws of law*. Thus far, we have been able to identity five such laws.

First Law of Law: The Disproportionate Prosecution Principle. *When society's laws are violated, the level of negative sanction directed against subordinates will be greater than that against dominants, everything else being equal.*

There is an overwhelming amount of empirical evidence consistent with this first law of law. This mountain of data suggests that, even after one controls for all other legally relevant factors (e.g., type and heinousness of crime, prior criminal record), subordinates will still face more severe sanctions than dominants. Furthermore, these differences manifest themselves in all stages of the criminal justice process, ranging from likelihood of arrest,[36] severity of charges filed,[37] the amount of bail set,[38] the likelihood of a plea bargain being offered,[39] likelihood of conviction,[40] severity of sentence imposed,[41] likelihood of probation,[42] and likelihood of early release and parole.[43] The empirical evidence also shows that this bias is most likely to occur at the earlier stages of the criminal justice process (e.g., when one is arrested, charged, and offered/not offered a plea bargain), rather than at the latter stages of the process (e.g., when the court imposes its penalty and when the likelihood of probation is determined).

A special case of this first principle is found in the *discretionary differential targeting effect*, which occurs when law enforcement authorities are much more keen on enforcing the law against subordinate than dominant communities.[44] For example, the general provisions of the American Anti-Drug Abuse Act of 1988 provides for the death penalty for those convicted of being "drug kingpins" (21 U.S.C. Section 848). In March 1994, a report issued by the House Judiciary Subcommittee of Civil and Constitutional Rights concluded that racial minorities were being prosecuted under this statute in numbers far exceeding their proportions in the general population, or even the population of criminal offenders. The report found that 75% of those convicted under the drug kingpin provision were White and 24% were Black. However, racial minorities represented almost 90% of those against whom the statute's death penalty provisions were sought.[45]

The dramatic and cumulative impact of these differential law enforcement policies within the United States is shown in Figure 8.2. This figure compares the overall drug use, drug arrests, drug convictions, and prison sentences for drug possession of African-Americans. While only about 13% of monthly drug users are African-American, African-Americans are targeted in 35% of drug possession arrests, 55% of drug possession convictions, and 74% of prison sentences for drug possession.[46] Together, the two low-status groups of Blacks and Latinos constitute almost 90% of all those sentenced to state prisons for drug possession in the United States.[47]

This pattern of more aggressive law enforcement within minority and subordinate communities is not simply restricted to drug violations, but also includes alleged criminal violations in general.[48] For example, Hardt conducted a comparative study of police activity against juvenile offenders within three different socioeconomic communities: low-income Blacks, low-income Whites, and middle-income Whites. He found that when rates of law violation were held constant, police apprehended a

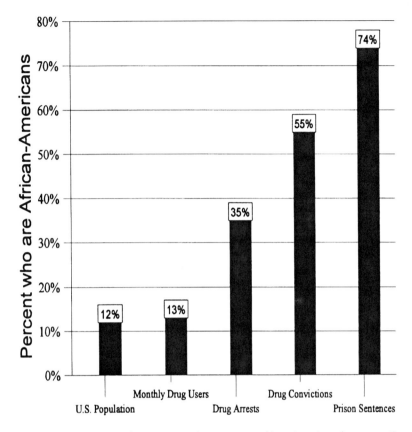

Figure 8.2. U.S. criminal justice system's response to African-American drug usage (Source: Mauer & Huling, 1995).

larger number of Black boys than White boys.[49] Similarly, statistics gathered in connection with a 1995 lawsuit filed by motorists in Maryland and New Jersey found that, while Blacks composed 14% of the drivers along a stretch of Interstate 95, they composed 73% of those stopped and searched by the police.[50]

While most of the studies conducted relevant to this first law of law (i.e., the disproportionate prosecution principle) have been American, the little research that has been conducted in other countries shows the same general pattern. For example, Junger and Polder[51] examined the degree of involvement in crime by boys (aged 12–17 years) from four ethnic groups in the Netherlands: Moroccans, Turks, Surinamese, and Dutch. Even after controlling for criminality factors, they found that the arrest rates of the subordinate boys were much higher than that of dominant (i.e., Dutch) boys. While the arrest rate was only 15% among Dutch boys, it was 22% among Turkish boys, 23% among Surinamese boys, and 34% among Moroccan boys.[52] Other Dutch research has shown that (a) criminal cases against foreigners are less likely to be dismissed than are cases against native Dutch defendants,[53] (b) once charged with a crime, foreigners were more likely to be remanded to custody rather than be released on bail,[54] and (c) once found guilty of the same crimes, foreigners were sentenced to longer prison sentences than native Dutch citizens.[55]

Data from Australia suggest that while Australian Aborigines (i.e., subordinates in Australia) represent only about 2% of the total population, they constitute more than 38.9% of the occupants of criminal institutions for juveniles.[56] Once again, while part of this overrepresentation is probably due to higher rates of criminality among Aborigines, a certain portion of this overrepresentation is also due to the discriminatory behavior of the Australian criminal justice system.[57]

Similarly, while Arab juveniles represent only 23% of Israel's juvenile population, they constitute 33% of those juveniles charged with criminal offenses. Israeli police are also more likely to arrest Arab juveniles than Jewish juveniles for similar offenses.[58] Likewise, while foreigners represent approximately 27% of the Saudi population, they constitute approximately 66% of those executed in Saudi Arabia. Furthermore, these executed foreigners are primarily from the low-status nations in Africa and Asia, rather than from high-status nations in the West.[59]

Evidence for the first law of law can even be found within a relatively egalitarian society such as Sweden. While foreign residents in Sweden represent only 5% of the population, they constitute 17% of those convicted of crimes. In addition, once convicted of crime, the average foreign resident receives a significantly longer prison sentence than the average Swede (7.7 months vs. 5.4 months). After being convicted of rape, native Swedes are more likely to be referred to psychiatric counseling, while immigrants are more likely to be condemned to prison.[60] Furthermore, in 1996 it was reported that in one Swedish prison (Norrtäljefängelset), as many as 75% of the prisoners were immigrants or ethnic minorities.[61] In line with the findings from other nations, even when one controls for factors such as age, gender, region of residence, and other legally relevant factors (e.g., type of crime), foreign residents still run a higher risk of being convicted than native Swedes.[62]

The same general relationship between group status and criminal justice outcome has been found in a comprehensive 1995 report on the criminal justice system in Ontario, Canada. Consistent with the general case, systemic racism was found at all stages of Ontario's criminal justice system, encompassing the likelihood of arrest, severity of charges filed, likelihood of being offered bail, likelihood of being found guilty, length of prison sentence served, likelihood and severity of institutional discipline being administered within prison, and likelihood of parole and early release. More important, these differential effects were found to hold even after all other legally relevant factors were considered. For example, the study found that "detention decisions about Blacks and Whites charged with the same offences suggest that accused Whites were more likely to be released by the police and less likely to be detained after a bail hearing. Accused Whites were treated more favorably although they were more likely than accused Blacks to have a criminal record and to have a more serious record." Just as in the United States, the most dramatic differences in the treatment of Black and White defendants within the Canadian criminal justice system were found in the prosecution of drug cases. For example, "the pre-trial admission rate for drug trafficking/importing charges [for Blacks] was 27 times higher than the White rate; for drug possession charges, the Black pre-trial admission rate was 15 times higher; and for obstructing justice charges, the Black pre-trial admission rate was 13 times higher."[63]

However, the most comprehensive and carefully done non-U.S. study of the differential effects of the criminal justice system we know of is covered in a 1992 report prepared by the Commission for Racial Equality in Great Britain.[64] In this study, the Hood Commission inspected a total of 2,884 criminal cases adjudicated by the Crown Court Centres covered by the West Midlands Police in 1989. The study examined the disposition of criminal cases involving Whites, Blacks (i.e., African-Caribbean people) and Asians (from the Indian subcontinent or "other" racial origin) and controlled for most legally relevant information about the cases. A rough inspection of incarceration data indicates that Asian and especially Black males occupy British prison cells at rates far exceeding their proportion in the general population. For example, the number of Black males imprisoned in Britain is between 8 and 9 times their representation in the British population. Detailed analyses of the data suggested that these differences were due both to the fact that Blacks commit a disproportionate number of crimes and to racial discrimination within the English criminal justice system. Similar to data from other nations, these data showed evidence of racial discrimination at all stages of the criminal justice process, from arrest to length of prison sentence served. For example, like the complaints often heard in the United States and Canada, the evidence suggests that Blacks in Britain are more likely than Whites to be stopped, questioned, and searched by the police.[65] Once arrested, Blacks are also more likely to be remanded to custody awaiting trial rather than released on bail. This effect holds even after one factors out all other legally relevant variables (e.g., seriousness of crime, previous criminal record, intention to contest the case at trial). What makes this remanding in custody factor so important is that, like in the United States and Canada, it has a major effect on the likelihood of receiving a prison sentence at trial, all other factors being equal. Once tried, and even after controlling for all other legally relevant factors, Blacks were more likely to be sentenced to prison than Whites.

However, it is important to note that this effect was not consistent across all levels of criminal severity. The differences in imprisonment rates for Whites and Blacks occurred only in the *intermediate range of criminal severity*. The most reasonable interpretation of this finding is that it is just within this intermediate range of severity that courts have the greatest degree of discretion. Institutional discrimination is most likely to occur when there is the greatest degree of individual discretion and consequently the greatest degree of freedom to express racial, class, and ethnic biases.[66]

In the British study, after controlling for all legally relevant variables, the data indicate that Black and Asian males were sentenced to more prison time than White males. This disparity was especially acute when the defendants pleaded not guilty. For example, everything else being equal, the average sentence given Asian males who pleaded not guilty was still 9 months longer than that given White males who pleaded not guilty.[67] On average, Black males who pleaded not guilty received a sentence 3.4 months longer than White males who pleaded not guilty.[68] Finally, there were also significant differences in the use of alternatives to prison terms such as discharge, fines, probation, community service, and suspended sentences, especially within the medium range of risk for imprisonment.

Similarly, data from the Canadian criminal justice report indicates that prison guards are more likely to subject Black prisoners to particularly harsh treatment. An interview with a correctional officer from this Canadian study gives some flavor of what this treatment is like:

The leading union official in my institution, on my very first day, made a point of coming to see me to say no CO (correctional officer) is trusted in this institution unless they have beaten up an inmate. In my time there, many CO's sat around telling me how much they hated niggers, how much they enjoyed beating them up.[69]

Quite consistent with other evidence reviewed here, the data from the Canadian criminal justice study indicate that Black prisoners were most often disciplined for infractions when the correctional officer had the greatest degree of interpretational discretion (e.g., willfully disobeying an order), rather than for infractions for which the correctional officer needed to show objective proof (e.g., possession of contraband).[70]

Subordinates not only are more likely to be put to death, but when options exist, are also more likely to be put to death in a particularly painful and demeaning fashion. Data supporting this assertion can be found in Espy and Smykla's unique data set of executions performed in the United States between 1608 and 1991.[71] Using this data set, we classified the method of execution into three levels of brutality: (a) relatively "humane" executions (i.e., by asphyxiation gas, shooting, lethal injection; $N = 306$), (b) moderately brutal executions (i.e., by hanging, electrocution; $N = 7,033$) and (c) very brutal executions (i.e., by crushing, breaking on the wheel, burning, hanging in chains, and bludgeoning; $N = 43$). We also controlled for the type of crime committed by examining only those executed for murder. Analysis of these data show that while 61% of those executed in relatively humane ways were White, only 39% were Black. Even more to the point, while only 11.6% of those gruesomely and brutally executed were White, fully 88.4% were Black.[72]

Another means of approaching the question of social status and institutional brutality is to examine the relationship between age of execution and race. Consistent with the fact that the United Nations and most nations of the world condemn the execution of children as a form of unacceptable barbarism, one can regard the execution of children and minors as another form of state-sponsored terror and brutality. Given this perspective, we have reason to expect that the U.S. criminal justice system is more likely to put subordinate children than dominant children to death. To explore this, we again used the Espy and Smykla death penalty data, examining only those executed for murder and blocking the data into five age cohorts. We defined *children and minors* as those less than 17 years of age. As expected, the data showed that the risk of execution as a function of age was not the same for Blacks and Whites.[73] While only 23.6% of those children and minors executed were White, fully 76.4% were Black.

Evidence of the differential execution rates of Blacks and Whites of all ages can be found throughout U.S. history, becoming more or less severe depending on the specific historical period. To demonstrate this, we examined the number of executions across seven historical periods in U.S. history: the colonial period (1608–1775), the revolutionary period (1776–1783), the founding and pre–Civil War period (1784–1860), the Civil War and Reconstruction period (1861–1876), the Jim Crow period (1877–1932), the New Deal and pre–civil rights period (1933–1963), and the civil rights period (1964–1991; see Figure 8.3).[74] Not surprisingly, Figure 8.3 shows that, compared with Whites, Blacks were most likely to be executed during

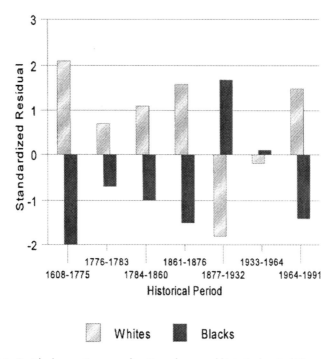

Figure 8.3. Residual executions as a function of race and historical period (Source: Espy & Symkla 1996).

the Jim Crow period (1877–1932). The Jim Crow era is that period of severe Southern backlash against Black political and economic empowerment in which almost all of the gains made during Reconstruction (1865–1876) were eliminated by both legal and extralegal means. On the other hand, contrary to what many people might expect, the degree to which Blacks were executed more than Whites was least severe during the earliest portion of U.S. history (1608–1775) and not during the most recent, civil rights period (1964–1991).

While many of our examples have shown race and ethnicity to be criteria of subordination, the first law of law extends to other types of arbitrary-set social categories. For example, the evidence shows that, even when controlling for race and ethnicity, differences in economic class alone will explain some differences in the severity of social sanctions imposed.[75]

Second Law of Law: The "Out of Place" Principle.   *When subordinates are accused of acts of violence against dominants, the accused face a particularly high risk of being found guilty and of suffering particularly severe punishment.*

There are two reasons we expect this principle to hold. First, within hierarchically organized social systems, the lives and well-being of dominants will be considered more valuable than those of subordinates. Because of this, crimes against the lives of dominants versus subordinates will also be judged as more serious. Second and perhaps even more fundamentally, acts of violence against dominants at the hands of subordinates will be considered more serious because such violence reaches beyond mere criminality and constitutes acts of sociopolitical insubordination. Such violent insubordination becomes a potential threat to the stability and integrity of the group-based system of social hierarchy itself.

There is a great deal of empirical evidence supporting the out of place principle. A large body of data from the United States suggests that this principle is particularly evident in capital murder and sexual assault cases. There has been a consistent line of research showing that Blacks who murder Whites are much more likely to face the death sentence than Blacks who murder Blacks, Whites who murder Blacks, or Whites who murder Whites.[76] In a major review of death penalty research, the U.S. Government Accounting Office (GAO) conducted a meta-analysis of studies concerning race and the application of the death penalty.[77] In this study, the GAO initially screened more than 200 studies of death penalty usage. In a second stage, all studies that were based on data collected prior to the *Furman*[78] decision or did not examine race in relation to the death penalty were eliminated. After this stage, the GAO was left with 53 studies. In a third stage, these 53 studies were examined for appropriateness and overall scientific quality. In the end, 28 studies were identified as having sufficient scientific merit for use in drawing conclusions concerning the relationship between race and application of the death penalty. The most unambiguous finding concerned the importance of the victim's race. Namely, in 82% of the studies, race of the victim was found to influence the likelihood of being charged with a capital offense and/or receiving the death penalty. Specifically, those who murdered Whites were significantly more likely to be sentenced to death than those who murdered Blacks. This result was found to hold "across data sets, states, data collection methods, and analytic techniques."[79] This *race of victim* effect was influential at all stages of the legal process and even after considering all other legally relevant factors such as prior criminal record, culpability level, heinousness of the crime, and the number of victims.[80] Once again, the data also showed that the largest race of victim effects appeared at the earlier rather than the latter stages of the criminal justice process. This is to say that race of the victim made a major difference in driving the prosecutor's decision to charge the defendant with a capital offense and whether to proceed to trial rather than accept a plea bargain.

Beyond the clear race-of-victim effect, the GAO report also found support for the out of place principle. Although less clear cut, the data suggested that the race-of-victim/race-of-defendant combination most likely to result in use of the death penalty was the case of a Black perpetrator and a White victim. Once again, the data showed that this race-of-victim/race-of-defendant effect is most likely to make itself felt at that stage where personnel within the criminal justice system have the greatest discretion. In capital murder cases, prosecutors enjoy the greatest degree of discretionary flexibility, (e.g., in comparison with judges), including what kind of charges to file (e.g., first-degree murder, second-degree murder, or manslaughter) or whether to offer a plea bargain.

The size of this early stage race-of-victim/race-of-perpetrator effect is most impressive in Paternoster's (1983) death penalty study. In this study of prosecutorial decisions in South Carolina, when Blacks were accused of killing Whites, prosecutors were 40 times more likely to recommend the death penalty than when Blacks were accused of killing other Blacks.[81] In a follow-up study, Paternoster examined data from 297 homicides in South Carolina involving an aggravating circumstance. The data showed that racial disparity was strongest in cases involving a single aggravating felony, rather than those involving multiple felonies. Furthermore, there was evidence that this racial effect reflected a different threshold of tolerance for White versus Black murders. Homicides with Black victims elicited death penalty requests only when they crossed a threshold of aggravation that was considerably higher than that for White victims.[82]

The out of place principle also applies to cases of sexual assault. For example, Williams and Farrell analyzed 43 cases of alleged sexual abuse by child care workers. Once again, there was an interaction between the victim's race and the perpetrator's race.[83] The jury was more likely to return a verdict of guilty for the combination of Black male perpetrator and White female victim. LaFree examined the interactive effect of the victim's race and the perpetrator's race in sexual assault cases from Indianapolis, Indiana. Again, the data showed that Black men who sexually assaulted White women were charged with more serious offenses and were sentenced to longer prison sentences than all other race-of-victim/race-of-perpetrator combinations. In addition, LaFree's data also showed that the least severe sanctions were applied in cases of Black men sexually assaulting Black women.[84]

The out of place principle applies not only to race, but to class. Using economic and occupational indicators of status, Farrell and Swigert divided homicide victims and perpetrators between 1955 and 1973 into high- and low-status groups.[85] They then examined the ability of five variables to distinguish among the four status-of-victim/status-of-offender categories. Controlling for factors such as trial by jury, use of private attorney, conviction severity, offender's prior record, and bail status, they found that of the four categories, low-status murderers of high-status victims received the most severe punishments.

Third Law of Law: The Social Dominance Orientation/Social Role Congruency Principle. *Within the criminal justice system, the level of social dominance orientation (SDO) among hierarchy enhancers will be relatively high, while the level of SDO among hierarchy attenuators will be relatively low.*[86]

For the criminal justice system to function effectively as a hierarchy-enhancing (HE) institution, it should tend to recruit people who are well suited to HE social roles. Among other things, such personnel should have particularly high levels of SDO. As a corollary, to the extent any component of the criminal justice system functions in a hierarchy-attenuating (HA) fashion, it should recruit personnel who are well suited to their roles, such as being relatively low on SDO. For example, because we regard police officers as hierarchy enhancers, we also expect them to have relatively high levels of SDO. On the other hand, because we regard public defenders as hierarchy attenuators, they should have relatively low levels of SDO.

To test this hypothesis, we sampled four populations within Los Angeles County: UCLA undergraduates (Sample 22), adults called to jury duty in Los Angeles County (Sample 21), street officers from the Los Angeles Police Department (Sample 20), and public defenders from the Los Angeles County Public Defenders' Office (Sample 19).[87] Within each of the four samples, we measured a range of social attitudes, including SDO.[88]

Our major hypotheses were that police officers (i.e., hierarchy enhancers) would have significantly *higher* levels of SDO than all other groups (i.e., jurors, students, and public defenders), and that public defenders (i.e., hierarchy attenuators) would have significantly *lower* SDO scores than all other groups. Inspection of the unadjusted means in SDO supports these expectations (see Figure 8.4). Analyses showed that there were highly significant differences among the four groups.[89] Specifically, police officers had significantly higher SDO scores than all other groups, and public defenders had significantly lower SDO scores than police officers and jurors.[90] Furthermore, these differences held even after controlling for major demographic differences between the groups (i.e., income, education, ethnicity).

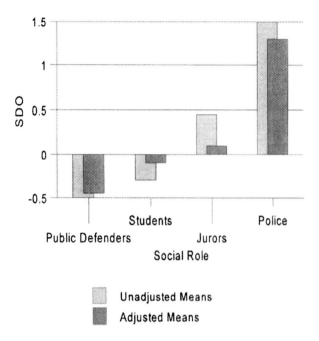

Figure 8.4. Social dominance orientation as a function of social role.

These results are also consistent with studies of police recruits. In one such study, Teahan[91] examined the attitudes of 97 White police officers over an 18-month period from the time of their entrance into the police academy. As police training progressed, the White officers became progressively more ethnocentric and hostile toward Blacks. In another study, Teahan[92] found the same general increase in anti-Black hostility among White police officers even in a training program ostensibly designed to increase racial understanding.

Fourth Law of Law: The Tolerance of Abuse Principle. *The degree of negative sanctions against security forces for abuses of power will tend to be exceedingly small, especially in cases of abuse against subordinates.*

While there has not been a great deal of empirical work devoted to this question, the work that has been done is highly consistent with this fourth law of law. For example, in a study of university campus police officers, Leitner and Sedlacek[93] found that racial prejudice was positively and significantly associated with the officers' performance evaluations by their supervisors, even when a number of other factors were controlled. Similarly, follow-up studies of civilian complaints about police brutality reveal that such brutality complaints rarely make a dent in a police officer's career path. Quite the contrary, police officers who are accused of brutality are often *rewarded* rather than *punished* by their departments,[94] at least as long as this brutality does not become a public issue. Similar evidence was found in the Warren Christopher Commission Report on the Los Angeles Police Department (LAPD) in 1991.[95] The Christopher Commission found that there were 3,419 complaints of excessive force or improper tactics leveled against the LAPD by members of the public between January 1986 and December 1990. In approximately 97% of these cases, the complaints were not sustained or were unfounded, or the officer involved was exonerated. Only 3% of the complaints were sustained. Of those complaints that were found to have merit, only 7.6% resulted in the removal of the police officer. Putting all this information together, we see that the probability of having an officer removed from the LAPD for complaints of excessive force or improper tactics is on the order of 0.00228, or essentially zero. Similar results have been found in New York City. Since its establishment in the summer of 1993, the New York Civilian Complaint Review Board has received some 20,000 complaints of police brutality. During that time, however, only one officer has ever been dismissed as a result of the Review Board's recommendations.[96] In other words, for all intents and purposes, police officers are almost completely invulnerable to dismissal as a result of citizen complaints of brutality.

The lack of accountability is not restricted to police in the United States, but is widely generalizable across a great number of countries. For example, Paul Chevigny conducted a cross-cultural examination of police violence across several police departments and nations of the Americas, including the United States, Brazil, Argentina, Jamaica, and Mexico. Among other things, Chevigny found that police terror against subordinates is relatively common and entails low risk. Consistent with the fourth law of law, rather than resulting in negative sanctions against the police, brutality against subordinates often results in institutional rewards.[97]

Fifth Law of Law: The Hierarchy–Terror Principle. *The greater the degree of social hierarchy, the greater the use of formal and informal terror there will be.*

As we discussed in Chapter 4, under normal circumstances, the consensual endorsement of HE ideologies (e.g., racism, classism) serves to maintain a group-based social hierarchy. However, hierarchical structure is not kept in place by ideological consensus alone, but ultimately by the threat and/or actual use of physical force and terror. Because ideological consensus cannot be expected to work perfectly and subordinates are still likely to resent and resist their lot,[98] everything else being equal, the more hierarchically structured a system is, the more subordinates will resist, and the more formal and informal terror will also be necessary to keep the system in place. Therefore, the greater the degree of group-based hierarchy, the more terror one should find.

Mitchell and Sidanius (1995) tested this idea by studying the use of the death penalty as a function of the degree of group-based social hierarchy, both in the United States and across several countries. Using the 50 states of the United States as the units of analysis, they first examined the number of prisoners executed in each state as a function of (a) degree of violent crime in each state, (b) the political conservatism of the state, (c) per capita income, (d) population size, (e) population density, (f) degree of education, (g) proportion of population that was White, (h) proportion of Whites killed (out of all those killed), and (i) the degree of social hierarchy within the state.[99] As expected, and even after controlling for demographic and criminality differences between states, there was a positive association between the degree to which a state was hierarchically structured and that state's propensity to put its citizens to death. The association between use of the death penalty and hierarchical social structure was not restricted to just the United States, but was also found to apply for nations around the world. Using 147 countries and controlling for the possible effects of demographic and criminality factors (e.g., murder rate), the evidence showed that the greater the economic inequality[100] within a nation, the more likely that nation was to put its citizens to death.

Fear of the State and Arbitrary-Set Social Status

If, as we claim, the criminal justice system is more likely to be used as an instrument of terror against subordinates than dominants, then subordinates should also experience this system as more fearsome and threatening.

To test this hypothesis, we examined whether fear of the police was greater among subordinates than dominants. We used a random telephone sample of adults from Los Angeles County in 1996 (Sample 39) in which respondents indicated how afraid they were of the police.[101] In the first analysis, we examined fear of the police as a function of ethnic status (White, Asian, Latino, and Black), while controlling for the other major demographic differences between the groups.[102] As Figure 8.5 indicates, dominants (i.e., Whites) showed the least amount of fear of the police, while the traditional subordinates (i.e., African-Americans) showed the greatest.[103]

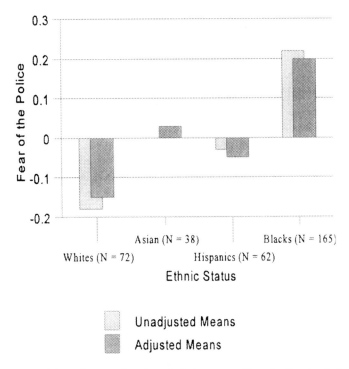

Figure 8.5. Fear of the police as a function of ethnic status, with and without adjustments for other demographic factors (Los Angeles County Sample 39).

In a second analysis, we examined fear of police in relation to economic status. Based on reported yearly family income before taxes, we defined three income classes: poor (below $10,000), middle class ($10,000–69,000), and wealthy ($70,000 and above).[104] Even when controlling for the effects of ethnicity and other demographic factors,[105] the evidence clearly showed that relatively wealthy people were least afraid of the police, while the poor were most afraid of the police (Figure 8.6).[106] We suggest that both types of subordinates (ethnic minorities and the poor) have a greater fear of the police due to the relatively high level of intimidation, abuse, and institutional discrimination they suffer within the legal system.

Gender and Age Exceptionalism

While there is now rather consistent evidence showing that subordinates are more likely to face harsh sanctions at the hands of the criminal justice system than dominants, this principle seems to apply only to those

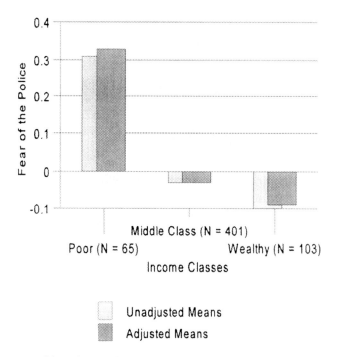

Figure 8.6. Fear of the police as a function of social class, with and without adjustments for other demographic factors (Los Angeles County Sample 39).

subordinates within the arbitrary-set system, rather than the age or gender systems. For example, there is no real evidence showing that young people are more severely punished than adults. In addition, while less univocal, the data also suggest that women face *less* severe social sanction than men.[107] For example, Daly and Bordt[108] reviewed 38 studies relating gender and sentence severity, while controlling for other legally relevant factors such as prior criminal record. They found that 45% of these studies showed evidence of sentencing differentials favoring women defendants. In addition, in an analysis also controlling for study quality, they found that 58% of the sentencing outcomes favored women, 5% favored men, and 37% showed no significant gender effects.[109] Similarly, for more than 10 offenses ranging from murder to traffic offenses, Australian men served much greater prison time than Australian women (i.e., 5.7 vs. 2.6 months).[110] Likewise, the Australian data also show that younger people (i.e., those under 20) tend to serve less prison time than older people, even after controlling for the offense.[111] However, it also appears that the relatively benign treatment of women by the criminal justice systems is limited to certain conditions. The data suggest that greater leniency toward women will be found only when women display gender-appropriate behavior and not when they deviate from stereotypic gender expectations.[112]

Subordinate Male Target Hypothesis and the Criminal Justice System

Once again, careful examination of the criminal justice evidence suggests that, to the extent there is discrimination against subordinate arbitrary sets, this discrimination is primarily directed against subordinate males rather than subordinate females. For example, in the very well carried out Hood and Cordovil Commission study of racial discrimination in England, it was found that, although a higher proportion of Black English women than White English women received prison sentences (29% vs. 23%), these differences could be completely accounted for in terms of legally relevant case characteristics such as crime severity and previous record. However, this was *not* the case for Black men. Even after all relevant legal factor were considered, Black men were still more likely to be charged, found guilty, and given longer prison sentences than comparable Whites.

Summary

While many continue to argue that the law essentially functions in a value-free and neutral manner,[113] we argue that the empirical data call this assertion into serious question. Not only does this view fail to account for the manner in which the law is both legislated and enforced within societies regarded as nondemocratic, but this value consensus model also fails to fully account for the manner in which the law functions within so-called democratic nations (e.g., the United States, Israel, Canada, Holland, Great Britain, New Zealand, Sweden). While we do not reject the value consensus model in its entirety, consistent with the general spirit of the pluralist and, especially, the class conflict models, social dominance theory suggests that the law must also be seen as a mechanism by which the rights and privileges of dominant groups are protected and the continued subordination of weaker groups is enforced and maintained. The net results of these HE and HA activities of the legal system is the substantial overrepresentation of subordinates within the prisons, dungeons, and gallows of all surplus-producing social systems. Like other elitist theories of social control, our perspective also argues that, because the instruments of state power are disproportionately manned and controlled by dominants, the coercive instruments of the state such as the police, secret police, and death squads should be seen as aspects of intergroup relations and as instruments used in the preservation of group-based and hierarchical social control.

Finally, while we have found fairly consistent evidence of discrimination and brutality against subordinates within the arbitrary-set system of social hierarchy, there is also evidence that this discrimination does *not* generalize to the other two systems of social hierarchy (i.e., the age system or the gender system). This is to say that institutional discrimination within the criminal justice system is largely restricted to subordinates defined in terms of arbitrary "otherness" such as race, ethnicity, religion, and social class. Young people and children are *not* more severely punished than adults, and consistent with the SMTH, women are generally *not* more severely punished than men. If anything, women and minors appear to be treated more leniently by the criminal justice system.

Altogether, although we have argued that the disproportionate use of negative sanctions against arbitrary-set subordinates is the result of subtle and sometimes not so subtle forms of institutional discrimination, as we detail in the next chapter, institutional discrimination is far from the *only* reason for the overrepresentation of arbitrary-set subordinates among the ranks of the damned. This overrepresentation is also strongly related to the higher levels of criminal and self-debilitating behaviors committed by arbitrary-set subordinates. In other words, consistent with the general theme of SDT, we argue that the construction and maintenance of group-based social hierarchy is very much a *cooperative* game.

OPPRESSION AS A COOPERATIVE GAME

9 | Social Hierarchy and Asymmetrical Group Behavior

In Part III we showed that discrimination makes a substantial and pervasive contribution to the unequal distribution of social resources and the subsequent establishment or maintenance of group-based hierarchy. However, there is another source of inequality besides discrimination. In this chapter we will argue that group-based social hierarchy is also maintained because people from dominant and subordinate groups actually behave differently. These behavioral differences are both a consequence of social hierarchy and a proximal cause of it.

Our analysis of group differences in behavior stems not from the assumption that there are basic or normal human proclivities that go awry in subordinate groups, or from the notion that people in dominant and subordinate groups have inherently different qualities or capacities. Rather, we argue that the behavioral differences between dominant and subordinate groups result from the fact that people within these groups live in profoundly different circumstances. Group-hierarchical societies are set up in ways that make life relatively easy for dominants and relatively difficult for subordinates. We saw clear evidence of this in Part III dealing with the "circle of oppression" and the pervasive group-based discrimination faced by subordinates. Less obvious, but still influential, are the ways that the most basic cultural, social, economic, and psychological tasks of life are made more difficult for subordinates and easier for dominants. These social conditions influence the psychological states and local social conditions of everyone in the society, causing, we argue, group differences in behavior, particularly in behavior that influences how well people do in life. In short, because they live under qualitatively different social circumstances, social dominance theory (SDT) predicts that dominants behave in ways that are more beneficial to themselves than subordinates do. We call this general thesis the *behavioral asymmetry hypothesis*.

For example, if a certain behavior, such as studying in school, is beneficial within a social context, the behavioral asymmetry hypothesis implies that this behavior should be more typical among dominants than among subordinates. Further, if another behavior, such as drug abuse, is harmful to oneself, one's family, or one's social group, this hypothesis implies that it will be more often displayed by subordinates than by dominants. As we examine empirical evidence consistent with this thesis, it will become clear that although dominants and subordinates may feel, believe, and behave differently, in a larger sense these differences may lead them to complement their positions vis-à-vis each other. There are at least three forms in which this behavioral asymmetry can express itself: *asymmetrical ingroup bias, ideological asymmetry,* and *group debilitating behavior.*

Asymmetrical Ingroup Bias

It has been clear to social scientists for a long time that people tend to value and favor ingroups more than outgroups. Sumner (1906) first labeled this apparently universal phenomenon *ethnocentrism.* Though ingroup favoritism is sufficient to produce discrimination and even group conflict, it is not sufficient to produce group hierarchy. A situation in which equally powerful groups each practiced ingroup favoritism to the same extent would merely maintain separate but equal relations. The asymmetrical ingroup bias hypothesis contradicts the expectation that everyone will show an equally strong tendency to favor the ingroup over the outgroup. Rather, because ingroup favoritism may be easier for and more valuable to dominants, our asymmetry hypothesis posits that ingroup favoritism will be stronger among dominants than among subordinates.

In its more extreme form, asymmetrical ingroup bias can actually lead subordinates to *outgroup favoritism,* or preference for the outgroup over the ingroup. A classical example of outgroup favoritism was found in the famous doll experiment of Clark and Clark (1947). In this study, U.S. Black children were asked to chose between a Black doll and a White doll on the assumption that choices between the dolls represent racial group preference and group identification among children. In direct contradiction to the notion that all people prefer their ingroups, the majority of the Black children (a) preferred to play with a White doll rather than a Black doll (67% vs. 32%), (b) thought that the White doll was nicer than the Black doll (59% vs. 38%), (c) thought that the Black doll looked bad (59% vs. 17%), and (d) thought that the White doll had a nicer color than the Black doll (60% vs. 38%). Furthermore, the preference for the White doll over the Black doll was stronger among the Black children attending racially integrated schools in the North than among Black children in racially segregated schools in the South. Rather than learning to admire and identify with their racial ingroup, the children in this study seemed to be developing attitudes and identities congruent with the unequal positions of Blacks and Whites in U.S. society.

Evidence of more outgroup favoritism and less ingroup favoritism has also been found among subordinates in several other groups, including Maori children of New Zealand, the Bnai Israel (or Ethiopian Jews of Israel), and Black children in the Caribbean.[1] Furthermore, the preference for Whites over Blacks has been found in many cultures around the world.[2]

It appears, then, that the psyches of subordinates reflect not only some normal human desire for positive regard and belonging, but also their group's inferior social position, just as the psyches of dominants mirror their privileged position in society. These group differences are not inherent, but reflect people's awareness of their group's relative power and status within the social system. As such, when group inequality is reduced, we expect group differences in ingroup preference to also be reduced. Consistent with this notion, research using the doll paradigm conducted during the middle and late 1960s, when the civil rights and Black Power movements were strongest, showed more symmetry in the doll preferences of Black and White children,[3] possibly reflecting the increased self-esteem and self-regard generated among African-Americans.

Using Clark and Clark's doll paradigm, Branch and Newcomb (1980) found that Black children whose parents *were* activists in the civil rights movement preferred the Black doll less frequently than children whose parents *were not* civil rights activists.[4] Branch and Newcomb explained their results by reasoning that the children of civil rights activists were most aware of the differential status of Whites and Blacks. Further, following the erosion of the Black Power movement and some of the gains made by the civil rights movement, the 1980s saw, once again, asymmetries in racial ingroup preference among U.S. children.[5] Both the group differences and the historical shifts in the degree of ingroup favoritism suggest that ingroup favoritism is more easily enabled when one's group has high social status.

Such asymmetrical ingroup bias has been found in other types of groups as well. In an experiment by Yee and Brown (1992), children participated in "egg/spoon" relay races and were then told by the experimenters – independently of their actual performance – that their teams were either fast or slow. Children on both the "fast" and the "slow" teams evaluated the fast group more positively than the slow group. Though children may be more susceptible than adults to reflecting reputational status differences in their evaluations of social groups, at times adults have been found to reflect group hierarchy differences in their group evaluations. Brown (1978) studied work groups that varied in status at a British aircraft factory. Again, rather than each group preferring itself, asymmetry was found in that lower-status work groups did not denigrate or discriminate against the higher-status work groups.

Though these status-group differences in ingroup favoritism are compatible with our asymmetry hypothesis, they contradict the general belief that all groups are equally ethnocentric and the expectations of social identity theory (SIT). SIT argues that when the boundary between low- and high-status groups is considered impermeable and legitimate, low-status groups will admit the superiority of the high-status group, as Ellemers and her colleagues have shown experimentally.[6] However, SIT predicts this within specific, status-relevant domains. Because people in low-status groups will still be motivated to have positive identity, SIT predicts that they should find an alternative dimension to maintain positive distinctiveness, and certainly should not adopt a belief in *general* outgroup superiority. Despite this, however, outgroup favoritism and disproportionate ingroup bias in favor of White rather than Black respondents has been documented in a variety of research settings.[7] As the asymmetry hypothesis implies, ingroup favoritism is most prevalent among groups that have equal or greater status than the outgroup. Outgroup favoritism occurs most often when the outgroup has higher status and when the social status hierarchy is perceived to be both legitimate and stable.[8] Together, both ingroup favoritism on the part of dominants and outgroup favoritism on the part of subordinates would seem to help maintain the system of group-based inequality.

Though the many studies just reviewed show that asymmetrical ingroup bias is consistent with the asymmetry hypothesis, some evidence appears to contradict this hypothesis. Specifically, Mullen, Brown, and Smith (1992) conducted a meta-analysis of 137 independent tests of ingroup bias. As SIT predicts, they found an overall pattern of ingroup favoritism, especially when the ingroup–outgroup distinction was highly salient.[9] Consistent with the asymmetry hypothesis, however, groups that had greater social status also showed more ingroup favoritism compared with groups with less social status, particularly among artificial ingroups (i.e., groups created by experimental manipulation). Within naturally occurring groups such as work groups and ethnic groups, however, this tendency was slightly reversed, with low-status groups showing slightly more ingroup favoritism than high-status groups. However, the pattern of group preference also depended on the dimension of group comparison. High-status groups were most favoring of ingroups on dimensions relevant to the status distinction between groups, while low-status groups exhibited greater ingroup bias on other, less relevant attributes.[10] This latter finding supports SIT's hypothesis that low-status groups will find alternative means of achieving positive distinctiveness. However, on overall evaluations of groups and on status-relevant dimensions – the dimensions that define the groups and are most valued by the society – greater ingroup favoritism by higher-status groups is the rule, as the asymmetry hypothesis predicts.

There have also been some historical shifts in whether White or Black Americans express more ingroup favoritism. As illustrated earlier, most studies prior to the 1960s and a substantial amount of research since the 1960s have shown greater ingroup bias among Whites than among Blacks,[11] with few exceptions.[12] But as SIT and, especially, SDT emphasize, group prejudice is a function of not only the status of the group in question, but also how legitimate its status is. Virtually all pollsters have found that White Americans' attitudes toward Blacks have become considerably more positive over the past 40 to 50 years,[13] and most researchers believe that expressing overtly anti-Black prejudice is now socially undesirable, especially among the college educated.[14] Therefore, it is not entirely surprising that in 1995 Judd et al. found greater levels of ethnocentrism among Blacks than among Whites in both student samples from small colleges and among randomly sampled adults from Cincinnati.[15] Because much of U.S. public discourse since the 1960s has made overt expressions of anti-Black racism illegitimate, we expect shifts in relative ingroup favoritism to have changed. However, we still predict asymmetries in how much ingroup favoritism each group expresses as a function of group status and how stable and legitimate group inequality appears.

To examine group asymmetry in ingroup favoritism, we used a large random sample of Los Angeles County adults (Sample 26). The first ingroup bias measure we used was based on comparisons of people's general affect ratings of, or feelings toward, different ethnic groups. For the main dominant group in Los Angeles (Whites) and two subordinate groups (Blacks and Latinos), we tested for ingroup preference by subtracting affective rating of ethnic outgroups from affective rating of one's ingroup. The initial results were similar to those of Mullen et al.[16] and Judd et al.[17] and fit the expectations of SIT. Namely, Blacks, arguably the group with the least social status, had slightly higher levels of affective ingroup bias than either Whites or Latinos.[18] Though that finding is at odds with the results of the doll studies and the asymmetry hypothesis, it is consistent with the social identity notion that Blacks will show relatively high affective ingroup bias to compensate for their low status.

However, there is reason to interpret these results cautiously. Experimental evidence suggests that Whites might express more warmth toward

Blacks and Latinos than they actually feel in order to appear unprejudiced. Research since the 1970s using Sigall and Page's (1971) *bogus pipeline* technique shows that when participants are told that their real opinions about ethnic groups are being monitored by electrodes attached to their bodies, Whites give significantly less positive evaluations of Blacks than when they are asked direct questions using traditional attitude surveys.[19] Similarly, implicit and uncontrollable expressions of racial attitudes are also less positive among Whites than their overt racial attitudes.[20] Thus, Whites may express more positive attitudes toward outgroups than they actually feel. We also suspect a complementary bias: that, to show ingroup solidarity, Blacks and Latinos may express more positive responses toward their ingroups than they actually feel. The result of both these biases would be the appearance of more positive attitudes toward Blacks and Latinos by all three groups, reducing status asymmetries on this measure.

Asymmetrical Opposition to Intergroup Marriage

Because of these possible validity problems, we also used another intergroup attitude measure that may be less susceptible to these self-presentational effects, namely respondents' willingness to have a close relative marry a person from a different race.[21] Using a large, random sample of Los Angeles County adults (Sample 26), we selected respondents from the four largest ethnic groups: Euro-Americans, Latino-Americans, Asian-Americans, and African-Americans. The asymmetry hypothesis leads us to expect a specific pattern: that members of more dominant groups should be more opposed to close relatives marrying members of relatively subordinate outgroups than members of relatively subordinate ingroups would be opposed to close relatives marrying members of relatively dominant outgroups.

This measure showed clear evidence of asymmetrical ingroup bias. Namely, when asked about intermarriage between two particular ethnic groups, members of higher-status ethnic groups were always more opposed to intermarriage with subordinate ethnic outgroups than the reverse (see Table 9.1). Table 9.1 shows that Euro-Americans were significantly more opposed to marrying Asian-Americans (2.97) than Asian-Americans were to marrying Euro-Americans (2.69).[22] Similarly, Asian-Americans were significantly more opposed to marrying African-Americans than African-Americans were opposed to marrying Asian-Americans (3.18 vs. 2.48). The same general pattern was found throughout, indicating, for all groups, greater aversion to marriage downward in the social status hierarchy than upward. The only pair-wise comparison that was not statistically reliable was the contrast between Asian-Americans and Latinos.

Table 9.1. Mean Opposition to Interracial Marriage as a Function of Ethnic Group (Los Angeles County Adults, Sample 26)

Intermarriage Combination	Participant's Ethnic Group				Comparison Statistics	
	Euro-American $N = 604$	Asian-American $N = 273$	Latino-American $N = 471$	African-American $N = 467$	F	η
Whites and Asians	2.97	2.69	—	—	13.11**	0.12
Whites and Latinos	2.80	—	2.44	—	36.60**	0.18
Whites and Blacks	3.17	—	—	2.26	166.88**	0.37
Asians and Latinos	—	2.91	2.79	—	2.25	n.a.[a]
Asians and Blacks	—	3.18	—	2.48	68.50**	0.29
Latinos and Blacks	—	—	2.94	2.39	60.49**	0.25

Note: Higher numbers mean greater opposition to intergroup marriage.
[a] Note that since there was no statistically significant relationship between ethnic group and interracial marriage opposition here, reporting the size of this noncorrelation is not appropriate.
** $p < .01$.

As indicated by the η-coefficient in Table 9.1,[23] the greatest degree of asymmetrical ingroup bias occurred with respect to Blacks, who were the least opposed to intermarriage themselves, but whom all other groups opposed marrying the most. The effect sizes concerning intermarriage with African-Americans, however, reflect the relative ordering of each racial group above Blacks in the United States: Whites and Blacks ($\eta = .37$), Asians and Blacks ($\eta = .29$), and Latinos and Blacks ($\eta = .25$).

We also tested asymmetrical ingroup bias in Israel in two groups of citizens, Israeli Jews (Sample 32) and Israeli Arabs (Sample 33). Because of the open nature of the Arab–Israeli conflict, we reasoned that there would be relatively little self-presentational pressure for Jews or Arabs to express substantially more positive affect toward the other group than they actually felt. Therefore, within each ethnic group (Israeli Jews and Israeli Arabs) we defined ingroup bias as the affect the respondents felt toward the ingroup, minus the affect they felt toward the outgroup. Consistent with the general expectation of ethnocentrism, both groups felt more

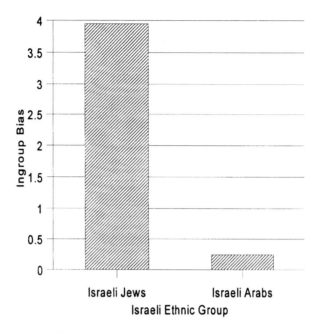

Figure 9.1. Degree of ingroup bias among Israeli Jews and Israeli Arabs.

positive affect toward the ingroup than toward the outgroup. However, the degree of ingroup bias was strongly asymmetrical. As can be seen in Figure 9.1, the degree of ingroup favoritism was substantially stronger among dominants (i.e., Jews) than among subordinates (Arabs; = 3.95 vs. 0.24).[24]

Ideological Asymmetry

One of the most central ideas within SDT is that legitimizing myths (LMs) provide intellectual and moral justification for either greater or smaller levels of group-based social inequality. These LMs affect not only the types of public policy and social allocations people are willing to support, but also how people feel about their own ingroups. However, the precise nature of the relationship between endorsement of legitimizing ideologies and attachment to one's own ingroup will depend on the relative status and power of one's ingroup and whether or not one is dealing with hierarchy-enhancing or hierarchy-attenuating legitimizing myths (HE-LMs or HA-LMs). For HE-LMs and members of dominant groups, the situation is relatively straightforward. Since HE-LMs support the

interests of dominant groups, one should expect that the more dominants endorse HE-LMs, the greater the degree of ingroup favoritism they
should show vis-à-vis subordinats groups. However, for members of subordinate groups, endorsement of HE-LMs implies support for the dominant outgroups and rejection of their subordinate ingroups. Therefore,
for members of subordinate groups, the more they endorse HE-LMs, the
less ingroup favoritism they should show vis-à-vis dominant groups. The
general notion that the degree and nature of asymmetrical ingroup bias
will be moderated or regulated by the LMs is known as the *ideological
asymmetry hypothesis*.

There are a number of different ways in which this ideological asymmetry effect should be manifested. For example, in a political environment
in which open oppression of subordinates is consensually considered fair
and legitimate, there should be strong evidence of asymmetric ingroup
bias. Under these circumstances dominants should show relatively strong
ingroup favoritism vis-à-vis subordinates, while subordinates show relatively weak ingroup favoritism vis-à-vis dominants. However, in sociopolitical environments in which open oppression of subordinates is not
considered legitimate and fair, there should be relatively little asymmetrical ingroup bias.

Using the same general reasoning, we should also expect that the degree of ingroup favoritism showed by dominants and subordinates will
vary as a function of their acceptance of HE-LMs. This is to say that the
more legitimate that individuals consider group-based hierarchy to be, the
more dominants will display ingroup favoritism and the *less* subordinates
will display ingroup favoritism.

How would we go about testing this notion of ideological asymmetry?
One approach would be to examine the degree to which people from dominant and subordinate groups display asymmetrical ingroup bias across
historical periods varying in how powerful and widely accepted certain
ideologies were. Unfortunately, the lack of historical polling data pre-
vents the direct application of such a strategy. However, we can do the
next best thing by examining people who were *socialized* during distinctly
different historical periods of ethnic relations. To accomplish this, we divided the respondents in our large random Los Angeles County sample
(Sample 26) into three age cohorts: a pre–civil rights cohort (those older
than 50 years of age), a civil rights cohort (those between 30 and 50 years
of age), and a post–civil rights cohort (those younger than 30 years of
age). The ideological asymmetry hypothesis implies that we should see
the most asymmetry in ingroup preference between Blacks and Whites
among those who came of age before the modern civil rights era (roughly

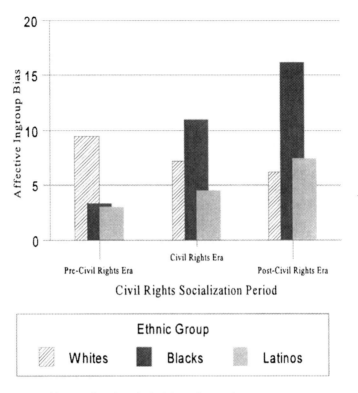

Figure 9.2. Ingroup bias as a function of ethnicity and age cohort.

1954), and that this group asymmetry should reverse among those who came of age in the civil rights and post–civil rights eras because overt anti-Black racism had by then become less legitimate and less consensually accepted.

The data in Figure 9.2 are consistent with these expectations. The first thing to note in Figure 9.2 is the presence of general ethnocentrism; all cohorts and racial groups preferred their racial ingroups over racial outgroups. More to the point, Figure 9.2 also shows the expected cohort differences in the degree of group asymmetry in ingroup preference. Among respondents who came of age before the modern civil rights era, Whites showed a substantially higher level of ingroup preference than that of either Blacks or Latinos (i.e., 9.39 vs. 3.11 and 3.00).[25] For those maturing when racial inequality had become less legitimate, this group asymmetry reversed, particularly for Blacks. Blacks who came of age during the civil rights and post–civil rights periods showed substantially greater ingroup preference than their White age-mates. These results held even after controlling for the effects of social class (indexed as income and education). Therefore, the degree of asymmetry in ingroup bias depends on the apparent legitimacy of the ethnic status hierarchy (as indexed by age cohort), even when using an ingroup bias measure that may show less ingroup bias among dominants than actually exists.

Another way to test whether the belief in legitimizing ideologies moderates the degree of asymmetrical ingroup bias is to examine individual differences in ideological endorsement within age cohorts. To do this, we used a sample of UCLA students (Sample 31) and explored the degree of asymmetry in ethnic ingroup preference as a function of two, major legitimizing ideologies: the belief that U.S. society is just and fair, and the belief that U.S. society is free of racial discrimination. If our general reasoning is correct, we should be able to show that the degree of asymmetrical ingroup bias in favor of dominants increases with increasing endorsement of HE-LMs. For illustrative purposes, we divided the sample into thirds in terms of the perceived fairness and equity of the U.S. political system (see Figures 9.3 and 9.4).

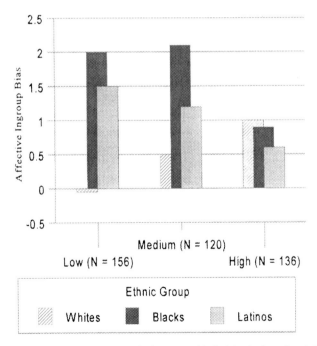

Figure 9.3. Ingroup bias as a function of ethnicity and belief that U.S. society is fair and just (Sample 31).

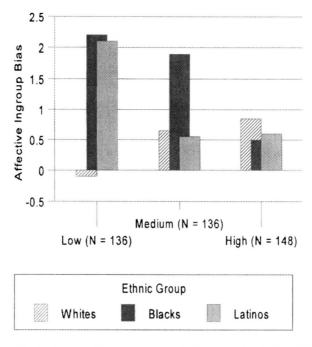

Figure 9.4. Affective ingroup bias as a function of ethnicity and belief that U.S. society is free of racial discrimination (Sample 31).

Although there was some tendency for Blacks and Latinos to display higher overall levels of ingroup bias than Whites,[26] there was also clear support for the ideological asymmetry hypothesis. Differences in ingroup preference among the ethnic groups were moderated by perceived legitimacy of the social system. That is, though the relationship between belief in system legitimacy and ingroup preference was positive among dominants, this relationship was negative among subordinates. Among those believing most strongly that U.S. society is just and fair, there was a slight tendency for dominants to show greater ingroup preference than subordinates (Figure 9.3).[27] However, among those most skeptical of societal justice, subordinates showed distinctly higher levels of ingroup preference than dominants. Similarly, and ironically, the more that dominants (Whites) believed U.S. society to be free of racial discrimination, the *more* they actually showed ingroup bias in favor of their racial ingroup. The opposite pattern was found among the two groups of subordinates. The more that Blacks and Latinos believed U.S. society to be free of racial and ethnic discrimination, the *less* they preferred their ethnic group over Whites (Figure 9.4).

Table 9.2. Regression of Ethnic Identification Ideological Beliefs and Within Ethnic Group, UCLA Students (Sample 31)

Legitimizing Ideology	Euro-Americans $n = 161$	Asian-Americans $n = 200$	Latino-Americans $n = 133$	African-Americans $n = 127$
Political conservatism	0.30**	0.19**	−0.18*	−0.27**
System legitimacy	0.20*	0.20*	−0.24***	−0.21**
System permeability	0.01	0.02	−0.30***	−0.28**
Protestant work ethic	0.07	0.05	−0.25***	−0.14+
Internal poverty attributions	0.23**	0.28**	−0.10*	−0.09*
L.A. riots caused by criminal elements	0.27*	0.02	−0.19+	−0.48***
Group competition	0.14+	0.17**	−0.07	−0.01
Patriotism	0.32***	−0.09	−0.21**	−0.27*
Nationalism	0.28***	0.03	−0.11*	0.05

Note: Entries for each ethnic group are unstandardized regression coefficients (i.e., *b*-coefficients).
+ $p < .10$, * $p < .05$, ** $p < .01$, *** $p < .001$ (one-tailed tests).

Extending this notion of ideological asymmetry slightly, we should expect ideological asymmetry with respect to not only ingroup bias, but also general attachment to the ingroup and an entire series of legitimizing ideologies. This extension would lead us to expect that, among dominants, psychological attachment to and identification with the ingroup should be positively related to their endorsement of HE-LMs. The *more* that dominants endorse these HE-LMs, the *greater* their psychological attachment to the ingroup. However, among subordinates, the exact opposite should be the case. The *more* that subordinates endorse the HE-LMs of the society, the *less* they should identify with their ingroups.

To explore these additional ideas, we again used the large UCLA sample (Sample 31) and examined the connection between ethnic identification and endorsement of a range of HE-LMs (Table 9.2). The legitimizing ideologies included (a) political conservatism, (b) system legitimacy (the

belief that U.S. society is just and fair), (c) system permeability (the belief that individual, upward mobility is possible in U.S. society), (d) the
Protestant work ethic (the belief that success is solely dependent on one's
individual effort), (e) internal attributions for poverty (the notion that
poverty in the United States is due to laziness and lack of intelligence),
(g) criminality attributions for the Los Angeles riots (the idea that they
were primarily caused by criminals), (h) group competition (the belief
that there is a built-in zero-sum conflict between U.S. ethnic groups),
(i) patriotism (love of country and its symbols), and (j) nationalism (the
desire to establish U.S. hegemony over other nations).

In general, the relationships between these ideologies and ethnic identification showed support for the notion of ideological asymmetry. The
relationships between ingroup identification and the HE-LMs were positive within the dominant and high-status groups and negative within
subordinate and low-status groups. For example, among Euro- and Asian-
Americans, the more politically conservative that respondents were, the
more positive they felt toward their own ethnic groups ($b = .30$ and $.19$,
respectively). However, among African- and Latino-Americans, the more
politically conservative that they were, the *less* they identified with their
own ethnic groups ($b = -.18$ and $-.27$, respectively). The same general
trend was found for each of the other legitimizing ideologies.

We performed formal tests of the ideological asymmetry hypothesis
by testing for differences between the size of the slopes for each ethnic group shown (see results in Table 9.3). For example, with respect to
the legitimizing ideology of political conservatism, all four comparisons
between higher- and lower-status groups were statistically significant.
The relationship between political conservatism and ethnic identification
was significantly more positive among Whites than among Latinos and
Blacks. Similarly, this relationship was significantly more positive among
Asian-Americans than among Latinos and Blacks.[28]

One of the most provocative and least obvious examples of ideological asymmetry involved the relationship between ethnic identification
and patriotism. Even though the patriotism measure was very tradition-
ally defined as love of one's country and implied nothing about social
hierarchy, we have argued that in societies organized as arbitrary-set hierarchies, such as the United States, love of country will also imply the
endorsement of that country's hierarchical ethos as well, at least among
members of dominant groups. Even if one has such a traditional interpretation of patriotism, one should not be surprised to find patriotism
positively correlated with identification with and attachment to one's

Table 9.3. Results of Pair-Wise Slope Comparisons Among U.S. Ethnic Groups

	Whites vs.		Asian-Americans vs.	
Legitimizing Ideology	**Latinos**	**Blacks**	**Latinos**	**Blacks**
Political conservatism	***	***	**	***
System legitimacy	***	***	***	***
System permeability	**	*	**	*
Protestant work ethic	**	*	**	+
Internal poverty attributions	***	***	***	**
L.A. riots caused by criminal elements	**	***	n.s.	**
Group competition	*	n.s.	**	n.s.
Patriotism	***	***	n.s.	n.s.
Nationalism	***	**	+	n.s.

Note: Entries of * or + represent a statistically significant difference in the slopes of the two compared groups.
$+ p < .10$, $* p < .05$, $** p < .01$, $*** p < .001$.

ethnic ingroup among Euro-Americans. However, expecting patriotism to be *negatively* correlated with identification with one's ethnic ingroup among African-Americans is far from obvious, especially when one considers the fact that the average African-American family has been in the United States considerably longer than the average Euro-American family. Nonetheless, among both African- and Latino-Americans, patriotic attachment to the nation clearly comes at the expense of disidentification with one's ethnic group. These findings then show that while patriotism implies the endorsement of the ethnic self among dominants and only mild rejection of the ethnic self among people with intermediate ethnic status (i.e., Asian-Americans), patriotism implies relatively strong rejection of the ethnic self among those at the bottom of the ethnic status continuum (i.e., Blacks in particular).[29]

Similar asymmetries were found among Jewish and Arab citizens of Israel (Samples 32 and 33, respectively). We examined four legitimizing ideologies: system legitimacy, belief in system permeability, patriotism, and nationalism. Because Jews are the dominants and Israeli Arabs (i.e., Arabs with Israeli citizenship) the subordinates within Israeli society, we expected HE ideologies to be positively associated with ethnic group

Table 9.4. Regression of Various LMs on Ethnic Identification and Pair-Wise Slope Comparisons Among Israeli Jews and Israeli Arabs

Hierarchy-Enhancing Legitimizing Myths	Jews	Arabs	Slope Test
System legitimacy	0.37***	−0.29***	***
System permeability	0.27***	−0.10	**
Nationalism	0.23***	−0.27*	***
Patriotism	0.36***	−0.32**	***

Note: Entries for each ethnic group are unstandardized regression coefficients of ideologies regressed on ingroup identification.
* $p < .05$, ** $p < .01$, *** $p < .001$.

identification among Israeli Jews and negatively associated with ethnic group identification among Israeli Arabs. Table 9.4 shows that the relationships between the legitimizing ideologies and ingroup identification reflect this ideological asymmetry. Among Israeli Jews, ingroup identification was consistently and positively related to support for HE ideologies. Among Israeli Arabs, on the other hand, ingroup identification was negatively related to support for HE ideologies, reliably so for three of the four relationships. Formal slope tests of these ideological asymmetries showed that these asymmetrical effects were statistically reliable in all four cases.

Finally, the expectation of ideological asymmetry concerning ingroup bias and ingroup identification should also extend to social dominance orientation (SDO). The more that dominants embrace group dominance motives, the more strongly they should identify with their ingroups. Of course, the exact opposite should be found for people from subordinate groups. In Figure 9.5 we have plotted the degree of affective ingroup bias among White and Latino students from UCLA (Sample 31) as a function of SDO. The data show quite clearly that at relatively low levels of SDO, dominants (i.e., Whites) have relatively low levels of ingroup bias (0.15). However, at relatively high levels of SDO, the degree of ingroup bias among dominants becomes substantially greater (1.01). Among subordinates (i.e., Latinos), we see the exact opposite trend; ingroup bias is high at low levels of SDO and low at high levels of SDO. This particular type of asymmetry also applies to dominant and subordinate groups in Israel. Figure 9.6 shows that, among Israeli Jews, the degree of affective ingroup bias is higher at higher levels of SDO than at lower levels of SDO. However, among Israeli Jews, the opposite pattern is found.

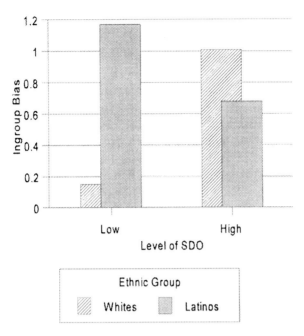

Figure 9.5. Affective ingroup bias as a function of ethnic status and SDO among Euro- and Latino-American students (Sample 31).

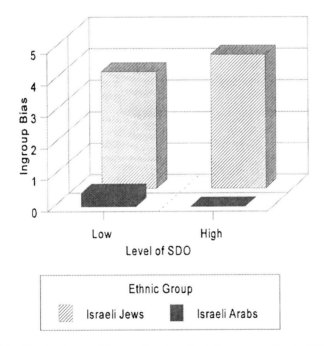

Figure 9.6. Affective ingroup bias as a function of ethnic status and level of SDO among Israeli Jews and Israeli Arabs (Samples 32 and 33).

This type of ideological asymmetry is also found in the relationship between SDO and ingroup identification. This specific hypothesis was first tested by Sidanius, Pratto, and Rabinowitz[30] using an older SDO scale, various measures of ethnic group salience and ethnic group attachment, and university students from UCLA (Sample 5) and San Jose State University (Sample 10). Pratto and Choudhury[31] extended these analyses using the SDO_5 and SDO_6 scales in several student samples. They predicted that differential group affiliation, that is, the difference between how close someone said they felt toward their ingroup minus how close they felt toward a relevant outgroup, would be positively related to SDO among high-status groups and negatively related to SDO among low-status groups.[32] They tested this hypothesis with respect to ethnic and gender groups and sexual orientation. We conducted the same analyses using the two, large random samples of Los Angeles adults (Samples 26 and 39).

Once again, the results of these analyses were consistent with the ideological hypothesis (see Table 9.5). Tests comparing the difference in the size of the regression weights between low-status and high-status groups showed that the difference in the relation between ingroup attachment and SDO was substantially different between the groups. Among dominants, the higher their SDO levels, the stronger their relative affiliations toward their ingroup in comparison with subordinate outgroups. Among subordinates, however, higher levels of SDO were associated with less identification with their ingroups in comparison with high-status dominant outgroups. These results, replicated across three group status designations and in multiple samples, are all strongly supportive of the ideological asymmetry hypothesis. Moreover, they suggest that adopting preferential attitudes toward dominant rather than subordinate people is associated with higher SDO levels for everyone.

In sum, the data from several independent samples and from different nations show that how strongly people prefer their ingroups depends jointly on their group's status and on how much individuals endorse the HE ideologies of their societies. The more that people endorse HE ideologies and are high on SDO, the more that people in dominant groups prefer their ingroups over subordinate outgroups and the less that members of subordinate groups prefer their ingroups over dominant outgroups.

This finding has several important ramifications for social theories of ingroup preference and ethnocentrism. First, the differences among status groups in the degree of ingroup preference suggests that what many approaches have theorized as normal, namely strong ingroup favoritism, is really normal only among dominants. Second, these results suggest

Table 9.5. Regression Slopes of Differential Ingroup Affiliation on SDO by Group Status

Group Type (Sample) Ethnicity	Low-Status Group Blacks and Latinos	High-Status Group Whites	*t*	df	*p*
UCLA students (Sample 5)	−0.15*	0.16**	3.02	439	.005
UCLA students (Sample 31)	−0.07	0.15**	2.19	472	.025
San Jose State University students (Sample 10)	−0.05	0.18*	3.77	225	.0015
Los Angeles adults (Sample 26)	−1.10	6.02**	4.98	1,402	.0001
Los Angeles adults (Sample 39)	−4.10	11.42**	2.21	539	.03
Gender	**Women**	**Men**			
Stanford University students (Samples 37 and 42)	−0.09	0.10	2.52	249	.01
Stanford University students (Sample 44)[a]	−0.16**	0.15*	6.75	568	.0001
Sexual Orientation	**Gays, Lesbians, Bisexuals**	**Heterosexuals**			
Stanford University students (Sample 44)	−0.25**	0.11*	3.00	567	.005
Stanford University students (Samples 37 and 42)	−0.70*	0.13*	7.03	247	.0005

Note: *T*-tests compare the difference between the slope for the high-status and low-status groups.

[a] Sample 44 was collected by anonymous email and consisted of a random sample of Stanford students plus students subscribing to special email lists of gay, lesbian, and bisexual communities at Stanford.

* $p < .05$, ** $p < 01$.

that dominant cultural ideologies do not function in the same way for all groups along the social status continuum. Among dominants, learning these ideologies may help them to bolster their own social positions, adopting high SDO levels and ethnocentrism as a consequence. But for subordinates, these ideologies may be fundamentally at odds with their abilities to adopt positive group identity and subsequently to behave in the best interests of their ingroups. Data from both the United States and Israel, then, are inconsistent with the multicultural ideal that all ethnic groups can be strongly and simultaneously attached to both their ethnic group and the nation as a whole. Instead, for subordinates, the rejection of their society's ideologies of subordination and even of the whole society may be necessary in order to facilitate positive group identity. Third, the results show that SDO is not equivalent to ingroup favoritism. Rather, SDO embodies a psychological orientation that favors dominants over subordinates, regardless of whether one's own group is dominant or subordinate.

Group Debilitating Behaviors

Perhaps the saddest evidence consistent with our status asymmetry hypothesis is in group differences in self-debilitating behaviors. Recall that our asymmetry hypothesis predicts that, on average, subordinates will engage in activities that are both directly and indirectly harmful to them at higher rates and with greater intensity than dominants. We next review evidence of behaviors that influence people's life outcomes in the domains of parenting styles, spousal abuse, education, health, and criminality.

Asymmetry in Parenting Styles and Spouse Abuse

There is fairly consistent evidence that parenting styles are related to one's general social status. The fact that parents from low-status and subordinate social groups tend to use more physical punishment and more authoritarian, punitive, and directive child-rearing patterns than middle-class parents has been known for some time. Middle-class parents are more likely to direct their children by using abstract reasoning and appealing to moral principles.[33] Although subordinate children are often socialized to obey authority figures without much question and without exercising their own critical reasoning abilities, middle-class and high-status children are generally given more leeway to question authority and exercise their moral and intellectual faculties. Subordinate children also obtain less mental stimulation because their parents are less likely to read stories to them, engage them in conversation, or expose them to books and other reading material at home, all of which are habits known to be associated with academic achievement.[34] Instead, children from subordinate groups are much more likely to spend their time in passive activities such as watching television.[35] For example, African-American children watch almost twice as much TV as Euro-American children at all levels of parental education.[36] These differences in television viewing habits are relevant to our discussion of debilitating behaviors because excessive television viewing has been shown to be related to relatively poor school achievement.[37] In addition, excessive TV viewing among Black children may create an additional risk because high levels of TV viewing are associated with low self-esteem among Black children, but not among White children.[38]

Children from subordinate groups are more likely to be abused and neglected by their parents as well. For example, using 1967 data, Gil found that 60% of families experiencing child abuse were recently on welfare.[39] In 1976, more than 76% of the 20,000 reported cases of child neglect and child abuse involved families either below or just above the poverty line.[40] Young found that 87% of the 1,202 reported cases of child abuse in Texas in the mid-1980s involved families at the bottom third of the income distribution.[41] Finally, Hampton analyzed 4,170 cases of child neglect and abuse between 1979 and 1980 among U.S. Whites, Blacks, and Latinos. Not only did the data show differential risks for child neglect and abuse between the different ethnic groups, but even when keeping ethnicity constant, lower socioeconomic status was associated with significantly greater risk of child neglect and abuse.[42] The child abuse found in these studies involved not only direct physical abuse (e.g., severe beatings), but emotional and psychological abuse as well (e.g., humiliating and demeaning treatment).[43]

Being a member of a subordinate group is associated with increased risk of spousal abuse as well.[44] While some recent scholarship has attributed this largely to the low IQ of the poor and certain ethnic minorities,[45] most of the scholarship in this area attributes the higher rates of child and spousal abuse within subordinate groups to their higher levels of stress and privation.

Asymmetry in Educational Behavior

Educational success is an important arena of life largely because it determines one's access to future occupational opportunities and thus one's position within the social hierarchy, especially in industrial and postindustrial societies. One of the most common findings in educational research is that children from dominant arbitrary-set groups enjoy higher academic success and achievement than children from subordinate arbitrary-set groups. This pattern has been found at various levels of industrial and postindustrial development and in a wide variety of countries, including Australia, Bangladesh, Belgium, Canada, Czechoslovakia, Denmark, England, France, Germany, Holland, Honduras, Hungary, India, Israel, Italy, Kenya, Luxembourg, New Zealand, Pakistan, Poland, Singapore, Sri Lanka, Sweden, Switzerland, Taiwan, the United States, and Wales.[46] For example, in line with Singapore's ethnic status hierarchy, 25% of the dominant Chinese population qualify for admission into the university, followed by 10% of the East Indian population and only 4% of the subordinate Malay population.[47] Research shows that there are several reasons for such group disparities, including group differences in intergenerational transfer of academic skills. Also, members of dominant groups have access to better schools, better teachers, higher teacher expectations, and richer social resources in general, while subordinate groups are subject to both direct and indirect discrimination (see Chapter 7).[48]

Another cause of inferior school success among subordinates is their own self-debilitating behavior. For example, subordinates have higher rates of school truancy, drop out of school earlier, devote greater time to television viewing, are less likely to start or complete homework assignments, and, when homework is given, give less time, care, and attention to these assignments. In one of the most detailed studies of the factors related to school performance to date, Laurence Steinberg and his colleagues followed more than 20,000 U.S. students from nine high schools during a 10-year period.[49] Consistent with much previous research in this area, a large number of demographic factors were related to the students' academic success, including social class, household composition (e.g., single-parent households), gender, and maternal employment. However, even after controlling for all other demographic factors, ethnic status was the single most important factor associated with the students' school success. The data showed that African-American and Latino students had significantly lower academic success than Euro-American and, especially, Asian immigrant students, who were even more academically successful than Euro-American students. Consistent with our behavioral asymmetry hypothesis, Steinberg's data show that the inferior academic performance of African- and Latino-American students is mainly due to their cutting classes more often, spending more class time with wandering minds, spending significantly less time doing homework, and generally being less engaged and dedicated to academic achievement.

Further, Steinberg's study showed that academic performance is substantially related to students' attribution for academic success. In the

United States, people generally attribute success or failure either to factors under the individual's control, such as effort, or to factors not under the individual's control, such as discrimination. A good deal of research has shown that students' attributional style is a strong correlate of academic success. In general, the more that students attribute their academic success to factors under their own control (e.g., hard work and effort), the greater academic success they will achieve.[50] Specifically, Steinberg's study found that the high-performing Asian students were significantly more likely to attribute their academic success to factors under their own control than African-American and Latino students, and were less likely to attribute academic failure to factors outside of their own control (e.g., luck, native intelligence). Most tellingly, compared with Asian immigrant children, U.S.-born children were far more likely to believe that academic success "is dependent upon native intelligence, that intelligence is fixed – either by genes or early experience."[51] However, it is also noteworthy that the more acculturated and immersed in U.S. culture immigrant students became, the more they ascribed academic success to native intelligence, rather than to effort, and the worse their academic performance became. The finding that the school success of immigrant children decreases with acculturation has also been confirmed in a recent study of immigrant children in San Diego, California.[52]

Such data show how important cultural beliefs influence behavior in ways that subsequently influence intergroup relations. Those students who believe that working hard can lead to success do in fact work harder at being good students, whereas those who believe they cannot influence their own outcomes behave in ways associated with poorer outcomes. Another very significant kind of cultural ideology that influences educational outcomes are stereotypes. In the United States, the stereotype of Black intellectual inferiority is still very widespread; in a recent national survey, Bobo and Kluegel found that 56% of Euro-Americans were willing to say that Blacks were less intelligent than Whites.[53] This stereotype can apparently undermine the school performance of Black students by making it part of the hurdle they must overcome when being evaluated.

For example, Irwin Katz and his colleagues found that Black students performed better on IQ tests when they believed these tests measured hand–eye coordination than when they thought the tests measured intelligence. Similarly, Black students performed better on IQ tests when they thought that their scores were to be compared with other Blacks than when they thought these scores were to be compared with Whites.[54] In follow-up studies, Steele and Aronson conducted a series of clever experiments comparing Black and White students matched for ability and interest.[55]

College students were given a rather difficult set of verbal problems to solve in a format identical to the Scholastic Aptitude Test under one of two conditions: (a) a diagnostic condition in which the students were told that their test results were indicative of their reading and verbal reasoning abilities, and (b) a nondiagnostic condition in which no mention was made of inherent aptitude and students were told instead that the purpose of the research was to better understand psychological factors associated with verbal problems. Steele and Aronson found that in the nondiagnostic condition, there was no difference in the tests scores between Black and White students. However, in the diagnostic condition, Black students performed significantly worse than White students (Figure 9.7).[56] Steele and Aronson reasoned that the presentation of the intellectual task as diagnostic of ability would trigger stereotypes of Black intellectual inferiority and put Blacks under "stereotype threat," distracting them from the test and undermining their performance as a consequence. Further, they expected the diagnostic condition to produce greater activation of other stereotypes about Blacks, greater concern about the cognitive ability of

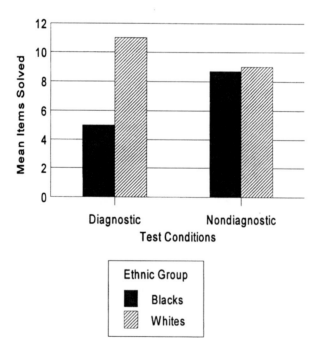

Figure 9.7. Mean test performance as a function of ethnicity and diagnosticity (Adapted from Steele & Aronson, 1995, Figure 2).

Blacks, and a greater use of external attributions for performance failure. The data were consistent with these expectations in almost all cases.

Most disturbing was Steele and Aronson's other experiment that showed how easily stereotype threat can be induced, even through the mildest form of race priming. In the "race-priming" condition, Black and White students answered a series of demographic questions about themselves (e.g., age, year in school), the last of which asked them to indicate their own race, followed by the performance task. In the condition in which race was not primed, students were asked the same set of demographic questions, but were not asked to indicate their race. Consistent with expectations, when the Black students were reminded of their ethnicity (and perhaps, consequently, of the negative stereotype of Blacks' performance in school), their performance scores were significantly worse than the scores of both White students and Black students who were not reminded of their race. When race was not primed, there was no significant difference in the performance scores between Black and White students (Figure 9.8). It is also noteworthy that Black students in the race-priming

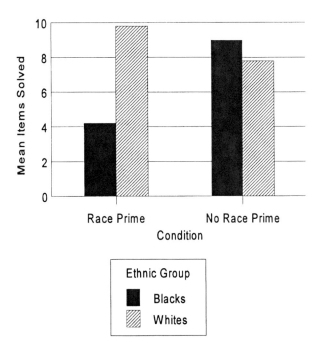

Figure 9.8. Mean number of items solved as a function of ethnicity and race-priming condition (Source: Steele & Aronson, 1995).

condition did not report expending less effort on the task or being more upset about indicating their race.

Finally, Steele and Aronson found evidence consistent with Louis Steinberg's attributional interpretation of school performance discussed earlier. Namely, under the diagnostic condition, Black students were more likely than White students to attribute their performance to external factors such as lack of sleep, lack of ability to focus, and unfair standardized tests. This series of studies suggests that being evaluated in the atmosphere of a negative group stereotype may lead to behavioral confirmation of that stereotype, both because of lowered performance and because of the development of attributions that may undermine future performance.

The invidious effects of stereotype threat on academic performance have been found to operate on women as well. For example, U.S. stereotypes suggest that women are not as good in mathematics as men. Relying on this stereotype, Spencer conducted a series of studies using students with very strong backgrounds in both math and English.[57] He examined how women and men performed on difficult math tests after they were told either that there were gender differences in results favoring men or that there were no gender differences at all. Consistent with the stereotype threat hypothesis, when told that the math test was gender-sensitive, men performed substantially better than women. However, when told that the math test was not gender-sensitive, men and women performed equally well and women scored higher than women who took the test under the stereotype threat. Here again, a group stereotype appeared to induce people to behave in ways that reconfirmed the stereotype.

The stereotype threat studies described are important because they indicate that stereotypes not only can induce people to behave in ways that confirm group stereotypes, but, in doing so, also help to reestablish the dominance relationships between groups. For example, a strong implication of Steele and Aronson's data is that the near-ubiquitous presence of the stereotype that Blacks are intellectually inferior systematically undermines Black intellectual performance, leading to the production of scientific "evidence" that this stereotype is true. Stereotype threat, then, is one more specific process through which stereotypes and other cultural and social beliefs influence people to behave in ways that "prove" the veracity of those beliefs and organize social relations according to those beliefs. Numerous other studies have shown additional intermediate processes contributing to this dynamically self-perpetuating relationship between social beliefs and intergroup relations. For example, Word, Zanna, and Cooper (1974) showed that when a White interviewer was uncomfortable interviewing a Black job candidate, that discomfort produced less than optimal performance in the job candidate – performance that one would expect to produce a poorer impression. Further, Bargh, Chen, and Burrows (1996) showed that subliminally priming Whites with faces of Blacks could invoke hostile behavior on the part of Whites. These authors speculated that such behavior could increase the possibility of aggressive responses in others. A number of other cognitive processes, including selective information seeking, selective memory, and misattribution, have been shown to increase the chance that people will end up believing in social stereotypes even when they think they are being open-minded.[58]

As described by Merton, stereotypes are "self-fulfilling prophecies."[59] Similarly, the anthropologist Peggy Sanday argues that gender roles are cultural scripts that organize the behavior and the social relations of everyone in societies. The notion that social beliefs not only describe, but also establish social relationships is one of the most important ideas that social scientists have developed.[60] Because of this importance, legitimizing ideologies play a very central role within SDT. Consensually shared stereotypes and other ideologies influence both subordinates and dominants to behave in ways that reconfirm group inequality. As we saw earlier (see Chapter 7), teachers tend to like a student who lives up to their stereotypical expectations, even when these expectations are quite negative. This kind of feedback mechanism can only be expected to further substantiate both group differences and the group stereotypes that prescribe those differences. This will then result in the further perpetuation of group-based social inequality.

Gender Exceptionalism

Although there is substantial evidence for behavioral asymmetry in education for arbitrary-set groups, such effects are somewhat less powerful and common for genders, again confirming the need for analyzing both gender and arbitrary-set social systems together. The degree to which women drop out of and are underrepresented in schools varies rather dramatically across different nations and cultures. In general, in the most gender-role-restrictive nations, even where primary and secondary education is mandatory for both sexes (e.g., Algeria, Kenya, India), girls experience higher school dropout rates and lower literacy rates than boys. For example, in Algeria, the school dropout rate is 6.4% for 11-year-old boys and 10.4% for girls in this age cohort. This trend is even more pronounced in rural areas of Algeria, where only 35.9% of girls attend primary school. Similar gender disparities exist in literacy as well. For example, around the world, while only 7.2% of boys aged 15 to 19 are illiterate, 25.3% of girls in this age cohort are illiterate.[61]

In societies that are substantially less gender role restrictive, for example, Sweden, Australia, Northern Europe, and the United States, with the exception of some specific subject domains, there is no evidence that females experience less academic success than males. Quite the opposite appears to be the case. For example, in the United States, girls drop out of school and are truant less and have higher average grades than boys at all grade levels.[62] Furthermore, as we recall from Chapter 7 and consistent with the SMTH, it is women from subordinate arbitrary-set groups who are most likely to outperform males from these subordinate groups. This relative success of subordinate females occurs at all levels of educational attainment, from elementary school to the doctoral degree.

In conclusion, the cumulative evidence seems to indicate that, besides their restricted access to economic, educational, and social resources, the behavior of members of subordinate arbitrary-set groups also contributes to lower academic performance. Negative stereotypes reflecting these performance differences are often used to justify resource allocation, and the stereotype threat research suggests that such stereotypes can contribute to these group differences. Therefore, we see that negative stereotypes not only serve as behavioral scripts for the denigration of subordinate groups by members of dominant groups, but also serve as behavioral scripts for subordinates themselves. As a consequence, the actions of subordinates help contribute to their own debilitation. Because some of the mediating mechanisms between the salience of negative group stereotypes and attenuated academic performance may be very subtle and beyond the individual's direct and conscious control, they may be all the more difficult to change. We suggest that this fact might help to explain the remarkable tenacity of the group-based system of social hierarchy.

Asymmetry in Health-Related Behaviors

As we discussed in Chapter 7, there is an apparent universal association between arbitrary-set social status and health outcomes. In each society examined, members of dominant arbitrary sets have lower morbidity and mortality rates than members of subordinate arbitrary sets. We have referred to this as the dominant/subordinate–health gradient. Furthermore, Chapter 7 also argued that a substantial portion of this gradient could be explained in terms of institutional discrimination against subordinates. However, here we will argue that other factors are also responsible for the association between social status and health outcomes.

As noted by Adler et al., there are at least three other mechanisms that might account for this association. First, it is possible that the relationship between social status and health is spurious, due, for example, to intelligent people being more healthy and achieving higher status. Second, the social status–health gradient might be due to what is known as the *drift hypothesis*, which suggests that poor health causes reduced socioeconomic status. While the empirical evidence supporting this process is relatively weak, the data supporting a third broad explanatory model is substantially stronger.[63] This model suggests that subordinate status may indirectly affect health outcomes by affecting a range of mediating variables. There are at least four categories of mediating variables involved: (a) Because of greater access to economic, social, and educational resources, higher status gives one greater capacity to successfully cope with any emerging health problems; (b) higher status gives one greater protection from potential health risks in the environment such as exposure to carcinogens, pathogens, hazardous materials, and higher levels of violence and aggression; (c) the negative experiences and greater experienced stress associated with subordinate status may influence affect and mood, which in turn may lead to less than optimal health outcomes; and (d) subordinate status may affect health outcomes by its association with risky behaviors such as cigarette smoking, poor eating habits, substance abuse, and lack of physical exercise.

We have discussed all four factors in Chapter 7, but here we take a closer look at how the suboptimal behaviors of subordinates themselves contribute to relatively poor health outcomes. For example, it is well known that cigarette smoking is associated with a wide range of health risks, including cardiovascular disease and cancer.[64] What is not as well known is the fact that, across the globe, social status is associated with smoking; the lower one's social status, the more likely one is to smoke.[65] For example, in a recent national survey of Australian Aborigines and Torres Straight Islanders, it was found that close to 50% of the sample smoked cigarettes.[66] Not only does the rate of smoking initiation increase with decreasing social status, but the lower one's social status, the less likely one is to even try to stop smoking.[67]

Physical activity and exercise are other health-linked behaviors that show group differences compatible with behavioral asymmetry. Lack of physical activity negatively influences health directly and indirectly, through effects from obesity.[68] Like the data for smoking, both U.S. and British health studies have shown that exercise and physical activity tend to increase with socioeconomic status.[69] In addition, there is evidence that even after controlling for other factors such as income and education, subordinates are still less likely than dominants to avail themselves of the health care available.

Alcohol consumption has a complex relation to health. Though alcohol consumption may increase the risk of certain health problems (e.g., cancer of the larynx and cirrhosis of the liver), moderate levels of alcohol consumption are actually associated with a lower risk of coronary heart disease, the leading cause of death in the United States and several other nations. Compatible with the behavioral asymmetry hypothesis, moderate levels of alcohol consumption are associated with higher and not lower levels of social status,[70] but extreme levels of alcohol consumption, including alcoholism, are consistently associated with low and not high social status.[71] This is a very consistent finding not only in the United States, but also in Germany, Denmark, Canada, Sweden, Chile, Australia, Italy, Poland, and Finland.[72]

Altogether, substantial evidence suggests that part of the relatively poor health outcomes of subordinates is due to their own behaviors. Nonetheless, it is important to point out that while such behaviors, plus the other contributing factors mentioned earlier (e.g., access to good health care, exposure to environmental toxins), account for a substantial portion of the dominant/subordinate–health gradient, the combination of all known factors does not completely explain this relation. This is to say that even after *all* known factors are accounted for, dominants still enjoy better health than subordinates.[73] Thus, substantially more research on the causes of the association between social status and health is needed.

Asymmetry in Criminal Activity

As we recall from Chapter 8, there is an apparently universal tendency for members of subordinate, arbitrary sets to be overrepresented in the world's prisons, dungeons, and execution chambers. Using what we called the five *laws of law*, we argued that one major reason for this overrepresentation is institutional discrimination within the criminal justice system. Another is that subordinates show disproportionate rates of criminal activity. In other words, the higher relative prosecution of subordinates is not simply the result of oppression from others, but also the result of cooperatively self-destructive and self-debilitating criminal behavior.

Criminal justice data from both the United States and Great Britain indicate that, on the whole, only about 22% of the racial disparity in the prison population can be attributed to the direct discriminatory behavior of the criminal justice system or its agents. This implies that approximately 78% of the overrepresentation of minority groups in the criminal justice system is a function of higher rates and more serious forms of criminal behavior within subordinate communities.[74] The higher rate of criminality among subordinates appears to be quite general, occurring among the Maori of New Zealand,[75] Aborigines of Australia,[76] Native Americans in the United States,[77] Native Americans in Canada,[78] Native Algerians under the French occupation,[79] Caribbean immigrants in England,[80] the Burakumin and Koreans of Japan,[81] foreign immigrants in the Netherlands,[82] Lapps in Finland,[83] and Arabs in Israel.[84] For example, over the past 20 years, African-Americans have committed between 44 and 47% of the violent crimes in the United States, even though they only represent about 12% of the population.[85]

In addition, as mentioned in Chapter 8, subordinates are more likely to be not only the perpetrators of crime, but also the direct victims of crime. Data from the United States consistently show that within all age cohorts, Blacks are substantially more likely to be victimized by violent crime than Whites. For example, the National Crime Victimization Survey shows that between 1987 and 1992, the average rate of handgun victimization among young Black males was 3 to 4 times that of young White males.[86] Furthermore, in 1992 Black males aged 12 to 24 were almost 10 times more likely to be victims of homicide than White males in the same age range (114.9 vs. 11.7 per 100,000).[87] More pertinent to our behavioral asymmetry hypothesis, however, the data also indicate that this extremely high rate of murder visited upon Blacks comes from within the Black community itself. For example, 82% of the violence inflicted on Black males aged 12 to 24 is committed by other Black males.

There are two broad approaches that have been offered to explain this disproportionate criminality within subordinate communities: the *inherency approach* and the *situational*, or *contingency*, approach.

The Inherency Approach

Proponents of the inherency paradigm would attribute the higher rates of criminality among subordinates to certain "inherent" features of these communities, such as lower impulse control or lower intelligence. One recent example of an inherency explanation that has become increasingly popular in the United States is implied in the book *The Bell Curve*.[88] The authors of this volume would argue that the high overlap between low group status and criminality is due to the relative inability of members of low-status groups to adjust to the increasingly complex demands of postindustrial society. In the new "information economy," a successful or even viable lifestyle will increasingly depend on one's intellectual ability to learn complex skills. According to supporters of this version of the inherency perspective, these are exactly the kinds of intellectual abilities for which the poor and certain ethnic minorities (e.g., Blacks) suffer inherent disadvantages. However, as has been forcefully argued elsewhere, there is also good reason to suspect that explanations of this type are based on a number of faulty analyses and interpretations of the empirical evidence that we do not have space to review here.[89]

The Situational Approach

Rather than regarding high criminality as inherent in the genes or cultures of subordinate groups, we regard models within the general situational approach as a more credible explanation. Such models emphasize the debilitating structural, situational, and psychosocial conditions under which subordinates live. Although the inherency and situational approaches differ in many ways, there is one important feature they have in common. Both approaches assume that a major reason for the differential rates of criminality between dominants and subordinates is due to their differential access to and command of the skills and resources necessary for successful coping within the legal system. In the postindustrial age, one of the most important general assets to have, besides access to accumulated financial capital, is investment in human capital such as a good education. For example, according to the U.S. Department of Justice, 50% of the inmates in federal and state prisons are completely illiterate. The major point of contention between the inherency and situational approaches then, hinges on the explanation of why members of low-status groups are so poorly educated and possess such relatively low levels of human capital. Within the situational approach, there are at least six non–mutually exclusive answers to this question.

The first major answer might be labeled a *resource accessibility* explanation. There are three prongs to this argument. People in subordinate groups tend to live in areas that are economically depressed and where there are relatively few socially acceptable jobs paying a living wage,[90] substandard educational opportunities,[91] and more obstacles to getting business loans and business experience from one's social network. There is some indication that the higher rate of criminality within subordinate communities is, in part, due to these economic and social realities. For example, a recent study by the Rand Corporation found that approximately two-thirds of the young Black males arrested for drug trafficking in Washington, D.C., were employed at the time of their arrest, mostly in low-paying jobs that provided a median income of $800 a month, which is less than a living wage in most large U.S. cities. Drug dealing had become a supplementary source of income for these young men, providing a median income of $2,000 a month for daily traders.[92]

The second major explanation within the general situational approach can be labeled the *culture of subordination model*. This model suggests that as a direct of result of oppression, subordinate communities have come to develop cultural values and interaction patterns that make it difficult for them to adequately realize and exploit their human potential. This culture of subordination is apparent in such self-debilitating behaviors as high rates of out-of-wedlock births, lower motivation for school achievement, higher rates of drug abuse (e.g., cigarette, cocaine, and alcohol abuse), higher rates of child and spousal abuse, and a greater tendency to use extreme violence in the resolution of disputes.[93] This model proposes that these self-debilitating behaviors are the result of self-loathing and inner-directed aggression resulting from severe and long-standing oppression and subordination.

A third and closely related explanation within the situational approach could be called the *false consciousness*, or *role-playing, model*. This model posits that consensual beliefs or stereotypes within hierarchically organized societies include the notion that subordinates are inherently inferior, dangerous, and incompetent. Because these consensually held stereotypes are shared by dominants and subordinates alike, these negative images are incorporated into the self-images and self-schemas of subordinates. Once part of one's self-image, these negative stereotypes of self serve as behavioral schemas helping to produce self-fulfilling prophecies.

The fourth model within the general situational family might be called the *oppositional identity model*. This perspective argues that, for example, among Black children from inner-city neighborhoods, high academic achievement will be interpreted as "trying to act White" and an act of ingroup disloyalty. John Ogbu has suggested that academic achievement among inner-city children will be discouraged not only by peers,[94] but, in more subtle ways, by family members as well (see Chapter 7).[95] A second component of this general approach is the idea that not investing in academic success is also a form of outgroup resistance and defiance. This defiance is directed against both teachers and school authorities, who are disproportionately members of the dominant group and whom subordinate students regard with a certain degree of suspicion and mistrust.

A fifth explanation concerns the effects of the physical environment on criminal behavior. Recent evidence suggests that exposure to environmental toxins, such as lead, may be the single most important cause of criminality, outweighing the effects of any other social or economic factor. In one recent study, 300 boys from Pittsburgh's inner city were tested for lifetime exposure to lead. Those with above-average levels of lead were found to be more aggressive and delinquent. Even small doses of lead were associated with the antisocial and delinquent behaviors of youth (e.g., vandalism, arson, theft, and fighting) that precede more violent adult criminality.[96] Moreover, the effects of lead were independent of race, suggesting that the relatively high criminality rates among African-American males do not result from them having a greater inherent predisposition toward crime, but rather from the fact that pollutants tend to accumulate in residential areas populated by members of low-status groups. In short, some antisocial and criminal behavior, while committed by members of subordinate groups, can still be regarded as ultimately resulting from the condition of subordination. Because of their relative lack of power, subordinates are more likely to be exposed to environmental hazards of all sorts, even when the deleterious effects of these environmental hazards are well known. Some have referred to this phenomenon as "environmental racism."

Finally, there is reason to suspect that the unusually high rate of subordinate imprisonment may itself further contribute to the deterioration of conditions within low-status communities. The Sentencing Project has pointed out that the extremely high incarceration rate of African-American males not only removes "criminals" from the street, but also has a number of damaging community-wide effects. Incarceration further undermines Black males' earning potential because the prison system fails to seriously increase their educational skills, which decreases their subsequent ability to earn legal, living wages upon release. Their inability to earn a living makes them less attractive as marriage partners and less able to provide for the children that they father. In addition, the incarceration rate of African-American males is now so high that spending time in prison may almost be considered a normal "rite of passage" for young Black men.

Therefore, from a general situational perspective, the ultimate causes of the relatively high levels of criminality among males from subordinate communities are to be found in the extreme levels of oppression and inequality suffered by these communities. At the present time, there is simply not enough empirical evidence to conclude which of these several situational explanations of the disproportionate level of criminality among subordinates is most correct. We suspect that several, if not all, of these propositions contain some grain of truth. This is another area in need of further empirical research.

General Conclusions

In sum, we are suggesting that self-destructive and self-debilitating behaviors are the primary means by which subordinates actively participate in and contribute to their own continued subordination. Because these behaviors can confirm group-based stereotypes and justify unequal treatment, they feed the ideologies that perpetuate discrimination, not only in the minds of dominants, but in those of subordinates as well. Therefore, rather than viewing institutional discrimination and self-debilitation as two independent processes, we argue that both processes are better seen as *interdependent and mutually reinforcing social mechanisms*. The net result of these processes is the continued stability and tenacity of group-based social hierarchy.

At the same time, however, this is not meant to imply that any given subordinate group will always remain subordinate, always behave in a self-debilitating manner, or always suffer from institutional discrimination. There are many examples of groups changing their relative positions within the social structure and subsequently ceasing to engage in self-debilitating behaviors and oppression at the hands of dominants. While the degree and precise configuration of group-based hierarchies are dynamic and forever changing, we argue that what does *not* change is the existence of the group-based social hierarchy itself. Within surplus-producing societies, it appears that there will always be *some group* that is both discriminated against by all major social institutions and that also cooperatively engages in a collage of self-debilitating behaviors. In other words, while specific actors may change the roles they play and the costumes they wear – the drama itself – remains the same.

Summary

In this chapter we examined how the actions taken by members of dominant and subordinate groups not only result from their unequal positions, but contribute to them. Systematic differences in the behavioral repertoires of dominants and subordinates tend to produce better outcomes for dominants and worse outcomes for subordinates. We refer to this general process as *behavioral asymmetry*. We reviewed behavioral asymmetry in three main areas: in differential degrees of ethnocentrism, in the degree to which ideologies give psychological justification for ingroup preference and SDO, and in behaviors influencing one's general well-being, including in educational, familial, legal, and health domains.

Though many psychological and social theories assume that everyone is motivated to prefer their ingroups, we saw evidence of asymmetries in this psychological stance. In numerous studies employing various measures of general attitudes toward ingroups and outgroups, dominants favored ingroups more than subordinates did, except for a brief period in the 1960s and 1970s, when U.S. racial inequality appeared to be waning. Consistent with our theory of how social beliefs serve to justify group dominance, among those socialized when racial inequality was perceived as most legitimate and among those who most endorse HE ideologies, we saw the greatest group asymmetries in ingroup preference. Thus, the more that people accept the dominant legitimizing ideologies of their society, the *more* that dominants display ingroup bias vis-à-vis subordinates and the *less* that subordinates display ingroup bias vis-à-vis dominants. In this conditional asymmetrical ingroup favoritism, we can see the importance of HE legitimizing ideologies. The more that people believe in such ideologies, the more likely they are to behave in ways that reinforce the hierarchical nature of group relations.

In ideological asymmetry, we also saw evidence that HE ideologies, including those such as patriotism and belief in the society's fairness that justify the entire society, are not as compatible with positive group identification for subordinates as for dominants. For members of dominant groups, the cultural ideologies of dominance, SDO, and identification with one's ingroup all appeared to be compatible. For members of subordinate groups, on the other hand, identification with one's ingroup and the acceptance of the dominant norms of the society were clearly incompatible. Such results suggest that positive social identity and adherence to one's culture's ideals are far more problematic for subordinates than for dominants.

Finally, we reviewed evidence of systematic asymmetry in behavior. In health-related habits, family relations, criminality, substance abuse, and education, we found that dominants behave in more self-advantageous ways than subordinates. For most such behaviors, these patterns were found across different cultures and different kinds of hierarchically structured groups. This in itself helps indicate that the causes of this pattern have to do with the psychosocial meaning of subordinate status. That is, it is unlikely that these behavioral differences are due to genetic inheritance and inferior intelligence among particular subordinate groups, as some have argued.[97] Instead, we posit that these effects are due to the difficulties resulting from subordinated group status itself, including the direct and indirect effects of discrimination and the resultant lack of material, social, and political resources. In addition, subordinated social status also produces difficulties in establishing a positive social identity and building a culture that is adaptive for one's group, while also fitting within one's larger society. While the direct effects of behavioral asymmetry on inequality may seem trivial compared with the institutional and coercive power of ruling elites and dominants, behavioral asymmetry plays a significant and important role in the continuation of the system of group dominance. Not only is behavioral asymmetry created and maintained by inequality and HE ideologies, but it also contributes to these ideologies.

10 | Sex and Power

The Intersecting Political Psychologies of Patriarchy and Arbitrary-Set Hierarchy

At the beginning of this book, we described group dominance societies as characterized by three distinct but interlocking forms of social group dominance: one based on an arbitrary-set distinction, one based on gender, and one based on age or, more specifically, the adult–child distinction. Understanding how the gender system relates to each of the other two dominance systems will reveal some important details about how group dominance societies work: why they contain each of the three forms of group dominance that they do, and how each form sustains and is sustained by the others. In this chapter we examine gender within dominance societies. In doing this, we explore gender differences in psychological orientations toward group dominance, political behavior, social roles that enhance or attenuate arbitrary-set hierarchy, sexual relationships, and parent–child relationships. In this exploration, we will provide theoretical and empirical evidence to substantiate our claim that gender is not simply another arbitrary-set distinction, but has unique properties not associated with that distinction. Although we do not reduce the psychology of gender to the psychology of arbitrary sets, we will argue that the psychology of gender is a crucial component of the psychology of intergroup politics. Finally, we will also provide a theoretical explanation for the subordinate male target phenomenon documented in many studies of institutional discrimination. To accomplish these goals, we will employ the conceptual framework of contemporary evolutionary psychology.

The Evolutionary Framework

Contemporary thinking within evolutionary psychology suggests that we should expect behavioral and psychological differences between males and females whenever reproductive success for each sex is optimized by different behavioral strategies.[1] In the evolutionary reasoning known as "parental investment theory," Trivers (1972) points out that, in many species, individual males can produce considerably more offspring than individual females because the act of reproduction is considerably more expensive for females than for males in terms of time and energy. For example, in humans, pregnancy and lactation require substantially more of mothers than of fathers. Because the reproductive constraints confronting females and males are so different, we are likely to observe differential reproductive behaviors among males and females. For example, to increase the likelihood that females' reproductive efforts are successful (i.e., produce a sexually mature next generation), Trivers suggests that females will be substantially more selective in their choice of mates than males will be. Females will prefer males with social and economic resources and who are willing to invest these resources in them and their offspring. For males, on the other hand, reproductive success is optimized by having sexual access to a large number of fertile and healthy females.

Not only do men and women display the kinds of *psychological differences* that evolutionary theory would expect, but these male–female differences also show a high degree of cross-cultural generalizability. For example, women tend to be much more selective and discriminating in their choices of sexual partners than men are. In choosing a mate, women place much greater weight on their prospective mates' social and economic status, whereas men place much greater emphasis on the physical attractiveness and youth of their prospective mates.[2] In addition to cross-cultural generality, some sex differences in mate preference strategies show a high degree of cross-species generalizability, having been found among other mammals, several species of birds, and even crustaceans.[3]

Several theorists have suggested that male reproductive success is increased not only by showing sexual interest in a relatively large number of females, but by certain additional strategies as well. These include trying to monopolize material and symbolic status resources, first as a means of making women dependent on the men for these resources, and second as a way to make themselves more appealing as mates compared with other men.[4] Laura Betzig (1993) pushes this argument even further and suggests that in an effort to increase reproductive success in the face of high female selectivity, male reproductive success is also increased by the expropriation of other men's labor. Thus, what is called *intrasexual competition* among males may encourage men not only to dominate women politically and economically and so control women's sexual and reproductive behavior, but also to form expropriative male coalitions against outgroup males. These activities will result both in the oppression of women and in class stratification among men. Betzig (1993) summarizes this line of reasoning by stating: "In short, reproductive inequality implies economic inequality. At the same time, economic inequality implies political inequality"

(p. 68). In other words, patriarchy and economic hierarchy are both partly the result of differential male/female reproductive strategies.

Fundamentally, then, the intrasexual and intersexual competition that stems from different male and female mating strategies suggests that many of the psychological predispositions, behaviors, and social practices characteristic of group dominance societies are adaptive.[5] A man's reproductive success is increased by having sexual access to several females, by the expropriation of other people's labor, and even by preventing other men from gaining access to the economic resources necessary to support their own families.

Together, female selection of high-status mates and male attempts to monopolize social and political resources may lead to the creation of exploitative social, economic, and political systems in which patriarchy and arbitrary-set stratification among males are assortative: adaptive for those who enjoy more social and economic resources and power, and maladaptive for those who do not. In other words and as depicted in Figure 10.1, patriarchy and arbitrary-set hierarchy are both partly the result of human reproductive strategies. This thesis has a number of empirically testable implications, which we shall explore in the body of this chapter.

Empirical Implications

This line of reasoning suggests at least four nonobvious and empirically testable implications. First, men and women should exhibit psychological and behavioral differences not only in sexual/reproductive strategies, but also in their general orientation toward expropriative social relations, systems of group-based social hierarchy, group oppression, and levels of social dominance orientation (SDO). Because the accumulation of economic resources, social power, and social dominance are most instrumental to male reproductive success, and because the actual achievement of social power will be facilitated by a psychological predisposition toward social power, we expect males to have higher levels of SDO than females.

Furthermore, the nature of this male–female difference in SDO should be of a qualitatively different character than the SDO difference between dominant and subordinate arbitrary sets. We recall that, due to their need to justify their superior position in society, arbitrary-set dominants are also expected to have higher average levels of SDO when compared with arbitrary-set subordinates. However, this higher SDO level among dominants will be highly contingent on situational and contextual factors. There are at least three reasons for this. First, the manner in which arbitrary sets are defined and the criteria for inclusion in one group versus

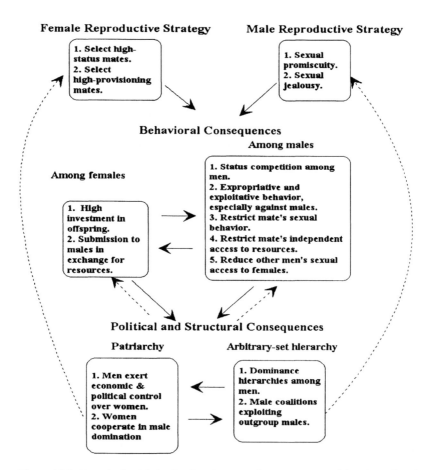

Figure 10.1. Hypothesized behavioral and structural consequences of female and male reproductive strategies.

the other are quite malleable, changing with different situational, cultural, and historical contexts. Second, any given arbitrary-set group that is dominant during one historical period or with respect to a given set of outgroups may well be subordinate within another historical period or with respect to another set of outgroups. Finally, there are no consistent functional or biologically driven behavioral differences between one arbitrary-set group and another.

Although the higher level of SDO among males compared with females may also be partly driven by the desire of males to justify their dominant position in society, our general evolutionary framework gives us reason to believe that higher levels of SDO among men are also part of the male reproductive strategy. Because the gender differences in reproductive strategies tend to be quite similar across cultures, societies, historical epochs, and even species, there is then reason to believe that the stability of gender differences in SDO will be substantially greater than the SDO differences between dominant and subordinate arbitrary-set groups. We label this the *invariance hypothesis*.

The second implication of this reasoning is that this robust male–female difference in SDO should help us better understand at least some of the sources of the political gender gap, or the tendency for men and women to have different sociopolitical preferences regarding left-wing political parties and support for issues such as war, welfare, and crime.[6]

Third, the concept of SDO will give us another way to understand not only the different sociopolitical choices that men and women make, but also gender differences in the choices of sexual and marriage partners and how these differences may be differentially related to SDO for men and women.

Fourth and finally, the use of this evolutionary view of male/female psychology will also give us a powerful, parsimonious, and logically coherent means of understanding the subordinate male target hypothesis (SMTH; see Chapters 2, 5–8).

Let us now more deeply explore each of these implications in turn.

The Invariance Hypothesis

The higher relative level of SDO among males is one of the most well-documented empirical findings generated by research on social dominance theory (SDT). We have examined the male–female difference in SDO in some 45 independent samples, using almost 19,000 respondents across 10 countries: Australia, Canada, Israel, Mexico, "Palestine" (i.e., West Bank, Gaza Strip), the People's Republic of China, New Zealand, the former USSR, Sweden, and the United States. Men were found to have a significantly higher average SDO in 39 of the 45 samples, and there was *not a single case* in which women were found to have statistically higher levels of SDO than men. The chances of this occurring by chance is on the order of 10^{-11}, or essentially zero.[7]

Contrasts Between Arbitrary-Set Interactionism and Gender Invariance

While social dominance theorists regard gender and arbitrary-set categories as distinctly different types of social constructions (see Chapter 2), most social scientists do not. Rather, most social scientists can be regarded as "cultural determinists," arguing that, to the degree that there are be-havioral differences between men and women, just as with other so-cially constructed distinctions (e.g., race), these differences are best un-derstood in terms of situational, contextual, and cultural factors, and *not* by evolved psychological predispositions.[8] While there are major differ-ences among the various models within the general cultural determinis-tic (CD) perspective,[9] all of these CD models share the assumption that male–female differences in group and social dominance behavior are con-tingent on specific social, cultural, and situational factors. For example, in one version of the CD perspective, the male–female difference in SDO is understood as an attitudinal difference between the powerful and the powerless (see Ward, 1995), and not in terms of evolved differences in male and female psychologies. This interpretation suggests that the de-gree to which males have higher SDO than females should be contingent on the degree to which men have more social and political power than women. In general, the CD perspective argues that, everything else being equal, the greater the degree to which groups (both genders and arbi-trary sets) are exposed to the same situational and cultural constraints and experiences, the smaller the SDO differences between these groups should be.[10]

While CD and SDT protagonists will tend to disagree about the factors responsible for the SDO differences between men and women, they do not disagree about the factors primarily responsible for the SDO differ-ences between arbitrary-set categories (e.g., races, social classes). Consis-tent with what we have already suggested and consistent with the thrust of Ward's (1995) argument, we expect that arbitrary-set dominants will have higher SDO scores than those of arbitrary-set subordinates. The reason for this has nothing to do with any evolved and relatively stable psychological differences between these arbitrary-set groups, but rather with the spe-cific set of power and status differences between these groups. As these differences between arbitrary-set groups change, we should expect a cor-responding change in the SDO differences between these groups. In other words, *while we do expect the SDO differences between arbitrary-set groups to be consistent with the interactionist perspective, we expect the SDO differences between males and females to be consistent with the invariance perspective.*

To demonstrate the sensitivity of arbitrary-set group differences in SDO to situational, status/power, and ideological distinctions, we be-gin by examining the SDO differences between U.S. ethnic groups as a function of the status differences between these groups. We asked UCLA students (Sample 31) to rate the perceived social status of four ethnic groups (Whites, Asians, Blacks, and Hispanics). We then compared the

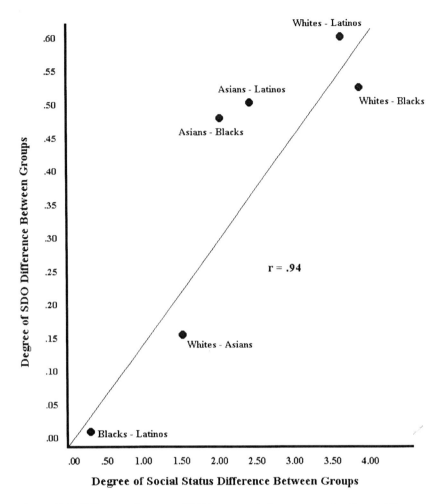

Figure 10.2. Differences in average SDO between ethnic groups as a function of difference in average perceived social status between these groups.

differences in rated social status between any two ethnic groups with the difference in the groups' mean levels of SDO.[11] Consistent with what we expect for arbitrary-set distinctions, Figure 10.2 shows that as the perceived difference in social status between any two ethnic groups increases, the difference in the average level of SDO between these groups increases in an almost perfectly linear fashion ($r = .94$).[12]

We also tested the interactionist model regarding arbitrary-set distinctions using a large sample of students from the University of Texas at Austin (Sample 4; $N = 5,655$). Here we examined the differences between

White and minority students (i.e., Blacks and Latinos) on a dimension entitled *group dominance orientation*,[13] as a function of three moderating variables: educational status, political ideology, and academic standing. Several previous studies have found that ethnocentrism, racism, and political conservatism decline with increasing levels of education.[14] One might well expect a similar decline in group dominance orientation. One ramification of the "liberalizing" effect of education on these social attitudes is that White and minority students should converge toward the same liberal position with increasing levels of education. In other words, we should expect an interaction between ethnic status and education level.

To test this, we examined the students' group dominance orientation as a function of their educational attainment. As shown in Figure 10.3, the arbitrary-set distinction of ethnicity interacted with educational level (see also Table 10.1).[15] As expected, group dominance was significantly lower among minorities than among Whites.[16] However, the magnitude of

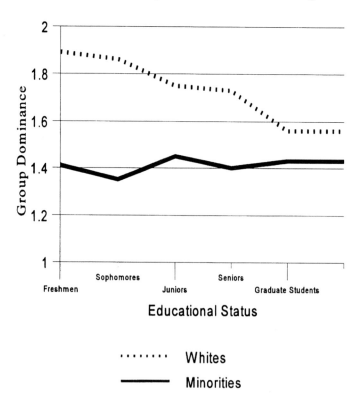

Figure 10.3. Group dominance orientation as a function of ethnicity and educational attainment (Texas Sample).

Table 10.1. Significance of Group Dominance Orientation as a Function of Interactions Between Arbitrary-Set Distinctions, Gender, and Interactions Between Arbitrary-Set Distinctions and Gender

	F-Coefficients and Significance Levels for Effects		
Social Distinctions	Effects for Interaction Between Arbitrary-Set Distinctions	Gender Effects	Effects for Interaction Between Arbitrary-Set Distinctions and Gender
University of Texas (Sample 4)			
Ethnicity and educational attainment	3.63**	n.a.	n.a.
Gender and educational attainment	n.a.	103.24**	<1 n.s.
Ethnicity and political conservatism	12.14**	n.a.	n.a.
Gender and political conservatism	n.a.	67.28**	<1 n.s.
Ethnicity and grade point average	3.85**	n.a.	n.a.
Gender and grade point average	n.a.	94.45**	1.25 n.s.
United States (Sample 2) vs. former USSR (Sample 14)			
Social class and nationality	17.43**	n.a.	n.a.
Gender and nationality	n.a.	30.55**	<1 n.s.
Sweden (Sample 1) vs. United States (Sample 2)			
Ethnicity and nationality	4.01*	n.a.	n.a.
Gender and nationality	n.a.	94.36**	2.28 n.s.
Israel (Sample 32) vs. United States (Sample 31)			
Ethnicity and nationality	8.31**	n.a.	n.a.
Gender and nationality	n.a.	23.28**	<1 n.s.

* $p < .05$, ** $p < .01$. N.a. means not applicable; n.s. means not significant.

this difference decreased with increasing educational level.[17] The same type of interaction was found between ethnicity and political ideology and between ethnicity and the students' academic achievement. Euro-American students had higher levels of group dominance orientation than minority students, but the size of this group difference decreased significantly as students became more politically liberal (see Table 10.1). White liberals had only marginally higher levels of group dominance orientation than liberals from ethnic minorities, whereas White conservatives had substantially higher levels of group dominance than conservatives from minority groups. Likewise, the greater the students' level of academic achievement (in terms of GPA), the smaller the group dominance differences between White and minority students.

In sum, all three of these analyses supported the notion that the degree of dominance differences between arbitrary-set categories is *contingent* upon a number of circumstances, including power differences between the groups, educational attainment, political ideology, and academic achievement. At the same time, however, and consistent with the invariance hypothesis, the data also showed that the group dominance differences between men and women were *not* contingent upon these factors. For example, Figure 10.4 shows that when examining the group dominance levels as a function of gender and educational attainment, men had significantly higher group dominance scores than women (see also Table 10.1)[18] and to the same extent across all educational levels.[19]

The results in Table 10.1 show that the same lack of significant interaction was found with respect to gender and political conservatism and with gender and grade point average. Thus, while there was a significant interaction between ethnicity and political conservatism,[20] there was no interaction between gender and political conservatism.[21] This absence of interaction is especially impressive in light of the very large size of Sample 4 ($N = 5,655$) and the very high resulting statistical power.

We were also able to contrast the effects of arbitrary-set and gender distinctions across cultural and national boundaries. We did this in three cross-national contrasts: the United States versus the former USSR, versus Sweden, and versus Israel.

United States Versus the Former USSR

We suspected that social class differences were smaller in the former Soviet Union than in the United States. Thus, we expected the difference in mean levels of group dominance orientation to be correspondingly smaller between Soviet social classes than between U.S. social classes. The data supported these expectations. While there was no real difference

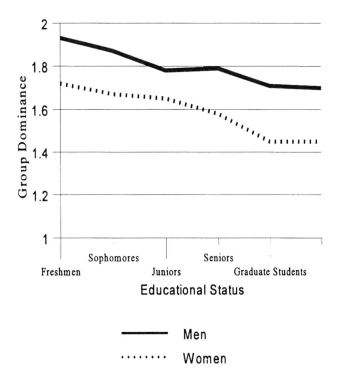

Figure 10.4. Group dominance orientation as a function of gender and educational attainment (Texas Sample).

in group dominance orientation between those describing themselves as "middle class" and "working class" in the former USSR, there was a significant difference between these two social categories in the United States, producing a significant interaction between social class and nationality (see Table 10.1).[22]

However, when we examined group dominance orientation as a function of nationality and gender, men were significantly more group dominance oriented than women in both countries[23] and to the same degree across the U.S.–Soviet national and cultural boundary.[24]

United States Versus Sweden

In comparing Sweden with the United States, we examined the stability of ethnic status differences in SDO across both nations versus the stability of the gender differences in SDO across these nations. We examined the relationship between a measure of group dominance orientation and ethnicity. In both countries we had respondents who would be considered members of either a high-status or a low-status ethnic group. In the Swedish sample (Sample 1), the high-status ethnic group was composed of those who were "historically Swedish" (i.e., individuals whose parents were both born in Sweden). The low-status group was composed of those with one or both parents who had immigrated to Sweden. In the U.S. sample (Sample 2), the high-status ethnic group was composed of Whites, and the low-status group was composed of Blacks.

Once again, while there was a significant interaction between ethnic status and nationality,[25] there was no interaction between gender and nationality. Both Swedish and U.S. men had significantly higher group dominance scores than women,[26] and these gender differences were basically constant across the national/cultural frontier.[27]

United States Versus Israel

Finally, we contrasted Israeli (Sample 32) and U.S. (Sample 31) students. In Israel the two arbitrary-set categories were Ashkenazic and Sephardic Jews, and in the United States the two arbitrary-set categories were Euro- and African-Americans. Since the status gap between Euro- and African-Americans in the United States is known to be substantially greater than the status gap between Ashkenazic and Sephardic Jews in Israel,[28] we expected and found the SDO differences between Euro- and African-Americans to be substantially greater than the SDO differences between Ashkenazic and Sephardic in Jews in Israel.[29] Once again, however, the data showed that males had significantly higher SDO scores than females[30] and that these differences were basically the same size in Israel as in the United States.[31]

Our final example of arbitrary-set interactionism and gender invariance was found in an experiment that Shana Levin conducted in Israel in 1994. In this study, Levin reminded Ashkenazic and Sephardic Jews of two different group conflicts: ethnic conflict and national conflict, before they completed the SDO_6 Scale. She expected the SDO difference between the two Jewish groups to vary as a function of political context. In the ethnic context, when the respondents were reminded of the conflict between Ashkenazic and Sephardic Jews, we expected the higher-status Ashkenazic Jews to have higher average SDO levels than the lower-status Sephardic Jews.[32] However, in the national context, where Jews were reminded of their common conflict with the lower-status Palestinians, the SDO difference between these two Jewish groups was expected to be substantially lower or disappear altogether.

The results were consistent with both predictions.[33] First, there was a significant effect for context, where respondents' SDO scores were significantly higher in the national context than in the ethnic context.[34] More

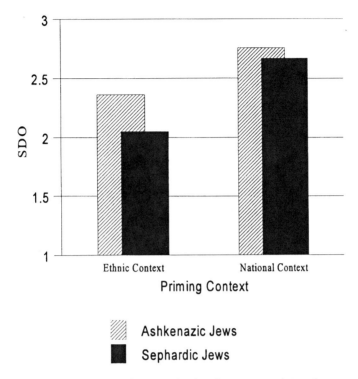

Figure 10.5. SDO as a function of ethnicity and political context (Israeli Sample).

importantly, there was also a significant interaction of the type expected[35] between group status and political context (see Figure 10.5). When confronted with a common subordinate group (i.e., Palestinians), the difference in SDO between Jewish groups all but disappeared. However, despite this clear interaction between the arbitrary-set category of ethnicity and political context, there was no corresponding interaction between gender and political context. Men had higher average SDO levels than women[36] and to the same degree across both political contexts[37] (see Figure 10.6).[38]

In sum, these analyses provide very clear and consistent support for the idea that, despite the fact that SDO differences between various arbitrary-set distinctions (e.g., social class, ethnicity, race) are sensitive to systematic differences in contextual, situational, or cultural factors, the SDO differences between men and women remain essentially unchanged over these factors.

Additional Support for the Invariance Hypothesis

In addition to the already discussed tests of the invariance hypothesis across ethnic, racial, and educational contexts, we also conducted

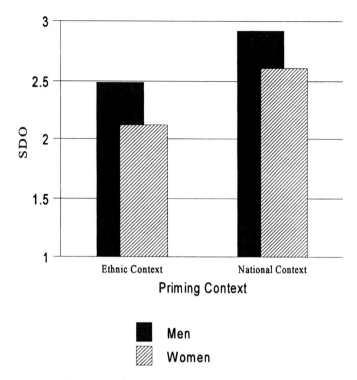

Figure 10.6. SDO as a function of gender and political context (Israeli Sample).

29 studies showing that gender differences in SDO do not vary across different situational, ideological, demographic, or contextual contingencies. For example, according to the socialization variant of the CD perspective, one substantial reason why men and women may have different levels of SDO is their different gender socialization experiences. Because gender roles have changed in the United States during the past 60 years, one might expect the size of the gender difference to depend on when people came of age, with smaller gender differences in SDO among younger people and larger differences among older people. However, the data showed no such age-by-gender interaction. Using two large samples of Los Angeles adults and breaking the samples into several age cohorts (e.g., 18–28 years, 28–38 years, etc.), men had higher SDO levels than women (see Table 10.2, Sample 26[39] and Sample 39).[40] More importantly however, Table 10.2 shows that these gender differences were basically of the same magnitude across the entire age continuum.[41]

  With virtually no exceptions, we observed the same lack of interaction between gender and the situational, contextual, and ideological factors

Table 10.2. Tests of Gender and Interaction Hypotheses Across 29 Situational, Cultural, Ideological, and Demographic Contingencies or Social Attitudes

Sample	Gender Effect (*F*-coefficient)	Interaction Effect: Gender × Contingency (*F*-coefficient)
Contingency: age		
U.S. adults (Sample 26)	8.20**	<1
U.S. adults (Sample 39)	7.65**	<1
Contingency: religiosity		
U.S. adults (Sample 26)	9.12**	1.08
U.S. adults (Sample 39)	7.73**	1.58
U.S. students (Sample 4)	98.98**	1.05
Israeli Jews (Sample 32)	21.61**	<1
Israeli Arabs (Sample 33)	9.81**	<1
Palestinian Arabs (Sample 34)	4.78**	<1
Contingency: ethnicity		
U.S. adults (Sample 26)	5.14**	<1
U.S. adults (Sample 39)	5.26**	1.51
U.S. students (Sample 31)	13.46**	1.63
Contingency: social role		
U.S. public defenders, police, jurors, and students (Samples 19–22)	34.50**	1.27
Contingency: income		
U.S. adults (Sample 26)	12.15**	1.26
U.S. adults (Sample 39)	6.55**	1.12
Swedish adolescents (Sample 1)	15.86**	1.30
Contingency: education		
U.S. adults (Sample 26)	14.64**	1.98
U.S. adults (Sample 39)	7.41**	2.15
Swedish adolescents (Sample 1)	19.10**	1.95
Contingency: national origin (i.e., immigrants to the United States)		
U.S. adults (Sample 26)	7.17**	<1
Contingency: nationality/culture		
Palestinian Arabs, Israeli Arabs, Israeli Jews, New Zealanders, Chinese, Americans (Samples 31–35, 38)	72.09**	1.03

(Continued)

Table 10.2. (*cont.*)

Sample	Gender Effect (*F*-coefficient)	Interaction Effect: Gender × Contingency (*F*-coefficient)
Soviets, Australians, Swedes, Americans (Samples 1–3, 14)	93.50**	5.93**
Contingency: child-rearing practices ("authoritarian" vs. "democratic")		
Swedish adolescents (Sample 1)	16.09**	<1
Contingency/social attitude: racism		
U.S. adults (Sample 26)	5.46**	<1
Contingency/social attitude: support for abortion		
U.S. adults (Sample 26)	10.60**	1.03
Contingency/social attitude: gender role attitudes		
U.S. students (Sample 4)	5.03*	<1
Contingency/social attitude: political conservatism		
U.S. adults (Sample 26)	7.22**	<1
U.S. adults (Sample 39)	8.39**	2.04
Swedish adolescents (Sample 1)	12.13**	<1
U.S. students (Sample 31)	26.14**	1.18

* $p < .05$, ** $p < .01$.

across the other 27 tests. These other factors included religiosity, ethnicity, social roles, income, education, national origin, nationality, types of child-rearing practices, racism, support for abortion, traditional versus nontraditional gender role attitudes, and political conservatism (see Table 10.2).

There are two analyses in Table 10.2 that are particularly striking. First, according to the social role version of the CD approach, these gender differences should be seen as a by-product of the different social roles that men and women occupy.[42] For example, because soldiers and police officers are usually men and are relatively punitive and xenophobic, any gender difference in these factors should be at least partly explained by these social roles. If we use this argument to understand the gender differences in SDO and related characteristics, then once we control for occupational role, the gender differences in SDO and related constructs should begin to fade. This should be particularly true if we choose professions that are strongly gendered and strongly associated with different

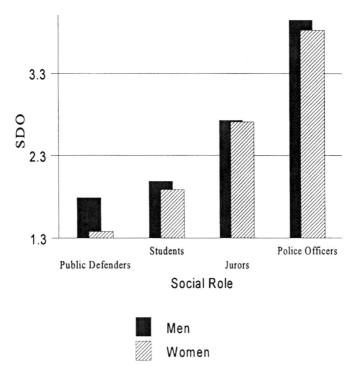

Figure 10.7. SDO as a function of gender and social role.

levels of SDO. We have two such professions: police officer and public defender.

We compared the SDO scores of people occupying the social roles of UCLA students, adults called to jury duty in Los Angeles County, members of the Los Angeles County Public Defenders Office, and members of the Los Angeles Police Department. As described in Chapter 3, the results were consistent with both predictions. Police officers had significantly higher SDO scores than those in all other categories, while members of the Public Defenders Office had significantly lower SDO scores than those in all other categories (see Figure 10.7). Because the social roles have been controlled within the police and public defender samples, but *not* in the student and juror samples, we should expect greater SDO differences in the latter two samples than within the former two samples. Figure 10.7 shows that this is *not* what happens. Across all social role categories, including police officer, women were still found to have significantly lower levels of SDO than men. If anything, the slight tendency toward interaction that the data suggest is exactly the opposite of what a social role interpretation of the data would imply. Because there is no control for social role within the juror and student samples, the social role model should expect to find *greater* male–female differences among students and jurors than among public defenders and police officers. However, the tendency toward interaction suggested the opposite.

Finally, we explored the plausibility of the invariance notion in some detail by examining the male–female SDO differences across five distinctly different nations: the United States, the People's Republic of China, New Zealand, Israel, and Palestine (i.e., West Bank and Gaza Strip). Cross-cultural comparisons of this sort would be relatively uninformative if there were no substantial differences in the degree of political equality between men and women across these cultures. To confirm that these nations really do differ in their relative degrees of patriarchy, we examined United Nations data on the political and social status of women around the world (see WISTAT, 1994). For the five nations involved, we averaged two indices from this database: the percentage of women with ministerial posts in the government, and the percentage of women in the lower house of the parliament or congress (see Table 10.3).

Although the United States can still be regarded as a patriarchical society, Table 10.3 nonetheless shows that there is more gender equality in the United States than in 87% of the other nations reviewed. On the other hand, the occupied Arab territories of the West Bank and the Gaza Strip (i.e., Palestine) are below the average in gender egalitarianism. Given this fact, a general CD perspective would expect larger gender differences in SDO with smaller levels of gender equality across nations, resulting in an interaction between nationality and gender. In contrast, the invariance

Table 10.3. Gender Equality Scores for Five Nations

Nation	% of Women in Ministerial Posts	% of Women in Lower Chamber of National Legislature	Percentile Rating of Generalized Gender Egalitarianism
United States	15	11	87
People's Republic of China	06	21	85
New Zealand	08	16	81
Israel	09	09	66
Palestine[a]	06	05	42

[a] The number in the first column represents the percentage of women in the PLO Executive Committee, and the number in the second column represents the percentage of women in the PNA Legislative Council.
Source: WISTAT (1994).

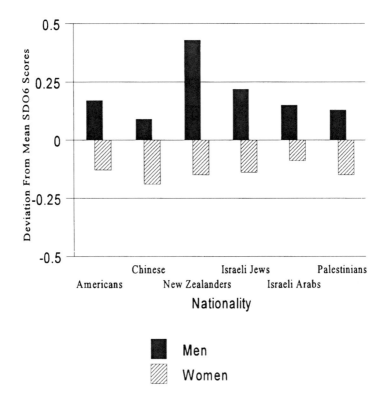

Figure 10.8. SDO as a function of gender and nationality.

hypothesis would expect no substantial variation in the size of the gender differences in SDO across these nations.

Statistical analysis of the results show that, although there are reliable male–female differences in SDO across nations,[43] the size of these differences is the same across nations.[44] Furthermore, Figure 10.8 shows that there is not even a tendency for the gender differences on SDO to increase as one moves from the relatively gender-egalitarian United States to the relatively gender-nonegalitarian Palestine.

Of the 29 analyses in Table 10.2, only 1 showed a significant interaction between gender and an arbitrary-set distinction. This analysis concerned gender differences in group dominance orientation across Sweden, the United States, the former Soviet Union and Australia (interaction $F = 5.93$, $p < .01$). However, even this single interaction provides no comfort for the general CD paradigm. Not only did men have significantly higher levels of dominance orientation within all four nations, but Sweden was the nation in which the male–female differences in group dominance were particularly large. The reason this fact offers no comfort to the CD

paradigm is because Sweden is among the most gender-egalitarian nations in the world (i.e., 97th percentile), a situation that should produce
very small rather than very large gender differences in group dominance
orientation.[45]

In sum, these analyses confirm the thesis of greater SDO among men.
Even more importantly, while the SDO differences between various arbitrary-set distinctions (e.g., race, social class, ethnicity) do tend to be sensitive to situational, contextual, ideological, and cultural factors, the SDO
differences between men and women appear to be largely impervious to
these factors.

The Gender Gap Revisited

The gender difference in SDO can also help us gain firmer purchase on
three important facets of group dominance. First, it provides us with another way of understanding the widely observed gender differences in social attitudes, voting patterns, proneness toward intergroup violence/war,
and occupational roles. Second, it provides us with deeper insight into the
manner in which patriarchy is distinct from, yet interfaces with, arbitrary-
set group dominance. Finally, this gender difference and the way it interfaces with arbitrary-set group dominance also implicate the third form of
group dominance, namely the adult–child distinction.

Sociopolitical Attitudes

Social scientists have become increasingly aware of the gender gap in
men's and women's sociopolitical preferences. For example, when controlling for other factors, women have been found to be more likely to vote
for liberal or socialist political parties and to be less militaristic, punitive,
and xenophobic, as well as more supportive of social welfare policies.[46]
We suggest that at least part of this gender gap in sociopolitical attitudes
is attributable to the gender difference in SDO.

To demonstrate this effect, we analyzed the connections between gender and several hierarchy-enhancing (HE) and hierarchy-attenuating
(HA) social attitudes across seven samples, five from the United States, one
from Sweden, and one from Israel. For example, in the Swedish data set
(Sample 1) males were significantly more politically conservative, punitive, and militaristic than females. We broke down these correlations between gender and social attitudes into two parts: that part attributable
to their common association with SDO, and the remaining direct relation
with gender. Table 10.4 shows that in each case there was a statistically

Table 10.4. Correlations Between Male Gender and HE Social Attitudes, Broken Down into Direct and Indirect (Mediated by Group Dominance Orientation/ Social Dominance Orientation) Components

HE Attitudes and/or Social Policies	Total Effect	Direct Effect	Indirect/Mediated Effect
Sweden (Sample 1). Mediator: Group Dominance Orientation Scale 1			
Conservatism	.09**	−.05 n.s.	.15**
Punitiveness	.21**	.07*	.14**
Support for the military	.21**	.07*	.14**
United States (Sample 4). Mediator: Group Dominance Orientation Scale 2			
Conservatism	.09**	.04**	.05**
Affirmative action opposition	.16**	.14**	.02**
Opposition to school busing	.10**	.07**	.03**
United States (Sample 10). Mediator: SDO_5 Scale			
Conservatism	.14**	.07	.07*
Opposition to racial policy	.21**	.11*	.11**
Opposition to gay and lesbian rights	.27**	.19**	.08**
Opposition to women's rights	.36**	.27**	.09*
Opposition to social welfare	.15**	.02 n.s.	.13**
Support for the military	.11*	.03 n.s.	.08*
United States (Sample 26). Mediator: SDO_4 Scale			
Conservatism	.21**	.14**	.07**
Harsher treatment of criminals is not the solution to crime	−.10**	−.03 n.s.	−.07**
Support for the death penalty	.10**	.02 n.s.	.08**
Support for the rehabilitation of criminals	−.16**	−.06*	−.10**
United States (Sample 31). Mediator: SDO_6 Scale			
Conservatism	.19**	.10**	.08**
Racism	.16**	.05*	.11**

(Continued)

Table 10.4. (*cont.*)

HE Attitudes and/or Social Policies	Total Effect	Direct Effect	Indirect/Mediated Effect
Antimiscegenation	.08**	.02 n.s.	.06**
Patriotism	.15**	.13**	.02**
Nationalism	.23**	.16**	.08**
Protestant work ethic	.14**	.07**	.06**
United States is fair	.19**	.09**	.10**
Anti-Black affect	.17**	.10**	.06**
Anti-Hispanic affect	.15**	.07**	.08**
White people have right to exclude minorities from neighborhood	.14**	.08**	.06**
Government should see to it that minorities get fair treatment in jobs	−.10**	−.01 n.s.	−.09**
Government should not pass laws concerning hiring of minorities	.11**	.06 n.s.	.05**
Government should ensure that Whites and minorities go to same school	−.17**	−.11**	−.06**
Government has no business trying to ensure racial integration in school	.13**	.05 n.s.	.08**
Government should do what it can to improve the economic condition of ethnic minorities	−.14**	−.05*	−.09**
Government has no business trying to improve the economic condition of ethnic minorities	.15**	.06*	.09**
Opposition to affirmative action	.19**	.12**	.07**

(*Continued*)

Table 10.4. (*cont.*)

HE Attitudes and/or Social Policies	Total Effect	Direct Effect	Indirect/Mediated Effect
Israel (Samples 32 and 33). Mediator: Group Dominance Orientation Scale 6			
Conservatism	.08	.02	.06*
Belief in legitimacy of Israeli society	.17**	.08	.09*
Sephardim are threat to Ashkenazim	.17**	.09*	.08*
United States (Sample 45). Mediator: Group Dominance Orientation Scale 6			
Conservatism	.13*	.06	.07*
Opposition to women's rights	.09*	.04	.05*
Less aid to the poor	.14*	.06	.08*
Support for the U.S. military	.17**	.12*	.05*
Opposition to higher taxes on the rich	.07	.01	.06*
Opposition to gay and lesbian rights	.16**	.09*	.07*
Government support for business	.12**	.12**	.00
Support for the death penalty	.10*	.04	.07*
Opposition to affirmative action	.13**	.07	.06*
Opposition to public day care	.12*	.06*	.06*

* $p < 0.05$, ** $p < 0.01$.

significant mediational role for the group dominance measure between gender and social attitudes. For example, the mediated effect of gender on opposition to welfare (via group dominance orientation) was 0.13, while the direct effect of gender on welfare opposition was statistically equivalent to zero (i.e., 0.02, Sample 10). This suggests that a major reason why men are more opposed to social welfare compared with women is attributable to men's higher levels of group dominance orientation.

This same pattern was found in several other samples (see Table 10.4). For example, in the UCLA sample (Sample 31), men were more likely than women to support the Protestant work ethic, or the notion that success in life is almost solely determined by one's own individual effort ($r = .14$). However, half of this relationship was mediated by the fact that men had higher levels of SDO (indirect effect $= .06$). Altogether, we performed 46 mediation analyses on the relationship between gender and social attitudes, and there was only one case in which social or group dominance orientation failed to have a statistically reliable mediating role between gender and social attitudes. On average, dominance orientation accounted for more than 50% of the covariation between gender and social attitudes.

Men and women show different attitudes with respect to not only social attitudes and social policy preferences, but also partisanship as well. For example, in the 1996 U.S. presidential election, 52% of married women and 66% of unmarried women voted for Bill Clinton, whereas only 44% of married men and 37% of unmarried men voted for him.[47] We believe that, just as with social attitudes, gender differences in political partisanship are attributable to gender differences in SDO. To demonstrate this, we surveyed Bay Area voters at election polls on November 3, 1992 (Sample 45). The participants were polled during the entire time the polls were open (i.e., 7 a.m. to 8 p.m.). The major presidential candidates were Bill Clinton, George Bush, and Ross Perot. Voters were asked to indicate which of the major candidates they voted for and their views on nine political policy positions. Because the nine political policy attitudes could distinguish Clinton voters from Bush and Perot voters, but could not distinguish between Bush and Perot voters, we clustered the latter two voter categories together.[48] Using structural equation modeling, we examined voting for Bush or Perot versus Clinton as a function of gender, SDO, political ideology,[49] and policy attitudes[50] in the manner depicted in Figure 10.9.[51] As can be seen in Figure 10.9, we were interested in explaining gender differences in vote choice as a function of how SDO influenced political ideology and policy issues. In this sample, as in the national election, a higher proportion of women than men voted for Clinton rather than for Perot or Bush.

As well as being associated with gender ($\gamma = .13$), SDO was also strongly associated with both political ideology ($\beta = .45$) and conservative policy positions ($\beta = .53$). Policy attitudes were directly related to vote choice ($\beta = .53$), and political ideology was related to vote choice both directly ($\beta = .23$) and through its relation to policy attitudes ($\beta = .38$). However, most relevant to our point, the model assuming that the relationship between gender and candidate choice is completely mediated by SDO was very consistent with the data.[52] This assumption was tested by adding a direct path from gender to vote choice. The addition of this direct path did

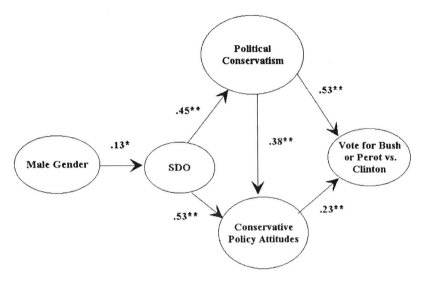

Figure 10.9. Political ideology model of candidate choice (SDO model; *$p < .05$, **$p < .01$; Source: Pratto, Stallworth, & Sidanius, 1997).

not substantially improve the fit of the model.[53] This shows that the relationship between gender and candidate choice was adequately accounted for by the mediating effects of SDO.

The adequacy of our model was further tested by comparison with a reasonable alternative model in which political ideology rather than SDO was the central and driving variable (see Figure 10.10). Though the hypothesized paths between gender and political conservatism ($\gamma = .14$), between political conservatism and conservative policy attitudes, and between SDO and candidate choice were found reliable, the model did not fit the data.[54] Adding a direct path from gender to candidate choice did not improve model fit. Further analyses showed that nothing could be done to improve the fit of this model as long as one avoided paths between SDO, on the one hand, and political policy attitudes and candidate choice, on the other hand.

Occupational Roles

We can also understand that some occupational segregation relates to the different functions for social hierarchy that men and women tend to play. In particular, we expect that men will predominate in occupations that help to enhance hierarchy (e.g., by channeling positive resources toward those better off or negative costs toward those worse off). For example,

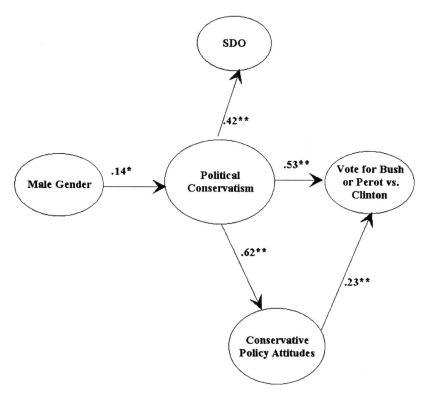

Figure 10.10. Political ideology model of candidate choice (Sample 45; *$p < .05$, **$p < .01$; Source: Pratto, Stallworth, & Sidanius, 1997).

as shown in Chapter 8, the criminal justice system disproportionately pe-
nalizes arbitrary-set subordinates (e.g., ethnic minorities and the poor).
Likewise, the military can be conceived of as a HE social institution because it helps to establish and/or maintain one nation's dominance over
other nations. In these and other HE institutional roles, we expect men to
be overrepresented. For example, 84% of U.S. police officers are men.[55]
There has never been a woman director of the FBI or CIA.[56] While 86% of
the U.S. military is male, fully 98% of the highest ranking officers in the
military are men.[57] Women are not even permitted in most of the world's
militaries and are rarely in positions of command even when permitted
to join. Furthermore, women rarely become police or prosecutors.[58]

   However, we expect women to be overrepresented in those sectors that
disproportionately aid subordinates. For example, in the United States
69% of social workers are women,[59] and a substantially higher proportion

Table 10.5. Correlations Between Male Gender and HE Social Roles, Broken Down into Direct and Indirect (Mediated by Group Dominance Orientation/ Social Dominance Orientation) Components (Sample 31)

Variable	Total Effect	Direct Effect	Indirect or Mediated Effect
Hierarchy-enhancing social roles			
Law enforcement officer	.11**	.10**	.02**
FBI agent	.13**	.10**	.03**
Business executive	.19**	.15**	.04**
Hierarchy-attenuating social roles			
Civil rights lawyer	−.17**	−.12**	−.05**
Lawyer for the poor	−.12**	−.07*	−.05**
Human rights advocate	−.17**	−.09**	−.08**

*$p < .05$, **$p < .01$.

of women than men donate money to charity and are actively involved in charity and social work.[60]

There are several different processes that probably contribute to this sort of gender segregation in hierarchy roles. First, men and women will chose occupations and social roles that reflect their own SDO levels. Because men and women differ on SDO, this self-selection will lead to more men choosing HE jobs and more women choosing HA jobs. We tested this idea several times by examining whether SDO mediates gender differences in preference for HE versus HA occupations. Self-selection is not the only process that contributes to gender segregation in hierarchy roles. Sex discrimination in hiring and the process of matching job applicants' apparent SDO levels to the role (see Chapter 3) also contribute.

For example, we asked UCLA students to indicate how attractive they found three hierarchy-enhancing and three hierarchy-attenuating jobs.[61] The hierarchy-enhancing jobs were law enforcement officer, FBI agent, and business executive, and the three hierarchy-attenuating jobs were civil rights lawyers, lawyer for the poor, and human rights advocate. Not surprisingly, Table 10.5 shows that hierarchy-enhancing-careers were more attractive to men, while HA-careers were more attractive to women. However, the data in Table 10.5 also show that a significant portion of this gender difference could be explained in terms of the gender difference on SDO. For example, women were more attracted to a career as a human rights advocate than men ($r = -.17$). However, almost half of this correlation could be accounted for in terms of lower levels of SDO in women (indirect effect $= -.08$).

Other Motives

The gender difference in SDO is but one reason that men and women might choose different kinds of careers. Other goals that men and women have for their work and the way such goals map onto the HA–HE distinction may also contribute to gender segregation in hierarchy roles. For example, there is a good deal of evidence that gaining personal status, prestige, and high income are more important to males than to females.[62] If HE jobs are seen as a way of enacting these desires, this would also contribute to gender assortment into hierarchy roles. We found data in support of this possibility in more controlled laboratory experiments. In this work, we examined choice of HE/HA jobs as a function of SDO and a number of other work values, such as having a high income, gaining personal prestige, having high social status, working with technology, being a mentor.[63] Within each of 10 occupations, participants chose either an HE or an HA job, but where the duties, salary, and work environment of the two jobs were comparable. Examples of the HE and HA job choices for two occupations are provided in Table 10.6.

Our results showed that across various occupations (e.g., public relations director, paralegal aide, real estate development), women chose more HA social roles than men, and men chose more HE social roles than women. When we examined hierarchy job choice as a simultaneous function of the participant's gender, SDO, and numerous work values, we found that those higher on SDO were more likely to select HE jobs (12% of variance explained). In addition, those valuing community service were more likely to select HA jobs (11% of variance), and those valuing status and prestige were more likely to select HA jobs (8% of variance). Thus, three values that men and women tend to differ on – SDO, desire for status and prestige, and desire to serve the community – contribute to and, in this study, completely accounted for gender differences in the selection of hierarchy roles.

Reproductive Strategies, Social Hierarchy, and Social Dominance Orientation

Finally, the robust gender difference in SDO has an additional and more subtle implication. As you will recall from the introduction to this chapter, parental investment theory implies that males and females pursue

Table 10.6. An Example of Paired Job Descriptions for Two Occupational Sectors

HA Description	HE Description
Occupation: public relations director	
Communications director, United Way: Produce videos, brochures, and pamphlets that present our cause to the public and to potential donors. Maintain contacts with the media. Educate the public about the need for community programs and about ongoing projects. You will be an important part of our program for community service.	Communications director, Shell Oil: Produce videos, brochures, and other public relations materials that present a positive company image to potential investors and consumers. Maintain contacts with the press. Publicize company actions and intervene to counteract negative publicity. We consider this job vital to the company and its shareholders.
Occupation: paralegal aide	
General assistant, Legal Aid Society: Assistant needed for lawyers whose client base consists of recent immigrants, lower-income families, and independent minors. Duties include assisting lawyers in directing clients to appropriate agencies and assisting clients in completing forms. Also, legal assistant will keep abreast of and advise attorneys and clients on new immigration regulations. Occasional delivery of papers to clients out of the office.	General assistant, Finney, Sutton, & Lara, Attorneys at Law: Legal assistant needed for growing firm specializing in workers' compensation fraud cases. We saved California companies over $1,000,000 last year by reducing the amount of workers' compensation they were required to pay to injured workers. Legal office research constitutes main part of duties; occasional errands for case investigations may be required.

qualitatively different mating strategies. While males have a predilection for sexual intercourse with a relatively large number of young and fertile females, females tend to be much more selective and concentrate their choices on resourceful, loyal, and high-status males.[64] When each sex selects different qualities in mates, this sets up competition within each sex along the dimensions relevant to mate selection. Because human females are the more selective sex, there should be substantial competition among men in the qualities that women desire in mates, such as social status and political and economic power.

Among other things, this thesis implies that reproductive outcomes should be associated with one's social status and political and economic power, especially for men. Support for this idea can be found in Betzig's (1993) historical study of the six earliest empires.[65] She found that men's social rank was directly related to the number of women they had as potential mates. Some emperors kept thousands of women, princes kept hundreds, men of the nobility kept 30 or more women, men of the upper middle class might have 6 to 12, while ordinary middle-class men had 3 or 4 women.[66] Because boys and girls are born in near equal proportions, this near monopolization of women by elite men was produced by their exploiting women from the lower-status segments of the society and from conquered peoples. Even in nonimperial societies there is a relationship between men's reproductive success and their social status.[67]

If, in fact, gender inequality and economic inequality are mutually enabling, we should find that the two are related not only in case studies of ancient societies, but even in comparisons of modern societies. Specifically, we predicted that the less the relative political power of women, the greater the degree of overall economic inequality. To test this idea, we used data from the United Nations database on the status of women.[68] We defined *female political power* as the proportion of women in the lower house of each nation's parliament or congress and defined each nation's *economic inequality* as the proportion of a nation's income held by the top-earning 10% of the population. Consistent with expectations, we found a small yet reliable correlation between the two. The less female political power within a society, the greater the degree of economic inequality within that society ($r = -.28$, $p < .01$, $N = 71$).

Another implication of this analysis concerns the relationship between mating strategies and SDO. If SDO was selected through human mating strategies, then it should also be associated with use of these mating strategies. In particular, male mating strategies (e.g., interest in having multiple sexual partners, sexual jealousy, and resistance to caring for other people's children), should be associated with SDO among men more so than among women. In addition, female strategies (e.g., desire for a high-status mate) should be associated with SDO among women more so than among men.

To test these hypotheses, Pratto (1996) conducted a series of studies using samples of heterosexual college students (Sample 10, Sample 23, and combined Samples 6, 7, 9, 11, and 12). In each sample, she assessed gender, SDO, and several preferences about potential mates. She regressed SDO on the relevant mate preference within each gender, and then tested whether the regression slopes for each gender differed in size. The results were consistent with her expectations.

Sexual Promiscuity and Social Dominance Orientation

Pratto asked respondents about the probability that they would have at least one affair while married. The respondents could answer from 0% (*No chance at all*) to 100% (*A certainty*). In general, men indicated they would be more likely to have an extramarital affair than women. In addition, those higher on SDO rated this even more likely. However, and as expected, this effect was greater among men than among women in both samples. These results are consistent with the notion that SDO is a stronger enabler of polygamous behavior among men than among women.

Sexual Jealousy and Social Dominance Orientation

In the same study, Pratto (1996) measured sexual jealousy in three ways: the likelihood that respondents would divorce an unfaithful spouse, the probability that their ideal spouse would have an extramarital affair, and the likelihood that their ideal spouse would be more sexually faithful than they. As expected, these sexual jealousy measures were associated with SDO. More importantly, the correlations were stronger among men than among women.

Caring for Children and Social Dominance Orientation

Consistent with expectations, SDO was negatively associated with respondents' willingness to adopt children who were not their biological offspring. Furthermore, this negative association was stronger among men than among women. In addition, SDO was also associated with the importance people assigned to their ideal mate having no children from previous relationships. Once again, however, this association was stronger among men than among women.

Desire for a High-Status Mate and Social Dominance Orientation

Within arbitrary-set dominance systems, people should prefer high-status mates. Furthermore, this preference should be more strongly associated with SDO among women than among men. Using standard measures in the literature, Pratto (1996) asked the students how important a number of characteristics in a mate were to them. A very clear social status factor emerged consisting of high social status, good education, and respectable family. Consistent with much prior research, women rated this dimension more important in a prospective mate than men did.[69] As expected, this dimension was positively related to SDO among both men and women, though among women more strongly. Using a separate measure, participants also rated the income range that they wished the ideal mate to earn. Once again, this status index was correlated with SDO among both women and men. However, the relationship was consistently stronger among women than among men.

Altogether then, we see that SDO may help enable the respective male and female mating strategies that Betzig (1993), Dickemann (1979), and others have shown to be characteristic of arbitrary-set group dominance societies. In particular, higher levels of SDO were found in women for whom social status in a mate was especially important. Higher SDO levels were found in men who expressed greater intention of having more than one mate, who reported higher levels of sexual jealousy, and who were less inclined to care for children they had not conceived. To the extent that each of these sexual strategies increases reproductive success, higher levels of SDO may be individually adaptive.[70]

Moreover, it is important to note that the evolutionary analysis suggests a dynamic and mutually enabling system that includes gender differences in mate preferences, gender inequality, social stratification, and SDO. Starting at any point in the system, we can see how each process contributes to the others. For example, female selection of high-status mates encourages competition among men for status and power, which makes female mate selection matter even more, which creates higher SDO levels in men. SDO biases people to act to establish arbitrary sets and gender inequality, and when those exist it is even more adaptive for women to select high-status mates, creating more competition among men for status, which further contributes to overall hierarchical social structure. Inasmuch as each component of the system helps perpetuate the others, the entire system will tend toward dynamic equilibrium over generations. This is, centrally, why we view gender, arbitrary-set, and adult–child dominance as mutually enabling systems.[71]

The Subordinate Male Target Hypothesis Revisited: Interface Between Patriarchy and Arbitrary-Set Hierarchy

The notion that both patriarchy and arbitrary-set hierarchy are, in part, a result of gender differences in mating strategies provides a useful theoretical context for understanding institutional discrimination, particularly discrimination against subordinate males. As we recall, the subordinate male target hypothesis (SMTH) predicts that arbitrary-set discrimination will be particularly severe against subordinate males, rather than subordinate females. Our review of the empirical evidence concerning institutional discrimination in Part III showed a great deal of evidence consistent with this view. Though women from subordinate arbitrary-set groups clearly suffer from *gender discrimination* along with women from dominant arbitrary-set groups, the *arbitrary-set discrimination* against these subordinate women is either relatively mild or nonexistent. The arbitrary-set discrimination that we do find is mainly directed against arbitrary-set men. This pattern was found in several types of data, including perceptions of discrimination, archival data, and well-controlled field experimentation, and across several domains, including employment and salary statistics, encounters with the police and the criminal justice system, housing, health care treatment, the banking and financial sectors, retail markets, and differential educational outcomes. This interaction between arbitrary-set status and gender is not restricted to African-Americans, but has also been found with respect to whatever ethnic group is subordinate within the society in question, including Native- and Latino-Americans, African, Arab, and Yugoslav immigrants to Sweden, and West Indian and Asian immigrants to the United Kingdom.

Recalling three concrete examples from Part III will help make this point very clear. First, in the best of its type yet done, the Hood and Cordovil (1992) study of the British criminal justice system disclosed that although there was rather strong evidence of racial discrimination against Black men, there was no evidence of such discrimination against Black women (see Chapter 8). Audit studies of housing discrimination show that people are less likely to sell a home to Black men than to Black women (see Chapter 5). Further clear and unambiguous experimental support for the SMTH was found in Ian Ayres's field studies of discrimination in the automobile retail market (see Chapter 5). As you will recall, this study found that while Black women were required to pay about $231 more for a given automobile than equivalent White women, Black men were required to pay more than $1,130 more for a given automobile than equivalent White men. Most tellingly, the evidence showed that, as opposed to the motives driving discrimination against both White and Black women, one of the primary motives driving discrimination against Black men was a desire to *harm*.

Why is arbitrary-set discrimination more strongly directed toward subordinate men than subordinate women? We suggest that the thesis of the differential male/female reproductive strategy might supply part of the answer to this riddle. Namely, dominant men will tend to view all females, from both dominant and subordinate arbitrary sets, as a reproductive resource. Though they may restrict women's economic and political power in order to increase the necessity of women relying on male mates, dominant men should do little to actually harm or debilitate women who may become mothers or caretakers to their children. The notion that gender discrimination is not motivated by animus or the desire to inflict damage is consistent with the recent survey work of Mary Jackman (1994). She found that men's attitudes toward equal economic and legal rights for women can be overwhelmingly described as "paternalistic," rather than as combative and conflictive. That is, the majority of men (approximately 60%) opposed equal rights for women *and simultaneously* expressed warm and positive feelings toward women, while only a few (3.5%) opposed equal rights for women *and simultaneously* expressed negative or hostile feelings toward women.[72] Furthermore, as shown in Chapter 6, though opposition to affirmative action for African-Americans was partly motivated by SDO (i.e., the desire to dominate, subordinate, and oppress), there was no evidence that opposition to affirmative action for women was motivated by these aggressive and debilitative motives.

Therefore, while there will certainly be some exceptions, this evidence suggests that discrimination against women may be an effort to limit their economic freedom and political prerogatives but not to debilitate women. This will apply to women in both dominant and subordinate groups alike. In contrast, there is now both theoretical and empirical reason to believe that discrimination against subordinate men is not simply motivated by a desire to restrict their economic and political prerogatives, but to *actually harm and debilitate them*. Thus, not only does arbitrary-set discrimination express ingroup favoritism, but we argue that arbitrary-set discrimination against outgroup men should be seen as a form of intergroup aggression. The evidence shows that the most extreme forms of intergroup aggression (e.g., lynching, deadly mutilation, warfare) are largely male versus male rather than female versus female or male versus female projects.[73] In addition, data show that less extreme forms of intergroup aggression, such as institutional discrimination, are also largely male projects. Thus, we should expect men to be disproportionately represented not only among outgroup aggressors, but also among the victims of these aggressors.

While there is little doubt that subordinate women certainly suffer from the effects of arbitrary-set discrimination and oppression, we are suggesting that subordinate women are not the primary targets of arbitrary-set discrimination. Rather, it appears that the negative effects of arbitrary-set discrimination on the lives of subordinate women are primarily the results of their association with subordinate men, in their roles of daughters, wives, sisters, lovers, mothers, and friends. None of this is to minimize the suffering of subordinate women and girls, but only to suggest that this suffering may be more incidental than deliberate.

All of this implies that gender and arbitrary-set dominance systems are neither reducible one to the other, nor purely additive. Rather, these two forms of oppression are highly interactive and conjoined. Moreover, because reproductive and child-rearing practices are the crux of mating strategy differences, the age system also intersects with the other two systems.

This suggests that a complete understanding of the psychology of gender cannot be realized until we appreciate the distinct gender differences in the generation and maintenance of arbitrary-set group-based hierarchies, including the gender difference on SDO, economic exploitation, war making, and other forms of outgroup aggression.

Summary

Using the general framework of sexual selection theory and evolutionary psychology, this chapter has made four arguments. First, we predicted and found that males should have higher average levels of SDO than females. In addition, while SDO differences between various arbitrary-set social distinctions (e.g., social class, ethnicity, race) systematically change as a function of the relevant changes in situational, contextual, and cultural factors, SDO differences between men and women were largely invariant across these factors.

Second, we argued that a substantial portion of the gender gap in social attitudes, political partisanship, and vote choices can be attributed to the effect of gender differences on SDO. Thus, for example, the pattern of men being more supportive of policies such as war and the death penalty and less supportive of social welfare policies and liberal political parties could be largely explained in terms of the higher levels of SDO found among men than among women. Likewise, the tendency for men to be more attracted to careers such as police officer and less attracted to careers such as social worker could also be substantially explained in terms of higher levels of SDO among men than among women.

Third, in analyzing the reproductive strategies that may be differentially optimal for men and women, we have suggested that patriarchy and arbitrary-set dominance systems may serve a particular, complementary mating system: one in which dominant men monopolize access to power and resources that would otherwise accrue to women and other men, but attract female mates due to the increased social status and power these accumulated social resources confer. We suggested that SDO may be a psychological facilitator of the behaviors that are associated with reproductive success for men and women within this mating system.

Consistent with this reasoning, we found that SDO was more related to intended promiscuity, sexual jealousy, and noninvestment in other people's children among men, whereas SDO was more strongly related to desire for a high-status mate among women.

Finally, application of evolutionary thinking has led us to conclude that both patriarchy and arbitrary-set hierarchy are partly the result of the interaction between male and female reproductive strategies. In particular, due to the female preference for high-status males, the reproductive interests of dominant males are optimized by the formation of coalitions with other ingroup and dominant males, not only to constrain the economic and political options of females, but also to exploit and debilitate outgroup males. We have labeled this latter phenomenon the subordinate male target hypothesis. Consistent with this hypothesis, analyses of discrimination data (Chapters 5–8) show that arbitrary-set discrimination seems to be particularly severe against subordinate men rather than subordinate women. Thus, we suspect that patriarchal and arbitrary-set discrimination are directed toward different goals. Discrimination against both dominant and subordinate women is not primarily driven by the desire to harm, destroy, or debilitate them, but to control them. On the other hand, discrimination against outgroup males appears to have a distinctly aggressive and debilitative character, suggesting that dominant men may regard subordinate men as potential threats and reproductive rivals. Both the theoretical analysis and the data we presented illustrate how the gender, arbitrary-set, and adult–child systems of social dominance work together to perpetuate each other.

11 | Epilogue

Our work on social dominance theory (SDT) has focussed on trying to answer two related questions: Why is group-based social dominance so common, and why is it so difficult to eliminate? In attempting to answer these two questions, we presume that, despite major and sometimes profound differences between societies and cultures, there is also a basic grammar and deep structure of social power that is shared by all societies.[1] Our work on SDT has been devoted to identifying what this grammar and deep structure consist of.

The historical and anthropological record suggests that most human societies contain three distinct but interlocking hierarchical systems: gender, age, and arbitrary sets, that is, the contextually dependent and arbitrarily defined social distinctions based on factors such as ethnicity, race, class, tribe, and nation. We have argued that these three systems of group-based dominance are not interchangeable or equivalent, but rather constitute three interlocking and mutually interdependent structural components of social life. Systems of group-based social dominance occur across a wide variety of historical periods, economies, and technologies. While gender and age hierarchies appear to be essentially universal across all known societies, arbitrary-set hierarchies largely occur only in societies in which people are able to generate and sustain an economic surplus. The consequent social stratification among arbitrary sets then further contributes to gender inequality and the establishment of patriarchy. For example, when the bush-living !Kung produced only enough to sustain themselves, they had a fairly flat social structure, with few status or power distinctions between men and women, among different groups, or even between adults and children. However, when the fundamental economic system of their society changed and they accumulated wealth, arbitrary-set status differentials and more severe forms of male dominance arose.[2] This same basic relationship between economic surplus and group discrimination has also been found in comparative cultural studies, as well as in more controlled experiments.[3] As soon as a society can produce an economic surplus, this surplus facilitates the development of role specialization, coalition formation among males, and the creation of arbitrary-set hierarchy.

Despite the fact that arbitrary sets can be defined using an almost limitless number of social distinctions, and despite the fact that no particular arbitrary set is permanently doomed to subordination while another is always privileged with dominance, the basic phenomenon of arbitrary-set social hierarchy itself appears always to re-create itself across time, culture, and geography.

Once any particular group dominance system becomes established, it is remarkably stable, even though the degree of this hierarchy might shift from one historical period to another as a result of cross-cultural contact and technological change. We suspect that group dominance societies are stable because such dominance systems are dynamic and adaptive and consist of interlocking and mutually reinforcing components. These features imply that a theory of group dominance should not rely solely on characteristics peculiar to specific societies, with specific histories of group conflict (e.g., the Jewish Holocaust), specific cultural values or beliefs (e.g., individualism), or particular economic systems (e.g., capitalism). Rather, SDT argues that certain key processes are likely to be found within all group dominance societies, including cultural beliefs, psychological prejudices, social roles, and discriminatory institutional allocations.

Levels of Analysis

Almost all theories of prejudice, stereotyping, ideologies, political systems, and intergroup conflict tend to be restricted to one of three conceptual levels: individual-psychological, social-situational, and social-structural. While this conceptual narrowness allows one a firm purchase on the details of some important processes, it also limits the utility of each type of theory. Theories that exclusively focus on individual motivation are able to show us how psychological prejudice intersects with both self-interest and group interest. However, such theory cannot explain the production of normative beliefs, social ideologies, or particular patterns of institutional discrimination or how all of these forces work together to produce and maintain group-based social inequality.

While social-situational analyses illustrate how specific aspects of social context, such as the social cuing of stereotypes and the salience of group boundaries, can evoke discriminatory behavior in individuals, such models are generally not well integrated with individual difference models below them or with social-structural or institutional models above them. The social-situational literature has rarely dealt with individual differences, nor has it adequately addressed how social context – especially social power – interfaces with social structure. Thus, it has no way of addressing system dynamics.

Structural analyses do allow one to discuss the aspects of social context that characterize the society and the real-life situations of different groups within it. However, previous models at this level of analysis often omit the actor and individual agency altogether, and so cannot incorporate the psychological motivations and cognitive processes that other literatures have shown to powerfully influence people's propensity to form groups, maintain group boundaries, and let group concerns govern their behaviors. To capitalize on the strengths and mend the weaknesses of each approach, we have developed SDT. Most importantly, we have tried to emphasize the way that processes at each level of analysis interface with the processes at other levels and how these interfaces help to both produce and maintain group-based social inequality.

Psychological Predispositions

One of the major influences on the kinds of societies that humans produce is the psychological nature of those people within society. There is a large body of social-cognitive work which suggests that normal human psychological biases, such as the tendency to exaggerate differences between social categories,[4] the tendency to favor ingroups over outgroups,[5] the motivation to reduce uncertainty,[6] the tendency to be especially responsive to threats rather than to potential gains,[7] all contribute to people's predilections to define social group boundaries, to stereotype outgroup members, and to discriminate against the generalized "other."

In addition, the consistency of group-based social hierarchy, across both human cultures and closely related hominoid species, suggests that hominoids have a psychological predisposition for noticing, understanding, and creating social dominance. This does not mean that every individual strives for social dominance. Rather, it suggests that people are sensitive to status and power cues and are psychologically equipped to respond to these cues. This cue sensitivity, coupled with other psychological biases, such as the motivation to reduce cognitive dissonance and to have positive social identity, implies that people easily learn different general value orientations toward group dominance. SDT examines how people in different positions within the social hierarchy develop different orientations toward group dominance and how, in turn, these orientations influence whether people contribute to or work against group dominance.

While our general approach does give more weight to psychological and individual difference phenomenon than has been popular in almost all sociological and even most recent social-psychological approaches, we have not "psychologized" the problem, have not implied that there are different types of SDO, or suggested that people with high levels of SDO are somehow abnormal, psychologically deviant, or morally suspect. This approach would not only give individual differences too much weight, but we suspect would also paint the psychological states that sustain group dominance as far more aberrant, unusual, and, therefore, more dismissable than they really are.

SDO is defined as the tendency for people to endorse group-based social inequality and the subordination of certain groups at the hands of dominant groups. Although SDO has a surface resemblance to more familiar concepts such as authoritarianism, political conservatism, racism, and individual dominance, we and others have shown that SDO is both conceptually and empirically distinct from these other constructs.[8] SDO is thus a generalized orientation toward the hierarchical relations among groups. Whatever SDO values one has developed about intergroup relations of one type (e.g., between races) are likely to be applied to intergroup relations of other types (e.g., between nations or minimal groups). This means that people will *re-create new hierarchical intergroup relations from the fragments of old hierarchical intergroup relations.*

Thus far, we have examined SDO in normal populations. The levels of SDO among even our "high" category (the top third of a distribution) are not high in absolute terms, nor are they statistically unusual – being no less common than those in the middle or low thirds. This suggests that extraordinarily high levels of SDO may not be necessary for the maintenance of group dominance. Rather, it is peoples' general tolerance of oppression and chronic group discrimination that accomplishes much of the work that sustains group dominance.

Social Context

Though psychological predispositions are important, they are always enacted within specific sociopolitical contexts. Social psychologists have identified a number of contextual conditions that instigate the formation and use of stereotypes, leading to group discrimination. We have argued that several of these conditions, including the presence of salient intergroup boundaries, group status differences, group segregation, and power differentials between social groups, are all normal aspects of social life within group-based dominance systems. Thus, much of the normal social context in which people live cues group-dominance-sustaining behaviors.

Unlike most social psychologists, we have also emphasized that shared ideologies – including stereotypes – are central to understanding discrimination and intergroup behavior. The shared cultural ideologies of a given society are cued by the everyday interaction patterns and symbols of those societies. Because many hierarchy-enhancing (HE) cultural ideologies are consensual enough that almost everyone endorses them to some degree, it is possible to cue people in their use on a regular basis. Once such ideologies are cued, people then act out their assigned dominant or subordinate social roles. Among other ways, people play out these social roles by discriminating against people from other groups and by behaving in self-destructive and self-debilitating ways. *Ideologies, then, are the genes of culture*: They describe the patterns of the culture and get people in the culture to reproduce these patterns.

Institutional Discrimination

The other main way we have recognized the cultural and societal aspect of group-based dominance systems is in our analysis of institutional discrimination. Contrary to broad public opinion, our review of the empirical evidence shows that institutional discrimination remains a very significant feature of modern "democratic" states. On average, major social institutions treat arbitrary-set dominants better than arbitrary-set subordinates, and treat men better than women. Despite recent claims to the contrary,[9] the research attesting to this discrimination is quite unambiguous and shows that dominants are favored over subordinates at essentially every turn and within every major domain of life, including the work place, the school, the health care system, the housing market, the retail market, the financial markets, and the criminal justice system. However, in line with a thesis we call the subordinate male target hypothesis, the data also show that arbitrary-set discrimination against subordinate males is particularly common and, at times, quite severe.

Sometimes institutional discrimination is overt and based explicitly on social group membership, even within so-called democratic states. However, most often, institutional discrimination within states with democratic pretensions is covert rather than overt. While not explicitly and openly targeted against subordinates, the social criteria on which favorable institutional responses are based are often so strongly linked to social group membership that it results in systematic, de facto discrimination against subordinates. At the same time, however, the explicit allocation criteria allow institutions to claim that their behaviors are "fair" and "equitable." Because the discriminatory effects of covert discrimination can be so easily masked and justified in terms of apparently legitimate arguments and criteria, the HE results of covert discrimination are quite powerful and difficult to change.

The Interactive Nature of Social Dominance Processes

We suggest that group-based hierarchy is not only the product of psychological, contextual, and institutional forces, but also the product of the mutually reinforcing interactions among these forces. First, the cognitive biases and motivational drives of humans appear to be so ordered that hierarchically organized ingroup–outgroup distinctions begin to appear whenever the conditions of economic surplus permit. Once such hierarchically organized systems emerge, the experiences of living in group dominance societies, in general, and having experiences associated with membership in dominant or subordinate groups, in particular, affect people's levels of social dominance orientation (SDO). The HE and HA tendencies of these orientations help to counterbalance each other within the social system, and thereby stabilize this hierarchical system.

The cultural ideologies that are part of group dominance societies are so thoroughly learned and so widely recognized that it is easy for one person to evoke the ideology in another person and so influence that person's behavior to enact that ideology. The discrimination that can result helps to re-create the social conditions that are likely to trigger the ideology in the future. This interplay between social context and individual psychologies also contributes to the stability of the social structure.

The constant confluence between individual psychological biases and social context not only leads individuals to discriminate, but also facilitates institutional discrimination. The roles that institutions require their members to play can themselves prescribe HE or HA behavior. Ensuring that the people who acquire those roles already have the general values and ideologies compatible with each role helps to further create and maintain the behavior prescribed by the role. Not only do institutional practices reify social structure, but this social structure also helps create the psychological states (e.g., SDO) and social conditions (e.g., group segregation) that further contribute to discriminatory behavior. The processes we have identified as sustaining group dominance are, then, mutually enabling, self-perpetuating, and, therefore, quite stable.

Despite the fact that SDT views the production and maintenance of group-based social hierarchy as a complex and interactive process, the theory can be summarized in a single, simple heuristic: *group inequality*. Like a fractal pattern observable from micro- to macro-levels of organization, group inequality is seen in psychological biases, in the effects of social contexts, in the biases of institutional discrimination, and, ultimately, in general social structure. At the individual level, we showed that one psychological contributor to group inequality, namely higher levels of SDO, is greater among dominant than among subordinate arbitrary sets, and also greater among men than among women. At the level of social context, the social conditions of group inequality, such as group segregation and power differences, contribute to social-cognitive processes that lead to more discrimination against subordinates and, therefore, to more inequality. At the institutional level, we saw ample evidence that central institutions treat people differently, depending on their group membership.

Comparisons with Other Theories

Unlike other theories of social identity, ideology, power, stereotyping, or discrimination, SDT has been dedicated to explaining why group-based dominance is such a common and robust form of human social organization. In confronting this issue, SDT provides some useful extensions and alternative conceptualizations of phenomena dealt with by other theories.

Social identity theory (SIT) has become a very powerful and popular framework for understanding intergroup discrimination, stereotyping, and social identity. This is probably because it does such a good job of examining how social-structural conditions (e.g., salience of group boundaries) intersect with psychological processes (e.g., creation of identity) and consequently produce behaviors such as intergroup discrimination. Nonetheless, we feel that expanding this theory to include some of the concerns of SDT would strengthen it considerably.

First, we argue that social status does not necessarily subsume social power. By presuming that these dimensions are one and the same, SIT has not examined how status and power translate into each other or the fact that it is power rather than a status differential that allows discrimination in the first place. Second, although SIT has tried to address the problem of group asymmetry – for example, in predicting that low- and high-status groups will resort to different means of generating positive identity – such theoretical predictions have not always been borne out by empirical data. Our ideological asymmetry hypothesis, concerning the interface between different processes, is a new and empirically robust improvement on understanding identity differences between groups differing in status and power. Third, because the hallmark of SIT has become the minimal groups paradigm, SIT has done relatively little to incorporate shared cultural ideologies and institutional discrimination in explaining social inequality – forces that we have shown to be both powerful and norma-tive. Fourth, our incorporation of systematic individual differences (i.e., as aggregated into SDO) enables us to examine motivations within as well as between groups. This provides another way of analyzing dynamic pro-cesses within group dominance societies.

Though SIT draws attention to social status as an important factor mod-erating people's social-psychological responses, much of the rest of social-psychological work in the areas of stereotyping and prejudice has not ad-dressed the larger structural context within which such processes occur. Most importantly, little work has been done on institutional discrimi-nation and the operation of social power, particularly the power that is situated in group membership. We hope that Part III, dealing with institu-tional discrimination, will inspire more serious social-psychological work as to its proximal causes, especially the differences between arbitrary-set and gender discrimination.

SDT obviously owes much to Marxist and elitist theories of ideology and social power. However, we have extended these analyses as well. It is not simply the case that consensual ideologies just reinforce social inequality. We propose that some consensual ideologies also work to at-tenuate this social hierarchy. This idea reinforces the notion that economic and structural forces are not the only factors that can attenuate inequal-ity, but that cultural and psychological factors can also contribute to this attenuation.

Second, while subordinates, by definition, have much less power than dominants, it is also true that subordinates are not completely powerless or without agency to affect the precise nature and severity of group-based social dominance.[10] However, the agency that subordinates do exercise is often self-debilitative. More precisely, our thesis, known as the behav-ioral asymmetry hypothesis, suggests that subordinates tend not to act in their own interest to the same extent as dominants do. We do not make this claim in order to "blame the victim" or to suggest that subordina-tion is really the result of some inherent moral or intellectual ineptitude on the part of the oppressed, an all too popular exercise at the close of the twentieth century. Rather, it is important to understand that subor-dinates' self-debilitative behaviors are most often the result of initial and very dramatic forms of oppression (e.g., slavery, military conquest). Once this oppression extends itself over time, self-debilitating behaviors will arise and then become part of one's normal behavioral repertoire. To a very significant degree then, the maintenance of dominance systems also depends on the self-debilitating behaviors of subordinates. More to the point, except for extreme cases of coercion, the persistence of group-based dominance rests on the coordinated and choreographed actions of both dominants and subordinates alike.

Another implication of these ideas is that one cannot make sense of psychological attitudes or group-associated behaviors outside of specific social and political contexts. For example, we showed how the relationship between SDO and ingroup affiliation depends on one's group status. Such results do not suggest that there is some general or normal psychological bias concerning ingroup affiliation, but rather suggest how this phenomenon is socially situated. The goal of understanding how psychological processes are influenced by group status is similar to the goals of the feminist movement and other "inclusivity" movements in science, and we are pleased that other social scientists are also turning their attention to this problem.

Material Versus Symbolic Group Conflict

Our theory can address a theoretical dilemma concerning whether group discrimination is fundamentally a real or a symbolic action. Realistic group conflict theory argues that group prejudice, stereotyping, and discrimination are the result of real groups fighting over real things (e.g., wealth), whereas SIT tends to view group conflicts as contests over the symbolic maintenance of group boundaries. SDT acknowledges the importance of conflicts over concrete material interests as well as conflicts within the symbolic realm in which ideologies and identities are constructed. Moreover, because we also consider social history to be an ongoing and dynamic process, we suggest that there will be a dialectical relationship between social ideology, on the one hand, and material social reality, on the other hand. Ideologies prescribe the behaviors that turn symbolic ideals into material and social reality, and concrete social realities in turn help shape social ideologies.

Future Directions for Research on Group Dominance

Though the work summarized in this book provides some insight into the internal dynamics of group dominance systems and suggests some reasons for why such systems tend to be so stable, this work also raises several important questions that will require additional theoretical and empirical effort to resolve. One such question concerns how people develop their orientation toward social dominance. We have shown that one's SDO is related to the power and status of one's primary social group. We have also speculated about how membership in one's group may contribute to SDO. While it is possible that SDO is also related to temperamental-emotional styles, attachment experiences, and certain kinds of socialization, we have yet to examine these processes in any detail. Experts in personality and social identity development, acculturation, and social psychology have the opportunity to make significant contributions to this problem.[11]

A second arena that bears further investigation concerns the subordinate male target hypothesis (SMTH), or that fact that institutional discrimination appears to be particularly severe when directed at subordinate males. Among the several questions provoked by this finding are the following: Do men and women show equal bias against subordinate males? Do dominants and subordinates show equal bias against subordinate males? What kinds of social beliefs and practices are particularly associated with this type of discrimination? What ramifications might this discrimination have for families, gender roles, and arbitrary-set group relations?

Third, the gender difference on SDO poses several puzzles. Though we have found ample evidence that men have higher SDO levels than women, we have been unable to find any moderator of this difference. This gender difference remains relatively stable regardless of one's particular culture, one's age, educational level, hierarchy role, or even how much power men have compared with women in their societies. While we have theoretical reasons to expect men to have higher average SDO than women, we have no reason to expect the size of this gender difference to be *quite* as impervious to contextual and situational factors as it appears to be. Perhaps other researchers will be able to identify the moderating factors that we have missed, and thereby enable us to better understand the precise mechanisms producing this gender difference and how it relates to other features of group-based dominance.

Though we have postulated that a single principle (i.e., differences in parental investment) may be able to explain the degree of gender inequality, we lack a single principle to explain the degree of arbitrary-set inequality. Clearly, these two forms of inequality affect one another. We need to better understand how various forms and degrees of arbitrary-set inequality influence and are influenced by various forms and degrees of gender inequality.

Most glaringly, because we have been so preoccupied with understanding why group dominance is so robust, we have yet to address adequately why some societies are more hierarchical than others. Similarly, we have yet to identify the factors responsible for changes in the degree of social hierarchy within any given society over historical time. Getting valid and powerful answers to these questions will be immensely important for deepening our understanding of the dynamics of oppression and group-based inequality.

Personal Statement

Our discussion of SDT would not be complete without a discussion of the political values of its authors. We feel this is especially important because, in describing how "well" group dominance works as a system and in reminding people that group dominance is one of the most predominant forms of social organization, we might also appear to be justifying social dominance. However, rather than trying to support and justify social inequality, our personal political biases are decidedly egalitarian.

We have focussed on the problems of inequality for two major reasons. First, it is exactly because we would like to see societies with democratic and egalitarian pretensions actually live up to these ideals that we have been so focussed on trying to better understand why the achievement of equality appears to be so mind-numbingly difficult. Second, we hope that by directing scientific attention on this problem, group dominance will be recognized for what it is. Calling social dominance by more palatable names, pretending that it is only a feature of other people's societies, assuming that it is due only to the actions of a "misguided" few, and presuming that it is merely a dying legacy of the past not only are exercises in self-delusion, but also contribute to the tenacity of group dominance by obfuscating its very existence, and thereby making it that much more difficult to change.

We judge it as considerably more harmful to the cause of equality and the fulfillment of democratic ideals to pay too little than too much attention to the dynamics of group dominance. It strikes us as slightly foolish to believe that the achievement of democratic ideals and true equality of opportunity can be realized by building our analyses on naïve or patently false assumptions. We suggest that is also wrongheaded to assume that we are inevitably and inextricably moving toward more inclusivity and greater equality of opportunity. The historical record shows that movement toward equality is decidedly not a linear or an inevitable process. Rather, the record shows that periods of greater equality are often followed by periods of greater inequality.[12] Therefore, it is exactly because we are committed to the principles of inclusiveness and social equality that we feel it is so crucial to truly understand how group dominance systems actually work. In trying to better understand the nature of group dominance, even to the point of revealing some uncomfortable similarities between so-called egalitarian and clearly nonegalitarian societies, we hope our work has helped reveal some of the consensually approved social practices and beliefs that prevent us all from realizing our collective democratic and inclusionary ideals.

Notes

Chapter 1.   From Viciousness to Viciousness

1. Crossette (1998).
2. See, e.g., Enzenberger (1994).
3. See, e.g., Staub (1989).
4. See, e.g., Jaensch (1938), W. Reich (1946).
5. Dollard, Miller, Doob, Mowrer, and Sears (1939).
6. Ibid., p. 1.
7. Dollard et al. (1939).
8. See esp. Dollard (1937), Hovland and Sears (1940).
9. For reviews, see Christie and Cook (1958), Christie and Jahoda (1954), Duckitt (1989), Kirscht and Dillehay (1967), Samelson (1986).
10. See, e.g., Peabody (1966).
11. See review by Stone (1980); see also Altemeyer (1981, 1988, 1996).
12. See Duckitt (1989) for a review.
13. Altemeyer (1981, 1988).
14. For a similar theme, see McClosky (1958).
15. Eysenck (1951, 1971, 1976), Eysenck and Coulter (1972), Dator (1969), Jackson and Kirby (1991), Nias (1972), Sidanius (1987), Sidanius and Ekehammar (1979), Sidanius, Ekehammar, and Ross (1979), Stone and Russ (1976), G. D. Wilson (1973), Wilson and Bagley (1973), Wilson and Lee (1974), Wilson and Patterson (1968).
16. Wilson (1973).
17. See, e.g., Eysenck (1944, 1951, 1971, 1976), Kerlinger (1984), McClosky (1958), Nias (1972), Ray (1983), Sidanius (1987), Sidanius and Ekehammar (1979), Sidanius, Ekehammar, and Ross (1979), Sidanius and Pratto (1993), Sirgo and Eisenman (1990), Wilson and Patterson (1968).
18. Note, while Eysenck also developed a typology related personality and political space, including racialism, this typology was far from a dynamic or integrated theory as to *why* these two spaces were related (see Eysenck, 1951).

19. See G. D. Wilson (1973), pp. 257–266.
20. For an overview, see Solomon, Greenberg, and Pyszczynski (1991).
21. See p. 135–136.
22. Greenberg et al. (1990, Study 1); see also Rosenblatt, Greenberg, Solomon, Pyszczynski, and Lyon (1989).
23. See Study 2; see also Greenberg, Simon, Pyszczynski, Solomon, and Chatel (1992, Study 1).
24. G. D. Wilson (1973).
25. See esp. Rokeach (1973), pp. 166–167.
26. Rokeach (1973).
27. Cochrane, Billig, and Hogg (1979), Searing (1979), Sidanius (1990).
28. See also Okanes (1974), Rokeach, Miller, and Snyder (1971), Sidanius, Devereux, and Pratto (1992).
29. Mirels and Garret (1971).
30. See Study 1; less independence was found among southern White college students.
31. They also found that completion of the Pro- or Anti-Black attitude measures could bias the subsequent general value measures.
32. See, e.g., S. T. Fiske (1997), Hilton and von Hippel (1996), Leyens, Yzerbyt, and Schadron (1994), Messick and Mackie (1989).
33. S. T. Fiske (1980).
34. Goffman (1959).
35. Lewicki (1986).
36. See Hilton and von Hippel (1996).
37. Ashmore and DelBoca (1981).
38. Devine (1989).
39. Fazio, Sanbonmatsu, Powell, and Williams (1995), Perdue, Dovidio, Gurtman, and Tyler (1990), Perdue and Gurtman (1990).
40. Note, however, that these two assertions are still under some debate; see Lepore and Brown (1997), Locke, MacCleod, and Walker (1994), Locke and Walker (1998), Wittenbrink, Judd, and Park (1997).
41. S. T. Fiske (1997).
42. D. L. Hamilton (1979), Pettigrew (1979).
43. Stephan (1987).
44. Taylor, Fiske, Close, Anderson, and Ruderman (1977).
45. See, e.g., Cantor and Mischel (1979).
46. Erber and Fiske (1984), Neuberg and Fiske (1987), Pratto and Bargh (1991).
47. Klatzky and Andersen (1988).
48. See, e.g., Ashmore and DelBoca (1981).
49. For exceptions, see Heilman (1983).

50. Pratto and Bargh (1991), Pratto, Stallworth, Sidanius, and Siers (1997).
51. See, e.g., van Dijk (1987).
52. Dovidio and Gaertner (1991), Kinder and Sanders (1996), McConahay (1986), Pettigrew (1989).
53. Schuman, Steeh, and Bobo (1985).
54. For a detailed discussion of these criticisms, see Bobo (1983), Sidanius et al. (1992), Sniderman and Tetlock (1986), Sniderman, Piazza, Tetlock, and Kendrick (1991). For the most recent attempt to address these criticisms, see Sears, van Laar, Carrillo, and Kosterman (1997).
55. See, e.g., Coser (1956), Sherif, Harvey, White, Hood, and Sherif (1961), Sumner (1906).
56. See, e.g., Bobo (1983), Sherif, et al. (1961).
57. Pratto, Shih, and Orton (1997), Tajfel, Billig, Bundy, and Flament (1971); see Brewer and Silver (1978) for an exception.
58. Brewer and Silver (1978), Tajfel, et al. (1971); for reviews, see Brewer (1979), Tajfel and Turner (1986).
59. Doise (1990), Turner and Bourhis (1996).
60. Sachdev and Bourhis (1985, 1987).
61. See, e.g., Crocker and Major (1994), Luhtanen and Crocker (1991).
62. Ng (1980).
63. Sachdev and Bourhis (1985, 1991).
64. See, e.g., Ellemers, van Knippenberg, de Vries, and Wilke (1988), van Knippenberg, and Wilke (1990).
65. See review by Hinkle and Brown (1990).
66. For similar comments, see Mummendey et al. (1992).
67. For a demonstration of this thinking, see Zubrinsky and Bobo (1996a, 1996b).
68. For a more detailed short description of Marxism, see Ollman (1996).
69. See also Davis (1981), Hamamsy (1957), Sacks (1971) for further data and extensions of this theory.
70. However, Lenski (1984) also suggests that there might be some tendency for social inequality to decrease slightly in advanced industrial societies.
71. Mosca (1896/1939). For an interesting modern discussion of this general perspective, see Tilly (1998).
72. Michels (1911/1962).
73. Pareto (1935/1963).
74. Burnham (1964).
75. "The more things change, the more they stay the same."
76. For evidence that is compatible with this assertion, see Collier (1988), Humphrey (1985).

77. Pettigrew (1979).
78. Campbell (1965), Reynolds, Falger, and Vine (1987), van den Berghe (1978b).
79. For important discussions of this point, see, e.g., Gould (1981), Kitcher (1985), Lewontin, Rose, and Kamin (1984).
80. For similar perspectives, see Oyama (1991). See also Somit and Peterson (1997).

Chapter 2. Social Dominance Theory

1. Adorno et al. (1950).
2. Rokeach (1979).
3. Blumer (1960).
4. Michels (1911/1962), Mosca (1896/1939), Pareto (1901/1979).
5. Tajfel and Turner (1986).
6. Reynolds, Falger, and Vine (1987).
7. van den Berghe (1978a).
8. Based on sex, age, descent, and marriage.
9. However, it should be noted that this age system is not completely linear. Very old people (i.e., 80 years and above) do not always dominate over somewhat younger people (e.g., 60-year-olds).
10. French (1996).
11. Gurr and Harff (1994).
12. Lenski (1984), van den Berghe (1978a).
13. Lenski (1984).
14. Ibid.
15. Buraku Liberation Research Institute (1994).
16. Bachofen (1861/1969), Gimbutas (1989).
17. Murdock (1949).
18. Busch (1990), Collier and Yanagisako (1987), Keegan (1993).
19. Johns (1947), Seagle (1947/1971).
20. See, e.g., Abel and Nelson (1990), Beck and Keddie (1978).
21. Mt. 19:21–30, New International Version.
22. See, e.g., Feagin and Feagin (1978).
23. Koch (1996).
24. Pomper (1970).
25. See, e.g., Scott (1990).
26. See, e.g., Rowell (1974), pp. 139–143.
27. See also Eibl-Eibesfeldt (1989).
28. See, e.g., Deane (1968).
29. Merton (1972). For a more detailed discussion of this point, see Chapter 9.

30. "Protective discrimination" is the Indian version of "affirmative action" designed to help India's scheduled castes achieve economic, social, and political equality (Karanth, 1996).
31. Durkheim (1893/1933), Gramsci (1971), Marx and Engels (1846/1970), Mosca (1896/1939), Moscovici (1981, 1988).
32. "And, behold, there are last which shall be first, and there are first which shall be last" (LK. 13:30, King James Version).
33. See, e.g., Kluegel and Smith (1986).
34. Biddiss (1970).
35. Gottfredson (1977), Herrnstein and Murray (1994), Rushton (1996), Shockley (1972).
36. Bouchard (1994), Loehlin (1993), Zahn-Waxler, Robinson, and Emde (1992).
37. See, e.g., Almquist (1975), Beale (1970).
38. Putnam (1976).
39. Ibid., pp. 31–35.
40. This sample will be referred to as Sample 5. See Chapter 3 for more details concerning the samples used.
41. $F(4,2824) = 1186.94$, $p < 10^{-10}$.
42. The intraclass correlation coefficient can be used to describe how well the assessments by a sample of judges correlate with one another.
43. Euro-Americans: $N = 242$; Asian-Americans: $N = 164$; Latino-Americans: $N = 137$; African-Americans: $N = 62$.
44. The intraclass correlation coefficient based on the mean status ratings of the five ethnic groups was as high as .990.
45. For a more complete description of this sample (Sample 31), see Chapter 3. The intraclass coefficient across all individual raters was .9995, and the intraclass coefficient based on the mean status ratings for respondents in each of the four major ethnic groups was .9948. See Kraus (1982).
46. See, e.g., Bercovitch (1991), Leonard (1979), Mazur (1985), Sapolsky (1993, 1995).
47. See, e.g., Kawanaka (1989).
48. Kawanaka (1982), Nadler (1988), Strier (1994).
49. There is only one known exception to the general rule of male dominance among hominoids. While individual Bonobo males often tend to dominate individual females, Bonobo society as a whole is more accurately characterized as a matriarchy rather than a patriarchy. This is because female Bonobos tend to form long-lasting political alliances with one another, while male Bonobos do not. This fact enables groups of females to easily dominant individual males. The opposite pattern tends to hold among other hominoid species (Waal, 1997).

50. See Rowell (1974).
51. See, e.g., Alberts and Altmann (1995), Lee and Oliver (1979).
52. J. A. Johnson (1987).
53. Marsden (1968).
54. See, e.g., Harcourt (1988), Leigh and Shea (1995).
55. Ghiglieri (1989), Wrangham (1987).

Chapter 3.   The Psychology of Group Dominance

1. See, e.g., Rokeach (1979).
2. These scales have also been referred to as group dominance orientation scales in our earlier work.
3. The instructions to this scale read: "Below are a series of statements with which you may either agree or disagree. For each statement, please indicate the degree of your agreement or disagreement by *circling* the appropriate number from 1 to 7. Once again, remember that your first responses are usually the most accurate." There was a seven-point response scale: 7 = "Very positive," 6 = "Positive," 5 = "Slightly positive," 4 = "Neither positive nor negative," 3 = "Slightly negative," 2 = "Negative," 1 = "Very negative."
4. Note that the anti-egalitarianism and early SDO scales (i.e., SDO_1 to SDO_4) are sometimes referred to as group dominance orientation scales.
5. $t < 1$.
6. The α-reliability of the SDO_6 Scale was .91.
7. This was done by use of principal components.
8. A confirmatory factor analysis is a means of testing the plausibility of a hypothesized factor structure. A factor structure is a means of understanding the interrelationships among several variables in terms of a smaller number of hypothetical dimensions, or "factors." For a fuller discussion of these terms see, for example, Tabachnick and Fidell (1996).
9. Rokeach (1979).
10. For other work placing great weight on the general value of "equality," see Verba et al. (1987).
11. $\alpha = .85$.
12. $\alpha = .77$.
13. $\alpha = .72$.
14. The items removed were "Equal opportunity for all" (giving everyone an equal chance in life) and "Greater economic equality" (lessening the gap between the rich and poor).

15. See G. D. Wilson (1973), pp. 12–15.
16. See *The American Heritage Dictionary*, third edition.
17. G. D. Wilson (1973).
18. Ibid.
19. It is interesting to note that, while he strongly condemned the French Revolution, he favored the American Revolution because of its more moderate character and its basic resistance to radical notions of social leveling.
20. See, e.g., Buckley and Kesler (1988).
21. A partial correlation analysis allows one to determine the degree to which two variables are related to one another net of the effects of a third variable.
22. See, e.g., Frenkel-Brunswik (1948a, 1948b).
23. Duckitt (1989).
24. Both the Altemeyer and Goertzel authoritarianism measures have shown themselves to have acceptable reliability and construct validity (see Altemeyer, 1981; Goertzel, 1987; Pratto et al., 1994).
25. McFarland and Adelson (1996).
26. See Altemeyer (1998).
27. In most cases, political conservatism was measured by asking respondents to identify their own political positions across three domains: economic issues, foreign policy issues, and social issues. For each question, there was a seven-point response scale: 1 = "Very liberal," 2 = "Liberal," 3 = "Slightly liberal," 4 = "Middle of the road," 5 = "Slightly conservative," 6 = "Conservative," 7 = "Very conservative"; ($\alpha = .72$).
28. Gough (1987), Jackson (1965).
29. Pratto and Choudhury (1998). See also Pratto (1999).
30. $F(1, 336) = 4.47$, $p < .04$, $\eta = .11$.
31. $F(1, 51) = 12.98$, $p < .001$, $\eta = .45$; see Sidanius, Liu, Shaw, and Pratto (1994).
32. The linearity was given by $F(1, 460) = 51.03$, $p < .0001$, and the deviation from linearity was not statistically significant: $F(2, 460) = 1.01$, n.s.
33. The Ashkenazic Jews come from Europe, the United States, and South Africa, and the Sephardic Jews are from Spain, Asia, Africa, and the Middle East. Although socioeconomic conditions have improved for all Jewish groups over the past few decades, compared with the Sephardim, the Ashkenazim continue to enjoy a disproportionate share of the nation's wealth, occupational prestige, and education opportunities, even after controlling for several confounding variables.

34. $F(4, 1005) = 7.43$, $p < .001$, $\eta = .17$.
35. All comparisons used the Scheffé test and the .10 significance level.
36. These experiments were part of Shana Levin's (1996) doctoral dissertation.
37. The split-half reliability of these two SDO scale halves was .96.
38. $p < .001$.
39. Using a two-way repeated measures ANOVA, with repeated measures over context, the interaction between ethnic group and social context was statistically significant: $F(2, 638) = 3.28$, $p < .04$.
40. $F(1, 638) = 112.14$, $p < .001$.
41. $\alpha = .73$.
42. McConahay (1986).
43. Katz and Hass (1988).
44. Sears (1988).
45. In China and Israel, ethnic prejudice was defined by use of preference for ethnic endogamy.
46. The items of this rape myth scale read: (a) "In the majority of rapes, the victim is promiscuous or has a bad reputation," (b) "Women who go out alone at night get what they deserve," (c) "When a woman goes around wearing a short skirt she is just asking for trouble," (d) "If a girl engages in necking or petting and she lets things get out of hand, it is her own fault if her partner forces sex on her," (e) I don't respect women who have one-night stands"; Median $\alpha = .80$.
47. Weiner (1986).
48. The stem question read: "Despite changes in social and economic policy, African- and Hispanic Americans still suffer much lower living standards than other groups. Several explanations have been suggested for this poverty. Using the scale below, indicate the degree to which you agree or disagree with each of these explanations."
49. The exact questions were – *internal attributions*: (a) "African-Americans are less intellectually able than other groups, (b) "African-Americans are lazier than other groups," (c) "Latinos are less intellectually able than other groups," (d) "Latinos are lazier than other groups." *External attributions*: (e) "African-Americans have poor schools and live in bad neighborhoods," (f) "African-Americans still suffer from the effects of past discrimination and racism," (g) "Latinos have poor schools and live in bad neighborhoods," (h) "Latinos still suffer from the effects of past discrimination and racism."
50. The "Fate" Scale was measured by four items: (a) "Being poor is just one's fate," (b) "The rich have been favored by the gods," (c) "The poor aren't deserving in the eyes of the gods," (d) "One must please the gods in order to be successful"; $\alpha = .72$.

51. The stem question read: "People give many reasons for their position on affirmative action. I am going to read you some of these reasons. For each one, please tell me how important this reason is for your position on affirmative action." For each reason read, the respondents were asked, "Is this consideration a very important reason, somewhat important reason, not very important reason, or not at all important reason for your position on affirmative action?"
52. Pratto, Orton, and Stallworth (1997).
53. A second experiment in which college students read pairs of essays for and against the policy showed the same type of interaction between HE/HA essay pair and participant SDO level.
54. Pratto et al. (1994).
55. For the exact wording of these questions, see Pratto et al. (1994), p. 753.
56. Robert Alton Harris, who was convicted of killing two teenage boys by the State of California in 1978, was to be the first person executed at the prison in 23 years.
57. See Sidanius, Pratto, Sinclair, and van Laar (1996) for more details and examples of each role type.
58. See Sidanius, Liu, Shaw, and Pratto (1994); see also Chapter 8.
59. Conducted with Sample 10 and with a combined sample using respondents from San Jose State University and Stanford University (Samples 16, 17, 18, and 23) to replicate the first findings from Sample 10.
60. These controls were deployed using sex as an independent variable in simultaneous regression-style analyses of variance with planned contrasts.
61. $F(1, 432) = 10.21, p < .01$.
62. Sidanius, Pratto, Sinclair, and van Laar (1996).
63. These controls were exercised by use of simultaneous, multiple regression analysis. Socioeconomic status was defined using two separate indices: respondent's yearly family income, and self-rated family class position. The latter index was rated with a question asking respondents to place their family into one of five social class positions ($\alpha = .58$). Using seven-point response scales, political conservatism was measured by the use of four indices: (a) "political party preference," (b) "self-rated degree of economic conservatism" (from *very liberal* to *very conservative*), (c) self-rated degree of social conservatism" (from *very liberal* to *very conservative*), and (d) degree of support for free-market capitalism (from *strongly disapprove* to *strongly favor*); $\alpha = .75$.
64. See Sidanius, Pratto, and Mitchell (1994) for details.

65. Pratto, Shih, and Orton (1997).
66. Among other things, principled conservatism theorists assert that po-
    litical conservatism and racism are essentially independent of one
    another. See, e.g., Cymrot (1985), Sniderman and Piazza (1993).
67. See, e.g., Adorno et al. (1950), G. D. Wilson (1973); see esp. Sidanius
    and Pratto (1993), Sidanius, Pratto, and Bobo (1996).
68. See, e.g., Dator (1969), Eysenck (1951, 1971, 1976), Eysenck and Coulter
    (1972), Jackson and Kirby (1991), Nias (1972), Sidanius (1987),
    Sidanius and Ekehammar (1979), Sidanius et al. (1979), Stone and
    Russ (1976), G. D. Wilson (1973), Wilson and Bagley (1973), Wilson
    and Lee (1974), Wilson and Patterson (1968).
69. This was the case at least as of the late 1970s, when much of this
    Swedish data was collected (Sidanius & Ekehammar, 1976, 1979).
70. The items defining each dimension and their associated LISREL fac-
    tor loadings (i.e., λs) were – *Anti-egalitarianism*: (a) "Increased social
    equality" ($\lambda = .67$), (b) "Social welfare" ($\lambda = .63$), (c) "Social equality"
    ($\lambda = .78$), and (d) "Increased democracy on the job" ($\lambda = .66$). *Political
    conservatism*: (a) "Increased socialization" ($\lambda = .89$), (b) "Socialism"
    ($\lambda = .89$), (c) "Capitalism" ($\lambda = .73$), (d) "Nationalization of private
    companies" ($\lambda = .55$), and (e) "Political party preference" (from com-
    munist to fascist; $\lambda = .80$). *Racism*: (a) "White superiority" ($\lambda = .83$)
    and (b) "Racial superiority" ($\lambda = .82$). All items used a seven-point
    response scale.
71. *Classical racism* was defined by the attributions used to explain the
    relatively poor social situation of Blacks compared with Whites: (a)
    "Because most Blacks have less in-born ability to learn" ($\lambda = .71$), (b)
    "Because other races are just more capable than Blacks" ($\lambda = .56$),
    (c) "Because most Blacks just don't have the motivation or willpower
    to pull themselves up out of poverty"; $\lambda = .70$. The responses were
    given on a five-point scale ranging from *strongly agree* to *strongly
    disagree*.
        Political conservatism was operationalized by use of three indices:
    (a) self-classification into one of seven categories (i.e., from 1 = *very
    liberal* to 7 = *very conservative*; $\lambda = .72$), (b) political partisanship (i.e.,
    from 1 = *strong Democrat*, to 7 = *strong Republican*; $\lambda = .69$), and
    (c) political issues positions. This was indexed as the respondents'
    average degree of support for/opposition to eight political issues,
    including (a) "Support for the death penalty," (b) "Spending to im-
    prove the environment," (c) "Spending for health care," (d) "Spending
    for educational improvement," (e) "Spending for social security," (f)
    "Spending for the poor," (g) "Spending for the military and defense,"

and (h) "Affective response to business executives" (i.e., using the standard feeling thermometer scale); $\lambda = .65$.

The items of the SDO$_4$ Scale and their associated factor loadings were as follows: (a) "Sometimes war is necessary to put other countries in their place" ($\lambda = .57$), (b) "This country would be better off if inferior groups stayed in their place" ($\lambda = .59$), (c) "Some people are just better cut out than others for important positions in society" ($\lambda = .46$), (d) "Some people are better at running things and should be allowed to do so" ($\lambda = .40$).

72. The items of the SDO$_6$ Scale and their associated factor loadings were as follows: (a) "If certain groups of people stayed in their place, we would have fewer problems" ($\lambda = .58$), (b) "It's probably a good thing that certain groups are at the top and other groups are at the bottom" ($\lambda = .62$), (c) "Sometimes other groups must be kept in their place" ($\lambda = .56$), (d) "Group equality should be our ideal" ($\lambda = .80$), (e) "We should do what we can to equalize conditions for different groups" ($\lambda = .80$), (f) "Increased social equality" ($\lambda = .80$).

Classical racism was defined using four indices: (a) "Blacks are inherently inferior" ($\lambda = .72$) and (b) "White superiority" ($\lambda = .70$). In addition, subjects were asked to rate several attributions for the lower standard of living among African-Americans: (c) "Blacks are less intellectually able than other groups" ($\lambda = .76$) and (d) "Blacks are lazier than other groups"; $\lambda = .76$.

Political conservatism was defined using four indices: (a) political party preference (i.e., $1 = $ *very liberal* to $7 = $ *very conservative*; $\lambda = .69$), (b) political partisanship (from $1 = $ *strong Democrat* to $7 = $ *strong Republican*; $\lambda = .77$), (c) degree of support for "Free-market capitalism" ($\lambda = .61$), and (d) the students' average degree of support for/opposition to five policy issues, including, "Greater assistance to the poor," "Increased taxation of the rich," "Universal health care," "Reduced public support for the homeless, and "Reduced benefits for the unemployed"; $\lambda = .93$.

73. SDO items and their associated factor loadings were as follows: (a) "To get ahead in life, it is sometimes necessary to step on other groups" ($\lambda = .58$), (b) "Inferior groups should stay in their place" ($\lambda = .51$), (c) "If certain groups stayed in their place, we would have fewer problems," ($\lambda = .50$), (d) "All groups should be given an equal chance in life" ($\lambda = .78$), (e) "Increased social equality" ($\lambda = .75$), and (f) "No one group should dominate in society" ($\lambda = .49$).

Political conservatism was measured by two items: (a) "Aid to the poor" ($\lambda = .91$) and (b) "Raise taxes for the rich" ($\lambda = .86$).

Anti-miscegenation attitudes were measured by two items: (a) "Interracial marriage" ($\lambda = .86$) and (b) "Interracial dating" ($\lambda = .42$). All items were measured on a seven-point scale ranging from *strongly agree* to *strongly disagree*.

74. *SDO* items and associated factor loadings were as follows: (a) "We should do what we can to equalize conditions for different groups" ($\lambda = .84$), (b) "Increased social equality" ($\lambda = .81$), (c) "We should strive to make incomes as equal as possible" ($\lambda = .62$), (d) "Sometimes other groups must be kept in their place" ($\lambda = .23$), (e) "Inferior groups should stay in their place" ($\lambda = .16$), (f) "It's probably a good thing that certain groups are at the top and other groups are at the bottom" ($\lambda = .27$).

Classical racism was defined by the attributions used to explain the relatively poor social situation of Blacks compared with Whites: (a) "Because most Blacks have less in-born ability to learn" ($\lambda = .47$) and (b) "Because most Blacks just don't have the motivation or willpower to pull themselves out of poverty" ($\lambda = .57$).

Political conservatism was measured by five items: (a) political party preference (from *strong Democrat* to *strong Republican*; $\lambda = .73$), (b) Political self-description (from *very liberal* to *very conservative*; $\lambda = .65$). In addition, we asked the respondents to indicate their degree of agreement with three sociopolitical policies: (c) "The government should guarantee that basic health care is available for all Americans" ($\lambda = .55$), (d) "The government should lower taxes" ($\lambda = .31$), (e) "The government has taken over too many things that should be handled by individuals, families, and private businesses" ($\lambda = .58$).

75. All correlations were significant at the .05 level or below.
76. These analyses used LISREL 8.
77. Sidanius, Pratto, and Bobo (1996).

Chapter 4. "Let's Both Agree That You're Really Stupid"

1. For an excellent discussion of this point, see Jackman (1994).
2. A similar argument could be made about the U.S. losses in the Vietnam War.
3. Jost (1995), p. 400.
4. Sanday (1971).
5. Merton (1972).
6. See, e.g., Nunnally and Bernstein (1994).
7. Ibid., pp. 237–239.

8. $F(9, 163) = 28.35$, $p < 10^{-5}$, $\eta = .22$. There were 10 ethnic/racial categories defined for these analyses: Whites ($N = 3,926$), Blacks ($N = 213$), Mexican-Americans ($N = 434$), Native Americans ($N = 28$), Asian-Americans ($N = 154$), European nationals ($N = 61$), Asian nationals ($N = 150$), Mideastern nationals ($N = 28$), and "Others" ($N = 84$).

9. $F(1, 297) = 934.10$, $p < 10^{-12}$, $\eta = .39$.

10. Besides using simply race and gender as predictor variables in the regression analyses, in order to extract that maximum amount of variance accountable in terms of social group membership, we also regressed the racism and sexism scores on other demographic and background variables such as religious denomination, the students' expected grades in the class, the students' grade point average, and the students' educational rank (freshman, sophomore, junior, senior, or graduate student).

11. Please note that the reliabilities here are estimated by use of Cronbach's α-coefficient. Since Cronbach's α defines reliability more in terms of domain sampling theory than classical measurement theory, these reliability estimates should be considered rough estimates.

12. Using a seven-point response scale ranging from *very positive* to *very negative*, the scale was formed from the following items – *Political conservatism*: (a) "Socialism," (b) "Capitalism," (c) "Totally free capitalism." *Racism*: (a) "Russian superiority," (b) "Racial equality," (c) "Interracial/interethnic marriage," (d) "Racially integrated neighborhoods," (e) "Racial/ethnic minorities are inherently inferior," (f) "Interracial dating." *Aid to minorities scale*: (a) "Less help to ethnic minorities," (b) "Reduced benefits for the unemployed," and (c) "Helping minorities get good educations is good for everyone."

13. This is seen by comparing the reliability of the consensual scores with that of the original scores. For example, while the reliability of the original SDO scores was .77, the reliability of the residual scores had only decreased to .73.

14. The respondents were asked to indicate their level of support for affirmative action on a five-point scale ranging from *very positive* to *very negative*.

15. Indexed by four items: (a) "greater assistance to the poor," (b) "universal health care," (c) "reduced public support for the homeless," and (d) "reduced benefits for the unemployed."

16. As indexed by five items: (a) "Government should see to it that minorities get fair treatment in jobs," (b) "Government should not pass laws concerning the hiring of ethnic minorities," (c) "Government should ensure that Whites and minorities go to the same school,"

(d) "Government should do what it can to improve the economic condition of poor ethnic minorities," and (e) "Affirmative action."

17. As indexed by two items: (a) "Government should ensure that minorities can go to any hotel or restaurant they can afford" and (b) "Government has no business trying to ensure minority access to hotels and restaurants."

18. Indexed by the question "What sentences did Officers Powell and Koon receive for the Rodney King beating?": (a) "Acquitted," (b) "Suspended sentence," (c) "6 months in jail," (d) "2 years in jail," (d) "5 years in jail," (e) "10 years in jail," (f) "15 years in jail," (g) "Don't know."

19. This item used a Tajfelian-type allocation matrix, and the question asked respondents to allocate $60 million to two social policies (i.e., more money to prisons and police, and more money to improve education in poor neighborhoods) in a long-term plan to alleviate the state's crime problem. The choices were (a) "$55 million to prisons and police versus $5 million to education," (b) "$50 million to prisons and police versus $10 million to education," (c) "$40 million to prisons and police versus $20 million to education," (d) "$30 million to prisons and police versus $30 million to education," (e) "$20 million to prisons and police versus $40 million to education," (f) "$10 million to prisons and police versus $50 million to education," (g) "$5 million to prisons and police versus $55 million to education."

20. This item consisted of a maximize-group-difference-type Tajfelian allocation matrix. The question read: "Assume that the Regents of the University of California have decided to allocate an unspecified amount of money to the support of various ethnic student organizations. Some of these organizations consist of predominantly White students, while others consist of primarily minority students." The allocation choices were (a) "$7 million to White groups versus $1 million to minority groups," (b) "$9 million to White groups versus $5 million to minority groups," (c) "$11 million to White groups versus $9 million to minority groups," (d) "$13 million to White groups versus $13 million to minority groups," (e) "$15 million to White groups versus $17 million to minority groups," (f) "$17 million to White groups versus $21 million to minority groups," and (g) "$19 million to White groups versus $25 million to minority groups."

21. The Los Angeles Police Department officers convicted of the beating of Rodney King.

22. Theses analyses were conducted by use of recursive LISREL 8 models. In each case, almost all elements of the Ψ-matrix were allowed to be

free. All elements of this matrix involving the social policy attitudes were fixed. This resulted in fully saturated models.

23. Including nonlinear and interactive specification.

Part III. The Circle of Oppression

1. J. M. Jones (1997).
2. For a more complex classification scheme of institutional discrimination, see Feagin and Feagin (1978).
3. Hochschild (1995).
4. See, e.g., D'Souza (1995), Loury (1985), Patterson (1997).

Chapter 5. " You Stay in Your Part of Town, and I'll Stay in Mine"

1. Lange (1996).
2. Please note that these figures are based only on the immigrants living in the large cities of Sweden.
3. See, e.g., Hraba, Hagendoorn, and Hagendoorn (1989).
4. Frey and Farley (1993).
5. Education: $r = .13$, $p < .01$; income: $r = .13$, $p < .01$. However, multiple regression analysis disclosed that of these two variables, education rather than income was the stronger. The number of Blacks in this subsample was 473.
6. Listokin and Casey (1980).
7. See *Civil Rights at the Department of Agriculture: A Report by the Civil Rights Action Team.* http://www.usda.gov/news/civil/wpindex.htm
8. The Boston Fed studies are reported by Munnell, Browne, McEneaney, and Tootell (1992).
9. For an example of criticism that should be taken less seriously, see Longhofer (1996).
10. There are several ways in which equation misspecification may occur, including assuming that the relationship between the outcome measure and a predictor variable is linear rather than curvilinear, failing to consider interactions among predictor variables, and failing to consider possible simultaneity effects in statistical equations.
11. See also Tootell (1996).
12. For a detailed discussion of these criticisms, see Carr and Magbolugbe (1994).
13. Tootell (1996).
14. Tajfel (1978, 1982), Tajfel and Turner (1979, 1986).
15. Note that some have even remarked that, rather than examining differential loan approval, a more appropriate test of mortgage

discrimination would be achieved by studying default rates instead. However, the logical and conceptual flaws of this approach have been clearly demonstrated and widely accepted (see detailed discussion by Yinger, 1986, pp. 39–43), even by those generally skeptical of the Boston Fed's findings.

16. Goering and Wienk (1996), Tootell (1996), Yinger (1995, 1996).
17. See McIntosh and Smith (1974).
18. The home purchase data are based on what is defined as "different treatment" for Whites as opposed to immigrants.
19. See Yinger (1996). See also Galster (1990).
20. McEntire (1960).
21. Wienk et al. (1979).
22. Ibid.
23. Yinger (1991a, 1991b).
24. Yinger (1996), p. 179.
25. This number was simply the number of housing units inspected by either dominants or subordinates.
26. For a more comprehensive comparison of the HDS and HMPS audits, see Elmi and Mikelsons (1991).
27. Reid (1987), Yinger (1986, 1995).
28. An *opportunity cost* is defined as the advantage forgone as the result of the acceptance of a given alternative. It is measured as the benefits that would result from the next best alternative use of the same resources that were rejected in favor of the one accepted. *Transaction costs* are defined as the costs associated with producing and selling goods and services. In the case of a housing search, we could define the transaction costs as the total costs associated with the search.
29. Yinger (1995), pp. 89–103.
30. For further evidence of housing discrimination, see Zubrinsky and Bobo (1996a, 1996b).
31. Governor's Commission report (1965), Sturdivant (1971), Sturdivant and Wilhelm (1968).
32. Ayres (1991).
33. Ayres (1995).
34. Thus, these numbers represent unstandardized regression coefficients for the dummy-variable-coded race–ethnicity combinations from a multiple regression equation.
35. Not significant at the 0.05 level.
36. A *reservation price* can be understood in the following terms: "The oldest pair of never-worn, never-washed Levi's jeans in the world is a discrete good. A consumer can only buy 0 or 1 unit of the good. If

the price is very high, a consumer would strictly prefer to purchase zero units. If the price is low enough, the consumer will strictly prefer to purchase one unit. At some price, the consumer will be indifferent between purchasing one unit or not purchasing it. The price at which the consumer is just indifferent, the highest price the consumer is willing to pay for a unit of the good, is called the reservation price" (Quintanilla, 1995).

37. Ayres and Siegelman (1995).

Chapter 6. "They're Just Too Lazy to Work"

1. Please note that these data are the average percentages of those who have experienced discrimination in the labor market at least once within the last five years.
2. D. J. Smith (1976), pp. 95–97.
3. Sandoval (1991).
4. ATSIC (1994).
5. These subordinates consisted primarily of Italian, Moroccan, French, and Turkish immigrants (Zegers de Beijl, 1990).
6. See, e.g., Sowell (1984, p. 116).
7. Zegers de Beijl (1990).
8. Commission Nationale Consultative des Droits de l'Homme (1990), Costa-Lascoux (1989).
9. Commission for Racial Equality (1996), Cross (1987).
10. Fase (1989), Roelandt and Veenman (1990).
11. See also Brassé and Sikking (1986), Veenman and Vijverberg (1982).
12. Cited in Zegers de Beijl (1990); see also Commission Nationale Consultative des Droits de l'Homme (1990).
13. W. J. Wilson (1996).
14. See, e.g., Adams (1979), Granotier (1979).
15. For similar findings in Germany, see Gillmeister, Kurthen, and Fijalkowski (1989).
16. Zegers de Beijl (1990).
17. Ibid., p. 44.
18. Fernandez (1975), Kluegel (1978), Mueller, Parcel, and Kazuko (1989).
19. Collins (1983, 1989), see also G. Wilson (1997).
20. R. A. Smith (1997).
21. Lattes (1989).
22. Verhaeren (1982).
23. Ramcharan (1976).
24. Mehrländer (1986).

25. See Zegers de Beijl (1990).
26. We are immensely grateful to Zegers de Beijl for supplying us with much of this background information.
27. D. J. Smith (1976), p. 87.
28. Koelewijn-Strattner (1991).
29. M. Reich (1981).
30. Bovenkerk (1992).
31. For a discussion of some of these methodological differences, see Bendick (1996).
32. D. J. Smith (1977).
33. Bendick (1996), Bendick, Jackson, and Reinoso (1994), Bendick, Jackson, Reinoso, and Hodges (1991), Cross et al. (1990), Fix and Bean (1990), Turner et al., (1991).
34. These controls were established by use of COANOVA.
35. The equation for this curve can be written as $1 - (1 - p)^n$, where p is the probability of being discriminated against in any given job search and n is the number of jobs applied for.
36. Bendick (1996), pp. 29–30.
37. See, e.g., Culp and Dunson (1986), Guion (1966).
38. Note that multiple regression analysis allows one to examine the effects on a single dependent variable (in this case net discrimination) as a simultaneous function of several independent variables (e.g., audit method used, gender of applicant).
39. Mean$_W$ indicates the weighted mean.
40. See, e.g., Gallaway (1971), Ramussen (1970), Thurow (1969).
41. These controls were employed by use of an analysis of covariance. Note also that only method and skill level were controlled because these factors proved to be the most relevant.
42. Goldberg et al. (1996)
43. Bovenkerk et al. (1994).
44. See, also Bendick (1996).
45. For a more modern elaboration of Becker's theory, see Sowell (1981).
46. See esp. R. A. Epstein (1992).
47. Goldberg et al. (1996).
48. See arguments about HA and HE roles; see also van Laar, Sidanius, Rabinowitz, and Sinclair (1999).
49. Bendick (1989).
50. Ibid. However, there are also some nonexperimental data indicating that firms announcing themselves to be equal opportunity employers do indeed discriminate less (Konrad and Linnehan, 1995).
51. $\chi^2(1) = 4.53$, $p < .03$.

52. The effect for target of affirmative action was statistically significant at the 0.001 level, $F(2, 596) = 13.05$.

53. It should also be noted that these differences were not affected by the respondents' gender, and the patterns of affirmative action opposition were essentially the same for both men and women.

54. Recall that multiple regression analysis examines an outcome variable (in this case affirmative action opposition with respect to a specific recipient) as a function of several independent variables.

55. These affective ratings used standard "feeling thermometer" ratings.

Chapter 7.   "They're Just Mentally and Physically Unfit"

1. Fort (1996).
2. Torney, Oppenheim, and Farnen (1975).
3. The only exception to this pattern we are aware of that uses large samples is the work of Magiste (1992). Even there, however, the second generation of immigrant children was found to be more isolated and have higher delinquency levels than a control group of native Swedes.
4. Lee (1991).
5. Shimahara (1991).
6. Ito (1967).
7. Ogbu (1978).
8. Ogbu (1991a).
9. Taylor (1995).
10. Kozol (1991).
11. Pyle (1997).
12. Kozol (1991).
13. Ibid., p. 208.
14. Ibid., pp. 208–209.
15. Ibid., p. 175.
16. Feagin and Feagin (1978).
17. See, e.g., Hansche, Gottfried, and Hansche (1982), Harry and Anderson (1995).
18. Kozol (1991), p. 119.
19. Serwatka, Deering, and Grant (1995).
20. Lanier and Wittmer (1977). For similar results with Latino children, see Zucker and Prieto (1977). However, there is also some exceptions to this evidence (see, e.g., Low and Clement, 1982).
21. Persell (1977), I. Smith (1981).
22. Sandoval (1991).
23. Shavit (1984).

24. Gamoran (1987).
25. Shavit (1984).
26. J. L. Epstein (1985).
27. Rosenthal and Jacobson (1968).
28. See, e.g., Brophy (1982, 1983), Darley and Fazio (1980), Harris and Rosenthal (1985), Jussim and Eccles (1992, 1995).
29. See, e.g., Allington (1980), Chaiken, Sigler, and Derlaga (1974).
30. See, e.g., Rubovits and Maehr (1973).
31. Ogbu (1991b).
32. See, e.g., Damstuen (1997), Magiste (1992), Steinberg (1996).
33. For similar results, see Woo (1997).
34. Simmons, Black, and Zhou (1991).
35. Gibson (1991).
36. U.S. Department of State Report on Human Rights in Australia (1997).
37. See, e.g., Manton, Patrick, and Johnson (1987).
38. For an in-depth and excellent review of literature concerning the socioeconomic status–health gradient, see Adler et al. (1994).
39. For similar findings in the United Kingdom, see, e.g., Adelstein (1980), Susser, Watson, and Hopper (1985).
40. See also studies by Pappas, Queen, Hadden, and Fisher (1993).
41. *Mortality* was here defined as the ratio between the number of observed deaths and the number of expected deaths.
42. Wilkinson (1992a, 1992b).
43. Somatization disorder is diagnosed as multiple physical complaints in multiple organ systems for which no organic cause can be found.
44. Blazer, Hughes, George, Swartz, and Boyer (1991).
45. Sapolsky (1993).
46. Munck, Guyre, and Holbrook (1984).
47. The reason that this HDL-C/LDL-C ratio is relevant to health outcomes is that it is widely recognized as being associated with atherosclerosis (which is a form of arteriosclerosis characterized by the deposition of atheromatous plaques containing cholesterol and lipids on the innermost layer of the walls of large and medium-sized arteries), and coronary heart disease among both baboons and humans (McGill, McMahan, Kruski, & Mott, 1981; Miller and Miller, 1975).
48. Manuck, Kaplan, Adams, and Clarkson (1988).
49. Bond, Bullock, Bellinger, and Hamm (1980), Kaplan, Adams, Clarkson, and Koritnick (1984).
50. Manuck et al. (1988).
51. See also Kaplan et al. (1984).

52. Murphy (1997).
53. S. Lindqvist (1997).
54. This institute was finally abolished in 1958 (Zaremba, 1997a).
55. Zaremba (1997a, 1997b).
56. Ruth (1997).
57. Zaremba (1997a).
58. "Ökat antal" (1997).
59. Hall (1997).
60. Herrnstein and Murray (1994).
61. Holhut (1996).
62. J. H. Jones (1993).
63. Peterson, Schwirian, and Bleda (1997).
64. This difference was statistically significant at the .001 level.
65. See, e.g., Gaston (1996), Gaston et al. (1994).
66. Geller et al. (1996).
67. $p < .001$ in both cases.
68. $p < .001$.
69. $p < .001$.
70. These ratios were significantly different from 1.00 in both cases (i.e., $p < .001$).
71. Lowe, Kerridge, and Mitchell (1995).
72. Kogan, Kotelchuk, Alexander, and Johnson (1994).
73. See also Krieger and Fee (1996).
74. See, e.g., Galap, Raveau, and Chiche (1985), Hughes and Hertel (1990), Hurtado (1994).
75. Glieberman, Harburg, Frone, Russell, and Cooper (1995). However, alternative explanations remain as well. For example, Gleiberman et al. point out that dark skin color may be a marker for genes of West African origin or be related directly to blood pressure through an as yet unknown biochemical pathway.
76. Hahn et al. (1996).

Chapter 8. "The More of 'Them' in Prison, the Better"

1. Older (1984).
2. Sanson-Fisher (1978), Walker (1989, 1994).
3. T. J. Young (1993).
4. Meyer (1992).
5. Fanon (1963).
6. Hood and Cordovil (1992).
7. Junger and Polder (1992).

8. Von Hofer and Tham (1991).
9. Poikolainen, Nayha, and Hassi (1992)
10. De Vos (1992), Kristof (1995).
11. U.S. Committee for Refugees (1996).
12. Sherer (1990).
13. Schiraldi, Kuyper, and Hewitt (1996).
14. Ibid.
15. Tillman (1987).
16. The "three-strikes" law stipulates that anyone convicted of three felonies is subject to a mandatory prison sentence of 25 years to life.
17. Schiraldi, Kuyper, and Hewitt (1996).
18. Davidson (1997), pp. 36–37.
19. These states were Rhode Island, Kansas, Texas, Utah, New Jersey, Nebraska, Illinois, Wisconsin, Connecticut, Pennsylvania, Iowa, and Minnesota; see ibid.
20. Espy and Smykla (1996).
21. Once again, these data are more consistent with the SMTH than with the double jeopardy hypothesis (see Chapter 2).
22. Voight, Thornton, Barrile, and Seaman (1994).
23. See, e.g., Durkheim (1933), Parsons (1951, 1962), Pound (1943/1959).
24. The specific question read, "Who do you think is treated more harshly in this country's criminal justice system – Blacks or Whites – or are they treated about the same?"
25. See, e.g., Turk (1969), Vold (1958/1979), Weber (1922).
26. See, e.g., Chambliss (1984), Dahrendorf (1959), Marx (1904), Quinney (1974, 1977).
27. See, e.g., Durkheim (1933), Parsons (1951, 1962), Pound (1943/1959).
28. For similar arguments, see Chevigny (1995), Ericson (1982).
29. See the *Pocket Oxford Dictionary of Current English*, seventh edition, 1991.
30. For a further discussion of other models of this type, see Vagged et al. (1994).
31. Miller (1993).
32. Hoig (1961).
33. Hedges (1994), McCuen (1988), Pauw (1991).
34. Glick (1989).
35. Brundage (1993), Finkelman (1992), Grant, (1975), Pomper (1970), Raper (1969), Wells-Barnett (1990).
36. Blumstein (1982), Bourg and Stock (1994), Hawkins and Jones (1989), Hepburn (1978), Holcomb and Ahr (1988), Hollinger (1984), Petersen et al. (1977), Sarri (1986), Schellenberg, Wasylenki, Webster, and

Goering (1992), Smith, Visher, and Davisdon (1984), Thornberry (1973), Visher (1983), Weisz, Martin, Walter, and Fernandez (1991).
37. Bourg and Stock (1994), Bradmiller and Walters (1985), Sorensen and Wallace (1995), Stewart (1985).
38. Ayres and Waldfogel (1994).
39. Sarri (1986).
40. Bernard (1979), Cohen and Peterson (1981), Kelly (1976), Lichtenstein (1982), Lipton (1983), Mazzella and Feingold (1994), Poulson (1990), Wilbanks (1988).
41. Austin (1985), Kelly (1976), Osborne and Rappaport (1985), Pruitt and Wilson (1983), Sidanius (1988), Stewart (1980, 1985), Sweeney and Haney (1992), Towers, McGinley, and Pasework (1992), Thornberry (1973), Uhlman (1979).
42. Austin (1985), Petersen and Friday (1975).
43. Dunwoody and Frank (1994), Myers (1985).
44. Lynch and Sabol (1994).
45. National Association of Criminal Defense Lawyers (1996).
46. Taken from Mauer and Huling (1995), p. 12. Note that these data are for 1992 or 1993, depending on the most recent data available.
47. Ibid., p. 2.
48. Mauer (1990); see also Reinarman (1995).
49. Hardt (1968), also Heussenstamm (1971).
50. ACLU (1997).
51. Junger and Polder (1992).
52. See also Mair (1986).
53. Maas and Stuyling de Lange (1989).
54. Bosma (1985).
55. Timmerman, Bosma, and Jongman (1986). For contradictory findings, see Beijers, Hille, and de Leng (1994).
56. Cunneen (1990), Walker (1994).
57. Sanson-Fisher (1978).
58. Sherer (1990).
59. Daniszewski (1997).
60. Guillou (1996a).
61. Guillou (1996b).
62. Von Hofer and Tham (1991).
63. Cole and Gittens (1995), p. iv.
64. Hood and Cordovil (1992).
65. See also Skogan (1990), Smith and Gray (1985).
66. Hood and Sparks (1970), Sherer (1990), Unnerver and Hembroff (1988).
67. $p < .002$.

68. $p < .06$.
69. Cole and Gittens (1995), p. 315.
70. Ibid., pp. 312–314.
71. Espy and Smykla (1996).
72. Needless to say, the overall relationship between race and execution brutality was statistically significant ($\chi^2(2) = 43.85$, $p < 0.0001$, $\Phi = .08$).
73. $\chi^2(4) = 73.88$, $p < 0.0001$, $\Phi = .15$.
74. Figure 8.3 contains a standardized residual, which provides a readily interpretable index of the degree to which the observed frequency in a cell deviates from the expected frequency for that cell. The standardized residual is given as:

$$z_p = \frac{x - \mu}{\sqrt{\mu}}$$

where x is the observed frequency for a cell and μ is the expected frequency for that cell. For large N, z_p is approximately normally distributed.
75. Chambliss (1973).
76. Arkin (1980), Baldus, Pulaski, and Woodsworth (1983), Baldus, Woodsworth, and Pulaski (1985), Bowers and Pierce (1980), Gross and Mauro (1989), Keil and Vito (1989), Paternoster (1984), Radelet (1981).
77. GAO (1990).
78. In *Furman v. Georgia*, 408 U.S. 238 (1972), the Supreme Court declared unconstitutional all death sentences imposed under state statutes that allowed juries to apply these sentences in an arbitrary or capricious manner. Subsequent to this ruling, states adopted new statutes that addressed these concerns of the Supreme Court.
79. *Furman v. Georgia* (1972), p. 6.
80. See also Rohrich and Tulsky (1996), Amnesty International (1998).
81. Paternoster (1983).
82. Paternoster (1984); see also Foley (1987), Sorensen and Wallace (1995).
83. Williams and Farrell (1990).
84. LaFree (1989); see also Sobral, Arce, and Farina (1989), Spohn (1994).
85. Farrell and Swigert (1978).
86. Note, this law is a revision of the third law of law as described in Sidanius (1993).
87. For a more detailed description of the samples and the overall study, see Sidanius, Liu, Shaw and Pratto (1994).

88. Most items used a seven-point response scale. For further details, see ibid.

89. These analyses were conducted by use of one-way ANOVA ($F(3, 591)$ $= 83.04$, $p < 0.001$, $\eta = .38$) and Sheffé posthoc comparisons.

90. These conclusions were reached by use of Scheffé posthoc comparisons ($p < 0.10$). Note, the only contrast that was not statistically reliable was between public defenders and university students.

91. Teahan (1975a).

92. Teahan (1975b).

93. Leitner and Sedlacek (1976).

94. Christopher (1991).

95. Ibid.

96. Kennedy (1997).

97. Chevigny (1995).

98. For a full treatment of this thesis, see Scott (1990).

99. Social hierarchy was operationalized by the use of three indicators: (a) class hierarchy (or the amount of economic inequality within each state), (b) caste hierarchy (the degree of economic inequality between Blacks and Whites and the degree to which Blacks were underrepresented in the state legislature), and (c) Confederacy (whether or not a state was part of the states of the Old Confederacy). For details of these analyses, see Mitchell and Sidanius (1995).

100. Social hierarchy was defined by the commonly used GINI index. This index "sums for each individual in the population the difference between where he is on the Lorenz curve, and where he would be expected to be in the case of democratic equality" (Alker, 1965). The greater the GINI index, the greater the inequality in the nation. The GINI index for the year 1970 was obtained from the *World Handbook of Political and Social Indicators* (Taylor and Jodice, 1983).

101. This question was worded as follows: "Some people are afraid of the police, while others are not. What are your feelings toward the police?" The response alternatives were "Very afraid," "Somewhat afraid," "Not very afraid," and "Not at all afraid."

102. These other demographic variables were education, political conservatism, income, gender, and citizenship (i.e., U.S. citizen vs. non–U.S. citizen).

103. The covariates of education, political conservatism, income, gender and citizenship were controlled by use of an analysis of covariance: $F(3, 528) = 3.71$, $p < 0.01$, $\eta = .16$, $\beta = .15$.

104. The poor and wealthy income classes were defined in terms of being one standard deviation below and above the mean.
105. Education, political conservatism, gender, and citizenship.
106. The covariates of ethnicity, education, political conservatism, gender, and citizenship were controlled by use of an analysis of covariance: $F(2, 558) = 4.02$, $p < .02$, $\eta = .12$, $\beta = .13$.
107. Daly (1994), Freyerhern (1981), Heilbrun (1982), Mann (1984), Nagel (1983), Visher (1983); for the exception to this general trend, see Meyer (1992).
108. Daly and Bordt (1991).
109. For similar findings, see Bureau of Justice Statistics Fact Sheet (1995).
110. Walker (1989).
111. Ibid.
112. Bernstein, Kick, Leung, and Schulz (1977), Visher (1983).
113. See, e.g., Gallup (1997).

Chapter 9.   Social Hierarchy and Asymmetrical Group Behavior

1. See Asher and Allen (1969), Ashmore (1970), Clark and Clark (1965), Gopaul-McNicol (1995), Munitz, Priel, and Henik (1985), Porter (1971), Stevenson and Stewart (1958), Vaughan (1978). See also the review by Brand, Ruiz, and Padilla (1974).
2. Mathur and Kalia (1984), Sparks-Davidson, Rahman, and Hildreth (1982).
3. See, e.g., Brand (1974), Fox and Jordan (1973), Gregor and McPherson (1966), Hraba and Grant (1970), Winnick and Taylor (1977).
4. Branch and Newcomb (1980).
5. Gopaul-McNicol (1988, 1995), Powell-Hopson and Hopson (1988, 1992).
6. Ellemers, van Riswijk, Roefs, and Simons (1997).
7. See the review by Brand, Ruiz, and Padilla (1974).
8. Brown (1978), Sachdev and Bourhis (1985), Skevington (1981), Turner and Brown (1978), van Knippenberg and van Oers (1984).
9. Cf. Brewer (1979).
10. Levin (1996).
11. Abel and Sahinkaya (1962), Asher and Allen (1969), Ashmore (1970), Brand, Ruiz, and Padilla (1974), Clark and Clark (1965), Coles (1965), Goodman (1952), Gopual-McNicol (1988), Horowitz (1936), G. B. Johnson (1950), Koslin (1970), Mussen (1950), Porter (1971), Powell-Hopson and Hopson (1988), Proenza and Strickland (1965), Richardson and Green (1971), Stevenson and Stewart (1958), Triandis and Triandis (1960), Vaughan (1978).

12. Greenwald and Oppenheim (1968), Gregor and McPherson (1966), Hraba and Grant (1970), Kline (1970).

13. See, e.g., Schuman et al. (1985), Sears and Kinder (1971).

14. See, e.g., Devine and Elliot (1995), Katz and Hass (1988).

15. Judd, Park, Ryan, Brauer, and Kraus (1995).

16. Mullen, Brown, and Smith (1992).

17. Judd, Park, Ryan, Brauer, and Kraus (1995).

18. The overall F-test was $F(2, 1534) = 4.26$, $p < 0.01$. However, the Scheffé posthoc comparisons showed that only the contrast between Blacks and Latinos was significant.

19. See also Mummendey, Bolten, and Isermann-Gerke (1982), Pavlos (1972, 1973), Roese and Jamieson (1993).

20. Devine (1989), Locke, MacLeod, and Walker (1994), Wittenbrink, Judd, and Park (1997).

21. The response scale ranged from $1 = $ *very much in favor of* to $5 = $ *very much opposed to*.

22. As can be seen in Table 9.1, the F-ratio for this difference was statistically significant ($F(1, 886) = 13.11$, $p < 0.0003$).

23. The η-coefficient, or generalized correlation coefficient, can be regarded as the degree of association or correlation between the independent variable (in this case ethnic group membership) and the dependent variable (in this case outmarriage opposition).

24. $F(1, 533) = 413.89$, $p < 10^{-10}$, $\eta = .66$.

25. This interaction effect was highly significant ($F(4, 1528) = 5.69$, $p < 0.0002$).

26. $F(2, 422) = 23.48$, $p < 10^{-10}$. The Scheffé posthoc comparisons showed all pair-wise comparisons to be statistically significant (i.e., $p < .10$).

27. The interaction between perceived system legitimacy and ethnicity was statistically significant ($F(4, 403) = 6.75$, $p < 0.00003$).

28. We used simple slopes analysis to test for the slope differences between groups. This was done using a two-step, hierarchical, multiple regression analysis. This latter technique was done by first entering the main effect terms of group status (coded as zero for the lower-status group and one for the higher-status group) and ethnic identification into a regression equation predicting the particular dependent variable of interest. At the second step, the group status by ethnic identification interaction term was entered. If the interaction term differed significantly from zero, this indicated that the two simple slopes (for the lower- and higher-status groups) differed reliably.

29. For some of the subtleties of these relationships, see Sidanius, Feshbach, Levin, and Pratto (1997).
30. Sidanius, Pratto, and Rabinowitz (1994).
31. Pratto and Choudhury (1998).
32. In the 1995 samples, these measures were differences between mean ratings for the relevant ingroup and outgroup for (a) how close one felt toward, (b) how different one felt than, and (c) how alienated one felt from other members of the groups, with the latter two ratings reverse coded.
33. Garfield and Helper (1962), Graudenz, Kraak, and Hauer (1976), Nettelbladt, Uddenberg, and Englesson (1981).
34. Heath (1980); see also Gottfried (1985), Gottfried and Gottfried (1986).
35. Neuman (1986), van Lil, Vooijs, and van der Voort (1994).
36. Tangney and Feshbach (1988).
37. Fetler (1984). However, we should note that the relationship between television viewing and academic achievement is not completely straightforward. Fetler's research (1984) shows that while excessive levels of TV viewing (i.e., >6 hours per day) appears to be associated with significantly lower academic achievement, moderate levels of TV viewing are associated with greater academic achievement than very low levels of TV viewing.
38. Tan and Tan (1979).
39. Gil (1970).
40. Pelton (1978).
41. G. Young (1988).
42. Hampton (1987).
43. See also S. E. Brown (1984), Pelton (1978).
44. Aldarondo and Sugarman (1996), Bauer and Ritt (1983), Bergman and Brismar (1993), Caesar (1988), Hotaling and Sugarman (1990), Kantor and Straus (1987), Lewis (1987).
45. Herrnstein and Murray (1994), pp. 203–233; see also Gottfredson (1997).
46. Bastenier et al. (1986), Brady (1996), Desai (1991), Dulaney and Bethune (1995), Jespersen and Herring (1994), Kirui (1982), Medina (1983), Poole and Low (1982), Shavit and Blossfeld (1993), Sohlman (1970), Spineux (1986).
47. Colvin (1997).
48. See, e.g., McGinn et al. (1991), Shavit and Blossfeld (1993), Sticht, Beeler, and McDonald (1992).
49. Steinberg (1996); see also Ortiz (1986).
50. See, e.g., Tuss et al. (1995).

51. Steinberg (1996), pp. 92–93.
52. Woo (1997).
53. Bobo and Kluegel (in press).
54. Katz, Epps, and Axelson (1964), Katz, Roberts, and Robinson (1965).
55. Steele and Aronson (1995).
56. Note that these performance scores were corrected for the students' SAT scores.
57. Spencer (1993).
58. See, e.g., Snyder and Uranowitz (1978); see Pettigrew (1979) for a review.
59. Merton (1972).
60. In addition to the previous discussions concerning group beliefs, other research has shown that individuals seek out social interactions and social relationships that help to reconfirm their own beliefs, even when these beliefs are negative (see, e.g., Hardin and Higgins, 1996; Swann, Pelham, and Krull, 1989; Swann and Read, 1981a; 1981b).
61. United Nations Children's Fund (1991); see also Ekstrand (1992), Kirui (1982).
62. Poole and Low (1982), Steinberg (1996).
63. Adler et al. (1994).
64. See, e.g., Centers for Disease Control (1987), Pugh, Power, Goldblatt, and Arber (1991), U.S. Department of Health, Education, and Welfare (1979).
65. Marmot et al. (1991), Matthews, Kelsey, Meilahn, Kuller, and Wing (1989), Winkleby, Fortmann, and Barrett (1990).
66. ATSIC (1994).
67. Escobedo, Anda, Smith, Remington, and Mast (1990), Kaprio and Koskenvuo (1988), Pugh et al. (1991).
68. U.S. Department of Health and Human Services (1989).
69. Cauley, Donfield, LaPorte, and Warheffig (1991), Ford et al. (1991), Marmot et al. (1991).
70. Cauley et al. (1991), Marmot et al. (1991), Matthews et al. (1989).
71. Drake and Vaillant (1988), Fitzgerald and Zucker (1995), Holzer, Shea, Swanson, and Leaf (1986), Jansen, Fitzgerald, Ham, and Zucker (1995), Mello (1982), Ortega and Rushing (1983), Yates, Booth, Reed, and Brown (1993).
72. Ambrozik (1983), Bianconi (1980), Cloninger, Sigvardsson, Bohman, and von Knorring (1982), Goodman, Siegel, Craig, and Lin (1983), Ladewig, Weidmann, and Hole (1975), Medina (1983), Munk-Jorgensen and Kaldau (1984), Pallavicini et al. (1982), Poikolainen and Vuori (1985), Seltzer and Langford (1984).

73. See, e.g., Adler et al. (1994).
74. The data seem to indicate that this discriminatory effect appears to be slightly higher in the United States (24%; see Blumstein, 1993) than in Great Britain (20%; see Hood and Cordovil, 1992). However, at least in the United States and Canada, the degree to which the criminal justice system functions in a discriminatory fashion varies radically as a function of the type of criminality involved. For example, recent U.S. data seem to indicate that, for drug offenses, approximately 50% of the racial disparity in imprisonment can be explained in terms of the discriminatory behavior of the criminal justice system (see Blumstein, 1993; for the Canadian case, see Cole and Gittens, 1995).
75. Older (1984).
76. Sanson-Fisher (1978).
77. T. J. Young (1993).
78. Meyer (1992).
79. Blumstein (1982).
80. Hood and Cordovil (1992).
81. Kristof (1995).
82. Junger and Polder (1992).
83. Poikalainen et al. (1992).
84. Sherer (1990).
85. Mauer and Huling (1995).
86. Bastian and Taylor (1994).
87. Ibid.
88. Herrnstein and Murray (1994).
89. Fischer et al. (1996), Fraser (1995), Gould (1981).
90. Annie E. Casey Foundation (1995), p. 6.
91. See, e.g., Cobb and Hops (1973), Love and Bachara (1975), Senna, Rathus, and Seigel (1974).
92. Reuter, MacCoun, and Murphy (1990); see also Myers (1992).
93. See, e.g., Moynihan (1967).
94. For similar negative peer group effects, see Steinberg, Dornbusch, and Brown (1992).
95. Ogbu (1991a, 1991b, 1994).
96. Maugh (1996).
97. See, e.g., Gottfredson (1997), Herrnstein and Murray (1994).

Chapter 10.   Sex and Power

1. See, e.g., Buss (1996), Malamuth (1996).
2. See, e.g., Buss (1992), Buss and Angleitner (1989), Buss and Barnes (1986), Coombs and Kenkel (1966), Feingold (1992), Kenrick, Sadalla,

Groth, and Trost (1990), Liston and Salts (1988), Murstein (1976), Wakil (1973).

3. See, e.g., Alatalo, Burke, Dann, Hanotte et al. (1996), Alatalo, Carlson, and Lundberg (1988), Backwell and Passmore (1996), Hakkarainen, Huhta, Lahti, Lundvall et al. (1996).

4. See, e.g., Parker (1987), Tiger and Fox (1972).

5. Ibid.

6. See, e.g., Ekehammar (1985), Furnham (1985), Marjoribanks (1981), Pratto, Stallworth, and Sidanius (1997), Whirls (1986).

7. This calculation uses the binomial distribution and assumes that the probability of males having significantly higher SDO is the same as the probability of females having significantly higher SDO (i.e., .50).

8. See especially Ward (1995).

9. See Sidanius et al. (1991) for a discussion of these models.

10. For some evidence consistent with this general interaction hypothesis within other situations, see Benton (1971), Kidder, Bellettirie, and Cohn (1977), Leventhal, Popp, and Sawyer (1973), Major and Adams (1984), Major, Bylsma, and Cozzarelli (1989), and Mikula (1974).

11. Not surprisingly, there was a highly significant relationship between ethnic group membership and SDO: the greater the perceived social status of one's ethnic group, the greater one's level of SDO_6 ($F(1, 594) = 63.63$, $p < 10^{-10}$, $r = .31$).

12. Note, even with as few as 4 degrees of freedom, an r of .94 is still highly significant (i.e., $p \leq .0026$).

13. AE-2 Scale; see Chapter 3.

14. See, e.g., Lipset (1982), Molin and Astin (1973).

15. $F = 3.63$, $p < .006$.

16. Ethnicity effect: $F(1, 4605) = 176.65$, $p < .001$.

17. Interaction effect: $F(4, 4605) = 3.63$, $p < .006$.

18. $F = 103.24$, $p. < .0001$.

19. Interaction effect: $F < 1$; see Table 10.1.

20. $F = 12.14$, $p < 0.01$.

21. $F < 1$.

22. $F = 17.43$.

23. $F = 30.55$, $p < .001$.

24. $F < 1$; see Table 10.1.

25. $F = 4.01$, $p < .053$, see Table 10.1.

26. $F = 30.55$, $p < .001$.

27. $F < 1$.

28. The interaction effect of nationality and perceived group status was highly significant ($F(1, 1166) = 170.76$, $p < 10^{-10}$).

29. $F = 8.31$; see Table 10.1.
30. $F = 23.20$, $p < 0.01$.
31. $F < 1$.
32. For status difference between Ashkenazic and Sephardic Jews, see Kraus (1982) and Smooha (1978).
33. Note that a repeated measures ANOVA was employed in these analyses, in which measures were assumed to be repeated over priming conditions.
34. $F(1, 552) = 136.46$, $p < .001$.
35. $F(1, 552) = 6.32$, $p < .01$.
36. Gender effect: $F(1, 545) = 18.48$, $p < .001$.
37. Interaction effect: $F(1, 545) < 1$.
38. $F(1, 530) = 1.88$, n.s.
39. $F = 8.20$, $p < .05$.
40. $F = 7.75$, $p < .01$.
41. $F < 1$ for both Sample 26 and Sample 39.
42. Eagly (1987), Eagly and Steffen (1984), Eagly and Wood (1991).
43. $F = 72.09$; see Table 10.2.
44. $F = 1.03$, n.s.
45. For details, see Sidanius, Pratto, and Brief (1995).
46. See, e.g., Ekehammar (1985), Eysenck (1971), Furnham (1985), Marjoribanks (1981), Powell and Stewart (1978), Sidanius et al. (1991), Sidanius and Ekehammar (1980, 1982).
47. *Family Policy* (1996).
48. For detailed discussion of these analyses, see Pratto (1996).
49. Political ideology was defined by (a) "Support for the Republican versus the Democratic Party" (i.e., 1 = "Strong Democrat," 2 = "Moderate Democrat," 3 = "Independent," 4 = "Moderate Republican," 5 = "Strong Republican") and (b) "Political self-description" (1 = *very liberal* to 5 = *very conservative*).
50. The policy attitudes were (a) "Equal rights for women," (b) "Less aid to the poor," (c) "The U.S. military," (d) "Higher taxes on the rich," (e) "Gay and lesbian rights," (f) "Government support for business," (g) "Death penalty," (h) "Affirmative action," (i) "Public day care."
51. This analysis was done by use of LISREL 6. Since vote choice was a dichotomous variable, the data were first analyzed by use of PRELIS in order to provide for distributed adjusted covariances.
52. $\chi^2(4) = 8.55$, $p < .07$, GFI = .992, AGFI = .969.
53. The change in model fit was not statistically significant ($\chi^2(1) = 0.37$).
54. $\chi^2(5) = 190.32$, $p < .001$, GFI = .865, AGFI = .585.
55. U.S. Bureau of Labor Statistics (1994).
56. *World Almanac and Book of Facts* (1993).

57. Schmittroth (1991).
58. *Compendium of Statistics and Indicators on the Situation of Women* (1989). The fact that women are severely underrepresented in high government positions the world over is also consistent with this general picture. See Norris (1987), Schmittroth (1991), Vianello and Siemienska (1990).
59. *Bureau of Labor Statistics* (1994), p. 205.
60. Schmittroth (1991).
61. See Sidanius, Pratto, Sinclair, and van Laar (1996).
62. Hales and Hartman (1978), Lyson (1984), Perron and St.-Onge (1991), Tittle (1982), Wijting, Arnold, and Conrad (1977).
63. See Pratto, Stallworth, Sidanius, and Siers (1997).
64. See, e.g., Buss (1996).
65. Mesopotamia (e.g., Sumeria, Babylon, Assyria), Egypt, the Aztec and Incan empires in the Americas, and the ancient empires of China and India.
66. Betzig (1993), pp. 41–42.
67. Rockwell (1976).
68. See WISTAT (1994).
69. $p < .05$.
70. See also Pratto and Hegarty (1998).
71. See Pratto (1996), Pratto, Sidanius, and Stallworth (1993).
72. Jackman (1994), p. 384, fig. 7.3.
73. See Keegan (1993, p. 76), Rodseth, Wrangham, Harrigen, and Smuts (1991), Wrangham (1982).

Chapter 11. Epilogue

1. For similar arguments, see A. P. Fiske (1991).
2. J. Brown (1970).
3. Lenski (1984), Yinger (1995).
4. See, e.g., Krueger and Rothbart (1988).
5. Tajfel and Turner (1986); see also Brewer and Miller (1996).
6. See, e.g., G. D. Wilson (1973).
7. See, e.g., Tversky and Kahneman (1973).
8. See Altemeyer (1998) and McFarland and Adelson (1996) for independent confirmation of this conceptual and empirical uniqueness.
9. See, e.g., Thernstrom and Thernstrom (1997).
10. Crocker and Major (1989); Scott (1990).
11. For some preliminary speculation along these lines, see Altemeyer (1998).
12. See, e.g., Williamson and Lindert (1980).

References

Abel, E., & Nelson, M. (1990). *Circles of care: Work and identity in women's lives.* Albany: State University of New York Press.

Abel, H., & Sahinkaya, N. (1962). Emergence of sex and race friendship preferences. *Child Development, 33,* 939–943.

ACLU. (1997). Legislation addresses "driving while Black" traffic offense. *ACLU Act Now* [On-line]. Available: www.aclu.org/action/drivingblack.html

Adamovic, K. (1979). Intellectual development and level of knowledge in Gypsy pupils in relation to the type of education. *Psychologia a Patopsychologia Dietata, 14,* 169–176.

Adams, A. (1979). Prisoners in exile: Senegalese workers in France. In R. Cohen, P. Gutkind, & P. Brazier (Eds.), *Peasants and proletarians, the struggle of third world workers* (pp. 307–330). London: Hutchinson.

Adelstein, A. M. (1980). Life-style in occupational cancer. *Journal of Toxicology and Environmental Health, 6,* 935–962.

Adler, N. E., Boyce, T., Chesney, M. A., Cohen, S., Folkman, S., Kahn, R. L., & Syme, L. S. (1994). Socioeconomic status and health: The challenge of the gradient. *American Psychologist, 49,* 15–24.

Adorno, T. W., Frenkel-Brunswik, E., Levinson, D. J., & Sanford, R. N. (1950). *The authoritarian personality.* New York: Norton.

Alatalo, R. V., Burke, T., Dann, J., Hanotte, O., et al. (1996). Paternity, copulation disturbance and female choice in lekking black grouse. *Animal Behaviour, 52,* 861–873.

Alatalo, R. V., Carlson, A., & Lundberg, A. (1988). The search cost in mate choice of the pied flycatcher. *Animal Behaviour, 36,* 289–291.

Alberts, S. C., & Altmann, J. (1995). Preparation and activation: Determinants of age at reproductive maturity in male baboons. *Behavioral Ecology and Sociobiology, 36,* 397–406.

Aldarondo, E., & Sugarman, D. B. (1996). Risk marker analysis of the cessation and persistence of wife assault. *Journal of Consulting and Clinical Psychology, 64,* 1010–1019.

Alker, H. (1965). *Mathematics and politics.* New York: Macmillan.

Allington, R. (1980). Teacher interruption behaviors during primary grade oral reading. *Journal of Educational Psychology, 72,* 371–377.

Allport, G. W. (1954). *The nature of prejudice.* Menlo Park, CA: Addison-Wesley.

Almquist, E. M. (1975). Untangling the effects of race and sex: The disadvantaged status of Black women. *Social Science Quarterly, 56,* 129–142.

Altemeyer, B. (1981). *Right-wing authoritarianism.* Manitoba: University of Manitoba Press.

Altemeyer, B. (1988). *Enemies of freedom: Understanding right-wing authoritarianism.* San Francisco: Jossey-Bass.

Altemeyer, B. (1996). *The authoritarian specter.* Cambridge, MA: Harvard University Press.

Altemeyer, B. (1998). The other "authoritarian personality." In M. P. Zanna (Ed.), *Advances in Experimental Social Psychology* (Vol. 30, pp. 48–92). New York: Academic.

Ambrozik, W. (1983). Sytuacja spoleczna dziecka rodziny alkoholicznej w kulturowo zaniedbanym rejonie wielkiego miasta [The social situation of a child in an alcoholic family in a culturally neglected quarter of a big town]. Uniwersytet Im. Adama Mickiewicza w Poznaniu: *Seria Psychologia i Pedagogika, no. 56,* 125.

Amnesty International (1998). *United States of America: Right for all.* New York: Amnesty International Publications.

Annie E. Casey Foundation. (1995). *Kids count in Michigan, 1995 data book: County profiles of child and family well-being.* Lansing, MI: Author.

Arkin, S. D. (1980). Discrimination and arbitrariness in capital punishment: An analysis of post-Furman murder cases in Dade County, Florida, 1973–1976. *Stanford Law Review, 33,* 75–101.

Asher, A., & Allen, V. (1969). Racial prejudice and social comparison processes. *Journal of Social Issues, 25,* 157–166.

Ashmore, R. D. (1970). The problem of intergroup prejudice. In B. E. Collins (Ed.), *Social psychology: Social influence, attitude change, group processes, and prejudice readings* (pp. 245–296). MA: Addison-Wesley.

Ashmore, R. D., & DelBoca, F. K. (1981). Conceptual approaches to stereotypes and stereotyping. In D. L. Hamilton (Ed.), *Cognitive processes in stereotyping and intergroup behavior* (pp. 1–35). Hillsdale, NJ: Erlbaum.

ATSIC. (1994). *Aboriginal and Torres Strait Islander Commission Annual Report,* Chapter 1.

Austin, T. L. (1985). Does where you live determine what you get? A case study of misdemeanant sentencing. *Journal of Criminal Law and Criminology, 76,* 490–511.

Ayres, I. (1991). Fair driving: Gender and race discrimination in retail car negotiations. *Harvard Law Review, 104,* 817–872.

Ayres, I. (1995). Further evidence of discrimination in new car negotiations and estimates of its cause. *Michigan Law Review, 94,* 109–147.

Ayres, I., & Siegelman, P. (1995). Race and gender discrimination in bargaining for a new car. *American Economic Review, 85,* 304–322.

Ayres, I., & Waldfogel, J. (1994). A market test for race discrimination in bail setting. *Stanford Law Review, 46,* 987–1047.

Bachofen, J. J. (1861/1969). *Das Mutterrecht: Eine Untersuchung uber die Gynaikokratie der altern Welt nach ihrer religiosen und rechtlichen Natur.* Bruxelles: Culture et Civilisation.

Backwell, P. R. Y., & Passmore, N. I. (1996). Time constraints and multiple choice criteria in the sampling behaviour and mate choice of the fiddler crab, *Uca annulipes. Behavioral Ecology and Sociobiology, 38,* 407–416.

Baldus, D. C., Pulaski, C. A., & Woodsworth, G. (1983). Comparative review of death sentences: An empirical study of the Georgia experience. *Journal of Criminal Law and Criminology, 74,* 661–753.

Baldus, D. C., Woodsworth, G., & Pulaski, C. A. (1985). Monitoring and evaluating contemporary death sentencing systems: Lessons from Georgia. *U.C. Davis Law Review, 18,* 1375–1407.

Bargh, J. A., Chen, M., & Burrows, L. (1996). Automaticity and social behavior: Direct effects of trait construct and stereotype activation on action. *Journal of Personality and Social Psychology, 71,* 230–244.

Bastenier, A., et al. (1986). *The vocational training of young migrants in Belgium, Denmark, France, Luxembourg, and the United Kingdom.* Synthesis report. Berlin: European Centre for the Development of Vocational Training.

Bastian, L. D., & Taylor, B. M. (1994). *Young Black male victims.* U.S. Department of Justice. Office of Justice Programs Bureau of Justice Statistics: Crime Data Brief, NCJ-147004.

Bauer, C., & Ritt, L. (1983). A husband is a beating animal: Frances Power Cobbe confronts the wife-abuse problem in Victorian England. *International Journal of Women's Studies, 6,* 99–118.

Beale, F. (1970). Double jeopardy: To be Black and female. In T. Cade (Ed.), *The Black woman* (pp. 90–100). New York: New American Library.

Beck, L., & Keddie, N. (1978). *Women in the Muslim world.* Cambridge, MA: Harvard University Press.

Beck, L. R., & St. George, R. (1983). The alleged cultural bias of PAT: Reading comprehension and reading vocabulary tests. *New Zealand Journal of Educational Studies, 18,* 32–47.

Becker, G. S. (1957). *The economics of discrimination.* London: University of Chicago Press.

Beijers, W. M. E. H., Hille, H., & de Leng, A. W. (1994). *Selectiviteit nader bekeken: Een onderzoek naar de OM-afdoening van strafzaken tegen verdachten behorende tot etnische minderheidsgroepen.* Amsterdam: Vrije Universiteit.

Bendick, M., Jr. (1989). Matching workers and job opportunities. In D. Dawden & F. Skidore (Eds.), *Rethinking employment policy* (pp. 81–108). Washington, DC: Urban Institute Press.

Bendick, M., Jr. (1996). Discrimination against racial/ethnic minorities in access to employment in the United States: Empirical findings from situation testing. *International Migration Papers, 12,* Geneva: Employment Department, International Labour Office.

Bendick, M., Jr., Jackson, C., & Reinoso, V. (1994). Measuring employment discrimination through controlled experiments. *Review of Black Political Economy, 23,* 25–48.

Bendick, M., Jr., Jackson, C., Reinoso, V., & Hodges, L. (1991). Discrimination against Latino job applicants: A controlled experiment. *Human Resource Management, 30,* 469–484.

Benson, C. (1995). Ireland's low IQ: A critique. In R. Jacoby & N. Glauberman (Eds.), *The bell curve debate* (pp. 222–233). New York: Times Books.

Benton, A. A. (1971). Productivity, distributive justice, and bargaining among children. *Journal of Personality and Social Psychology, 18,* 68–78.

Bercovitch, F. B. (1991). Social stratification, social strategies, and reproductive success in primates. *Ethology and Sociobiology, 12,* 315–333.

Bergman, B., & Brismar, B. (1993). Assailants and victims: A comparative study of male wife-beaters and battered males. *Journal of Addictive Diseases, 12,* 1–10.

Bernard, J. L. (1979). Interaction between the race of the defendant and that of jurors in determining verdicts. *Law and Psychology Review, 5,* 103–111.

Bernstein, I., Kick, E., Leung, J., & Schulz, B. (1977). Charge reduction: An intermediary stage in the process of labeling criminal defendants. *Social Forces, 56,* 362–384.

Betzig, L. (1993). Sex, sucession, and stratification in the first six civilizations: How powerful men reproduced, passed power on to their sons, and used power to defend their wealth, women and children. In L. Ellis (Ed.), *Social stratification and socioeconomic inequality: A comparative biosocial analysis* (pp. 37–74). New York: Praeger.

Bianconi, S. (1980). Anomia e alcoolismo: Contributo alla sociopatologia della intossicazione etilica cronica [Anomie and alcoholism: Contribution to the sociopathological study of chronic alcoholic intoxication]. *Lavoro Neuropsichiatrico, 67,* 119–126.

Biddiss, M. D. (1970). *Father of racist ideology: The social and political thought of Count Gobineau.* London: Weidenfeld & Nicolson.

Blazer, D. G., Hughes, D., George, L. K., Swartz, M., & Boyer, R. (1991). Generalized anxiety disorder. In L. N. Robins & D. A. Regier (Eds.), *Psychiatric disorders in America: The Epidemiological Catchment Area Study* (pp. 180–203). New York: Free Press.

Blumer, H. (1960). Race prejudice as a sense of group position. *Pacific Sociological Review, 1,* 3–5.

Blumstein, A. (1982). On the racial disproportionality of United States' prison populations. *Journal of Criminal Law and Criminology, 73,* 1259–1281.

Blumstein, A. (1993). Racial disproportionality of U.S. prison populations revisited. *University of Colorado Law Review, 64,* 743–759.

Bobo, L. (1983). Whites' opposition to busing: Symbolic racism or realistic group conflict? *Journal of Personality and Social Psychology, 45,* 1196–1210.

Bobo, L., & Kluegel, J. R. (in press). Status, ideology and dimensions of Whites' racial beliefs and attitudes: Progress and stagnation. In S. Tuck & J. K. Martin (Eds.), *Racial attitudes in the 1990s: Continuity and change.* Greenwood, CT: Praeger.

Bodman, P. M. (1995). *Estimating frictional unemployment for Australia and its states using a stochastic frontier approach.* Working paper, Department of Economics, University of Queensland, St. Lucia, Brisbane, Australia.

Bond, M. D., Bullock, B. C., Bellinger, D. A., & Hamm, T. E. (1980). Myocardial infarction in a large colony of nonhuman primates with coronary artery atherosclerosis. *American Journal of Pathology, 101,* 675–692.

Bosma, J. J. (1985). *Allochtonen en straftoemeting.* Groningen: Uitgave Criminologisch Instituut Groningen.

Bouchard, T. J. (1994). Genes, environment, and personality. *Science, 264*, 1700–1701.

Bourg, S., & Stock, H. V. (1994). A review of domestic violence arrest statistics in a police department using a pro-arrest policy: Are pro-arrest policies enough? *Journal of Family Violence, 9*, 177–189.

Bovenkerk, F. (1992). *A manual for international comparative research on discrimination on the grounds of "race" and ethnic origin.* Geneva: International Labour Office.

Bovenkerk, F., Gras, M. J. I., & Ramsoedh, D. (1994). Discrimination against migrant workers and ethnic minorities in access to employment in the Netherlands. *International Migration Papers, 4,* Geneva: Employment Department, International Labour Office.

Bowers, W. J., & Pierce, G. L. (1980). Arbitrariness and discrimination under post-*Furman* capital statutes. *Crime and Delinquency, 26*, 563–635.

Bradmiller, L. L., & Walters, W. S. (1985). Seriousness of sexual assault charges: Influencing factors. *Criminal Justice and Behavior, 12*, 463–484.

Brady, P. (1996). Native dropouts and non-native dropouts in Canada: Two solitudes or a solitude shared? *Journal of American Indian Education, 35*, 10–20.

Braithwaite, V. A., & Law, H. G. (1985). Structure of human values: Testing the adequacy of the Rokeach value survey. *Journal of Personality and Social Psychology, 49*, 250–263.

Branch, C., & Newcomb, N. (1980). Racial attitudes of Black preschoolers as related to parental civil rights activism. *Merrill Palmer Quarterly, 26*, 425–428.

Brand, E. S. (1974). Psychological correlates of ethnic esteem among Anglo, Black and Chicano, second-grade and fifth-grade children. Unpublished doctoral dissertation, University of Missouri. (University Microfilms No. 74-1742)

Brand, E. S., Ruiz, R. A., & Padilla, A. M. (1974). Ethnic identification and preference: A review. *Psychological Bulletin, 81*, 860–890.

Brassé, P., & Sikking, E. (1986). *Positie en kansen van etnische minderheden in Nederlandse ondernemingen.* Rijswijk: Ministerie van Sociale Zaken en Werkgelegenheid.

Brewer, M. B. (1979). In-group bias in the minimal intergroup situation: A cognitive-motivational analysis. *Psychological Bulletin, 86*, 307–324.

Brewer, M. B., & Miller, N. (1996). *Intergroup relations.* Pacific Grove, CA: Brooks-Cole.

Brewer, M. B., & Silver, R. (1978). Ingroup bias as a function of task characteristics. *European Journal of Social Psychology, 8*, 393–400.

Brophy, J. (1982). *Research on the self-fulfilling prophecy and teacher expectations.* Paper presented at the annual meeting of the American Educational Research Association. New York.

Brophy, J. (1983). Research on the self-fulfilling prophecy and teacher expectations. *Journal of Educational Psychology, 75*, 631–661.

Brown, J. (1970). Economic organization and the position of women among the Iroquois. *Ethnohistory, 17*, 151–167.

Brown, R. (1978). Divided we fall: An analysis of relations between sections of a factory work-force. In H. Tajfel (Ed.), *Differentiation between social groups:*

Studies in the social psychology of intergroup relations (pp. 395–429). London: Academic.

Brown, S. E. (1984). Social class, child maltreatment, and delinquent behavior. *Criminology: An Interdisciplinary Journal, 22,* 259–278.

Brundage, W. F. (1993). *Lynching in the new South.* Urbana: University of Illinois Press.

Buckley, W. F., Jr., & Kesler, C. R. (Eds.). (1988). *Keeping the tablets: Modern American conservative thought.* New York: Perennial Library.

Buraku Liberation Research Institute. (1994). *The reality of Buraku discrimination in Japan.* Osaka: Author.

Bureau of Justice Statistics Fact Sheet. (1995). *Husbands accused of killing spouses convicted more often than wives.* Available: http://aspensys. aspensy.. ncjrs/data/spousfac.txt

Burke, E. (1790/1955). *Reflections on the revolution in France.* Chicago: Regnery.

Burnham, J. (1964). *Suicide of the West.* New York: John Day.

Busch, R. C. (1990). *Family systems: Comparative study of the family.* New York: P. Lang.

Buss, D. M. (1992). *Evolution and human mating.* New York: Basic.

Buss, D. M. (1996). Sexual conflict: Evolutionary insights into feminism and the "battle of the sexes." In D. M. Buss & N. M. Malamuth (Eds.), *Sex, power and conflict: Evolutionary and feminist perspectives* (pp. 296–318). New York: Oxford University Press.

Buss, D. M., & Angleitner, A. (1989). Mate selection preferences in Germany and the United States. *Personality and Individual Differences, 10,* 1269–1280.

Buss, D. M., & Barnes, M. (1986). Preferences in human mate selection. *Journal of Personality and Social Psychology, 50,* 559–570.

Caesar, P. L. (1988). Exposure to violence in the families-of-origin among wife-abusers and maritally nonviolent men [Special issue: Wife assaulters]. *Violence and Victims, 3,* 49–63.

Campbell, D. T. (1965). Ethnocentric and other altruistic motives. In D. Levine (Ed.), *Nebraska Symposium on Motivation* (pp. 283–311). Lincoln: University of Nebraska Press.

Cantor, N., & Mischel, W. (1979). Prototypes in person perception. In L. Berkowitz (Ed.), *Advances in experimental social psychology* (Vol. 12, pp. 3–52). New York: Academic.

Caplovitz, D. (1963). *The poor pay more.* New York: Free Press.

Caporael, L. R., & Brewer, M. B. (1991). Reviving evolutionary psychology: Biology meets society. *Journal of Social Issues, 47,* 187–195.

Carr, J. H., & Magbolugbe, I. F. (1994). *A research note on the Federal Reserve Bank of Boston study on mortgage lending.* Washington, DC: Federal National Mortgage Association, Office of Housing Research.

Carter, D. J., & Wilson, R. (1994). *Minorities in higher education.* Washington, DC: American Council on Education.

Cauley, J. A., Donfield, S. M., LaPorte, R. E., & Warheftig, N. E. (1991). Physical activity by SES in two population-based cohorts. *Medicine and Science in Sports and Exercise, 23,* 343–352.

Centers for Disease Control. (1987). *Smoking tobacco and health: A fact book.* Rockville, MD: U.S. Department of Health and Human Services, Public Health Service, Office on Smoking and Health.

Chaiken, A., Sigler, E., & Derlaga, V. (1974). Nonverbal mediators of teacher expectation effects. *Journal of Personality and Social Psychology, 30,* 144–149.

Chambliss, W. J. (1973). The saints and the roughnecks. *Society, 11,* 24–31.

Chambliss, W. J. (1984). *Criminal law in action* (2nd ed.). New York: Wiley.

Chevigny, P. (1995). *Edge of the knife: Police violence in the Americas.* New York: New Press.

Christie, R., & Cook, P. (1958). A guide to published literature relating to the authoritarian personality through 1956. *Journal of Psychology, 45,* 1717–1799.

Christie, R., & Jahoda, M. (1954). *Studies in the scope and method of "The Authoritarian Personality."* Glencoe, IL: Free Press.

Christopher, W. et al. (1991). *Report of the Independent Commission on the Los Angeles Police Department.* Los Angeles: Independent Commission on the Los Angeles Police Department.

Clark, K. B., & Clark, M. P. (1947). Racial identification and preference in Negro children. In T. M. Newcomb & E. L. Hartley (Eds.), *Readings in social psychology* (pp. 169–178). New York: Holt, Rinehart, & Winston.

Clark, K. B., & Clark, M. P. (1965). Racial identification and preference in Negro children. In H. Proshansky & B. Seidenberg (Eds.), *Basic studies in social psychology* (pp. 308–317). New York: Holt, Rinehart, & Winston.

Cloninger, C. R., Sigvardsson, S., Bohman, M., & von Knorring, A. (1982). Predisposition to petty criminality in Swedish adoptees: II. Cross-fostering analysis of gene–environment interaction. *Archives of General Psychiatry, 39,* 1242–1247.

Cobb, J. A., & Hops, H. (1973). Effects of academic survival skill training on low achieving first graders. *Journal of Educational Research, 67,* 108–113.

Cochrane, R., Billig, M., & Hogg, M. (1979). British politics and the two-value model. In M. Rokeach (Ed.), *Understanding human values* (pp. 179–191). New York: Free Press.

Cohen, D. L., & Peterson, J. L. (1981). Bias in the courtroom: Race and sex effects of attorneys on juror verdicts. *Social Behavior and Personality, 9,* 81–87.

Cole, D. P., & Gittens, M. (1995). *Report of the Commission on Systemic Racism in the Ontario Criminal Justice System.* Ontario: Queen's Printer of Ontario.

Coles, R. (1965). It's the same, but it's different. *Daedalus, 94,* 1107–1132.

Collier, J. (1988). *Marriage and inequality in classless societies.* Stanford, CA: Stanford University Press.

Collier, J., & Yanagisako, S. J. (Eds.). (1987). *Gender and kinship: Essays toward a unified analysis.* Stanford, CA: Stanford University Press.

Collins, S. M. (1983). The making of the Black middle class. *Social Problems, 30,* 369–381.

Collins, S. M. (1989). The marginalization of Black executives. *Social Problems, 36,* 317–331.

Colvin, R. L. (1997, February 21). Why Singapore is at top of class. *Los Angeles Times,* p. 1.

Commission for Racial Equality. (1996). *How much discrimination is there?* Available: www.open.gov.uk/cre/discrim/htm

Commission Nationale Consultative des Droits de l'Homme. (1990). *Rapport au premier ministre sur la lutte contre le racisme et la xénophobie.* Paris.

Compendium of statistics and indicators on the situation of women, 1986. (1989). New York: United Nations.

Coombs, R. H., & Kenkel, W. F. (1966). Sex differences in dating aspirations and satisfaction with computer-selected partners. *Journal of Marriage and the Family, 28,* 62–66.

Coser, L. A. (1956). *The functions of social conflict.* Glencoe, IL: Free Press.

Costa-Lascoux, J. (1989). *De l'immigré au citoyen.* Notes et études documentaires, No. 4886. Paris: La Documentation Française.

Crocker, J., & Major, B. (1989). Social stigma and self-esteem: The self-protective properties of stigma. *Psychological Review, 96,* 608–630.

Crocker, J., & Major, B. (1994). Reactions to stigma: The moderating role of justifications. In M. P. Zanna & J. M. Olson (Eds.), *The psychology of prejudice: The Ontario Symposium: Vol. 7. Ontario Symposium on Personality and Social Psychology* (pp. 289–314). Hillsdale, NJ: Erlbaum.

Cross, H., et al. (1990). *Employer hiring practices: Differential treatment of Hispanic and Anglo job seekers.* Washington, DC: Urban Institute.

Cross, M. (1987). Generation jobless: The need for a new agenda in ethnic relations policy. *New Community, 14,* 123–127.

Crossette, B. (1998, June 14). Violation: An old scourge of war becomes its latest crime. *New York Times,* section 4, p. 1.

Culp, J., & Dunson, B. (1986). Brothers of a different color: A preliminary look at employer treatment of Black and White youth. In R. Freeman & H. Holzer (Eds.), *The Black youth employment crisis* (pp. 233–259). Chicago: University of Chicago Press.

Cunneen, C. (1990). Aborigines and law and order regimes [Special edition series: Contemporary race relations]. *Journal for Social Justice Studies, 3,* 37–50.

Cymrot, D. J. (1985). Does competition lessen discrimination? Some evidence. *Journal of Human Resources, 20,* 605–612.

Dahrendorf, R. (1959). *Class and conflict in industrial society.* Stanford, CA: Stanford University Press.

Daly, K. (1994). *Gender, crime, and punishment.* New Haven, CT: Yale University Press.

Daly, K., & Bordt, R. L. (1991). *Gender, race and discrimination research: Disparate meanings of statistical "sex" and "race effects" in sentencing.* Unpublished manuscript, University of Michigan at Ann Arbor.

Damstuen, E. (1997, February 10). Norsk välfärd inget för invandrare. *Dagens Nyheter,* Dnet. Available: www.dn.se/DNet/articles/14400–14499/14495/index.html

Daniszewski, J. (1997, September 29). Death penalty for Briton poses Saudi dilemma. *Los Angeles Times,* pp. A1, A11.

Dar, Y., & Resh, N. (1991). Socioeconomic and ethnic gaps in academic achievement in Israeli junior high schools. In N. Bleichrodt & P. Drenth (Eds.),

Contemporary issues in cross-cultural psychology. Amsterdam: Swets & Zeitlinger.

Darley, J. M., & Fazio, R. H. (1980). Expectancy confirmation processes arising in the social interaction sequence. *American Psychologist, 35,* 867–881.

Das, J. P., & Khurana, A. K. S. (1988). Caste and cognitive processes. In S. H. Irvine & J. W. Berry (Eds.), *Human abilities in cultural context* (pp. 487–508). Cambridge University Press.

Das, S. (1994). Level-I abilities of socially disadvantaged children: Effects of home-environment, caste and age. *Social Science International, 10*(1), 69–74.

Das, S., & Padhee, B. (1993). Level II abilities of socially disadvantaged children: Effects of home-environment, caste and age. *Journal of Indian Psychology, 11,* 38–43.

Dator, J. A. (1969). Measuring attitudes across cultures: A factor analysis of the replies of Japanese judges to Eysenck's inventory of conservative-progressive ideology. In G. Shubert & D. J. Danelski (Eds.), *Comparative judicial behavior* (pp. 71–102). New York: Oxford University Press.

Davidson, J. (1997, October). Crime pays big time. *Emerge,* 36–46.

Davis, A. (1981). *Women, race, and class.* New York: Vintage.

Dawkins, R. (1989). *The selfish gene.* Oxford: Oxford University Press.

Deane, P. C. (1968). The persistence of Uncle Tom: An examination of the image of the Negro in children's fiction series. *Journal of Negro Education, 37,* 140–145.

DeFreitas, G. (1985). Ethnic differentials in unemployment among Hispanic-Americans. In G. T. Borjas & M. Tienda (Eds.), *Hispanics in the U.S. economy* (pp. 127–157). New York: Academic.

Deprét, E. F., & Fiske, S. T. (1993). Social cognition and power: Some cognitive consequences of social structure as a source of control deprivation. In G. Weary, F. Gleicher, & K. Marsh (Eds.), *Control motivation and social cognition* (pp. 176–202). New York: Springer-Verlag.

Desai, U. (1991). Determinants of educational performance in India: Role of home and family. *International Review of Education, 37,* 245–265.

Devine, P. G. (1989). Stereotypes and prejudice: Their automatic and controlled processes. *Journal of Personality and Social Psychology, 56,* 5–18.

Devine, P. G., & Elliot, A. J. (1995). Are racial stereotypes really fading? The Princeton trilogy revisited. *Personality and Social Psychology Bulletin, 21,* 1139–1150.

De Vos, G. A. (1992). *Social cohesion and alienation: Minorities in the United States and Japan.* Boulder, CO: Westview.

DeVos, G. A., & Wetherall, W. O. (1983). *Japan's minorities.* London: Minority Rights Group.

Dickemann, M. (1979). Female infanticide, reproductive strategies, and social stratification: A preliminary model. In N. A. Chagnon & W. Irons (Eds.), *Evolutionary biology and human social behavior: An anthropological perspective* (pp. 321–367). North Scituate, MA: Duxbury.

Doise, W. (1990). Social biases in categorization processes. In J. P. Caverni, J. M. Fabre, & M. Gonzalez (Eds.), *Cognitive biases: Advances in psychology* (Vol. 68, pp. 305–323). Amsterdam: North-Holland.

Dolan, M. (1998, June 4). Study finds death penalty unevenly applied. *Los Angeles Times*, p. A33.

Dollard, J. W. (1937). *Caste and class in a southern town*. New Haven, CT: Yale University Press.

Dollard, J. W., Miller, N. E., Doob, L. W., Mowrer, O. H., & Sears, R. R. (1939). *Frustration and aggression*. New Haven, CT: Yale University Press.

Dovidio, J. F., & Gaertner, S. L. (1991). Changes in the expression and assessment of racial prejudice. In H. J. Knopke, R. J. Norrell, & R. W. Rogers (Eds.), *Opening doors: Perspectives on race relations in contemporary America* (pp. 119–148). Tuscaloosa: University of Alabama Press.

Drake, R. E., & Vaillant, G. E. (1988). Predicting alcoholism and personality disorder in a 33-year longitudinal study of children of alcoholics. National Institute on Alcohol Abuse and Alcoholism and the American Research Society on Alcoholism. *British Journal of Addiction, 83*, 799–807.

D'Souza, D. (1995). *The end of racism: Principles for a multiracial society*. New York: Free Press.

Duckitt, J. (1989). Authoritarianism and group identification: A new view of an old construct. *Political Psychology, 10*, 63–84.

Dulaney, C., & Bethune, G. (1995). *Racial and gender gaps in academic achievement: An updated look at 1993–94 data*. Report summary. Wake County Public Schools System, Raleigh, NC. Department of Evaluation and Research.

Duncan, D. G., & Wachter, S. M. (1995, February). Evaluating the evidence. *Mortgage Banking, 55*, 67–74.

Dunwoody, P. T., & Frank, M. L. (1994). Effects of ethnicity on prison sentencing. *Psychological Reports, 74*, 200.

Durkheim, E. (1933). *The division of labor in society* (G. Simpson, Trans.). New York: Macmillan. (Original work published 1893)

Eagly, A. H. (1987). *Sex differences in social behavior: A social-role interpretation*. Hillsdale, NJ: Erlbaum.

Eagly, A. H., & Steffen, V. J. (1984). Gender stereotypes stem from the distribution of women and men into social roles. *Journal of Personality and Social Psychology, 46*, 735–754.

Eagly, A. H., & Wood, W. (1991). Explaining sex differences in social behavior: A meta-analytic perspective [Special issue: Meta-analysis in personality and social psychology]. *Personality and Social Psychology Bulletin, 17*, 306–315.

Eibl-Eibesfeldt, I. (1989). *Human ethology*. New York: de Gruyter.

Ekehammar, B. (1985). Sex differences in socio-political attitudes revisited. *Educational Studies, 11*, 3–9.

Ekstrand, G. (1992). *Drop-out in schools in India: Minor field studies in Orissa, 1990*. Educational and Psychological Interactions. No. 112. Lund University, Malmo (Sweden). Department of Educational and Psychological Research.

Ellemers, N., van Knippenberg, A., de Vries, N., & Wilke, H. (1988). Social identification and permeability of group boundaries. *European Journal of Social Psychology, 18*, 497–513.

Ellemers, N., van Knippenberg, A., & Wilke, H. (1990). The influence of permeability of group boundaries and stability of group status on strategies of individual mobility and social change. *British Journal of Social Psychology,* *29*, 233–246.

Ellemers, N., van Riswijk, W., Roefs, M., & Simons, C. (1997). Bias in intergroup perceptions: Balancing group identity with social reality. *Personality and Social Psychology Bulletin, 23*, 188–198.

Elmi, A. H. N., & Mikelsons, M. (1991). *Housing discrimination study: Replication of 1997 measures using current data.* Washington, DC: U.S. Department of Housing and Urban Development, Office of Policy Development and Research.

Engels, F. (1884/1902). *The origin of the family, private property, and the state* (E. Untermann, Trans.). Chicago: E. H. Kerr.

Enzenberger, H. M. (1994). *Civil wars: From L.A. to Bosnia.* New York: New Press.

Epstein, J. L. (1985). After the bus arrives: Resegregation in desegregated schools. *Journal of Social Issues, 41*, 23–43.

Epstein, R. A. (1992). *Forbidden grounds: The case against employment discrimination laws.* Cambridge, MA: Harvard University Press.

Erber, R., & Fiske, S. T. (1984). Outcome dependency and attention to inconsistent information. *Journal of Personality and Social Psychology, 47*, 709–726.

Ericson, R. (1982). *Reproducing order: A study of police patrol work.* Toronto: University of Toronto Press.

Escobedo, L. G., Anda, R. F., Smith, P. F., Remington, P. L., & Mast, E. E. (1990). Sociodemographic characteristics of cigarette smoking initiation in the United States. *Journal of the American Medical Association, 264*, 1550–1555.

Espy, M. W., & Smykla, J. O. (1996). *Executions in the United States, 1608–1991: The Espy file.* Inter-university Consortium for Political and Social Research, Ann Arbor, MI (ICPSR 8451).

Eysenck, H. J. (1944). General social attitudes. *Journal of Social Psychology, 19*, 207–227.

Eysenck, H. J. (1951). Primary social attitudes as related to social class and political party. *British Journal of Sociology, 11*, 198–209.

Eysenck, H. J. (1971). Social attitudes and social class. *British Journal of Social Psychology, 10*, 201–212.

Eysenck, H. J. (1976). Structure of social attitudes. *Psychological Reports, 39*, 463–466.

Eysenck, H. J., & Coulter, T. T. (1972). The personality and attitudes of working class British communists and fascists. *Journal of Social Psychology, 87*, 59–73.

Family Policy. (1996). Gender politics. (Vol. 9, No. 6). Family Research Council, Washington, DC. Available: http: // www.heritage.org/frc/fampol/fp96lpl.html

Fanon, F. (1963). *The wretched of the earth.* New York: Grove.

Farley, R., & Allen, W. R. (1987). *The color line and the quality of life in America.* New York: Russell Sage.

Farrell, R., & Swigert, V. (1978). Legal disposition of inter-group and intra-group homicides. *Sociological Quarterly, 19*, 565–576.

Fase, W. (1989). Young migrants between school and work: Recent trends in Holland. In F. Schmidt & G. Chomé (Eds.), *Initial and continuing vocational training and work migration in Europe* (pp. 83–117). CEDEFOP document,

Luxembourg, Office for Official Publications of the European Communities.

Fazio, R. H., Sanbonmatsu, D. M., Powell, M. C., & Williams, C. J. (1995). Variability in automatic activation as an unobtrusive measure of racial attitudes: A bona fide pipeline? *Journal of Personality and Social Psychology, 69,* 1013–1027.

Feagin, J. R., & Feagin, C. B. (1978). *Discrimination American style: Institutional racism and sexism.* Englewood Cliffs, NJ: Prentice-Hall.

Feingold, A. (1992). Gender differences in mate selection preferences: A test of the parental investment model. *Psychological Bulletin, 112,* 125–139.

Fernandez, J. P. (1975). *Black managers in White corporations.* New York: Wiley.

Fetler, M. (1984). Television viewing and school achievement. *Journal of Communication, 34,* 104–118.

Finkelman, P. (Ed.). (1992). *Lynching, racial violence, and law.* New York: Garland.

Fischer, C. S., Hout, M., Jankowski, M. S., Lucas, S. R., Swidler, A., & Voss, K. (1996). *Inequality by design: Cracking the bell curve myth.* Princeton, NJ: Princeton University Press.

Fiske, A. P. (1991). *Structures of social life: The four elementary forms of human relations: Communal sharing, authority ranking, equality matching, market pricing.* New York: Free Press.

Fiske, S. T. (1980). Attention and weight in person perception: The impact of negative and extreme behavior. *Journal of Personality and Social Psychology, 38,* 889–906.

Fiske, S. T. (1997). Stereotyping, prejudice, and discrimination. In D. T. Gilbert, S. T. Fiske, & G. Lindzey (Eds.), *The handbook of social psychology* (4th ed., pp. 357–411). New York: McGraw-Hill.

Fitzgerald, H. E., & Zucker, R. A. (1995). Socioeconomic status and alcoholism: The contextual structure of developmental pathways to addiction. In H. E. Fitzgerald, B. M. Lester, & B. S. Zuckerman (Eds.), *Children of poverty: Research, health, and policy issues* (pp. 125–148). New York: Garland.

Fix, M., & Bean, F. (1990). The findings and policy implications of the GAO report and the Urban Institute hiring audit. *International Migration Review, 24,* 817–827.

Foley, L. A. (1987). Florida after the *Furman* decision: The effect of extralegal factors on the processing of capital offense cases. *Behavioral Sciences and the Law, 5,* 457–465.

Ford, E. S., Merritt, R. K., Heath, G. W., Powell, K. E., Washburn, R. A., Kriska, A., & Haile, G. (1991). Physical activity behaviors in lower and higher socioeconomic status populations. *American Journal of Epidemiology, 133,* 1246–1256.

Fort, B. (1996). *Reading in the margins: The politics and culture of literacy in Georgia, 1800–1920.* Department of History, University of Virginia. Charlottesville, VA. Available: http://wsrv.clas.virginia.edu/~jbf2p/disspros.html

Fox, D. J., & Jordan, V. B. (1973). Racial preference and identification of Black, American, Chinese, and White children. *Genetic Psychology Monographs, 88,* 229–286.

Fraser, S. (1995). *The bell curve wars: Race, intelligence, and the future of America.* New York: Basic.

French, H. W. (1996, September 18). A neglected region loosens ties to Zaire. *New York Times,* pp. A1, A4.

Frenkel-Brunswik, E. (1948a). A study of prejudice in children. *Human Relations, 1,* 295–306.

Frenkel-Brunswik, E. (1948b). Tolerance of ambiguity as a personality variable. *American Psychologist, 3,* 268.

Frey, W. H., & Farley, R. (1993). *Latino, Asian, and Black segregation in multi-ethnic metro area findings from the 1990 census.* Ann Arbor: Population Studies Center, University of Michigan.

Freyerhern, W. (1981). Gender differences in delinquency quantity and quality. In L. H. Bowker (Ed.), *Women and crime in America.* New York: Macmillan.

Fromm, E. (1941). *Escape from freedom.* New York: Holt.

Furnham, A. (1985). Adolescents' sociopolitical attitudes: A study of sex and national differences. *Political Psychology, 6,* 621–636.

Galap, J., Raveau, F. H., & Chiche, J. (1985). Ethnicité antillaise: De l'émigration à la deuxième génération (West Indians' ethnicity: From emigration to second generation). *Cahiers d'Anthropologie et Biométrie Humaine, 3,* 123–188.

Gallaway, L. (1971). *Manpower economics.* Homewood, IL: Irwin.

Gallup. (1997). Black/White relations in the United States: A Gallup poll social audit. Dateline: June 10.

Galster, G. C. (1990). Racial discrimination in housing markets during the 1980s: A review of the audit evidence. *Journal of Planning Education and Research, 9,* 165–175.

Gamoran, A. (1987). The stratification of high school learning opportunities. *Sociology of Education, 60,* 135–155.

Garfield, S. L., & Helper, M. M. (1962). Parental attitudes and socio-economic status. *Journal of Clinical Psychology, 18,* 171–175.

GAO. (1990). *Death penalty sentencing: Research indicates patterns of racial disparities.* Report to Senate and House Committees on the Judiciary. (GAO/GGD-90-57).

Gaston, R. S. (1996). Factors affecting renal allograft survival in African Americans. *Blood Purification, 14,* 327–333.

Gaston, R. S., Shroyer, T. W., Hudson, S. L., Deierhoi, M. H., Laskow, D. A., Barber, W. H., Julian, B. A., Curtis, J. J., Barger, B. O., & Diethelm, A. G. (1994). Renal retransplantation: The role of race, quadruple immunosuppression, and the flow cytometry cross-match. *Transplantation, 57,* 47– 54.

Geller, A. C., Miller, D. R., Lew, R. A., Clapp, R. W., Wenneker, M. B., & Koh, H. K. (1996). Cutaneous melanoma mortality among the socioeconomically disadvantaged in Massachusetts. *American Journal of Public Health, 86,* 538–544.

Ghiglieri, M. P. (1989). Hominoid sociobiology and hominid social evolution. In P. G. Heltne & L. A. Marquardt (Eds.), *Understanding chimpanzees* (pp. 370–379). Cambridge, MA: Harvard University Press.

Gibson, M. A. (1991). Ethnicity, gender and social class: The school adaptation patterns of West Indian youths. In M. Gibson & J. Ogbu (Eds.), *Minority status and schooling: A comparative study of immigrant and involuntary minorities* (pp. 169–203). New York: Garland.

Gil, D. G. (1970). *Violence against children: Physical child abuse in the United States.* Cambridge, MA: Harvard University Press.

Gillmeister, H., Kurthen, H., & Fijalkowski, J. (1989). *Ausländer-beshschäftigung in der Krise?* Berlin: Edition Sigma.

Gimbutas, M. A. (1989). *The language of the goddess: Unearthing the hidden symbols of Western civilization.* New York: Harper & Row.

Gleiberman, L., Harburg, E., Frone, M. R., Russell, M., & Cooper, M. L. (1995). Skin colour, measures of socioeconomic status, and blood pressure among Blacks in Erie County, NY. *Annals of Human Biology, 22,* 69–73.

Glick, B. (1989). *Covert action against U.S. activists and what we can do about it.* Boston: South End Press.

Goering, J., & Wienk, R. (1996). An overview. In J. Goering & R. Wienk (Eds.), *Mortgage lending, racial discrimination, and federal policy* (pp. 3–28). Washington, DC: Urban Institute Press.

Goertzel, T. G. (1987). Authoritarianism of personality and political attitudes. *Journal of Social Psychology, 127,* 7–18.

Goffman, E. (1959). *The presentation of self in everyday life.* Garden City, NY: Doubleday.

Goldberg, A., Mourinho, D., & Kulke, U. (1996). Labour market discrimination against foreign workers in Germany. *International Mirgration Papers,* 7. Employment Department: International Labour Office, Geneva.

Goodman, A. B., Siegel, C., Craig, T. J., & Lin, S. P. (1983). The relationship between socioeconomic class and prevalence of schizophrenia, alcoholism, and affective disorders treated by inpatient care in a suburban area. *American Journal of Psychiatry, 140,* 166–170.

Goodman, M. (1952). *Race awareness in young children.* Cambridge, MA: Addison-Wesley.

Gopaul-McNicol, S. (1988). Racial identification and racial preference of Black preschool children in New York and Trinidad. *Journal of Black Psychology, 14,* 65–68.

Gopaul-McNicol, S. (1995). A cross-cultural examination of racial identity and racial preference of preschool children in the West Indies. *Journal of Cross-Cultural Psychology, 26,* 141–152.

Gornick, M. E., Eggers, P. W., Reilly, T. W., Mentnech, R. M., Fitterman, L. K., Kucken, L. E., & Vladeck, B. C. (1996). Effects of race and income on mortality and use of services among Medicare beneficiaries. *New England Journal of Medicine, 335,* 791–799.

Gotowiec, A., & Beiser, M. (1993). Aboriginal children's mental health: Unique challenges. *Canada's Mental Health, 41,* 7–11.

Gottfredson, L. S. (1997). Paired review of prescription for failure: Race relations in the age of social science. *Political Psychology, 18,* 209–214.

Gottfried, A. W. (1985). Measures of socioeconomic status in child development research: Data and recommendations. *Merrill-Palmer Quarterly, 31,* 85–92.

Gottfried, A. W., & Gottfried, A. E. (1986). Home environment and children's development from infancy through the school entry years: Results of contemporary longitudinal investigations in North America. *Children's Environments Quarterly, 3,* 3–9.

Gough, H. (1987). *California Personality Inventory: Administrator's guide*. Palo Alto, CA: Consulting Psychological Press.

Gould, S. J. (1981). *The mismeasure of man*. New York: Norton.

Governor's Commission on the Los Angeles Riots. (1965). *Violence in the city: An end or a beginning?* Los Angeles, CA.

Gramsci, A. (1971). *Selections from the prison notebooks*. London: Wishart.

Granotier, B. (1979). *Les travailleurs immigrés en France*. Paris: Maspero.

Grant, D. L. (1975). *The anti-lynching movement, 1883–1932*. San Francisco: R & E Research.

Graudenz, I., Kraak, B., & Hauer, D. (1976). Scale to measure child-rearing practices and attitudes of mothers of five- to six-year-old preschool children. *Psychologie in Erziehung und Unterricht, 23*, 70–79.

Greenberg, J., Pyszczynski, T., Solomon, S., Rosenblatt, A., Veeder, M., Kirkland, S., & Lyon, D. (1990). Evidence for terror management theory: II. The effects of mortality salience reactions to those who implicitly or explicitly threaten or support the cultural world view. *Journal of Personality and Social Psychology, 58*, 308–318.

Greenberg, J., Simon, L., Pyszczynski, T., Solomon, S., & Chatel, D. (1992). Terror management and tolerance: Does mortality salience always intensify negative reactions to others who threaten one's world view? *Journal of Personality and Social Psychology, 63*, 212–220.

Greenwald, H. J., & Oppenheim, D. B. (1968). Reported magnitude of self-misidentification among Negro children: Artifact? *Journal of Personality and Social Psychology, 8*, 49–52.

Gregor, A. J., & McPherson, D. A. (1966). Racial attitudes among White and Negro children in a Deep South standard metropolitan area. *Journal of Social Psychology, 68*, 95–106.

Gross, M. (1978). Cultural concomitants of preschoolers' preparation for learning. *Psychological Reports, 43*, 807–813.

Gross, S. R., & Mauro, R. (1989). *Death and discrimination: Racial disparities in capital sentencing*. Boston: Northwestern University Press.

Guillou, J. (1996a, January). 60 döms varje år för våldtäkt. *Aftonbladet*. Available: http://www.aftonbladet.se/nyheter/guillou/guillou9.html

Guillou, J. (1996b, January). Därför är fängelserna fyllda med utlänningar. *Aftonbladet*. Available: http://www.aftonbladet.se/nyheter/guillou/guillou6.html

Guion, R. (1966). Employment test and discrimination hiring. *Industrial Relations, 5*, 20–37.

Gupta, A., & Jahan, Q. (1989). Differences in cognitive capacity among tribal and non-tribal high school students of Himachal Pradesh. *Manas, 36*, 17–25.

Gupta, D. (1990). *The economics of political violence: The effect of political instability on economic growth*. New York: Praeger.

Gurr, T. R., & Harff, B. (1994). *Ethnic conflict in world politics*. Boulder, CO: Westview.

Hahn, R. A., Eaker, E. D., Barker, N. D., Teutsch, S. M., Sosniak, W. A., & Krieger,

N. (1996). Poverty and death in the United States. *International Journal of Health Services, 26*, 673–690.

Hakkarainen, H., Huhta, E., Lahti, K., Lundvall, P., et al. (1996). A test of male mating and hunting success in the kestrel: The advantages of smallness? *Behavioral Ecology and Sociobiology, 39*, 375–380.

Hales, L., & Hartman, T. (1978). Personality, sex and work values. *Journal of Experimental Education, 47*, 16–21

Hall, T. (1997, August 29). Österrike steriliserar än i dag. *Dagens Nyheter.* Available: http://www.dn.se/DNet/firstframe.html

Hamamsy, L. S. (1957). The role of women in changing Navaho society. *American Anthropologist, 59*, 101–111.

Hamilton, D. L. (1979). A cognitive-attributional analysis of stereotyping. *Advances in Experimental Social Psychology, 12*, 53–85.

Hamilton, D. L., & Gifford, R. K. (1976). Illusory correlation in interpersonal perception: A cognitive basis of stereotypic judgments. *Journal of Experimental Social Psychology, 12*, 392–407.

Hamilton, D. L., & Rose, T. L. (1980). Illusory correlation and the maintenance of stereotypic beliefs. *Journal of Personality and Social Psychology, 39*, 832–845.

Hamilton, W. D. (1964). The genetical evolution of social behavior. *Journal of Theoretical Biology, 7*, 1–16 and 17–52.

Hampton, R. L. (1987). Race, class and child maltreatment. *Journal of Comparative Family Studies, 18*, 113–126.

Hansche, J. H., Gottfried, N. W., & Hansche, W. J. (1982). A multiple discriminant analysis of special education classification. *Southern Psychologist, 1*, 41–52.

Harcourt, A. H. (1988). Alliances in contests and social intelligence. In R. W. Byrne & A. Whiten (Eds.), *Machiavellian intelligence: Social expertise and the evolution of intellect in monkeys, apes, and humans* (pp. 132–152). Oxford: Clarendon Press.

Hardin, C. D., & Higgins, E. T. (1996). Shared reality: How social verification makes the subjective objective. In R. M. Sorrentino & E. T. Higgins (Eds.), *Handbook of motivation and cognition: The interpersonal context* (Vol. 3, pp. 28–84). New York: Guilford.

Hardt, R. H. (1968). Delinquency and social class: Bad kids or good cops. In I. Deutscher & E. J. Thompson (Eds.), *Among the people: Encounters with the poor* (pp. 132–145). New York: Basic.

Harris, M. J., & Rosenthal, R. (1985). Mediation of interpersonal expectancy effects: 31 meta-analyses. *Psychological Bulletin, 97*, 363–386.

Harry, B., & Anderson, M. G. (1995). The disproportionate placement of African-American males in special education programs: A critique of the process [Special issue: Pedagogical and contextual issues affecting African-American males in school]. *Journal of Negro Education, 63*, 602–619.

Hawkins, D. F., & Jones, N. E. (1989). Black adolescents and the criminal justice system. In R. L. Jones (Ed.), *Black adolescents* (pp. 403–425). Berkeley, CA: Cobb & Henry.

Heath, S. B. (1980). What no bedtime story means: Narrative skills at home and school. In B. B. Schieffelin & E. Ochs (Eds.), *Language socialization across cultures: Studies in the social and cultural foundations of language* (pp. 97–124). Cambridge University Press.

Hedges, C. (1994, January 24). Dozens of Islamic rebel suspects slain by Algerian death squads. *New York Times.*

Heilbrun, A. B. (1982). Female criminals: Behavior and treatment within the criminal justice system. *Criminal Justice and Behavior, 9,* 341–351.

Heilman, M. E. (1983). Sex bias in work settings: The lack-of-fit model. *Research in Organizational Behavior, 5,* 269–298.

Henry, F., & Ginzberg, E. (1985). *Who gets the work? A test of racial discrimination in employment.* Toronto: Social Planning Council of Metropolitan Toronto.

Hepburn, J. R. (1978). Race and the decision to arrest: An analysis of warrants issued. *Journal of Research in Crime and Delinquency, 15,* 54–73.

Herrnstein, R. J., & Murray, C. A. (1994). *The bell curve: Intelligence and class structure in American life.* New York: Free Press.

Heussenstamm, F. K. (1971). Bumper stickers and cops. *Transaction, 8,* 32–33.

Hilton, J. L., & von Hippel, W. (1996). Stereotypes. *Annual Review of Psychology, 47,* 237–271.

Hinkle, S., & Brown, R. (1990). Intergroup comparisons and social identity: Some links and lacunae. In D. Abrams & M. Hogg (Eds.), *Social identity theory: Constructive and critical advances* (pp. 48–70). London: Harvester Wheat Sheaf.

Hochschild, J. L. (1995). *Facing up to the American dream: Race, class, and the soul of the nation.* Princeton, NJ: Princeton University Press.

Hoig, S. (1961). *The Sand Creek massacre.* Norman: University of Oklahoma Press.

Holcomb, W. R., & Ahr, P. R. (1988). Arrest rates among young adult psychiatric patients treated in inpatient and outpatient settings. *Hospital and Community Psychiatry, 39,* 52–57.

Holhut, R. T. (1996). Challenging the racist science of "the bell curve." Available: http://www.mdle.com/WrittenWord/rholhut/holhut27.htm

Hollinger, R. C. (1984). Race, occupational status, and pro-active police arrest for drinking and driving. *Journal of Criminal Justice, 12,* 173–183.

Holzer, C. E., Shea, B. M., Swanson, J. W., & Leaf, P. J. (1986). The increased risk for specific psychiatric disorders among persons of low socioeconomic status [Special issue: Psychiatric epidemiology]. *American Journal of Social Psychiatry, 6,* 259–271.

Hood, R., & Cordovil, G. (1992). *Race and sentencing: A study in the Crown Court– A report for the Commission for Racial Equality.* Oxford: Clarendon Press.

Hood, R., & Sparks, R. (1970). *Key issues in criminology.* London: Weidenfeld & Nicholson.

Horowitz, E. L. (1936). The development of attitude toward the Negro. *Archives of Psychology, 194,* 1–47.

Hotaling, G. T., & Sugarman, D. B. (1990). A risk marker analysis of assaulted wives. *Journal of Family Violence, 5,* 1–13.

Hovland, C. I., & Sears, R. R. (1940). Minor studies of aggression: VI. Correlation of lynching with economic indices. *Journal of Psychology, 9,* 301–310.

Hraba, J., & Grant, G. (1970). Black is beautiful: A re-examination of racial preference and identification. *Journal of Personality and Social Psychology, 16*, 398–402.

Hraba, J., Hagendoorn, L., & Hagendoorn, R. (1989). The ethnic hierarchy in the Netherlands: Social distance and social representation. *British Journal of Social Psychology, 28*, 57–69.

Hughes, M., & Hertel, B. R. (1990). The significance of color remains: A study of life chances, mate selection, and ethnic consciousness among Black Americans. *Social Forces, 68*, 1105–1120.

Humphrey, R. (1985). How work roles influence perception: Structural-cognitive processes and organizational behavior. *American Sociological Review, 50*, 242–252.

Hurtado, A. (1994). Does similarity breed respect? Interviewer evaluations of Mexican-descent respondents in a bilingual survey. *Public Opinion Quarterly, 58*, 77–95.

Ito, H. (1967). Japan's outcasts in the United States. In G. A. DeVos & H. Wagatsuma (Eds.), *Japan's invisible race* (pp. 200–221). Berkeley: University of California Press.

Jackman, M. (1994). *The velvet glove: Paternalism and conflict in gender, class and race relations.* Berkeley: University of California Press.

Jackson, D. N. (1965). *Personality research form.* Goshen, NY: Research Psychologists Press.

Jackson, J. S., & Kirby, D. (1991, August). *Models of individual outgroup rejection: Cross-national Western Europe–United States comparisons.* Paper presented at the Symposium on the Social Psychology of Intergroup Relations, ASA annual meeting, Cincinnati, OH.

Jaensch, E. R. (1938). *Der Gegentypus.* Leipzig: J. A. Barth.

James, W. (1890). *Principles of psychology* (Vol. 1). New York: Holt.

Jansen, R. E., Fitzgerald, H. E., Ham, H. P., & Zucker, R. A. (1995). Pathways into risk: Temperament and behavior problems in three- to five-year-old sons of alcoholics. *Alcoholism: Clinical and Experimental Research, 19*, 501–509.

Jespersen, S., & Herring, R. D. (1994). International counseling: An opportunity for culture-specific counseling with the New Zealand Maori. *Journal of Multicultural Counseling and Development, 22*, 17–27.

Johns, C. H. W. (1947). *Babylonian and Assyrian laws, contracts, and letters.* New York: Scribner.

Johnson, G. B., Jr. (1950). The origin and development of the Spanish attitudes toward the Anglo and the Anglo attitudes toward the Spanish. *Journal of Educational Psychology, 41*, 429–439.

Johnson, J. A. (1987). Dominance rank in juvenile olive baboons, *Papio anubis*: The influence of gender, size, maternal rank and orphaning. *Animal Behaviour, 35*, 1694–1708.

Jones, J. H. (1993). *Bad blood: The Tuskegee syphilis experiment.* New York: Free Press.

Jones, J. M. (1997). *Prejudice and racism* (2nd ed.). New York: McGraw–Hill.

Jost, J. T. (1995). Negative illusions: Conceptual clarification and psychological evidence concerning false consciousness. *Political Psychology, 16*, 397–424.

Jost, J. T., & Banaji, M. R. (1994). The role of stereotyping in system-justification and the production of false-consciousness. *British Journal of Social Psychology, 33*, 1–27.

Judd, C. M., Park, B., Ryan, C. S., Brauer, M., & Kraus, S. (1995). Stereotypes and ethnocentrism: Diverging interethnic perceptions of African-American and White American youth. *Journal of Personality and Social Psychology, 69*, 460–481.

Junger, M., & Polder, W. (1992). Some explanations of crime among four ethnic groups in the Netherlands. *Journal of Quantitative Criminology, 8*, 51–78.

Jussim, L., & Eccles, J. (1992).Teacher expectations: II. Construction and reflection of student achievement. *Journal of Personality and Social Psychology, 63*, 947–961.

Jussim, L., & Eccles, J. (1995). Naturally occurring interpersonal expectancies. In N. Eisenberg (Ed.), *Social development: Review of personality and social psychology* (pp. 74–108). Thousand Oaks, CA: Sage.

Kantor, G. K., & Straus, M. A. (1987). The "drunken bum" theory of wife beating. *Social Problems, 34*, 213–230.

Kaplan, J. R., Adams, M. R., Clarkson, T. B., & Koritnik, D. R. (1984). Psychosocial influences on female "protection" among cynomolgus macaques. *Atherosclerosis, 53*, 283–295.

Kaprio, J., & Koskenvuo, M. (1988). A prospective study of psychological and socioeconomic characteristics, health behavior and morbidity in cigarette smokers prior to quitting compared to persistent smokers and non-smokers. *Journal of Clinical Epidemiology, 41*, 139–150.

Karanth, G. K. (1996). Caste in contemporary rural India. In M. N. Srinivas (Ed.), *Caste: Its twentieth century avatar* (pp. 87–109). New Delhi: Penguin.

Katz, I., Epps, E. G., & Axelson, L. J. (1964). Effect upon Negro digit symbol performance of anticipated comparison with Whites and with other Negroes. *Journal of Abnormal and Social Psychology, 69*, 963–970.

Katz, I., & Hass, R. G. (1988). Racial ambivalence and American value conflict: Correlational and priming studies of dual cognitive structures. *Journal of Personality and Social Psychology, 55*, 893–905.

Katz, I., Roberts, S. O., & Robinson, J. M. (1965). Effects of task difficulty, race of administrator, and instructions on digit-symbol performance of Negroes. *Journal of Personality and Social Psychology, 2*, 53–59.

Katz, I., Wackenhut, J., & Hass, R. G. (1986). Racial ambivalence, value duality, and behavior. In J. F. Dovidio & S. L. Gaertner (Eds.), *Prejudice, discrimination, and racism* (pp. 35–59). New York: Academic.

Kawanaka, K. (1982). Further studies on predation by chimpanzees of the Mahale Mountains. *Primates, 23*, 364–384.

Kawanaka, K. (1989). Age differences in social interactions of young males in a chimpanzee unit-group at the Mahale Mountains National Park, Tanzania. *Primates, 30*, 285–305.

Keegan, J. (1993). *The history of warfare*. New York: Knopf.

Keil, T. J., & Vito, G. F. (1989). Race, homicide severity and application of the death penalty: A consideration of the Barnett Scale. *Criminology, 27*, 511–531.

Kelly, H. E. (1976). A comparison of defense strategy and race as influences in differential sentencing. *Criminology: An Interdisciplinary Journal, 14*, 241–249.

Kelsey, J. (1995) *The New Zealand experiment: A world model for structured adjustments*. Auckland: Auckland University Press.

Kennedy, R. (1997, August 29). Civilian police review unit is criticized as ineffectual. *New York Times*. Available: http://www.nytimes.com/yr/mo/day/news/national/nyc-police-board.html

Kenrick, D. T., Sadalla, E. K., Groth, G., & Trost, M. R. (1990). Evolution, traits, and the stages of human courtship: Qualifying the parental investment model [Special issue: Biological foundations of personality: Evolution, behavioral genetics, and psychophysiology]. *Journal of Personality, 58,* 97–116.

Kerlinger, F. N. (1984). *Liberalism and conservatism: The nature and structure of social attitudes*. Hillsdale, NJ: Erlbaum.

Kidder, L. H., Bellettirie, G., & Cohn, E. S. (1977). Secret ambitions and public performances: The effects of anonymity on reward allocations made by men and women. *Journal of Experimental Social Psychology, 13,* 70–80.

Kinder, D. R., & Sanders, L. M. (1996). *Divided by color: Racial politics and democratic ideals*. Chicago: University of Chicago Press.

Kirschenman, J., & Neckerman, K. M. (1991). "We'd love to hire him but . . . ." The meaning of race for employers. In C. Jencks & P. E. Peterson (Eds.), *The urban underclass*. Washington, DC: Brookings Institution.

Kirscht, J. P., & Dillehay, R. C. (1967). *Dimensions of authoritarianism: A review of research and theory*. Lexington: University of Kentucky Press.

Kirui, P. M. K. (1982). A study of the factors that influence the increasing repetition and dropout rates in primary schools in the Nandi district of Kenya. *African Studies in Curriculum Development and Evaluation*, no. 67. African Curriculum Organisation. German Agency for Technical Co-Operation, Nairobi (Kenya). Kenya Institute of Education, Nairobi. Nairobi University (Kenya).

Kitagawa, E. M., & Hauser, P. M. (1973). *Differential mortality in the United States: A study in socioeconomic epidemiology*. Cambridge, MA: Harvard University Press.

Kitcher, P. (1985). *Vaulting ambition: Sociobiology and the quest for human nature*. Cambridge, MA: MIT Press.

Klatzky, R. L., & Andersen, S. M. (1988). Category-specificity effects in social typing and personalization. In T. K. Srull & R. S. Wyer, Jr. (Eds.), *A dual process model of impression formation: Advances in social cognition* (Vol. 1, pp. 91–101). Hillsdale, NJ: Erlbaum.

Klich, L. Z. (1988). Aboriginal cognition and psychological science. In S. H. Irvine & J. W. Berry (Eds.), *Human abilities in cultural context* (pp. 427–452). Cambridge University Press.

Kline, H. K. (1970). An exploration of racism in ego-ideal formation. *Smith College Studies in Social Work, 40,* 211–215.

Kluegel, J. R. (1978). The causes and cost of racism exclusion from job authority. *American Sociological Review, 43,* 285–301.

Kluegel, J. R., & Smith, E. R. (1986). *Beliefs about inequality: Americans' views of what is and what ought to be*. New York: Aldine De Gruyter.

Koch, E. (1996). How murder became mere routine: De Kock trial. *Electronic Mail and Guardian.* Available: www.mg.co.za/mg/newss/96feb/27feb-dekock.html

Koelewijn-Strattner, G. J. (1991). *Race and gender in the chemistry profession: Double jeopardy or double negative.* Washington, DC: American Sociological Association.

Kogan, M. D., Kotelchuck, M., Alexander, G. R., & Johnson, W. E. (1994). Racial disparities in reported prenatal care advice from health care providers. *American Journal of Public Health, 84,* 82–88.

Kolb, L. (1932). The intelligence of immigrants as measured by tests. *Proceedings and Addresses of the American Association for the Study of Feeblemindedness, 37,* 395–407.

Konrad, A., & Linnehan, F. (1995). Formalized HRM structures: Coordinating equal employment opportunity or concealing organizational practices? *Academy of Management Journal, 55,* 187–195.

Koslin, S. C., Amarel, M., & Ames, N. (1970). The effect of race on peer evaluation and preference in primary grade children: An exploratory study. *Journal of Negro Education, 39,* 346–350.

Kozol, J. (1991). *Savage inequalities: Children in America's schools.* New York: Harper Perennial.

Kraus, V. (1982). Ethnic origin as a hierarchical dimension of social status and its correlates. *Sociology and Social Research, 66,* 50–71.

Krieger, N., & Fee, E. (1996). Measuring social inequalities in health in the United States: A historical review, 1900–1950. *International Journal of Health Services, 26,* 391–418.

Krieger, N., & Sidney, S. (1996). Racial discrimination and blood pressure: The CARDIA Study of Young Black and White Adults. *American Journal of Public Health, 86,* 1370–1378.

Kristof, N. D. (1995, November 30). Japanese outcasts better off than in past but still outcast. *New York Times,* p. A1.

Krueger, J., & Rothbart, M. (1988). Use of categorical and individuating information in making inferences about personality. *Journal of Personality and Social Psychology, 55,* 187–195.

Kugelman, S., Lieblich, A., & Bossik, D. (1974). Patterns of intellectual ability in Jewish and Arab children in Israel. *Journal of Cross-Cultural Psychology, 5,* 184–198.

Ladewig, D., Weidmann, M., & Hole, G. (1975). Occupation, social level, and free-time activity of depressives and drug addicts: A social psychiatric study in hospitalized patients. *Social Psychiatry, 10,* 145–152.

LaFree, G. D. (1989). *Rape and criminal justice: The social construction of sexual assault.* Belmont, CA: Wadsworth.

Lagendijk, J. (1986). *Opinie onderzoek, het FEM Lagendijk ondernemerspanel, Raadpleging over het tweede kwartaal.* Apeldoorn, Lagendijk's Opinie Onderzoek.

Lanfranchi, A. (1993). "...Wenigstens in meinem Dorf ist es Brauch ...": Von der Stagnation zur Transformation familialer Wirklichkeitskonstrukte bei Immigranten. *Praxis der Kinderpsychologie und Kinderpsychiatrie, 42,* 188–198.

Lange, A. (1996). *Invandrare om diskriminering: II. En enkät- och intervjuunder- sökning om etnisk diskriminering på uppdrag av Diskrimineringsombudsmannen (DO).* CEIFO Skriftserie nr. 70. Edsbruk, Sweden: Akademitryck AB.

Lanier, J., & Wittmer, J. (1977). Teacher prejudice in referral of students to EMR programs. *School Counselor, 24,* 165–170.

Lattes, J. (1989). *La principe de non-discrimination en droit de travail.* Toulouse: Université de Toulouse.

Lee, P. C., & Oliver, J. I. (1979). Competition, dominance and the acquisition of rank in juvenile yellow baboons (*Papio cynocephalus*). *Animal Behaviour, 27,* 576–585.

Lee, Y. (1991). Koreans in Japan and the United States. In M. Gibson & J. Ogbu (Eds.), *Minority status and schooling: A comparative study of immigrant and involuntary minorities* (pp. 131–167). New York: Garland.

Leigh, S. R., & Shea, B. T. (1995). Ontogeny and the evolution of adult body size dimorphism in apes. *American Journal of Primatology, 36,* 37–60.

Leitner, D. W., & Sedlacek, W. E. (1976). Characteristics of successful campus police officers. *Journal of College Student Personnel, 17,* 304–308.

Lenski, G. E. (1984). *Power and privilege: A theory of social stratification.* Chapel Hill: University of North Carolina Press.

Leonard, J. W. (1979). A strategy approach to the study of primate dominance behavior. *Behavioural Processes, 4,* 155–172.

Lepore, L., & Brown, R. (1997). Category and stereotype activation: Is prejudice inevitable? *Journal of Personality and Social Psychology, 72,* 275–287.

Leventhal, G. S., Popp, A. L., & Sawyer, L. (1973). Equity or equality in children's allocation of reward to other persons? *Child Development, 44,* 753–763.

Levin, S. L. (1996). A social psychological approach to understanding inter- group attitudes in the United States and Israel. Unpublished doctoral dis- sertation, Department of Psychology, UCLA.

Levine, R. A., & Campbell, D. T. (1972). *Ethnocentrism: Theories of conflict, ethnic attitudes and group behavior.* New York: Wiley.

Lewicki, P. (1986). Processing information about covariations that cannot be articulated. *Journal of Experimental Psychology: Learning, Memory, and Cogni- tion, 12,* 135–146.

Lewis, B. Y. (1987). Psychosocial factors related to wife abuse. *Journal of Family Violence, 2,* 1–10.

Lewontin, R. C., Rose, S., & Kamin, L. J. (1984). *Not in our genes: Biology, ideology, and human nature.* New York: Pantheon.

Leyens, J. P., Yzerbyt, V., & Schadron, G. (1994). *Stereotypes and social cognition.* Thousand Oaks, CA: Sage.

Lichtenstein, K. R. (1982). Extra-legal variables affecting sentencing decisions. *Psychological Reports, 50,* 611–619.

Lindqvist, S. (1997, August 30). Välfärd stoppade steriliseringar. *Dagens Nyheter.*

Lipset, S. M. (1982). The academic mind at the top: The political behavior and values of faculty elites. *Public Opinion Quarterly, 46,* 143–168.

Lipton, J. P. (1983). Racism in the jury box: The Hispanic defendant. *Hispanic Journal of Behavioral Sciences, 5,* 275–290.

Listokin, D., & Casey, S. (1980). *Mortgage lending and race: Conceptual and analytical perspectives on the urban financing problem.* New Brunswick, NJ: Rutgers University Press.

Liston, A., & Salts, C. J. (1988). Mate selection values: A comparison of Malaysian and United States students. *Journal of Comparative Family Studies, 19,* 361–370.

Locke, V., MacLeod, C., & Walker, I. (1994). Automatic and controlled activation of stereotypes: Individual differences associated with prejudice. *British Journal of Social Psychology, 33,* 29–46.

Locke, V., & Walker, I. (1998). Stereotyping, processing goals, and social identity: Inveterate and fugacious characteristics of stereotypes. In D. Abrams & M. Hogg (Eds.), *Social identity and social cognition.* London: Blackwell.

Loehlin, J. C. (1993). What has behavioral genetics told us about the nature of personality? In T. J. Bouchard & P. Propping (Eds.), *Twins as a tool of behavioral genetics* (pp. 109–119). Chichester: Wiley.

Longhofer, S. D. (1996, August 15). Discrimination in mortgage lending: What have we learned? *Economic Commentary.* Available: http://www.clev.frb.org/research/com/081596.htm

Loury, G. C. (1985). The moral quandary of the Black community. *Public Interest, 79,* 9–22.

Love, W., & Bachara, G. (1975). Delinquents with learning disabilities. *Youth Re.* Washington, DC: Department of Health Education and Welfare.

Low, B. P., & Clement, P. W. (1982). Relationships of race and socioeconomic status to classroom behavior, academic achievement, and referral for special education. *Journal of School Psychology, 20,* 103–112.

Lowe, M., Kerridge, I. H., & Mitchell, K. R. (1995). "These sorts of people don't do very well": Race and allocation of health care resources. *Journal of Medical Ethics, 21,* 356–360.

Luhtanen, R., & Crocker, J. (1991). Self-esteem and intergroup comparisons: Toward a theory of collective self-esteem. In J. Suls & T. A. Wills (Eds.), *Social comparison: Contemporary theory and research* (pp. 211–234). Hillsdale, NJ: Erlbaum.

Lynch, J. P., & Sabol, W. J. (1994, November). *The use of coercive social control and changes in the race and class composition of U.S. prison populations.* Paper presented at the meeting of the American Society of Criminology, Miami, FL.

Lynn, R., Hampton, S., & Magee, M. (1984). Home background, intelligence, personality and education as predictors of unemployment in young people. *Personality and Individual Differences, 5,* 549–557.

Lyson, T. A. (1984). Sex differences in the choice of a male or female career line: An analysis of background characteristics and work values. *Work and Occupations, 11,* 131–146.

Maas, C., & Stuyling de Lange, J. (1989). Selectiviteit in de rechtsgang van buitenlandse verdachten behorende tot ethnische groepen. *Tijdschrift voor Criminologie, 1,* 1–13.

Magiste, E. (1992). Social isolation and juvenile delinquency in second generation immigrants. *Studia Psychologica, 34,* 153–165.

Mair, G. (1986). Ethnic minorities, probation and the magistrates' courts: A pilot study. *British Journal of Criminology, 26,* 147–155.

Major, B., & Adams, J. B. (1984). Situational moderators of gender differences in reward allocations. *Sex Roles, 11,* 869–880.

Major, B., Bylsma, W. H., & Cozzarelli, C. (1989). Gender differences in distributive justice preferences: The impact of domain. *Sex Roles, 21,* 487–497.

Malamuth, N. M. (1996). The confluence model of sexual aggression: Feminism and evolutionary perspectives. In D. M. Buss & N. M. Malamuth (Eds.), *Sex, power and conflict: Evolutionary and feminist perspectives* (pp. 269–295). New York: Oxford University Press.

Mann, C. R. (1984). Race and sentencing of female felons: A field study. *International Journal of Women's Studies, 7,* 160–172.

Manton, K. G., Patrick, C. H., & Johnson, K. W. (1987). Health differentials between Blacks and Whites: Recent trends in mortality and morbidity. *Milbank Quarterly, 65,* 129–199.

Manuck, S. B., Kaplan, J. R., Adams, M. R., & Clarkson, T. B. (1988). Studies of psychosocial influences on coronary artery atherogenesis in cynomolgus monkeys. *Health Psychology, 7,* 113–124.

Marjoribanks, K. (1981). Sex-related differences in socio-political attitudes: A replication. *Educational Studies, 7,* 1–6.

Marmot, M. G., Smith, G. D., Stansfeld, S., Patel, C., North, F., Head, J., White, I., Brunner, E., & Feeney, A. (1991). Health inequalities among British civil servants: The Whitehall II Study. *Lancet, 337,* 1387–1393.

Marsden, H. M. (1968). Agonistic behaviour of young rhesus monkeys after changes induced in social rank of their mothers. *Animal Behaviour, 16,* 38–44.

Marx, K. (1904). *A contribution to a critique of political economy.* London: Charles Kerr.

Marx, K., & Engels, F. (1846/1970). *The German ideology.* New York: International Publishers.

Mathur, S. S., & Kalia, A. K. (1984). Colour consciousness among nursery school children in relation to sex and income level. *Asian Journal of Psychology and Education, 13,* 30–33.

Matthews, K., Kelsey, S., Meilahn, E., Kuller, L., & Wing, R. (1989). Educational attainment and behavioral and biologic risk factors for coronary heart disease in middle-aged women. *American Journal of Epidemiology, 129,* 1132–1144.

Mauer, M. (1990). Testimony of Marc Mauer, Assistant Director, the Sentencing Project, before the Subcommittee on Legislation and National Security and the Subcommittee on Government Information, Justice and Agriculture of the House Government Operations Committee, May 2, 1990, Washington, DC.

Mauer, M., & Huling, T. (1995, October). *Young Black Americans and the criminal justice system: Five years later.* Washington, DC: Sentencing Project.

Maugh, T. H., II. (1996). Study says lead exposure may contribute to crime. *Los Angeles Times,* p. A13.

Mazur, A. (1985). A biosocial model of status in face-to-face primate groups. *Social Forces, 64,* 377–402.

Mazzella, R., & Feingold, A. (1994). The effects of physical attractiveness, race, socioeconomic status, and gender of defendants and victims on judgments of mock jurors: A meta-analysis. *Journal of Applied Social Psychology, 24,* 1315–1344.

McBean, A. M., & Gornick, M. (1994). Differences by race in the rates of procedures performed in hospitals for Medicare beneficiaries. *Health Care Financing Review, 15,* 77–90.

McClosky, H. (1958). Conservatism and personality. *American Political Science Review, 52,* 27–45.

McConahay, J. B. (1986). Modern racism, ambivalence, and the modern racism scale. In S. L. Gaertner & J. F. Dovidio (Eds.), *Prejudice, discrimination, and racism: Theory and research* (pp. 91–125). New York: Academic.

McCuen, G. E. (1988). *Political murder in Central America: Death squads and U.S. policies.* Hudson, WI: McCuen.

McEntire, D. (1960). *Residence and race.* Berkeley: University of California Press.

McFarland, S. G., & Adelson, S. (1996, July). *An omnibus study of personality, values and prejudices.* Paper presented at the annual convention of the International Society for Political Psychology, Vancouver, British Columbia.

McGill, H. C., Jr., McMahan, C. A., Kruski, A. W., & Mott, G. E. (1981). Relationship of lipoprotein cholesterol concentrations to experimental atherosclerosis in baboons. *Arteriosclerosis, 1,* 3–12.

McGinn, N. F., et al. (1991). *Attending school and learning or repeating and leaving: A study about the determinants of grade repetition and dropout in primary school in Honduras—Synthesis of the study.* Cambridge, MA: Harvard University, Institute for International Development.

McIntosh, N., & Smith, D. J. (1974). *The extent of racial discrimination.* London: PEP, the Social Science Institute.

Medina, C. E. (1983). Salud mental en Chile: Estado actual y perspectivas [Mental health in Chile: Actual state and perspectives]. *Revista Chilena de Neuro-Psiquiatría, 21,* 77–90.

Mehrländer, U. (1986). *Situation der ausländer: Arbeitnehmer und ihrer familienangehšrigen in der Bundesrepublik Deutschland. Repräsentativeuntersuchung '85.* Bonn: Bundesministerium für Arbeit und Sozialordung.

Mello, N. K. (1982). An examination of some etiological theories of alcoholism. *Academic Psychology Bulletin, 4,* 467–474.

Merton, R. (1972). The self-fulfilling prophecy. In E. P. Hollander & R. G. Hunt (Eds.), *Classic contributions to social psychology* (pp. 260–266). New York: Oxford University Press.

Messick, D. M., & Mackie, D. M. (1989). Intergroup relations. *Annual Review of Psychology, 40,* 45–81.

Meyer, S. (1992, July/October). Race, gender, and homicide: Comparisons between aboriginals and other Canadians. *Canadian Journal of Criminology,* 387–402.

Michels, R. (1911/1962). *Political parties: A sociological study of the oligarchical tendencies of modern democracy.* New York: Free Press.

Mikula, G. (1974). Nationality, performance, and sex as determinants of reward allocation. *Journal of Personality and Social Psychology, 29,* 435–440.

Miller, G. (1993, August 28). U.S. denounces Baghdad for violating rights of Shiites. *Los Angeles Times*.

Miller, N. E., & Miller, G. J. (1975). Letter: High-density lipoprotein and atherosclerosis. *Lancet, 1*, 1033.

Mirels, H. L., & Garrett, J. B. (1971). The Protestant ethic as a personality variable. *Journal of Consulting and Clinical Psychology, 36*, 40–44.

Mitchell, M., & Sidanius, J. (1995). Social hierarchy and the death penalty: A social dominance perspective. *Political Psychology, 16*, 591–619.

Molin, L. D., & Astin, A. W. (1973). Personal characteristics and attitude changes of student protestors. *Journal of College Student Personnel, 14*, 239–249.

Mosca, G. (1896/1939). *The ruling class: Elements of political science*. New York: McGraw-Hill.

Moscovici, S. (1981). On social representation. In J. P. Forgas (Ed.), *Social cognition: Perspectives on everyday understanding* (pp. 181–209). London: Academic.

Moscovici, S. (1988). Notes towards a description of social representations. *European Journal of Social Psychology, 18*, 211–250.

Moynihan, D. P. (1967). The Negro family: The case for national action. In L. Rainwater & W. L. Rainwater (Eds.), *The Moynihan Report and the politics of controversy* (pp. 41–64). Cambridge, MA: MIT Press.

Mueller, C. W., Parcel, T. L., & Kazuko, T. (1989). Particularism in authority outcomes of Black and White supervisors. *Social Science Research, 18*, 1–20.

Mullen, B., Brown, R., & Smith, C. (1992). Ingroup bias as a function of salience, relevance, and status: An integration. *European Journal of Social Psychology, 22*, 103–122.

Mummendey, A., Simon, B., Dietze, C., Grunert, M., et al. (1992). Categorization is not enough: Intergroup discrimination in negative outcome allocation. *Journal of Experimental Social Psychology, 28*, 125–144.

Mummendey, H. D., Bolten, H., & Isermann-Gerke, M. (1982). Experimentelle uberprufung des bogus-pipeline-paradigmas: Einstellungen gegenuber Turken, Deutschen und Hollandern. *Zeitschrift fur Sozialpsychologie, 13*, 300–311.

Munck A., Guyre, P. M., & Holbrook, N. J. (1984). Physiological functions of glucocorticoids in stress and their relation to pharmacological actions. *Endocrine Reviews, 5*, 25–44.

Munitz, S., Priel, B., & Henik, A. (1985). Color, skin color preferences and self color identification among Ethiopian- and Israeli-born children [Special issue: Ethiopian Jews and Israel]. *Israel Social Science Research, 3*, 74–84.

Munk-Jorgensen, P., & Kaldau, R. (1984). Sammenligning af sociale forhold for et forstegangsklientel ved to arhusianske alkoholambulatorier [Summary of the social status of first referrals in an outpatient clinic for alcoholics in Arhus]. *Nordisk Psykiatrisk Tidsskrift, 38*, 393–400.

Munnell, A., Browne, L. E., McEneaney, J., & Tootell, G. M. B. (1992). *Mortgage lending in Boston: Interpreting HMDA data*. Federal Reserve Bank of Boston. Working paper 92-07, October.

Murdock, G. P. (1949). *Social structure*. New York: Macmillan.

Murphy, D. E. (1997, September 2). A victim of Sweden's pursuit of perfection. *Los Angeles Times*.

Murstein, B. I. (1976). Qualities of desired spouse: A cross-cultural comparison between French and American college students. *Journal of Comparative Family Studies, 7*, 455–469.

Mussen, P. H. (1950). Some personality and social factors related to changes in children's attitudes toward Negroes. *Journal of Abnormal and Social Psychology, 45*, 423–444.

Myers, S. L. (1985). Statistical tests of discrimination in punishment. *Journal of Quantitative Criminology, 1*, 191–218.

Myers, S. L. (1992, April). Crime, entrepreneurship, and labor force withdrawal. *Contemporary Policy Issues, 10* (2).

Nadler, R. D. (1988, August). *Sexual aggression in the great apes*. Paper presented at the conference of the New York Academy of Sciences: Human sexual aggression – Current perspectives (1987, New York, NY). *Annals of the New York Academy of Sciences, 528*, 154–162.

Nagel, I. H. (1983). The legal/extra legal controversy: Judicial decisions in pretrial release. *Law and Society Review, 17*, 481–515.

National Association of Criminal Defense Lawyers. (1996). *Racism in the criminal justice system*. Available: www.criminaljustice.org/LEGIS/leg17.htm

National Research Council. (1995). *Doctorate record file*. 2101 Constitution Avenue NW, Washington, DC 20418.

Neto, F., & Mullet, E. (1982). Résultats d'une enquête sur les conditions de vie des migrants Portugais. *Orientation Scolaire et Professionnelle, 11*, 355–368.

Nettelbladt, P., Uddenberg, N., & Englesson, I. (1981). Sex-role patterns, paternal rearing attitudes and child development in different social classes. *Acta Psychiatrica Scandinavica, 64*, 12–24.

Neuberg, S. L., & Fiske, S. T. (1987). Motivational influences on impression formation: Outcome dependency, accuracy-driven attention, and individuating processes. *Journal of Personality and Social Psychology, 53*, 431–444.

Neuman, S. B. (1986). The home environment and fifth-grade students' leisure reading. *Elementary School Journal, 86*, 335–343.

Ng, S. H. (1980). *The social psychology of power*. New York: Academic.

Nias, D. K. B. (1972). The structuring of social attitudes in children. *Child Development, 43*, 211–219.

Norris, V. P. (1987). *Politics and sexual equality: The comparative position of women in Western democracies*. Boulder, CO: Rienner.

Nunnally, J. C., & Bernstein, I. H. (1994). *Psychometric theory* (3rd ed.). New York: McGraw-Hill.

Ogbu, J. U. (1978). *Minority education and caste: The American system in cross-cultural perspective*. New York: Academic.

Ogbu, J. U. (1991a). Minority coping responses and school experience. *Journal of Psychohistory, 18*, 433–456.

Ogbu, J. U. (1991b). Minority education. In M. Gibson & J. Ogbu (Eds.), *Minority status and schooling: A comparative study of immigrant and involuntary minorities*. New York: Garland.

Ogbu, J. U. (1994). From cultural differences in cultural frame of reference. In P. M. Greenfield & R. R. Cocking (Eds.), *Cross-cultural roots of minority child development* (pp. 365–391). Hilldale, NJ: Erlbaum.

Okanes, M. M. (1974). Machiavellian attitudes and choice of values among students in a business college. *Psychological Reports, 34,* 1342.

Ökat antal steriliseras in Nya Zeeland. (1997, August 30). *Dagens Nyhter.*

Older, J. (1984). Reducing racial imbalance in New Zealand universities and professions. *Australian and New Zealand Journal of Sociology, 20,* 243–256.

Oliver, M. L., & Shapiro, T. M. (1995). *Black wealth/White wealth: A new perspective on racial inequality.* New York: Routledge.

Ollman, B. (1996). Marxism. *Grolier's Multimedia Encyclopedia.* Danbury, CT: Grolier.

Ortega, S. T., & Rushing, W. A. (1983). Interpretation of the relationship between socioeconomic status and mental disorder: A question of the measure of mental disorder and a question of the measure of SES. *Research in Community and Mental Health, 3,* 141–161.

Ortiz, V. (1986). Reading activities and reading proficiency among Hispanic, Black and White students. *American Journal of Education, 95,* 58–76.

Osborne, Y. H., & Rappaport, N. B. (1985). Sentencing severity with mock jurors: Predictive validity of three variable categories. *Behavioral Sciences and the Law, 3,* 467–473.

Oyama, S. (1991). Bodies and minds: Dualism in evolutionary theory. *Journal of Social Issues, 47,* 27–42.

Pallavicini, J., et al. (1982). Estudio comparativo sobre alcoholismo y otros hábitos de beber, Santiago 1958 y 1982 [Comparative study of alcoholism and drinking habits, Santiago, 1958 and 1982]. *Revista de Psiquiatría Clínica, 20,* 48–66.

Pappas, G., Queen, S., Hadden, W., & Fisher, G. (1993). The increasing disparity in mortality between socioeconomic groups in the United States, 1960 and 1986. *New England Journal of Medicine, 329,* 103–109.

Pareto, V. (1901/1979). *The rise and fall of the elites.* New York: Arno.

Pareto, V. (1935/1963). *The mind and society: A treatise on general sociology.* New York: Dover.

Parker, S. T. (1987). A sexual selection model of hominid evolution. *Human Evolution, 2,* 235–253.

Parsons, T. (1951). *The social system.* Gencoe, IL: Free Press.

Parsons, T. (1962). The law and social control. In W. M. Evan (Ed.), *Law and sociology: Exploratory essays* (pp. 56–72). New York: Free Press.

Paternoster, R. (1983). Race of victim and location of crime: The decision to seek the death penalty in South Carolina. *Journal of Criminal Law and Criminology, 74,* 754–785.

Paternoster, R. (1984). Prosecutorial discretion in requesting the death penalty: A case of victim-based racial discrimination. *Law and Society Review, 18,* 437–478.

Patterson, O. (1997). *The ordeal of integration: Progress and resentment in America's "racial" crisis.* Washington, DC: Civitas Counterpoint.

Pauw, J. (1991). *In the heart of the whore: The story of apartheid's death squads.* Midrand: Halfway House, Southern Book Publications.

Pavlos, A. J. (1972). Racial attitude and stereotype change with bogus pipeline paradigm. *Proceedings of the Annual Convention of the American Psychological Association, 1972, 7,* 291–292.

Pavlos, A. J. (1973). Acute self-esteem effects on racial attitudes measured by rating scale and bogus pipeline. *Proceedings of the 81st Annual Convention of the American Psychological Association, Montreal, Canada, 8,* 165–166.

Peabody, D. (1966). Authoritarianism scales and response bias. *Psychological Bulletin, 65,* 11–23.

Pelton, L. H. (1978). Child abuse and neglect: The myth of classlessness. *American Journal of Orthopsychiatry, 48,* 608–617.

Perdue, C. W., Dovidio, J. F., Gurtman, M. B., & Tyler, R. B. (1990). Us and them: Social categorization and the process of intergroup bias. *Journal of Personality and Social Psychology, 59,* 475–486.

Perdue, C. W., & Gurtman, M. B. (1990). Evidence for the automaticity of ageism. *Journal of Experimental Social Psychology, 26,* 199–216.

Perron, J., & St.-Onge, L. (1991). Work values in relation to gender and forecasted career patterns for women. *International Journal for the Advancement of Counseling, 14,* 91–103.

Persell, C. H. (1977). *Education and inequality: A theoretical and empirical synthesis.* New York: Free Press.

Petersen, D. M., & Friday, P. C. (1975). Early release from incarceration: Race as a factor in the use of "shock probation." *Journal of Criminal Law and Criminology, 66,* 79–87.

Petersen, D. M., Schwirian, K. P., & Bleda, S. E. (1977). The drug arrest: Empirical observations on the age, sex and race of drug law offenders in a midwestern city. *Drug Forum, 6,* 371–386.

Peterson, E. D., Shaw, L. K., DeLong, E. R., Pryor, D. B., Califf, R. M., & Mark, D. B. (1997). Racial variation in the use of coronary-revascularization procedures: Are the differences real? Do they matter? *New England Journal of Medicine, 336,* 480–486.

Pettigrew, T. F. (1979). The ultimate attribution error: Extending Allport's cognitive analysis of prejudice. *Personality and Social Psychology Bulletin, 5,* 461–476.

Pettigrew, T. F. (1989). The nature of modern racism in the United States. *Revue Internationale de Psychologie Sociale, 2,* 291–303.

Poikolainen, K., Nayha, S., & Hassi, J. (1992). Alcohol consumption among male reindeer herders of Lappish and Finnish origin. *Social Science and Medicine, 35,* 735–738.

Poikolainen, K., & Vuori, E. (1985). Risk of fatal alcohol poisoning by marital and occupational status. *Alcohol and Alcoholism, 20,* 329–332.

Pomper, G. N. (1970). *Elections in America.* New York: Dodd, Mead.

Poole, M. E., & Low, B. C. (1982). Who stays? Who leaves? An examination of sex differences in staying and leaving. *Journal of Youth and Adolescence, 11,* 49–63.

Porter, J. (1971). *Black child, White child: The development of racial attitudes.* Cambridge, MA: Harvard University Press.

Poulson, R. L. (1990). Mock juror attribution of criminal responsibility: Effects of race and the guilty but mentally ill (GBMI) verdict option. *Journal of Applied Social Psychology, 20,* 1596–1611.

Pound, R. A. (1943/1959). A survey of social interests. *Harvard Law Review, 57,* 1–39.

Powell, G. E., & Stewart, R. A. (1978). The relationship of age, sex, and personality to social attitudes in children aged 8–15 years. *British Journal of Social and Clinical Psychology, 17,* 307–317.

Powell-Hopson, D., & Hopson, D. S. (1988). Implications of doll color preferences among Black preschool children and White preschool children. *Journal of Black Psychology, 14,* 57–63.

Powell-Hopson, D., & Hopson, D. S. (1992). Implications of doll color preferences among Black preschool children and White preschool children. In K. H. Burlew, W. C. Banks, H. P. McAdoo, & D. Ajani ya Azibo (Eds.), *African-American psychology: Theory, research, and practice* (pp. 183–189). Newbury Park, CA: Sage.

Pratto, F. (1996). Sexual politics: The gender gap in the bedroom, the cupboard and the cabinet. In D. M. Buss & N. M. Malamuth (Eds.), *Sex, power and conflict: Evolutionary and feminist perspectives* (pp. 179–230). New York: Oxford University Press.

Pratto, F. (1999). The puzzle of continuing group inequality: Piecing together psychological, social, and cultural forces in social dominance theory. In M. P. Zanna (Ed.), *Advances in experimental social psychology, 31,* 191–263. NY: Academic Press.

Pratto, F., & Bargh, J. A. (1991). Stereotyping based on apparently individuating information: Trait and global components of sex stereotypes under attention overload. *Journal of Experimental Social Psychology, 27,* 26–47.

Pratto, F., & Choudhury, P. (1998). *A group status analysis of ingroup identification and support for group in equality: Ethnicity, sex, and sexual orientation.* Unpublished manuscript, University of Connecticut.

Pratto, F., & Hegarty, P. (1998). *The politics of mating: Social dominance and mating strategies.* Unpublished manuscript, University of Connecticut.

Pratto, F., Orton, J., & Stallworth, L. M. (1997). *Issue-framing and social dominance orientation in persuasion.* Unpublished manuscript, University of Connecticut.

Pratto, F., Shih, M., & Orton, J. (1997). *Social dominance orientation, group salience, and implicit and explicit group discrimination.* Unpublished manuscript, University of Connecticut.

Pratto, F., Sidanius, J., & Stallworth, L. M. (1993). Sexual selection and the sexual and ethnic basis of social hierarchy. In L. Ellis (Ed.), *Social stratification and socioeconomic inequality: A comparative biosocial analysis* (pp. 111–137). Westport, CT: Praeger.

Pratto, F., Sidanius, J., Stallworth, L. M., & Malle, B. F. (1994). Social dominance orientation: A personality variable predicting social and political attitudes. *Journal of Personality and Social Psychology, 67,* 741–763.

Pratto, F., Stallworth, L. M., & Sidanius, J. (1997). The gender gap: Differences in political attitudes and social dominance orientation. *British Journal of Social Psychology, 36,* 49–68.

Pratto, F., Stallworth, L. M., Sidanius, J., & Siers, B. (1997). The gender gap in occupational role attainment: A social dominance approach. *Journal of Personality and Social Psychology, 72,* 37–53.

Proenza, L., & Strickland, B. R. (1965). A study of prejudice in Negro and White college students. *Journal of Social Psychology, 67,* 273–281.

Pruitt, C. R., & Wilson, J. Q. (1983). A longitudinal study of the effect of race on sentencing. *Law and Society Review, 17,* 613–635.

Pugh, H., Power, C., Goldblatt, P., & Arber, S. (1991). Women's lung cancer mortality, socio-economic status and changing smoking patterns. *Social Science and Medicine, 32,* 1105–1110.

Putnam, R. D. (1976). *The comparative study of political elites.* Englewood Cliffs, NJ: Prentice-Hall.

Pyle, A. (1997, July 28). Book shortage plagues L.A. Unified: High school students often don't have texts for classes, despite state law. *Los Angeles Times,* pp. A1, A16, A17.

Quinney, R. (1974). *Criminal justice in America.* Boston: Little, Brown.

Quinney, R. (1977). *Class, state, and crime.* New York: David McKay.

Quintanilla, C. (1995, September 6). All you will need is a 36 waist, a 33 inseam and a thick wallet. *Wall Street Journal.* Available: http://www.wwnorton.com/wsj/varian/09-06-95/090695q1.htm

Radelet, M. L. (1981). Racial characteristics and the imposition of the death penalty. *American Sociological Review, 46,* 918–927.

Ramcharan, S. (1976). The economic adaptation of West Indians in Toronto, Canada. *La Revue Canadienne de Sociologie et d'Anthropologie/The Canadian Review of Sociology and Anthropology, 13,* 295–304.

Raper, A. F. (1969). *The tragedy of lynching.* Chapel Hill: University of North Carolina Press.

Raskin, C. (1993). *De facto discrimination, immigrant workers and ethnic minorities: A Canadian overview.* World Employment Programme working paper. Geneva: International Labour Office.

Rasmussen, D. (1970). A note on the relative income of non-White men, 1948–1964. *Quarterly Journal of Economics, 84,* 166–172.

Raven, J. (1989). The Raven progressive matrices: A review of national norming studies and ethnic and socioeconomic variation within the United States. *Journal of Experimental Measurement, 26,* 1–16.

Ray, J. J. (1983). A scale to measure conservatism of American public opinion. *Journal of Social Psychology, 119,* 293–294.

Reich, M. (1981). *Racial inequality: A political-economic analysis.* Princeton, NJ: Princeton University Press.

Reich, W. (1946). *The mass psychology of fascism.* New York: Orgone Institute Press.

Reid, C. E. (1987, July). *An analysis of racial discrimination in rental housing markets.* Unpublished manuscript, Grinnell College, Grinnell, IA.

Reinarman, C. (1995). The crack attack: America's latest drug scare, 1986–1992.

In J. Best (Ed.), *Images of issues: Typifying contemporary social problems* (2nd ed., pp. 147–186). Hawthorne, NY: Aldine.

Reuter, P., MacCoun, R., & Murphy, P. (1990). *Money from crime: A study of the economics of drug dealing in Washington, DC.* Santa Monica, CA: Rand.

Reynolds, V., Falger, V., & Vine, I. (1987). *The sociobiology of ethnocentrism: Evolutionary dimensions of xenophobia, discrimination, racism, and nationalism.* Athens: University of Georgia Press.

Richardson, S. A., & Green, A. (1971). When is black beautiful? Colored and White children's reactions to skin color. *British Journal of Educational Psychology, 41,* 62–69.

Robins, L. N., & Regier, D. A. (1991). *Psychiatric disorders in America: The Epidemiologic Catchment Area Study.* New York: Free Press.

Rockwell, R. C. (1976). Historical trends and variations in educational homogamy. *Journal of Marriage and the Family, 38,* 83–95.

Rodseth, L., Wrangham, R. W., Harrigan, A. M., & Smuts, B. B. (1991). The human community as a primate society. *Current Anthropology, 32,* 221–254.

Roelandt, T., & Veenman, J. (1990). *Allohtonen van school naar werk.* Gravenhage: SDU Uitgeverij.

Roese, N. J., & Jamieson, D. W. (1993). Twenty years of bogus pipeline research: A critical review and meta-analysis. *Psychological Bulletin, 114,* 363–375.

Rohrich, T., & Tulsky, F. (1996, December 3). Not all L.A. murder cases are equal. *Los Angeles Times,* p. A1.

Rokeach, M. (1973). *The nature of human values.* New York: Free Press.

Rokeach, M. (1979). The two-value model of political ideology and British politics. In M. Rokeach (Ed.), *Understanding human values: Individual and social* (pp. 192–196). New York: Free Press.

Rokeach, M., Miller, M. G., & Snyder, J. A. (1971). The value gap between police and policed. *Journal of Social Issues, 27,* 155–171.

Rosenblatt, A., Greenberg, J., Solomon, S., Pyszczynski, T., & Lyon, D. (1989). Evidence for terror management theory: I. The effects of mortality salience on reactions to those who violate or uphold cultural values. *Journal of Personality and Social Psychology, 57,* 681–690.

Rosenthal, R., & Jacobson, L. (1968). *Pygmalion in the classroom: Teacher expectations and pupils' intellectual development.* New York: Holt, Rinehart, & Winston.

Rowell, T. E. (1974). The concept of social dominance. *Behavioral Biology, 11,* 131–154.

Rubovits, P. C., & Maehr, M. L. (1973). Pygmalion black and white. *Journal of Personality and Social Psychology, 25,* 210–218.

Rushton, J. P. (1996). Race differences in brain size. *American Psychologist, 51,* 556.

Ruth, A. (1997, September 15). När demokratin töms på värden. *Dagens Nyheter.* Available: http://www.dn.se/DNet/firstframe.html

Sachdev, I., & Bourhis, R. Y. (1985). Social categorization and power differentials in group relations. *European Journal of Social Psychology, 15,* 415–434.

Sachdev, I., & Bourhis, R. Y. (1987). Status differentials and intergroup behavior. *European Journal of Social Psychology, 17,* 277–293.

Sachdev, I., & Bourhis, R. Y. (1991). Power and status differentials in minority and majority group relations. *European Journal of Social Psychology, 21*, 1–24.

Sacks, K. (1971). Engels revisited: Women, the organization of production, and private property. In R. R. Reiter (Ed.), *Toward an anthropology of women* (pp. 211–234). New York: Monthly Review Press.

Samelson, F. (1986). Authoritarianism from Berlin to Berkeley: On social psychology and history. *Journal of Social Issues, 42*, 191–208.

Sanday, P. R. (1981). *Female power and male dominance.* Cambridge University Press.

Sandoval, S. A. M. (1991). Mechanisms of racial discrimination in the labor market: The case of urban Brazil. *Estudios Sociologicos, 9*, 35–60.

Sanson-Fisher, R. (1978). Aborigines in crime statistics: An interaction between poverty and detection. *Australian and New Zealand Journal of Criminality, 11*, 71–80.

Sapolsky, R. M. (1993). The physiology of dominance in stable versus unstable social hierarchies. In W. A. Mason & S. P. Mendoza (Eds.), *Primate social conflict* (pp. 171–204). Albany: State University of New York Press.

Sapolsky, R. M. (1995). Social subordinance as a marker of hypercortisolism: Some unexpected subtleties. In G. P. Chrousos, R. McCarty, K. Pacak, G. Cizza, E. Sternberg, P. W. Gold, & R. Kvetnansky (Eds.), *Stress: Basic mechanisms and clinical implications. Annals of the New York Academy of Sciences* (Vol. 771). New York: New York Academy of Sciences.

Sarri, R. C. (1986). Gender and race differences in criminal justice processing [Special issue: Women and the law]. *Women's Studies International Forum, 9*, 89–99.

SCB Statiska Centralbyrån. (1998). Available: www.scb.se/scbswe/vhtm/valf%/5f5fi.htm

Schellenberg, E. G., Wasylenki, D., Webster, C. D., & Goering, P. (1992). A review of arrests among psychiatric patients. *International Journal of Law and Psychiatry, 15*, 251–264.

Schiraldi, V., Kuyper, S., & Hewitt, S. (1996). *Young African-Americans and the criminal justice system in California: Five years later.* San Francisco: Center on Juvenile and Criminal Justice.

Schmittroth, L. (1991). *Statistical record of women worldwide.* Detroit, MI: Gale.

Schuman, H., Steeh, C., & Bobo, L. (1985). *Racial attitudes in America: Trends and interpretation.* Cambridge, MA: Harvard University Press.

Scott, J. C. (1990). *Domination and the arts of resistance: Hidden transcripts.* New Haven, CN: Yale University Press.

Seagle, W. (1947/1971). *Men of law, from Hammurabi to Holmes.* New York: Hafner.

Searing, D. D. (1979). A study of values in the British House of Commons. In M. Rokeach (Ed.), *Understanding human values* (pp. 154–178). New York: Free Press.

Sears, D. O. (1988). Symbolic racism. In P. A. Katz & D. A. Taylor (Eds.), *Eliminating racism: Profiles in controversy* (pp. 53–84). New York: Plenum.

Sears, D. O., & Kinder, D. R. (1971). Racial tensions and voting in Los Angeles. In W. Z. Hirsch (Ed.), *Los Angeles: Viability and prospects for metropolitan leadership* (pp. 51–88). New York: Praeger.

Sears, D. O., Lau, R. R., Tyler, T. R., & Allen, H. M. (1980). Self interest vs. symbolic politics in policy attitudes and presidential voting. *American Political Science Review, 74*, 670–684.

Sears, D. O., van Laar, C., Carrillo, M., & Kosterman, R. (1997). Is it really racism? The origins of White Americans' opposition to race-targeted policies. *Public Opinion Quarterly, 61*, 16–53.

Sedlacek, W. E., & Brooks, G. C. (1976). *Racism in American education: A model for change*. Chicago: Nelson-Hall.

Sellin, T. (1938). *Culture, conflict and crime*. New York: Social Science Research Council.

Seltzer, A., & Langford, A. (1984). Forensic psychiatric assessments in the Northwest Territories. *Canadian Journal of Psychiatry, 29*, 665–668.

Senna, J., Rathus, S. A., & Seigel, L. (1974). Delinquent behavior and academic investment among suburban youth. *Adolescence, 36*, 481–491.

Serwatka, T. S., Deering, S., & Grant, P. (1995). Disproportionate representation of African-Americans in emotionally handicapped classes. *Journal of Black Studies, 25*, 492–506.

Shavit, Y. (1984). Tracking and ethnicity in Israeli secondary education. *American Sociological Review, 49*, 210–220.

Shavit, Y., & Blossfeld, H. P. (1993). *Persistent inequality: Changing educational attainment in thirteen countries*. Boulder, CO: Westview.

Sherer, M. (1990). Criminal activity among Jewish and Arab youth in Israel. *International Journal of Intercultural Relations, 14*, 529–548.

Sherif, M., Harvey, O. J., White, B. J., Hood, W. R., & Sherif, C. (1961). *Intergroup conflict and cooperation: The Robbers' Cave experiment*. Norman: Institute of Group Relations, University of Oklahoma.

Shimahara, N. K. (1991). Social mobility and education: Burakumin in Japan. In M. A. Gibson & J. U. Ogbu (Eds.), *Minority status and schooling: A comparative study of immigrants and involuntary minorities* (pp. 227–256). New York: Garland.

Shockley, W. (1972, January). Dysgenics, geneticity, raceology: A challenge to the intellectual responsibility of educators. *Phi Delta Kappan*, 297–307.

Shyam, R. (1986). Variations in concentrations of "g" level abilities among different groups. *Journal of Personality and Clinical Studies, 2*, 123–126.

Sidanius, J. (1987). Social attitudes and political party preferences among Swedish youth. *Scandinavian Political Studies, 10*, 111–124.

Sidanius, J. (1988). Intolerance of ambiguity, conservatism and racism – Whose fantasy, whose reality?: A reply to Ray. *Political Psychology, 9*, 309–316.

Sidanius, J. (1990). Basic values and sociopolitical ideology: A comparison of political experts and political novices. *Perceptual and Motor Skills, 71*, 447–450.

Sidanius, J. (1993). The psychology of group conflict and the dynamics of oppression: A social dominance perspective. In S. Iyengar & W. McGuire (Eds.), *Explorations in political psychology* (pp. 183–219). Durham, NC: Duke University Press.

Sidanius, J., Cling, B. J., & Pratto, F. (1991). Ranking and linking as a function of sex and gender role attitudes. *Journal of Social Issues, 47*, 131–149.

Sidanius, J., Devereux, E., & Pratto, F. (1992). A comparison of symbolic racism theory and social dominance theory: Explanations for racial policy attitudes. *Journal of Social Psychology, 132*, 377–395.

Sidanius, J., & Ekehammar, B. (1976). Cognitive functioning and socio-political ideology: A multidimensional and individualized analysis. *Scandinavian Journal of Psychology, 17*, 205–216.

Sidanius, J., & Ekehammar, B. (1979). Political socialization: A multivariate analysis of Swedish political attitude and preference data. *European Journal of Social Psychology, 9*, 265–279.

Sidanius, J., & Ekehammar, B. (1980). Sex-related differences in socio-political ideology. *Scandinavian Journal of Psychology, 21*, 17–26.

Sidanius, J., & Ekehammar, B. (1982). Test of a biological model for explaining sex differences. *Journal of Psychology, 110*, 191–195.

Sidanius, J., Ekehammar, B., & Ross, M. (1979). Comparisons of socio-political attitudes between two democratic societies. *International Journal of Psychology, 14*, 225–240.

Sidanius, J., Feshbach, S., Levin, S., & Pratto, F. (1997). The interface between ethnic and national attachment: Ethnic pluralism or ethnic dominance? *Public Opinion Quarterly, 61*, 102–133.

Sidanius, J., Liu, J., Shaw, J., & Pratto, F. (1994). Social dominance orientation, hierarchy-attenuators and hierarchy-enhancers: Social dominance theory and the criminal justice system. *Journal of Applied Social Psychology, 24*, 338–366.

Sidanius, J., & Pratto, F. (1993). Racism and support of free-market capitalism: A cross-cultural analysis. *Political Psychology, 14*, 383–403.

Sidanius, J., Pratto, F., & Bobo, L. (1996). Racism, conservatism, affirmative action and intellectual sophistication: A matter of principled conservatism or group dominance? *Journal of Personality and Social Psychology, 70*, 476–490.

Sidanius, J., Pratto, F., & Brief, D. (1995). Group dominance and the political psychology of gender: A cross-cultural comparison. *Political Psychology, 16*, 381–396.

Sidanius, J., Pratto, F., & Mitchell, M. (1994). Ingroup identification, social dominance orientation, and differential intergroup social allocation. *Journal of Social Psychology, 134*, 151–167.

Sidanius, J., Pratto, F., & Rabinowitz, J. (1994). Gender, ethnic status, ingroup attachment and social dominance orientation. *Journal of Cross-Cultural Psychology, 25*, 194–216.

Sidanius, J., Pratto, F., Sinclair, S., & van Laar, C. (1996). Mother Teresa meets Genghis Khan: The dialectics of hierarchy-enhancing and hierarchy-attenuating career choices. *Social Justice Research, 9*, 145–170.

Sigall, H., & Page, R. (1971). Current stereotypes: A little fading, a little faking. *Journal of Personality and Social Psychology, 18*, 247–255.

Simmons, R. G., Black, A., & Zhou, Y. (1991). African-American versus White children and the transition into junior high school [Special issue: Development and education across adolescence]. *American Journal of Education, 99*, 481–520.

Sirgo, H. B., & Eisenman, R. (1990). Perceptions of governmental fairness by liberals and conservatives. *Psychological Reports, 67*, 1331–1334.

Skevington, S. (1981). Intergroup relations and nursing. *European Journal of Social Psychology, 11*, 43–59.

Skogan, W. (1990). *The police and public in England and Wales: A British crime survey report*. Home Office Research Study, No. 117, pp. 26–37.

Smith, D. A., Visher, C. A., & Davisdon, L. A. (1984). Equity and discretionary justice: The influence of race on police arrest decisions. *Journal of Criminal Law and Criminology, 75*, 234–249.

Smith, D. J. (1976). *The facts of racial disadvantage: A national survey*. PEP Report, vol. 42. London: Berridge.

Smith, D. J. (1977). *Racial disadvantage in Britain: The PEP Report*. Harmondsworth: Penguin.

Smith, D. J., & Gray, J. (1985). *Police and people in London*. Aldershot: Policy Studies Institute Report.

Smith, I. (1981). Educational differentiation and curricular guidance: A review. *Educational Studies, 7*, 87–94.

Smith, R. A. (1997). *Race and job authority: An analysis of men and women, 1972–1994*. Rutgers University, School of Management and Labor Relations, New Brunswick, NJ.

Smith, T. W. (1991). *What do Americans think about Jews? Working papers on contemporary anti-semitism*. New York: American Jewish Committee, Institute of Human Relations.

Smooha, S. (1978). *Israel: Pluralism and conflict*. London: Routledge & Kegan Paul.

Sniderman, P. M., & Piazza, T. (1993). *The scar of race*. Cambridge, MA: Harvard University Press.

Sniderman, P. M., Piazza, T., Tetlock, P. E., & Kendrick, A. (1991). The new racism. *American Journal of Political Science, 35*, 423–447.

Sniderman, P. M., & Tetlock, P. E. (1986). Symbolic racism: Problems of motive attribution in political analysis. *Journal of Social Issues, 42*, 129–150.

Snyder, M., & Uranowitz, S. W. (1978). Reconstructing the past: Some cognitive consequences of person perception. *Journal of Personality and Social Psychology, 36*, 941–950.

Sobral, J., Arce, R., & Farina, F. (1989). Aspectos psicosociales de las decisiones judiciales: Revisión y lectura diferenciada (Psychosocial aspects of judicial decisions: Revision and differentiated reading). *Boletín de Psicología, 25*, 49–74.

Sohlman, A. (1970). *Differences in school achievement and occupational opportunities: Explanatory factors – A survey based on European experience*. Paper presented at the Conference on Policies for Educational Growth (Paris, France, June 3–5). Paris: Organisation for Economic Cooperation and Development.

Solomon, S., Greenberg, J., & Pyszczynski, T. (1991). A terror management theory of social behavior: The psychological functions of self-esteem and cultural world views. In M. P. Zanna (Ed.), *Advances in Experimental Social Psychology* (Vol. 24, 93–159). San Diego: Academic.

Somit, A., & Peterson, S. A. (1977). *Darwinism, dominance and democracy: The biological bases of authoritarianism*. Westport, CT: Praeger.

Sorensen, J. R., & Wallace, D. H. (1995). Capital punishment in Missouri: Examining the issue of racial disparity. *Behavioral Sciences and the Law, 13*, 61–80.

Sowell, T. (1981). *Markets and minorities*. New York: Basic.

Sowell, T. (1984). *Civil rights: Rhetoric or reality*. New York: Morrow.

Sparks-Davidson, Z. A., Rahman, P. Z., & Hildreth, G. J. (1982). Extension of color bias research to young, Malay-Malaysian children. *Southern Psychologist, 1*, 20–26.

Spencer, S. J. (1993). *The effect of stereotype vulnerability on women's math performance*. Unpublished doctoral dissertation, University of Michigan, Department of Psychology.

Spineux, A. (1986). *Vocational training of young migrants in Luxembourg*. Berlin: European Centre for the Development of Vocational Training.

Spohn, C. (1994). Crime and the social control of Blacks: Offender/victim race and the sentencing of violent offenders. In G. S. Bridges & M. A. Myers (Eds.), *Inequality, crime, and social control: Crime and society* (pp. 249–268). Boulder, CO: Westview.

Staub, E. (1989). *The roots of evil: The origins of genocide and other group violence*. Cambridge University Press.

Steele, C. M., & Aronson, J. (1995). Stereotype threat and the intellectual test performance of African Americans. *Journal of Personality and Social Psychology, 69*, 797–811.

Steinberg, L. (1996). *Beyond the classroom: Why school reform has failed and what parents need to do*. New York: Simon & Schuster.

Steinberg, L., Dornbusch, S. M., & Brown, B. B. (1992). Ethnic differences in adolescent achievement: An ecological perspective. *American Psychologist, 47*, 723–729.

Stephan, W. G. (1987). The contact hypothesis in intergroup relations. In C. Hendrick (Ed.), *Group processes and intergroup relations: Review of personality and social psychology* (pp. 13–40). Beverly Hills, CA: Sage.

Stevenson, H. W., & Stewart, E. C. (1958). A developmental study of racial awareness in young children. *Child Development, 29*, 399–409.

Stewart, J. E. (1980). Defendant's attractiveness as a factor in the outcome of criminal trials: An observational study. *Journal of Applied Social Psychology, 10*, 348–361.

Stewart, J. E. (1985). Appearance and punishment: The attraction–leniency effect in the courtroom. *Journal of Social Psychology, 125*, 373–378.

Sticht, T. G., Beeler, M. J., & McDonald, B. A. (1992). *The intergenerational transfer of cognitive skills: Vol. 2. Theory and research in cognitive science*. Norwood, NJ: Ablex.

Stone, W. F. (1980). The myth of left-wing authoritarianism. *Political Psychology, 2*, 3–19.

Stone, W. F., & Russ, R. C. (1976). Machiavellianism as tough mindedness. *Journal of Social Psychology, 98*, 213–220.

Stoneman, E. T. (1929). *State psychological clinic: Annual report for the year ending 30th of June, 1929*. Perth, Western Australia: Department of Public Health.

Strier, K. B. (1994). Brotherhoods among atelins: Kinship, affiliation, and competition. *Behaviour, 130*, 151–167.

Sturdivant, F. D. (1971). Discrimination in the marketplace: Another dimension. *Social Science Quarterly, 52,* 625–630.

Sturdivant, F. D., & Wilhelm, W. T. (1968). Poverty, minorities, and consumer exploitation. *Social Science Quarterly, 49,* 643–650.

Sumner, W. G. (1906). *Folkways: A study of the sociological importance of usages, manners, customs, mores and morals.* Boston: Ginn.

Susser, M., Watson, W., & Hopper, K. (1985). *Sociology in medicine* (3rd ed.). Oxford: Oxford University Press.

Swann, W. B., Pelham, B. W., & Krull, D. S. (1989). Agreeable fancy or disagreeable truth? Reconciling self-enhancement and self-verification. *Journal of Personality and Social Psychology, 57,* 782–791.

Swann, W. B., & Read, S. J. (1981a). Acquiring self-knowledge: The search for feedback that fits. *Journal of Personality and Social Psychology, 41,* 1119–1128.

Swann, W. B., & Read, S. J. (1981b). Self-verification processes: How we sustain our self-conceptions. *Journal of Experimental Social Psychology, 17,* 351–370.

Sweeney, L. T., & Haney, C. (1992). The influence of race on sentencing: A meta-analytic review of experimental studies. *Behavioral Sciences and the Law, 10,* 179–195.

Tabachnick, B. G., & Fidell, L. S. (1996). *Using multivariate statistics* (3rd ed.). New York: HarperCollins.

Tajfel, H. (1978). Social categorization, social identity and social comparison. In H. Tajfel (Ed.), *Differentiation between social groups* (pp. 61–76). London: Academic.

Tajfel, H. (1981). *Groups and social categories.* Cambridge University Press.

Tajfel, H. (1982). Social psychology of intergroup relations. *Annual Review of Psychology, 33,* 1–30.

Tajfel, H., Billig, M., Bundy, R., & Flament, C. (1971). Social categorization and intergroup behavior. *European Journal of Social Psychology, 5,* 5–43.

Tajfel, H., & Turner, J. C. (1979). An integrative theory of intergroup conflict. In W. G. Austin & S. Worchel (Eds.), *The social psychology of intergroup relations* (pp. 33–47). Monterey, CA: Brooks-Cole.

Tajfel, H., & Turner, J. C. (1986). The social identity theory of intergroup behavior. In S. Worchel & W. G. Austin (Eds.), *Psychology of intergroup relations* (pp. 7–24). Chicago: Nelson-Hall.

Tan, A. S., & Tan, G. (1979). Television use and self-esteem of Blacks. *Journal of Communication, 29,* 129–135.

Tangney, J. P., & Feshbach, S. (1988). Children's television-viewing frequency: Individual differences and demographic correlates. *Personality and Social Psychology Bulletin, 14,* 145–158.

Taylor, C. L., & Jodice, D. A. (1983). *World handbook of political and social indicators.* New Haven, CN: Yale University Press.

Taylor, P. (1995, January 29). South Africa quietly integrates schools. *The Washington Post.*

Taylor, S. E., Fiske, S. T., Close, M., Anderson, C., & Ruderman, A. (1977).

Solo status as a psychological variable: The power of being distinctive. Unpublished manuscript, Harvard University, Cambridge, MA.

Teahan, J. E. (1975a). A longitudinal study of attitude shifts among Black and White police officers. *Journal of Social Issues, 31,* 47–56.

Teahan, J. E. (1975b). Role playing and group experience to facilitate attitude and value changes among Black and White police officers. *Journal of Social Issues, 31,* 35–45.

Thernstrom, S., & Thernstrom, A. (1997). *America in black and white: One nation, indivisible.* New York: Simon & Schuster.

Thomas, E. J. (1982). The status of immigrant workers in France. In E. J. Thomas (Ed.), *Immigrant workers in Europe: Their legal status* (pp. 41–82). Paris: UNESCO.

Thornberry, T. P. (1973). Race, socioeconomic status and sentencing in the juvenile justice system. *Journal of Criminal Law and Criminology, 64,* 90–98.

Thurow, L. (1969). *Poverty and discrimination.* London: Brookings Institution.

Tiger, L., & Fox, R. (1972). *The imperial animal.* New York: Henry Holt.

Tillman, R. (1987). The size of the "criminal population": The prevalence and incidence of adult arrest. *Criminality, 25,* 561–579.

Tilly, C. (1998). *Durable inequality.* Berkeley, CA: University of California Press.

Timmerman, H., Bosma, J. J., & Jongman, R. W. (1986). Minderheden voor de rechter. *Tijdschrift voor Criminologie, 2,* 57–72.

Tittle, C. K. (1982). Career, marriage, and family: Values in adult roles and guidance. *Personnel and Guidance Journal, 61,* 154–158.

Tootell, G. M. B. (1996). Turning a critical eye on the critics. In J. Goering & R. Wienk (Eds.), *Mortgage lending, racial discrimination, and federal policy* (pp. 143–182). Washington, DC: Urban Institute Press.

Torney, J. V., Oppenheim, A. N., & Farnen, R. F. (1975). *Civic education in ten countries: International studies in evaluation* (Vol. 4). Stockholm: Almqvist & Wiksell.

Towers, T., McGinley, H., & Pasewark, R. A. (1992). Insanity defense: Ethnicity of defendants and mock jurors. *Journal of Psychiatry and Law, 20,* 243–256.

Triandis, H., & Triandis, L. M. (1960). Race, social class, religion, and nationality as determinants of social stress. *Journal of Abnormal and Social Psychology, 61,* 110–118.

Trivers, R. (1972). Parental investment and sexual selection. In B. Campbell (Ed.), *Sexual selection and the descent of man* (pp. 136–179). New York: Aldine.

Turner, J., & Bourhis, R. Y. (1996). Social identity, interdependence, and the social group: A reply to Rabbie et al. In W. P. Robinson (Ed.), *Social groups and identities: Developing the legacy of Henri Tajfel* (pp. 25–63). Boston: Butterworth-Heinemann.

Turk, A. (1969). *Criminality and the legal order.* Chicago: Rand McNally.

Turner, J., & Brown, R. (1978). Social status, cognitive alternatives and intergroup relations. In H. Tajfel (Ed.), Differentiation between social groups: Studies in the social psychology of intergroup relations. *European Monographs in Social Psychology, 14.* London: Academic.

Turner, M., Fix, M., & Struyk, R. (1991). *Opportunities diminished, opportunities denied.* Washington, DC: Urban Institute.

Tuss, P., et al. (1995). Causal attributions of underachieving fourth-grade students in China, Japan, and the United States. *Journal of Cross-Cultural Psychology, 26,* 408–425.

Tversky, A., & Kahneman, D. (1973). Availability: A heuristic for judging frequency and probability. *Cognitive Psychology, 5,* 207–232.

Uhlman, T. (1979). *Racial justice.* Lexington, MA: Heath.

United Nations Children's Fund. (1991). *The girl child: An investment in the future* (Revised ed.). New York: United Nations.

Unnerver, J. D., & Hembroff, L. A. (1988). The prediction of racial/ethnic sentencing disparities: An expectation states approach. *Journal of Research in Crime and Delinquency, 25,* 53–82.

U.S. Bureau of Labor Statistics. (1994, January). *Employment and earnings, 41.* Washington, DC: U.S. Department of Labor.

U.S. Bureau of the Census. (1998a, October 10). Table 12. Total Money Earnings in 1994 of Persons 25 Years Old and Over, by Educational Attainment, Sex, Region, and Race. Available: http://www.census.gov/population/socdemo/ race/black/tabs95/tab12a.txt

U.S. Bureau of the Census. (1998b, October 10). Table 19. Mean Earnings of Workers 18 Years Old and Over, by Educational Attainment, Race, Hispanic Origin, and Sex: 1975 to 1994." Available: http://www.census.gov/population/socdemo/education/table19.txt

U.S. Committee for Refugees. (1996). Ethnic cleansing, massacres continue in Zaire: 3,000 ethnic Tutsi surrounded by attackers. Available: http://www.reliefweb.int

U.S. Department of Education/NCES. (1988). *National Education Longitudinal Study of 1988: First follow-up student survey.* Washington, DC: U.S. Government Printing Office.

U.S. Department of Health and Human Services. (1989). *Promoting health/ preventing disease: Year 2000 objectives for the nation.* Washington, DC: U.S. Government Printing Office.

U.S. Department of Health, Education, and Welfare. (1979). *Smoking and health: A report of the Surgeon General, 1979* (USDHEW Publication No. 79-50066). Washington, DC: U.S. Government Printing Office.

U.S. Department of State. (1997). *Australia report on human rights practices for 1996.* Released by the Bureau of Democracy, Human Rights, and Labor, January 30. Washington, DC: Available: http://www3.itu.int/MISSION/US/hrc/australi.html

van den Berghe, P. L. (1978a). *Man in society: A biosocial view.* New York: Elsevier North Holland.

van den Berghe, P. L. (1978b). Race and ethnicity: A sociobiological perspective. *Ethnic and Racial Studies, 1,* 401–411.

van Dijk, T. A. (1987). *Communicating racism: Ethnic prejudice in thought and talk.* Newbury Park, CA: Sage.

van Knippenberg, A., & van Oers, H. (1984). Social identity and equity concerns in intergroup perceptions. *British Journal of Social Psychology, 23,* 351–361.

van Laar, C., Sidanius, J., Rabinowitz, J., & Sinclair, S. (1999). The three r's of academic achievement: Reading, 'riting, and racism. *Personality and Social Psychology Bulletin, 25,* 139–151.

van Lil, J. E., Vooijs, M. W., & van der Voort, T. H. (1994). Parental attitudes towards television and the guidance of children's television viewing. *Medienpsychologie: Zeitschrift fur Individual- & Massenkommunikation, 6,* 2–14.

Vaughan, G. M. (1978). Social change and intergroup preferences in New Zealand. *European Journal of Social Psychology, 8,* 297–314.

Veenman, J. (1990). The labour market position of migrants in the Netherlands, with special reference to Moluccans. Unpublished doctoral thesis, Erasmus University, Rotterdam, Netherlands.

Veenman, J., & Vijverberg, C. H. T. (1982). *De arbeidsmarktproblemtiek van Molukkers: Een verkennend onderzoek.* Rotterdam, Netherlands: Erasmus University.

Verba, S., Orren, G. R., Miyake, I., Watanuki, J., Kabashima, I., & Ferree, G. D., Jr. (1987). *Elites and the idea of equality: A comparison of Japan, Sweden and the United States.* Cambridge, MA: Harvard University Press.

Verhaeren, R. E. (1982). L'immigration Algérienne et la crise économique en France. In *Annuaire de l'Afrique du Nord* (pp. 121–142). Paris: Education du Centre National de la Recherche Scientifique.

Verster, J. M., & Prinsloo, R. J. (1988). The diminishing test performance gap between English speakers and Afrikaans speakers in South Africa. In S. H. Irvine & J. W. Berry (Eds.), *Human abilities in cultural context* (pp. 534–560). Cambridge University Press.

Vianello, M., & Siemienska, R. (1990). *Gender inequality: A comparative study of discrimination and participation.* Newbury Park, CA: Sage.

Visher, C. A. (1983). Gender, police arrest decisions, and notions of chivalry. *Criminology: An Interdisciplinary Journal, 21,* 5–28.

Voigt, L., Thornton,W. E., Jr., Barrile, L., & Seaman, J. M. (1994). *Criminology and Justice.* New York: McGraw-Hill.

Vold, G. (1958/1979). *Theoretical criminality.* New York: Oxford University Press.

Von Hofer, H., & Tham, H. (1991). *Foreign citizens and crime: The Swedish case.* Stockholm: Statistiska Centralbyrån Promemoria, 1991: 4 ISSN 0280-7327.

Waal, F. B. M. de (1997). *Bonobo: The forgotten ape.* Berkeley: University of California Press.

Wakil, S. P. (1973). Campus mate selection preferences: A cross-national comparison. *Social Forces, 51,* 471–476.

Walker, J. (1989). Prison sentences in Australia: Estimates of the characteristics of offenders sentenced to prison in 1987–88. *Trends and Issues in Crime and Criminal Justice,* no. 20. Woden: Australian Institute of Criminology.

Walker, J. (1994). The overrepresentation of Aboriginal and Torres Strait Islander people in prison. *Criminology Australia, 6,* 13–15.

Walker, S., Spohn, C., & Delone, M. (1996). *The color of justice: Race, ethnicity, and crime in America.* San Francisco: Wadsworth.

Ward, D. (1995). *Social dominance theory: Are the genes too tight?* Paper presented at the Eighteenth Annual Meeting of the International Society of Political Psychology, Washington, DC., July 4–8. Available: http://ispp.org/ISPP/wardispp95.html

Weber, M. (1922). *Max Weber on law in economy and society* (M. Rheinstein, Ed.). Cambridge, MA: Harvard University Press.

Weiner, B. (1986). *An attributional theory of achievement motivation and emotion.* New York: Springer-Verlag.

Weisz, J. R., Martin, S. L., Walter, B. R., & Fernandez, G. A. (1991). Differential prediction of young adult arrests for property and personal crimes: Findings of a cohort follow-up study of violent boys from North Carolina's Willie M Program. *Journal of Child Psychology and Psychiatry and Allied Disciplines, 32,* 783–792.

Wells-Barnett, I. B. (1990). *On lynchings: Southern horrors, a red record, mob rule in New Orleans.* Salem, NH: Ayer.

Whirls, D. (1986). Reinterpreting the gender gap. *Public Opinion Quarterly, 50,* 316– 330.

Wienk, R. E., et al. (1979). *Measuring discrimination in American housing markets: The Housing Market Practices Survey.* Washington, DC: U.S. Department of Housing and Urban Development.

Wijting, J. P., Arnold, C. R., & Conrad, K. A. (1977). Relationships between work values, socio-educational and work experiences, and vocational aspirations of 6th, 9th, 10th, and 12th graders. *Journal of Vocational Behavior, 11,* 51–65.

Wilbanks, W. (1988). Are elderly felons treated more leniently by the criminal justice system? *International Journal of Aging and Human Development, 26,* 275–288.

Wilkinson, R. G. (1992a). National mortality rates: The impact of inequality? *American Journal of Public Health, 82,* 1082–1084.

Wilkinson, R. G. (1992b). Income distribution and life expectancy. *British Medical Journal, 304,* 165–168.

Wilkinson, R. G. (1996). *Unhealthy societies: The afflictions of inequality.* New York: Routledge.

Williams, L. M., & Farrell, R. A. (1990). Legal response to child sexual abuse in day care. *Criminal Justice and Behavior, 17,* 284–302.

Williamson, J. G., & Lindert, P. H. (1980). *American inequality.* New York: Academic.

Wilson, G. (1997). Pathways to power: Racial differences in the determinants of job authority. *Social Problems, 44,* 38–54.

Wilson, G. D. (1973). *The psychology of conservatism.* San Diego, CA: Academic.

Wilson, G. D., & Bagley, C. (1973). Religion, racialism and conservatism. In G. D. Wilson (Ed.), *The psychology of conservatism* (pp. 117–128). London: Academic.

Wilson, G. D., & Lee, H. S. (1974). Social attitude patterns in Korea. *Journal of Social Psychology, 94,* 27–30.

Wilson, G. D., & Patterson, J. R. (1968). A new measure of conservatism. *British Journal of Social and Clinical Psychology, 7,* 264–269.

Wilson, P. (1991). Trauma of Sioux Indian high school students. *Anthropology and Education Quarterly, 22,* 367–383.

Wilson, W. J. (1996). *When work disappears: The world of the new urban poor.* New York: Knopf.

Winkleby, M., Fortmann, S., & Barrett, D. (1990). Social class disparities in risk factors for disease: Eight-year prevalence patterns by level of education. *Preventive Medicine, 19,* 1–12.

Winnick, R. H., & Taylor, J. A. (1977). Racial preference: 36 years later. *Journal of Social Psychology, 102,* 157–158.

WISTAT. (1994). *United Nations women's indicators and statistical database.* New York: United Nations.

Wittenbrink, B., Judd, C., & Park, B. (1997). Evidence for racial prejudice at the implicit level and its relationship with questionnaire measures. *Journal of Personality and Social Psychology, 72,* 262–274.

Woo, E. (1997, June 16). School success of immigrants' children tracked. *Los Angeles Times,* p. A1.

Word, C. O., Zanna, M. P., & Cooper, J. (1974). The nonverbal mediation of self-fulfilling prophecies in interracial interaction. *Journal of Experimental Social Psychology, 10,* 109–120.

World almanac and book of facts. (1993). New York: Pharos Books.

Wrangham, R. W. (1982). Mutualism, kinship and social evolution. In *Current problems in sociobiology* (Edited by King's College Sociobiology Group, pp. 269–289). Cambridge University Press.

Wrangham, R. W. (1987). The significance of African apes for reconstructing human social evolution. In W. G. Kinsey (Ed.), *The evolution of human behavior: Primate models* (pp. 51–71). Albany: State University of New York Press.

Yates, W. R., Booth, B. M., Reed, D. A., & Brown, K. (1993). Descriptive and predictive validity of a high-risk alcoholism relapse model. *Journal of Studies on Alcohol, 54,* 645–651.

Yee, M. D., & Brown, R. (1992). Self-evaluations and intergroup attitudes in children aged three to nine. *Child Development, 63,* 619–629.

Yinger, J. (1986). Measuring discrimination with fair housing audits: Caught in the act. *American Economic Review, 76,* 881–893.

Yinger, J. (1991a). *Housing discrimination study: Incidence and severity of unfavorable treatment.* Washington, DC: U.S. Department of Housing and Urban Development, Office of Policy Development and Research.

Yinger, J. (1991b). *Housing discrimination study: Incidence of discrimination and variation in discriminatory behavior.* Washington, DC: U.S. Department of Housing and Urban Development, Office of Policy Development and Research.

Yinger, J. (1995). *Closed doors, opportunities lost: The continuing costs of housing discrimination.* New York: Russell Sage.

Yinger, J. (1996). Discrimination in mortgage lending: A literature review. In J. Goering & R. Wienk (Eds.), *Mortgage lending, racial discrimination, and federal policy* (pp. 29–73). Washington, DC: Urban Institute Press.

Young, G. (1988). Neighborhood impoverishment and child maltreatment: An analysis from the ecological perspective. *Journal of Family Issues, 9,* 240–254.

Young, T. J. (1993). Alcohol misuse and criminal violence among Native Americans. *Psychiatric Forum, 16,* 20–26.

Zahn-Waxler, C., Robinson, J. L., & Emde, R. N. (1992). The development of empathy in twins. *Developmental Psychology, 28*, 1038–1047.

Zaremba, M. (1997a, August 20). Rasren in välfärden. *Dagens Nyheter.* Available: http://www.dn.se/DNet/firstframe.html

Zaremba, M. (1997b, August 21). De olönsamma skars bort. *Dagens Nyheter.* Available: http://www.dn.se/DNet/firstframe.html

Zegers de Beijl, R. (1990). *Discrimination of migrant workers in Western Europe.* Geneva, Switzerland: International Labour Office.

Zubrinsky, C. L., & Bobo, L. (1996a). Attitudes on residential integration: Perceived status differences, mere in-group preference, or racial prejudice? *Social Forces, 74*, 883–909.

Zubrinsky, C. L., & Bobo, L. (1996b). Prismatic metropolis: Race and residential segregation in the City of the Angels. *Social Forces, 25*, 335–374.

Zucker, S. H., & Prieto, A. G. (1977). Ethnicity and teacher bias in educational decisions. *Journal of Instructional Psychology, 4*, 2–5.

Author Index

Subject Index

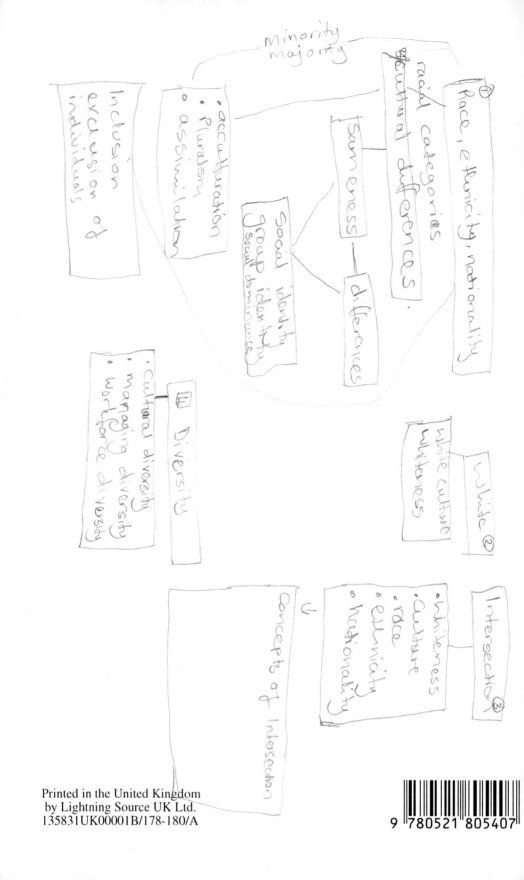

Printed in the United Kingdom
by Lightning Source UK Ltd.
135831UK00001B/178-180/A